The Long Road to Baghdad

Also by Lloyd C. Gardner

Economic Aspects of New Deal Diplomacy

Architects of Illusion: Men and Ideas in American Foreign Affairs, 1941–1949

The Creation of the American Empire
(with Walter LaFeber and Thomas McCormick)

American Foreign Policy Present to Past

Looking Backward: A Reintroduction to American History
(with William O'Neill)

Imperial America: American Foreign Policy, 1898–1976

A Covenant with Power: America and World Order from Wilson to Reagan

*Safe for Democracy: The Anglo-American Response
to Revolution, 1913–1923*

Approaching Vietnam: From World War II to Dienbienphu

Spheres of Influence: The Great Powers Partition Europe from Munich to Yalta

Pay Any Price: Lyndon Johnson and the Wars for Vietnam

The Case That Never Dies: The Lindbergh Kidnapping

Edited by Lloyd C. Gardner

The Great Nixon Turnaround

America in Vietnam: A Documentary History (with Walter LaFeber,
Thomas McCormick, and William Appleman Williams)

Redefining the Past: Essays in Honor of William Appleman Williams

On the Edge: The Early Decisions in the Vietnam War (with Ted Gittinger)

International Perspectives on Vietnam (with Ted Gittinger)

Vietnam: The Search for Peace (with Ted Gittinger)

The New American Empire: A 21st Century Teach-In on U.S. Foreign Policy
(with Marilyn B. Young)

Iraq and the Lessons of Vietnam: Or, How Not to Learn from the Past
(with Marilyn B. Young)

The Long Road to Baghdad

*A History of U.S. Foreign Policy from
the 1970s to the Present*

LLOYD C. GARDNER

THE NEW PRESS

NEW YORK
LONDON

To my grandchildren,
Jamie, Dylan, Kyle, and Asha

Requests for permission to reproduce selections from this book should be mailed to:
Permissions Department, The New Press, 38 Greene Street, New York, NY 10013.

Published in the United States by The New Press, New York, 2008
Distributed by W. W. Norton & Company, Inc., New York

LIBRARY OF CONGRESS CATALOGING-IN-PUBLICATION DATA

Gardner, Lloyd C., 1934–
  The long road to Baghdad : a history of U.S. foreign policy from the 1970s to the present
/ Lloyd C. Gardner.
    p.   cm.
  Includes bibliographical references and index.
  ISBN 978-1-59558-404-5 (hc.)
    1. Iraq War, 2003—Causes. 2. United States—Politics and government—2001– I. Title.
DS79.76.G366 2008
956.7044'31—dc22

2008004344

The New Press was established in 1990 as a not-for-profit alternative to the large,
commercial publishing houses currently dominating the book publishing industry.
The New Press operates in the public interest rather than for private gain,
and is committed to publishing, in innovative ways, works of educational, cultural,
and community value that are often deemed insufficiently profitable.

www.thenewpress.com

Composition by NK Graphics
This book was set in Goudy

Printed in the United States of America

2   4   6   8   10   9   7   5   3   1

*To contemplate war is to think about the most horrible of human experiences.
On this February day, as this nation stands at the brink of battle, every American on some level must be contemplating the horrors of war.*

*Yet, this Chamber is, for the most part, silent—ominously, dreadfully
silent. There is no debate, no discussion, no attempt to lay out for the nation
the pros and cons of this particular war. There is nothing.*

*We stand passively mute in the United States Senate, paralyzed by our
own uncertainty, seemingly stunned by the sheer turmoil of events. Only on
the editorial pages of our newspapers is there much substantive discussion of
the prudence or imprudence of engaging in this particular war.*

*And this is no small conflagration we contemplate. This is no simple attempt
to defang a villain. No. This coming battle, if it materializes, represents a turning
point in U.S. foreign policy and possibly a turning point in the recent history
of the world.*

—Senator Robert F. Byrd, February 12, 2003

CONTENTS

Acknowledgments   ix

Introduction   1

1: Beyond Baghdad: The Sacred Metaphor of "Making Progress"   9

2: Zbig at the Khyber Pass, or the Last Flight of the Persian Rug   32

3: The First Gulf War, in Which the Realists
Make Their Last Stand   62

4: The End(s) of History, in Which the
Theory and Practice Conflict   92

5: Axis of Evil, in Which the Nation's Enemies Are Revealed   116

6: Shock and Awe, in Which We Learn How Some
Democracies Go to War   149

7: The Occupation, in Which We Learn What
Followed Shock and Awe   177

8: The Dream Dies Hard, in Which the Administration
Loses the Mandate of the People   213

9: What Lies Ahead, in Which the Meaning of the
War Is Revealed   247

Notes   273

Index   297

ACKNOWLEDGMENTS

No man is an island, and no book is ever written without inspiration from friends and colleagues. In writing about contemporary subjects, moreover, no book is written without the Web. The ability to access documents and articles in a trice is real fun and encourages an author enormously. What happens then, of course, is the hard work. Walter LaFeber, Thomas McCormick, and I began a conversation more than fifty years ago in graduate school. It continues to this day. Warren Kimball keeps my eyes and ears open for the impact of nationalism and political economy. Paul Miles enlightens me during our lunch discussions on all sorts of topics related to the military and other questions. Gerry MacCauley is an agent for all seasons.

In recent years I have enjoyed collaborating with Marilyn Young on two readers published by The New Press. Our work on those books was instrumental in my willingness to undertake this project, and it has profited from her comments on early drafts of many of the chapters. At The New Press, Marc Favreau has seen the book develop from our first discussions through its evolution to the final product. His suggestions and those of the copy editor, Rachel Burd, have sharpened my ideas, and made it a better read, I hope. My wife, Nancy, is the title master in the family, and she has done it again. For all this help, and for her love, I am very thankful.

INTRODUCTION

On the eve of war, George W. Bush confided to the Spanish prime minister that Saddam Hussein was testing him and America. "He thinks that I am very weak. But the people around him know that things are otherwise. They know his future is in exile or a coffin." Defense Secretary Donald Rumsfeld also liked to think out loud about the personal challenges ahead. He had wanted to get rid of the Iraqi dictator even before the fateful attacks on 9/11. But he was more intrigued about how the earth looked from an observation point far away. He showed visitors a satellite picture of the two Koreas taken at night that he kept under a clear plastic cover on his desk. Rumsfeld delighted in pointing out how the south was a blaze of lights, while in the north only Pyongyang, the capital, showed up, as a pinpoint against the vast dark background. The comparison between the light and dark places, he believed, explained the world and where matters stood. "Anyone looking down from Mars sees that the countries that are providing the greatest opportunity for people are the freer countries." The threat to Western culture, therefore, emanated from all those who hated such freedoms, and who lived in the dark places. "It isn't just the United States," he argued, that faced such threats, "it's a way of life."

Breaking Saddam Hussein's grip on Iraq was the right thing to do, but only an intermediary goal in the New American century's mission for the world's benefit. That should have been apparent from the aftermath of the brief war that toppled the Taliban regime in Afghanistan, when the decision was made to stop chasing Osama bin Laden and shift resources for an attack on Iraq. In early 2002, at the time of President Bush's "axis of evil" State of the Union speech, this shift was well under way, as Senator Bob Graham would tell the Council on Foreign Relations; he was let in on the secret after a briefing at the headquarters of the Central Command at MacDill Air Force Base. "Senator," one of the commanders confided, "we have stopped fighting the war on terror in

Afghanistan. We are moving military and intelligence personnel and re-sources out of Afghanistan to get ready for a future war in Iraq." He ex-plained that pursuing the originator of the 9/11 attacks was not what they were trained to do, "Senator, what we are engaged in now is a man-hunt, not a war, and we are not trained to conduct a manhunt."

There would be many other explanations of why the search for Osama bin Laden failed to reach the al Qaeda leader's lair. The day of the 9/11 attacks Rumsfeld would propose going after Saddam Hussein at the same time. Sweep it all up, he would say. "There aren't any good targets in Afghanistan and there are lots of good targets in Iraq." What were those targets? Certainly Rumsfeld did not want to bomb the oil fields, and in-deed Gulf War II was planned so that there would be no repeat of what had happened in the earlier war, when Hussein managed to set a great many oil fields afire. Supposedly no one really knew where the suspected weapons of mass destruction were actually located, though Rumsfeld would claim he knew in general the area where they were hidden.

So what were the targets for bombing?

That is the central question I am concerned with in the chapters that follow. The road to Iraq began, I will argue, in the aftermath of the Viet-nam War. During that war Walt Whitman Rostow represented a strong tradition in American thought about the nature of revolutions and the need for outside forces to kick off the process of economic growth in what were labeled backward areas. In Woodrow Wilson's time, his con-fidante, Colonel Edward M. House, attempted to stave off a world con-flagration by enlisting the industrial powers then at odds, Germany and Great Britain, to join in a sort of "coalition of the willing" to take charge of what he called in his diary the "waste places of the earth." He failed, of course, but the idea was at the center of the American sacred meta-phor of progress.

Vietnam was a traumatic intellectual and political experience. It was something no one wanted to repeat. But Zbigniew Brzezinski, Rostow's successor as national security advisor in the Carter administration, fo-cused attention on a different area, the "arc of crisis" centered on the Persian Gulf, with its rich oil resources. But he also imagined it a place where the Cold War's outcome could be determined. Zbig also worked hard to strengthen the national security advisor's role, much in the fash-ion, interestingly, that someone like Dick Cheney would approve of, with his concern for "reclaiming" the supposedly lost powers of the president, a casualty of the Vietnam debacle. The 1979 Iranian Revolution spoiled his plans, however, and led to further humiliations, followed by the beginnings of a conflict with Islamic fundamentalism. For a decade the United States struggled with a dual containment policy toward both Iran and Iraq, while casting wary glances at events in Saudi Arabia. That policy came apart when Saddam Hussein took out his grievances against fellow Arab countries and the United States by invading Kuwait.

Gulf War I was George H.W. Bush's triumphal moment, but it did not last. He had managed the end of the Cold War with considerable skill, and he hoped that the new world order would be solidified by his actions in repelling Saddam Hussein's challenge. Dual containment might be over, but the task of finding a policy to deal with the aftermath of Gulf War I left the elder Bush (and his successor, Bill Clinton) without an answer. George H.W. Bush failed, said his critics, because he pursued outdated Cold War policies dominated by a containment worldview. His decision not to press on to Baghdad and remove the tyrant only stored up trouble for the future, especially after it was discovered that Iraq had been closer than anyone expected to developing a nuclear capability. The containment policy, it was argued, had only prolonged the Cold War, and was now totally irrelevant. National Security Advisor Brent Scowcroft had urged patience when the war stopped short of removing Saddam Hussein. The president and his advisers had hoped Hussein would be removed by an Iraqi-managed operation that would not blow the lid off a potentially dangerous situation and produce chaos in this crucial oil-rich country that lacked historical roots as a nation and was deeply fissured by ethnic identities and hatreds. Bush's critics had little but scorn for an argument that left the final decisions in the hands of others, whether inside Iraq or in other places like the United Nations. It was, they said, both dangerous to national security and unworthy of the American dream—now not a dream, but as self-evident as the physical world itself.

Indeed, Gulf War I turned out to be the last stand for Cold War realism. It fell before an onslaught of ideologues, sometimes called neoconservatives, who espoused, ironically, a new form of liberationist theory suitable for a reigning superpower, one supposedly able to remake the world in its image, but only if it cast off the remnants of pre-Reagan thinking. Accordingly, some of the most assertive voices condemning Bush's supposed timidity in facing up to post–Cold War challenges proclaimed the end of history, in the sense that the great ideological strug-gles of the ninteenth and twentieth centuries had finally produced a winner.

The neocons asserted that the real takeoff point of the American as-cendancy had come with Ronald Reagan's stigmatizing of the Soviet Union as an illegitimate "evil empire," and his innovative Star Wars program that forced the Kremlin to spend itself into oblivion. Applied to the Iraqi situation, the Reagan lesson was taken to mean that a brittle tyrannical system far less powerful than the Soviet Union could easily be overthrown by a shove from without. But, said his critics, George H.W. Bush had refused the opportunity to prove that he was really serious about a New World Order. And so had Bill Clinton. Whether George W. Bush would have gone to war the way he did without 9/11 can be de-bated. It proved very easy to convince him, however—indeed he asked to be convinced—that the Iraqi dictator was behind the attacks. There is little doubt, as we will see, that he had targeted Saddam Hussein for re-moval from the very outset, and was searching for a rationale to make it happen.

Despite the shock of 9/11 and the ostensible immediate reason for war, weapons of mass destruction, both Gulf Wars were long in the mak-ing. In the aftermath of Gulf War II, probably too many of the war's crit-ics look back at Cold War realism as an alternative to the policies of George W. Bush in Iraq. But the realist worldview emerged in the Cold War and was specific to that era. Besides, it was the realists, after all, who came into the Kennedy administration determined to revitalize the American dream after the supposed lethargy of the Eisenhower years, and wound up in Vietnam—on equally dubious premises, it can be ar-gued, as those that motivated George Bush to move into Iraq.

But even leaving that argument unresolved, if Gulf War II had lasted only a few months, the failure to find the weapons of mass destruction would not have mattered. No one who had the president's ear ever ex-pected to be engaged in a counterinsurgency that would last longer than World War II. Equally important, if the war had lasted only a short time, the long-term objective of gaining a stronghold and permanent bases for American "strategic interests" would have remained on the back pages, if in the newspapers at all, and would not need to have been argued out in embarrassing fashion before a public grown skeptical and war-weary. Even now, while it has become permissible—in fact mandatory for political candidates—to criticize the way the war has been fought, and to challenge the original premise for going to war, there are few indications of a deeper willingness to come to terms with the larger question of why the nation's leaders put themselves on the road to Baghdad.

It is up for debate, in other words, whether it will be enough to say, yes, we are in fact an empire with all that entails in terms of understanding ourselves. But the important thing now, it is already argued, is to cease harping on past errors and find a safe exit, one that does not abandon the Iraqi people to chaos and that protects present and future interests in the Middle East, whether access to oil resources, blocking Iranian ambitions, or protecting Israel's ability to exist in a hostile environment.

Quite possibly—indeed, undoubtedly, most would say—we have gone about the Iraq question all wrong, but talking about past errors, votes on Capitol Hill, or White House failures will not help us protect American interests. After several years of egregious errors, George W. Bush hit upon something when he asked General David Petraeus to take charge of the surge. It seems—at least to many in the public—to be working. The decline in violence in Baghdad is indeed welcome, however temporary and however achieved by payments to Sunni mercenaries or restraint by Shiite leaders. But it cannot last forever, and then what?

One answer to "What next?" was given by a retired general who had previously criticized the administration. "We deserve a comprehensive strategy that is focused on victory and guided by decisive leadership," he said. "America must succeed in Iraq and Afghanistan, but we cannot focus too narrowly on those conflicts. We need a regional and global strategy to defeat worldwide Islamic extremism to ensure a safer world today and for future generations."[1]

It was, in a sense, a circular argument, one that posited the need for a global response as a justification for continuing a local war. While it was true that American intervention had made Iraq, as one critic put it, the Super Bowl of terrorism, it was not also true that "victory . . . guided by decisive leadership" would do anything about "Islamic extremism." That was the last-ditch argument made by President Bush and Vice President Dick Cheney.

Similar arguments were made about Vietnam and the worldwide communist conspiracy at the time of the first expansion of the war, in 1965. At the national teach-in that spring historian Arthur M. Schlesinger Jr., of all people, made such a statement to the effect that it was time to stop arguing about how the United States became involved, and discuss how to get out without hurting the cause, which of course would limit one's thinking, because how it all began is essential to thinking about exit corridors. The problem for policy makers is that these usually lead away from a stage on which actors proclaim victory. The axis of evil speech deliberately suggested a connection with World War II, and looked forward in this case to Bush heralding "mission accomplished."

As matters developed in quite a different direction, the president attempted to rally his supporters with assertions to friendly audiences that this struggle was still connected to the good war; it was the supreme ideological face-off between a new form of totalitarianism—"Islamofascism," he called it—and the free world. The enemy planned to reestablish the caliphate in Baghdad as the center of a world-threatening Islamic menace. In Australia, Prime Minister John Howard, a close ally of George Bush, lost an election to Kevin Rudd, who had vowed to bring home Aussie soldiers. Howard had asserted that Osama bin Laden was praying for Barack Obama to become president. Obama called his bluff, and in doing so raised a central issue about the war's meaning. "My understanding," said Obama, "is that Mr. Howard has deployed fourteen hundred. So if he's ginned up to fight the good fight in Iraq, I would suggest that he call up another twenty thousand and send them to Iraq. Otherwise, it's just a bunch of empty rhetoric."[2]

Bush had summoned his coalition of the willing after the UN and Old Europe had denied him support for the invasion. And as in Vietnam, they were well paid to come into the ring for a few rounds. "From 2003 to early 2007," it was reported, "the United States spent $1.5 billion to support the Iraq contingents of 20 countries . . . with about two-thirds of the money devoted to Polish forces." But it was not only cash. "Many nations value the equipment they get from the United States in Iraq and hope their loyalty will be rewarded in the future through help in joining international organizations for instance."[3]

As early as 2004, only a year into the war, however, nations began to join the unwilling, starting with Spain, which, under a new government began removing its 1,400-man contingent. Poland announced in 2005 it would start bringing its force home, which at times had numbered nearly 10,000; the same year the Netherlands, the Ukraine, and Bulgaria decided to withdraw. After another change of government in early 2008, Australia said it would withdraw its small contingent of 500.

The defections from the ranks of the coalition of the willing helped to clarify the war as driven by the same assumptions that had led America to send half a million troops into Southeast Asia four decades earlier—but under the guise of a World War II–type crusade to eradicate a new axis of evil. In Vietnam, the "many flags campaign" preceded the Iraqi coalition of the willing. In both cases, Washington's associates were paid for their services, which were most useful—it was hoped—in providing an ideological cover for what looked more and more like a continuation of a neocolonial hundred years' war. The United States, ambivalently, and despite its insistence that its vision and purpose were different, had truly succeeded the old colonial powers of Britain and France. Wherein, one should ask, was this self-proclaimed mission different from what the British or French had proclaimed to be their civilizing missions? September 11 provided an electrifying moment that enabled proponents to argue with passion that the United States was responding to an assault more horrifying in its immediate and long-term consequences than Pearl Harbor, rather than expanding its efforts to dominate areas to secure political and economic advantage in imitation of nineteenth-century imperialism.

Like previous presidents from the time of Woodrow Wilson, President George W. Bush insisted that the United States wanted no territory, but at the time of his administration the nation's military owned or enjoyed unlimited access to more than seven hundred bases abroad, enabling Washington to move quickly to trouble spots with far greater ease than at any time in the classical imperialist era. Imperialism had always been about enjoying markets and raw materials and political stability without interference. In the twenty-first century it was characterized by a new emphasis on producing cheap manufacturing abroad, controlling energy resources, and selling expensive hi-tech weapons to compradors. These were the signature marks of the quest for a new American century.

Methods of control were different, mostly, from those of the imperial age, but revelations about Abu Ghraib suggested that ways of obtaining information from terrorist suspects were no different from what, for example, the French had used during France's long colonial wars in Indochina and Algeria. Interpretations of imperialism and neo-imperialism fill libraries with books thick and thin in an effort to explain the forces that motivate states to control their destiny by achieving a superior position on the international playing field. During the Cold War it was said that economic interpretations of imperialism failed because the costs of maintaining an empire outweighed the profits on any fairly drawn balance sheet. Looking at the costs—immediate and long-term—of the Iraq War would seem to suggest that was the case. But such calculations assumed that costs were spread across the population from the drugstore on Main Street to the offices of Halliburton Inc. Specific economic motives, moreover, while they are there for all to see, do not explain all the considerations that put America on the road to Baghdad and beyond. Such interests do attach themselves with amazing alacrity to policies initiated for a complex set of purposes. In the case of the Iraq Wars, the quest has been to find a safe landing zone for American influence throughout the Middle East in the aftermath of the 1979 Iranian Revolution. Such a quest does not diminish the significance of the need to control oil resources, and, indeed, demonstrates the impossibility of separating motives in a discussion of how foreign policy is designed to promote what is called a global free marketplace.

And finally, future historians will look closely at how the second Gulf War completed the transformation of the American military into something quite different from all earlier wars, with consequences that changed the very conception of a citizen army in a democracy, raising questions about whether the new military could be controlled by civilian authority—the essential ethos of the founders of the American republic—or whether the ability of the Pentagon to portray not just the war in ways it sees fit will alter political reality and create a permanent imperial presidency to replace the republic.

These are the questions that confront us today. Whatever one takes away from this book, my hope in writing it is to engage readers in a serious dialogue about the meaning of our times. Chapters 1 and 2 continue this introduction by focusing on two national security advisors, Walt Rostow and Zbigniew Brzezinski, as concrete universals of the ideas shaping the framework for understanding what started us on the road to Baghdad.

Lloyd Gardner
Newtown, Pennsylvania
April 2008

1

BEYOND BAGHDAD: THE SACRED METAPHOR OF "MAKING PROGRESS"

Our success in the Gulf will shape not only the new world order we seek but our mission here at home.

—George H.W. Bush, January 1991

And so I—the notion that somehow we're not making progress I just don't subscribe to.

—George W. Bush, January 2005

A retired CIA analyst who worked on declassifying Vietnam War national intelligence estimates—some of which he helped to write—spoke of his increasingly bitter feelings as he went over the record of America's longest war, and the failure of policy makers to heed the warnings. The volume they were preparing, he said, ought to have a cover depicting the view from an automobile rear seat. Driving the car, he went on, would be Vice President Cheney, with President Bush in the passenger's seat. Through the windshield one could see a minaret and palm trees. In the rearview mirror was the American embassy in Saigon, with the last helicopter lifting off in 1975. The legend at the bottom of the mirror read "Objects in the Mirror Are Closer than You Think."

Iraq is not Vietnam. The wars are not the same, but the image is disturbing nevertheless, because it challenges a deeply held conviction dating back to the nation's origins: American history is a narrative of steady progress, and, therefore, exceptional in all ways. In the American political tradition, moreover, science, as technology, is never at odds with faith, comprising a belief in a uniquely inspired mission for the nation to fulfill. This is true especially in foreign policy, because there it is possible to externalize evil completely, unlike in domestic politics, where ordinarily, but not always, the art of compromise has been accepted as a necessary evil. At the dawn of the atomic age, when faith in technology reached new heights, Harry Truman celebrated the coming of the bomb by declaring, "This is the greatest thing in history." Press releases prepared months in advance for the day after the first bomb was delivered made it clear that only in America could the bomb have been developed: "It is doubtful if such another combination could be got together in the world. What has been done is the greatest achievement of organized science in history."[1]

For Ronald Reagan, as for Truman, American ingenuity could overcome *any* technological or *any* political difficulty. His most insightful biographer, Lou Cannon, made the connection nicely: "He had been an ideal spokesman for General Electric, where the motto was, 'Progress Is Our Most Important Product,' in part because he accepted the inevitability of scientific progress as an article of faith." Confronted by a university student who complained that his generation was out of touch with reality, because it grew up in a world without computers, Reagan, who was governor of California at the time, smiled, "It's true . . . we didn't grow up . . . with those things. We invented them."[2]

The Russians tested their own bomb four years after Truman's boast, but there was a ready explanation that preserved the metaphor. They had not out-progressed America; they had stolen the secret! Didn't the arrests of atom spies Julius and Ethel Rosenberg prove it? And with their conviction and execution came a Cold War obsession with the internal threat to national security that actually bolstered the search for the next big thing, the H-bomb. Something else emerged from the atomic spy case as a counterpart to the idea of progress—the agent theory of international relations. The theory not only explained why the Russians got the bomb sooner than they ought to have, it also seemed to account for the growth of anti-Americanism in the later years of the Cold War, when the front lines shifted to the third world.

If America could not count on always having everyone cheering its policies, that was because its critics feared losing out to a better worldview, and they did not have enough to offer materially or morally in the struggle between capitalism and communism for the right to determine the world's direction. Secretary of State John Foster Dulles, ruminating in 1954 about the differences between Europe's traditional approach to world affairs and the American mission, thought his country's exceptional place among nations stemmed from a pervasive religious influence on national thought. In a private meditation, "The 'Big Three' Alliance," he wrote, "There is a very definite loosening of the ties which unite Great Britain, France and the United States in the field of foreign policy. The causes of this are not superficial, such as disagreement about tactics or clashes of personalities, but they are fundamental, and need to be understood if our policies are to be wise and adequate:"

> The American people, far more than the people of either Britain or France, are a religious people who like to feel that their international policies have a moral quality. By and large throughout our history we have stood for policies which could be expressed in moral terms. Perhaps there has been an element of hypocrisy in this respect but also there is a very genuine dedication to moral principles as contributing the element of "enlightenment" to what is called "enlightened self-interest."
>
> There is a particular antipathy in the American people to the so-called "colonial" policies of the Western Europe powers. The U.S. is the first colony to win independence and feels sympathetic to the aspirations of colonial and dependent peoples and . . . [feels] strongly vexed at the leadership which communism is giving to these aspirations, while we seem inhibited from giving that leadership because of our alliance with the colonial powers.[3]

As he mulled over what he had written, it seemed not yet enough. So Dulles added in longhand, "There is also strong opposition to giving moral approval to Soviet rule over captive peoples, as seems implicit in U.K. attitudes." Compare that to a more recent rumination on coalitions by Secretary of Defense Donald Rumsfeld in an early November 2001 speech to the Center for Security Policy—one of the many such think tanks that proliferated across Washington in the post–Cold War era. Coalitions were fine, he said, because America needed help with its mission. "I used the word in the plural form," he alerted them, "not the singular." That was because in the Afghan war just concluded—and implicitly in the war against Iraq to come—the coalitions would be different. "It's important because if it were a single coalition, and a coalition member decided not to participate in one way or another, it would be charged that the coalition was falling apart." If that happened, the weakest link in the chain would end the mission, and the American cause would be betrayed. "Which is why we don't have a single coalition, we have flexible coalitions for different aspects of the task. In this way, the mission determines the coalition; the coalition must not determine the mission. [Applause.]"[4]

Closely related to Rumsfeld's description of America's future relationship to coalitions was the notion of "creative destruction" espoused by the new-age muscular Wilsonians influencing foreign policy in the Bush II administration. Instead of continuity and containment, they believed, a sharp blow was the only way to break through to change societies frozen in underdevelopment, prolonged in that unhappy state by evil leaders dedicated to developing weapons of mass destruction. Such a description applied to both the Soviet Union and Saddam Hussein's Iraq. Here is Secretary of State Condoleezza Rice writing after the Cold War about prospects for German reunification, as a former Russian specialist in the first Bush administration: "The harsh truth was that the American goal could be achieved only if the Soviet Union suffered a reversal of fortunes not unlike a catastrophic defeat in a war."[5]

Whenever President George W. Bush and Secretary of State Condoleezza Rice speak about the failed policy of seeking to preserve stability as leading only to the rise of al Qaeda and desperate acts of terrorism, they are expressing sentiments John Foster Dulles would have understood fully, and fully approved. "What we're seeing here, in a sense," Rice responded to a question, when things did not seem to be going well some time after the fall of Baghdad, "is the growing—the birth pangs of a new Middle East, and whatever we do we have to be certain that we're pushing forward to the new Middle East, not going back to the old one." Pushing forward was the traditional way of expressing the westward movement of American pioneers and what schoolchildren are taught about inevitable progress.[6]

But perhaps it was Secretary of Defense Robert McNamara who set forth the boldest expression of the need to unify the world behind American leadership, suggesting in a memorandum to President Lyndon Johnson that the stakes in Vietnam could not be higher.

The role we have inherited and have chosen for ourselves for the future is to extend our influence and power to thwart ideologies that are hostile to these aims [open societies] and to move the world, as best we can, in the direction we prefer. Our ends cannot be achieved and our leadership role cannot be played if some powerful and virulent nation—whether Ger-

many, Japan, Russia or China—is allowed to organize their part of the
world according to a philosophy contrary to ours.[7]

When McNamara wrote those words no one was talking about an American empire, whether exceptional in its pervasive religious content, as
Dulles described the differences with old European empires, or in any
other way ambitious to determine how the world was organized. In the
years subsequent to 9/11, however, American policy makers used phrases
similar to McNamara's to explain how the realist interpretation of world
affairs, with its supposed emphasis on balance-of-power multipolarity
and stability, or any other containment formula, did not fit the era of the
new American century. The phrase "coalitions of the willing," coined
when it became clear there would be no UN mandate for war with Iraq,
suited the White House, and was, in fact, more congenial, to use former
secretary of state Dean Rusk's word, to the American concept of progress
and the self-imposed burden of meeting the world's aspirations.

Rusk had used the word to separate the American experience from the
agent theory of revolution to answer a question from Senator Frank
Church in 1966 about the struggle in Vietnam. Church had suggested
that Vietnam presented an entirely different challenge than what had
taken place in Europe and Korea after World War II, and then asked if it
wasn't naive to expect that any amount of money or military force could
prevent guerrilla uprisings. "We will have to live in a world afflicted with
such revolutions for a long time to come." They could not be prevented
entirely, agreed Rusk, but the challenge must be met, because what was
going on in Vietnam was not a true revolution; it was fomented by a
harsh totalitarian regime in China. So there was a fundamental difference between that kind of fraudulent revolution, he said, "and the kind
of revolution which is congenial to our own experience, and fits into the
aspirations of ordinary men and women right around the world."[8]

It was no great distance from Rusk's pronouncement, or Dulles's med-
itations, to President George W. Bush's assertion of America's world mission, on January 28, 2003, the eve of the invasion of Iraq.

> Americans are a free people, who know that freedom is the right of every
> person and the future of every nation. The liberty we prize is not Amer-
> ica's gift to the world, it is God's gift to humanity. [Applause.]
>
> We Americans have faith in ourselves, but not in ourselves alone. We

do not know—we do not claim to know—all the ways of Providence, yet we can trust in them, placing our confidence in the loving God behind all of life, and all of history.

May He guide us now. And may God continue to bless the United States of America.

Bush equates American foreign policy here with God's will, a claim very few felt willing to challenge, either because the shock of 9/11 had jarred loose normal sensibilities, or because the effort would not be worth it, since everyone expected an easy victory, like Gulf War I. To those who might question just a little whether the war was a just war, the answer was: "[W]e do not claim to know all the ways of Providence, yet we can trust in them." Statements like these, fairly radiating with the conviction that he is submitting himself to God's ordination to bring American freedom to the peoples of the Middle East, so long held in bondage by the cruelest of tyrants, should have raised alarms.

But they did not, in part because of a false syllogism. "God is not on the side of any nation," the president acknowledged on one occasion, "yet we know He is on the side of justice. And it is the deepest strength of America that from the hour of our founding, we have chosen justice as our goal."[9] God is on the side of justice; America has chosen the side of justice as its goal; therefore, God will bless American policy. Obstacles to this mission were only to be expected from forces on the wrong side of history.

Truman to Tet

President Truman had raised high expectations about America's capabilities to push forward the cause of freedom in the aftermath of the atomic bombs dropped on Hiroshima and Nagasaki, telling French leader Charles de Gaulle in August 1945 that the old diplomacy was dead. De Gaulle came to Washington to ask for negotiations on a security treaty, but was rebuffed by a comment that such pacts were no longer important. "The United States possessed a new weapon," the president said, "the atomic bomb, which would defeat any aggressor." France should get in line, literally, for economic aid, and figuratively, by removing Communists from its government and welcoming American businessmen, who had thus far found their way blocked in resuming operations.[10]

As the Cold War developed, things did not work out as Truman suggested they would, of course, because the atomic bomb could not easily
be shrunk to fit into the challenges of the Berlin blockade or Korea. But
the distaste for diplomacy and the preference for negotiations only from
strength led to a decision to build the H-bomb, not only to preempt the
Soviets in the arms race but also to insure against a supposed weakening
of national will—a persistent issue during the Cold War, and after. The
H-bomb, of course, was an even less usable weapon than the A-bomb,
except as the key component of mutually assured destruction (MAD).
The steady downgrading of the State Department as the source of foreign
policy decisions, despite strong personalities such as Dean Acheson and
John Foster Dulles at its head in the early Cold War, in favor of the Pentagon and its related agencies was probably inevitable in an era of glam-
orous high-tech weapons systems. These systems, in turn, stood atop a
pyramid of influence that rested in part on the increased use of MAAGs
(military assistance advisory groups) that fostered military-to-military
negotiations as the dominant pattern of foreign relations. The diplomacy (or denial) of arms sales was a perfect fit with the diplomacy of values, and the use of military power in the cause of spreading freedom.

The creation of the offices of the secretary of defense and the director
of the Central Intelligence Agency came in the same year, 1947, as the
Truman Doctrine, when the U.S. government told the world that its
mission was to come to the aid of all countries who were threatened not
only by foreign aggression but also by internal subversion. Under-Secretary
of State Dean Acheson pretty well summed it all up in testimony on the
Truman Doctrine, combining the questions of competing values, the uses
of military aid in Greece and Turkey (and elsewhere in the future), and
the burden of the American mission: "We are willing to help people who
believe the way we do, to continue to live the way they want to live."[11]

The Cold War era began with American military men as viceroys in
Germany and Japan, as ambassador to the Soviet Union, and as head of
the Central Intelligence Agency as well as the Department of State. But
the high-tension power lines in the capital would soon run from the
White House to the Department of Defense through an office located in
the basement of the executive mansion that had no specific bureaucratic
mandate other than a self-defined one, the office of the national security
advisor. McGeorge Bundy's close relationship with Defense Secretary
Robert McNamara was typical, and though Dean Rusk was every bit as

hawkish as Bundy (if not more so), it was the national security advisor who framed the policy alternatives at the outset of the Vietnam War,

The real father of creative destruction was not some Bush II official but Walt Rostow, an economic theorist and Bundy's successor, who persuaded LBJ he was definitely on the right track in Vietnam. Even after Richard Nixon tried and failed to "save" either Vietnam or his presidency, Rostow urged a last-ditch effort. The United States, he said in a CBS television interview on April 4, 1975, should "land two Marine divisions in North Vietnam and keep them there" to make sure Hanoi abided by the 1973 Paris peace accords. President Gerald Ford should do this "as a matter of conscience."[12]

Hawk-eyed Optimist

To answer the question why Rostow clung to his hopes for saving South Vietnam after nearly all the other hawks had abandoned that perch involves confronting issues that also explain a good deal about the origins of the Iraq crusade. Above all, Walt Rostow was a theorist, one who believed he had a mission to fulfill to save the world from false prophets, particularly Marxist tempters who had flooded into places like Southeast Asia in the wake of failed colonial regimes. A first-generation immigrant and the son of a baker who named his two boys Walt Whitman Rostow and Eugene V. Debs Rostow, Walt became convinced during his early years delivering bread to the black ghetto in New Haven that liberal political thought needed military backbone to make it stand up against competing ideologies. He also believed, more particularly, that the only way to jolt traditional socieities into moving toward what he called the takeoff point economically and politically was through outside force.

Educated at Yale and Oxford, during World War II Rostow was a target planner for the Army Air Force in Europe. After the war he settled in at the Massachusetts Institute of Technology and was a co-founder of its Cold War think tank, the Center for International Studies, the sort of place that became a model for conservative think tanks such as the American Enterprise Institute where so many idea men found places to reach and be reached by political elites. Through his work at the center Rostow established very good contacts with C.D. Jackson, a psychological war expert from Henry Luce's Time-Life-Fortune empire on loan to the Eisenhower administration.

"C.D." Jackson called upon Rostow for ideas at the time of Stalin's death in 1953 in order to exploit a presumed opportunity to promote the breakup of the Soviet bloc in Eastern Europe, and perhaps steer events in the direction of ending the Cold War altogether. One result was the "Chance for Peace" speech Ike gave in April 1953 heralding the opportunity Moscow had to change course. After discussing the divergent paths the United States and the Soviet Union had pursued after World War II, and the strength of a determined West to confront Russian expansionist efforts, the president turned to specific requirements for Moscow besides ending the Korean War: "It should mean, no less importantly, an end to the direct and indirect attacks upon the security of Indochina and Malaya. For any armistice in Korea that merely released aggressive armies to attack elsewhere would be fraud."

"I strongly feel," Rostow advised Jackson in explaining why Moscow could be held to account for revolutions outside its actual sphere of influence, "that the basic strength of the United States lies in the fact that our interests, properly formulated and properly explained, do coincide with the interests of people everywhere. This includes the people of Russia and China."[13]

That assumption said it all so far as Rostow was concerned. It energized American policy, but it was only good so long as there was a powerful military force behind it. Rostow was always a liberationist thinker, never a containment Cold War realist. By comparison, Dulles was cautious and measured, a litigator with a brief; Rostow was freewheeling and assertive, an innovator with a cause. He was the author of Eisenhower's Open Skies proposal to the Soviet Union, for example, which Ike threw out at the 1955 Geneva summit conference, a proposition designed solely to put the Russians on the defensive. The Open Skies proposal was a perfect example of how psychological warfare worked, both abroad and at home. In essence, Eisenhower offered to allow Soviet reconnaissance planes over the United States if the Soviet Union would grant reciprocal rights. No one really expected the Soviet leaders to agree, but the idea got terrific publicity. The United States kept pressing it as a major step toward ending the threat of nuclear war, until the end of the Eisenhower years. Russian efforts to point out that the American proposal excluded foreign bases seemed nitpickish.

As he awaited a call to Washington, Rostow wrote big-idea books, the most famous of which, published in 1960, was *The Stages of Economic*

Growth, boldly subtitled *A Non-Communist Manifesto*. *Stages* brought him instant attention in political circles as well as among academic contemporaries. The review-catching phrase, "takeoff" stage, described the point where traditional societies suddenly began to leave their centuries-old fatalism behind and grasp the possibilities of modernization. What forces trigger such a process, asked Rostow? Sometimes they boiled up from inside the traditional society, he wrote, but mostly they came from the outside: "The more general case in modern history . . . saw the stage of preconditions arise not endogenously but from some external intrusion by more advanced societies. These invasions—literal or figurative—shocked the traditional society and began or hastened its undoing; but they also set in motion ideas and sentiments that initiated the process by which a modern alternative to the traditional society was constructed out of the old culture." "I decided when I was eighteen," Rostow once told a congressional committee, "that when I learned enough I was going to do an alternative to Marxism, because I knew a lot of people in the world were taken in by this theory, and I finally took my shot at it." The underlying assumption of *Stages of Economic Growth* was that the American Revolution was the *only* revolution the world needed, or could live with in safety.

Stages appeared at a time when the Eisenhower administration seemed to have run out of ideas and had only a short time left in any event. Russian successes in space and in playing godfather to Fidel Castro's Cuban Revolution alarmed Americans. Rostow was immediately drawn to Jack Kennedy as someone who would welcome big ideas for getting lost momentum back. Kennedy needed a winning campaign slogan, and Rostow offered one: "This country is ready to get moving again—and I'm prepared to lead it." Shortened to "Let's get this country moving again," it became JFK's battle cry. Rostow was also the source of the phrase "The New Frontier."

Invited to join Mac Bundy's NSC shop in the White House as an Asian specialist, Rostow was soon immersed in planning for a bigger U.S. role in Indochina—a fateful beginning for both him and the country. After the embarrassing flop at the Bay of Pigs in mid-April 1961, Rostow had some tough advice. The problem, as he saw it, was where to pick the place to start afresh. There was no time to lose, because delay would give the impression "that we are up against a game we can't handle." "A clean-cut success in Viet-Nam [sic] would do much to hold the line in Asia while permitting us—and the world—to learn how to deal with indirect aggression." His job, as he would say, was to anticipate where communist forces might find openings, and thwart their purposes with whatever methods necessary. In Vietnam that meant injecting military forces to counter a rival effort to overturn a traditional society, and, as in Iraq later, provide a breathing space for political development.[14]

Rostow went to Vietnam in 1961 along with General Maxwell Taylor. There he met the American-backed leader Ngo Dinh Diem, and came away troubled. Diem had problems, but most were not of his making. Locked in "Oriental" ways, Diem did not have the right temperament to encourage the new generation of technocrats, men who could be instrumental in saving his country from the communists. The key problem, however, Rostow concluded, was that he faced an impossible situation. No nation since Napoleonic times, he insisted, had ever won a counterinsurgency war when faced with an open frontier that allowed insurgents to cross back and forth with impunity. The only way to win such a war was by sending troops to close the frontier with Laos and Cambodia, and to halt infiltration from North Vietnam—an idea he would pursue even as war weariness and disillusionment descended over Washington fifteen years later. He held to this conviction until Saigon fell and afterward, as he criticized former colleagues in the Johnson administration for abandoning the cause. Rostow's belief that defeat in Vietnam was not inevitable but the result of mistaken timidity and a failure of will shaped his successors' outlooks down to Iraq.

Rostow and Taylor came back home in 1961 to urge an immediate effort using American troops to seal the Laos border. Their report triggered a debate still going on at Kennedy's death, and into the early months of the Johnson administration. While President Johnson may have envisaged the 1964 Gulf of Tonkin resolution Congress gave him (after hardly a sentence of debate) as insulation against Republican attacks for running away from a fight, and an easy way to achieve a huge margin of victory so as to get on with his Great Society domestic program, Rostow saw it very differently: as an opportunity to move forward in Vietnam, not unlike later enabling resolutions Bush presidents used to wage war in the Middle East.

Rostow wished to bring an end to uncertainty about American determination to save South Vietnam. Tit-for-tat responses would never do the job. Instead, the Tonkin resolution would open a new page. "They [leaders in Hanoi and Beijing] should now feel they confront an LBJ who has made up his mind. Contrary to the anxiety expressed at an earlier stage, I believe it quite possible to communicate the limits as well as the seriousness of our intentions," he wrote to Secretary of Defense Robert McNamara, without stirring fears that we intend to land troops in China itself.[15]

Rostow hoped that when the inevitable decision came to send troops their mission would include closing South Vietnam's open frontiers with Laos. When LBJ sent the first one hundred thousand men in July 1965 to attempt the rescue of Saigon's increasingly inept regimes, which came and went with dreary frequency, Rostow had little hope that policy alone would do the job. Nearly a year later he succeeded Mac Bundy as national security advisor when there was already talk about a developing quagmire. He was not discouraged by such talk, but he felt the president should go to the country for a new mandate. Johnson should tell the people "We are all being tested by this crisis." Americans must learn, he said, in words that might have come right out of *The Stages of Economic Growth*, or from speeches during later years in the second Gulf War, "to understand the nature of the war; to understand the confusing but essentially constructive struggle of a democratic nation to bloom; and, above all, by the fact that the Communists are counting on us to despair and give up. . . . If our people really understand, I believe they would be quite tolerant of the birth pangs."[16]

It was remarkable indeed how Rostow's conception of the problem facing an American leader in a war gone sour, and even his precise phrase concerning the need to be "quite tolerant of the birth pangs," would be reprised by Secretary of State Condoleezza Rice as she attempted to summon up American will to stay the course in Iraq. Both Rostow and Rice eagerly sought out audiences to refute critics.

In February 1967 Rostow went to Leeds University to proclaim the passing of the era of guerrilla wars, promising his British audience that Vietnam marked an end to the historic struggle with communism for supremacy in the third world. Indeed, the very concept of wars of national liberation was "old-fashioned." "It is being overtaken not merely by the resistance of the seven nations fighting there, but also by history and by increasingly pervasive attitudes of pragmatism and moderation." The Chinese communist offensive in the developing world had fallen apart, "leaving the war in Viet Nam [sic] perhaps the last major stand of Mao's doctrine of guerrilla warfare." Even so, one had to be aware that failure in Vietnam "could destroy the emerging foundation for confidence and regional cooperation in Asia, with further adverse consequences on every continent."[17]

One hears in these words an argument very like the "end of history" assertions in the Bush era, with the same edgy caveat that the consequences of failure were incalculable. There were other similarities. Foreshadowing later disputes, Rostow, like Vice President Dick Cheney in Gulf War II, had a running battle with the CIA when the intelligence agency's conclusions did not fit well with the idea of progress. This was hardly surprising given the way that the role of national security advisor had evolved, for the position required someone who could reduce complicated reality to just a few alternatives. Cheney played that role more than Condoleezza Rice did, and neither he nor Walt Rostow lacked confidence in their ability to condense and simplify choices.

In Rostow's view, the CIA and the State Department had irritating habits of nay-saying, and, it sometimes seemed to a troubled White House, were actually disloyal to the American mission. Rostow's feud erupted several times, but one incident is worth discussing in detail. CIA director Richard Helms sent Johnson in September 1967 a memorandum that challenged the very premise of the war, the simplistic domino thesis that Eisenhower had almost casually announced at a 1954 press conference, suggesting that nations close to Vietnam would topple over into communism's evil empire all the way to Japan if America pulled out. Helms tried to soften the message with an ambivalent nod to Oval Office convictions. "We are not defeatist out here [at Langley]," he assured LBJ. But gradual withdrawal could be managed so as to minimize damage to the nation's position abroad and lessen the domestic political fallout. "If the analysis here advances the discussion at all, it is in the direction of suggesting that the risks [of an unfavorable outcome] are probably more limited and controllable than most previous argument has indicated."[18]

With Walt Rostow standing close by his side, Johnson gave Australian journalists to understand that he believed the domino thesis. That was his answer to those who would run out on the American mission. Summarize for these people the consequences of pulling out of Vietnam, he ordered Rostow. The national security advisor did so with a new spin on the domino thesis, suggesting there would be "an immediate and profound political crisis," not in Vietnam, however, but in the United States. Out of this turmoil would emerge a powerful isolationist surge unless we finished the job in the right way. Johnson nodded, and urged him to go on: "They would say our character had worn out?" Rostow replied, "Yes." And while we were divided and preoccupied by the debilitating debate, Johnson declared, the USSR and China would seize dangerous initiatives? Yes, and NATO "could never hold up" as America lost self-confidence. On and on Rostow continued this litany of disasters, countering all the arguments advanced in the Helms memo.[19]

Rostow offered the president a chart he had devised demonstrating that the "crossover point" was approaching—that inevitable moment when American troop reinforcements surpassed North Vietnamese and Vietcong ability to replace their losses. According to his chart, infiltration had fallen off dramatically in the first eight months of 1967, from a monthly average the previous year of between 7,000 and 8,000, to between 4,000 and 5,000. From such statistics it was possible to glimpse the crossover point just beyond the next rice paddy. But Johnson never got there. The president even brought his commander, General William Westmoreland, back to Washington at the end of 1967 to assure Congress and the public that the moment was nearly at hand. The general made speeches, gave television interviews, and was guided along by Johnson at a congressional briefing. "We feel that we are somewhat like the boxer in the ring," Westmoreland told congressional leaders, "where we have got our opponent almost on the ropes. And we hear murmurs to our rear as we look over the shoulder that the second wants to throw in the towel."[20]

Forty years later, on August 22, 2007, George W. Bush addressed a friendly audience, the Veterans of Foreign Wars, and said much the same thing as he spoke about his war in Iraq and the supposed success of the latest escalation, the surge.

Our troops are seeing this progress that is being made on the ground. And as they take the initiative from the enemy, they have a question: Will their elected leaders in Washington pull the rug out from under them just as they're gaining momentum and changing the dynamic on the ground in Iraq? Here my answer is clear: We'll support our troops, we'll support our commanders, and we will give them everything they need to succeed. [Applause.]

When General Westmoreland went back to Vietnam, he left the United States with a promise of light at the end of the tunnel. Then came the Tet offensive. Rostow was grim—but still determined. The debates inside the president's tightest circle had become centered on what kind of speech Johnson should give to announce his new decisions on the war. Some drafts had him hunkering down, as he liked to say, like a jackrabbit in a dust storm. But over a period of days LBJ began moving in the direction of a peace speech. Rostow at one point passed a note to CIA director Richard Helms:

> Dick:
> About the only hope we've got, I conclude, is that:
> —the North Vietnamese *do* mount a big offensive (B-3, Hue, Quang Tri, Khe Sanh);
> —the 101, Airmobile, and the marines clobber them between now and May 15.
> —Just like Lincoln in 1864.
>
> Walt[21]

The infuriating thing about the war had always been the asymmetrical challenge. Rostow ached for the enemy to mount a big offensive that could be met by conventional forces—and to do so before the presidential campaign got fully under way. The results in the early primaries suggested, however, that if there was such an offensive, Johnson's position would actually worsen. Besides, after Tet it was unlikely that the enemy could put together a new offensive, having suffered heavy losses in the battles around South Vietnam. It was increasingly clear, finally, that Johnson was leaning in another direction, though he would not tell his national security advisor he was contemplating combining an invitation to peace talks with an announcement he would not seek another term.

Upset by evidence that everything had come apart, Johnson appealed to Rostow for understanding. "What the hell do they want me to do? What *can* we do that we're not doing?" The national security advisor saw his opening, perhaps his last chance. "Well, Mr. President, you know, as we've talked about before," and launched into the case for invading North Vietnam and Laos. An aide, Harry McPherson, was present, and he reported Johnson's reaction: "Johnson just *flinched*, just *jumped*." He did not even want McPherson to hear such things. "No, no, no, I don't want to talk about that," he said. The president did not want somebody going public with the idea of a surge into North Vietnam, saying, "Oh, my God, we're going to invade North Vietnam."[22]

The war would go on for nearly five more years after Johnson returned to the hill country of Texas to sort out his memories. Rostow accompanied him to Austin, where he set up a new office in the Johnson Presidential Library, amid the archives holding the policy papers he had written. Twenty years later Rostow had some final words to say in "The Case for the Vietnam War." The occasion for this essay in the War College Quarterly, *Parameters*, was the publication of Robert McNamara's first volume of memoirs, *In Retrospect: The Tragedy and Lessons of Vietnam*. Rostow listed McNamara's arguments about why the war was unwinnable, then added his refutation, "To a degree impossible to determine, his conclusion, by his own account, was influenced also by the anti-war sentiment in the country which extended to his immediate family." However couched in praise for McNamara, this was an accusation. It indicted the former defense secretary, but also all those who had come to see the war as a futile and tragic encounter with forces beyond the nation's ability to overcome. Vietnam had been a shattering blow to Rostow's core assumptions about the evolution of the world, and the central place of the American guiding hand in that evolution.

What happened could have been avoided. Rostow reminded readers of the recommendation he had made in 1961, when JFK had sent him to Saigon for his first close-up encounter with a war of national liberation. His conclusion thirty-five years later was the same: "Another weakness of McNamara's book is his failure to discuss systematically the gift of sanctuary which rendered the war inevitably 'long and inconclusive.' There have been no examples in which a guerrilla war (or a war dependent on external supply) has been won in which one side was granted sanctuary by the other." Just think how American support for the Afghan defenders through Pakistan had turned the tide in the war against the Russians, he wrote. "Those who advocated blocking the trails on the ground [primarily Rostow himself] believed that action would force a concentration of North Vietnamese troops to keep the trails open, and two or three reinforced U.S. divisions together with air supremacy could deal with them."

He ended with one final thrust at the antiwar movement through the screen of McNamara's supposed inner turmoil. "One returns to the wild card in this story: the manner in which the United States, including Mc-Namara's own family, was driven into painful controversy over the war. And that is part of the equation that all Americans must weigh for themselves. In fact, only McNamara can weigh all the factors which have driven him into the position that, whatever the cost, the United States should have withdrawn its troops from Vietnam."[23]

No More Vietnams

As in so many other ways, the rationalizations that emerged in critiques of the *way* the war was waged protected the metaphor of progress from any lasting trauma inflicted by Vietnam. From this perspective it was more appropriate and satisfying that Defense Secretary Dick Cheney arrived fifteen years later in the Middle East, at the outset of Gulf War I, wearing Western cowboy boots and jeans. The Cold War was over, but doubts lingered about whether the United States could always win what were now to be called the "savage wars of peace." "The only acceptable outcome is absolute, total victory," he declared, meaning not only the immediate conflict but also victory over the stalemates that had characterized the Cold War from Korea, the bad outcome in Vietnam, and the MAD standoff of the arms race. It was important, furthermore, to have such an "absolute, total victory" over Iraq to erase any doubts that military power had ultimately defeated the Soviet Union and brought the evil empire crashing in a heap of its Stalinist concrete.

In Cheney's view—and that of many other conservatives—the pressing issue after the Cold War was the danger of a letdown, combined with a fear of using American troops connected to the so-called Vietnam syndrome that inhibited presidential initiative. Indeed, Ronald Reagan himself had engendered doubts in some quarters by cozying up to Mikhail Gorbachev, and was too hasty about dismantling and ordering a partial stand-down of the Strategic Air Command.[24] The new world order President George H.W. Bush envisioned was threatened by those who eagerly embraced the idea of a peace dividend, as if America's mission had finished with the fall of the Evil Empire, when it had only really begun. Gulf War I, therefore, would have two redeeming features, beyond Kuwait's immediate liberation from Iraqi occupation: first, it would eradicate the last bad memories of Vietnam: and, second, as President Bush told a questioner, there was always the problem of the "siren's call" to be overcome:

I think we've got to guard against the siren's call, "Now is the time to slash defense spending. . . . If there's ways that we can save money in defense, I'll be right out front. I've told the American people we're going to do it, and we have done it. We have cut defense. But I'm not going to cut into the muscle of defense of this country in a kind of an instant sense of budgetary gratification so that we can go over and help somebody when the needs aren't clear and *when we have requirements that transcend historic concerns about the Soviet Union* [emphasis added].[25]

It appeared to be an ironic twist when the wrath of the neoconservatives fell on the first President Bush for his failure to take advantage of the supposed opportunity to topple Saddam Hussein from power. But was that really so? In truth, there is no substantive "realist" tradition in American history. The tradition ran along other lines, combining faith and experience, faith in technology, and the experience of ever-expanding frontiers. While the neoconservatives now held aloft the banner under which the second President Bush would go to war to finish the job, it displayed the same set of beliefs that Walt Rostow had put at the top of his policy papers when he penned the slogan "The New Frontier" and urged Lyndon Johnson not to forsake the cause of progress in Vietnam.

What was ironic, perhaps, was the alliance that formed between British prime minister Tony Blair, who renamed his party "new" Labour, and the Texas-style Republican George W. Bush. On one level, it was not at all surprising that Blair—who broke with many party attachments to a socialist vision—would seek common ground with Bush. British political leaders hardly wished to repeat any of the Vietnam experience, when Harold Wilson and Lyndon Johnson were barely on speaking terms. But there was a fascinating conjunction of ideological assumptions that made the Blair story a clue to understanding the development of the Bush administration's quest to transform the Middle East area into modernizing states that reached toward political democracy and the free marketplace.

Indeed, in the aftermath of 9/11, that conjunction emerged clearly in the speeches of Blair and National Security Advisor Condoleezza Rice, and demonstrated how the events of that tragic day reenergized policy makers to pursue their goals to transform the Middle East. "I tell you," Blair instructed his cabinet, "we must steer close to America. If we don't we will lose our influence to shape what they do." Blair could see that

Britannia no longer ruled the waves. But narrow self-interest was not the most important reason for Blair's unstinting support—"I'm there to the very end," he told Bush. As early as 1999, before anyone had really paid much attention to a Texas governor as a presidential candidate, the prime minister had outlined a Blair doctrine that discounted the historic principle of noninterference by one state in another state's internal affairs as inadequate in an age of rapid globalization. From the outset he was as much a believer in the metaphor of progress as anyone on the other side of the Atlantic still contemplating finishing the job in Iraq. "We are continually fending off the danger of letting wherever CNN roves," he said in a Chicago speech, "be the cattle prod to take a global conflict seriously."[26]

Since the end of the Cold War, Blair went on, "Our armed forces have been busier than ever—delivering humanitarian aid, deterring attacks on defenseless people, backing up UN resolutions, and occasionally engaging in major wars as we did in the Gulf in 1991 and are currently doing in the Balkans." Were these aftershocks of the Cold War, he asked, or a future pattern? Many of the problems had been caused by "two dangerous and ruthless men—Saddam Hussein and Slobodan Milošević," who had waged vicious campaigns "against sections of their own community. . . . Instead of enjoying its oil wealth Iraq has been reduced to poverty, with political life stultified through fear."

America had emerged as by far the strongest state, but with no dreams of world conquest or colonies, he concluded, and, if anything, after the Cold War, "too ready to see no need to get involved in the affairs of the rest of the world." But that was fatally shortsighted. "Now our actions are guided by a more subtle blend of mutual self-interest and moral purpose in defending the values we cherish. In the end values and interests merge. . . . The spread of our values makes us safer."

The 2000 Bush campaign seemed to prove Blair's point, as the Republican candidate called for less use of the American military in "nation-building" missions around the world. "I would be guarded in my approach. I don't think we can be all things to all people in the world." He said that he would not use force against one of Blair's two major villains, Milošević, who was a problem for the people in that part of the world (including the Russians), and his references to Saddam Hussein sometimes seemed limited to suggestions that his plan for Alaskan oil drilling and greater use of American coal resources would reduce U.S.

involvement—at least in the Gulf region. "Today we import one million barrels [a day] from Saddam Hussein," he said in the first presidential debate. "I would rather that a million come from our own hemisphere, have it come from our own country as opposed to Saddam Hussein."[27]

Having surrounded himself with policy figures then usually associated with the realist approach, such as Condoleezza Rice and Colin Powell, Bush gave an impression that his administration would, if it departed at all from Clinton's policies, move in the direction of greater circumspection. It was a false impression, of course, but no doubt Tony Blair was deeply concerned, as once in the White House Bush moved swiftly to disassociate the United States from the Kyoto treaty limiting carbon emissions into the atmosphere, and took other steps that observers might label as isolationist. From this perspective Bush was changed instantly into an internationalist by 9/11. But a better understanding of the president's positions disclose instead that the tragedy released him from constraints that had been in place since Gulf War I, when his father built the international coalition that swept Saddam Hussein's army out of Kuwait in less than one hundred hours. The attacks on the World Trade Center and the Pentagon made it unnecessary to justify a new war as in any way part of the old politics or a compromise with any ally.

In a speech to the British International Institute for Strategic Studies in London on June 26, 2003, National Security Advisor Condoleezza Rice began by recalling President Bush's *pre-* 9/11 remarks to a European audience: "We share more than an alliance. We share a civilization. Its values are universal, and they pervade our history and our partnership in a unique way." The bankruptcy of all twentieth-century "isms" has "given way to a paradigm of progress." The United States, its allies, and its friends all over the world, now "share a broad commitment to democracy, the rule of law, a market-based economy, and open trade":

> And since September 11, the world's great powers see themselves as falling on the same side of a profound divide between the forces of chaos and order.

Then she made the point in another way in order to demonstrate the complete transformation from Cold War politics and alliances into a confluence of common interests that began with 9/11. The tragedy had created a historic opportunity to break the destructive pattern of great power rivalry going back to the rise of the nation-state in the seventeenth century, she said, almost quoting Blair's words. It was more than an opportunity, it was an obligation. Some had spoken almost nostalgically about "multipolarity," as if it should be desired for its own sake, as something inherently good. She was troubled by this false note seeping into the political discourse.

> The reality is that multipolarity was never a unifying idea, or a vision. It was a necessary evil that sustained the absence of war but it did not promote the triumph of peace. Multipolarity is a theory of rivalry; of competing interests—and at its worst—competing values.[28]

The compelling vision, the demanding dream, it was all coming true in these years to demonstrate that Vietnam as a defeat had never happened, only a failure of will, just as Rostow had insisted all along. Addressing the seventy-fifth anniversary of the Woodrow Wilson School at Princeton University, Rice, now secretary of state, urged: "If you believe, as I do, and as President Bush does, that the root cause of September 11 was the violent expression of a global extremist ideology, an ideology rooted in oppression and despair of the modern Middle East, then we must seek to remove the source of this terror by transforming that troubled region. If you believe as we do, then it cannot be denied that we are standing at an extraordinary moment in history."[29]

Tony Blair was true to his word, staying loyal to Bush's vision of a new world emerging out of the Gulf War. He could hardly take back anything he said, even as domestic criticism mounted about London's enabling role in the Iraq War. It was Blair who had described the origins of the modern state system in the 1648 Treaty of Westphalia, which established the principle of nonintervention by one state in another's affairs, and the need to seek a new understanding of international and intranational affairs. Rice's glancing reference to the rise of nation-states reprised the prime minister's comments on Westphalia, and her attack on nostalgia for multipolarity resonated with his argument about the inseparability arising from globalization. He certainly did not want to be seen as falling on the wrong side of the boundary between chaos and order.

The Military Lead

Rice put a question to her Princeton audience about the realist-minded nostalgists. "Why would anyone who shares the values of freedom seek to put a check on those values?" No one should seek to do so, even if that meant using force. "Power in the service of freedom is to be welcomed, and powers that share a commitment to freedom can—and must—make common cause against freedom's enemies."

As the Iraq War unfolded into a drawn-out struggle that more and more looked like the Vietnamese struggle, Rice and President Bush insisted that the only thing to fear was a failure of will. Traveling to Hanoi for an Asian economic conference in November 2006, Bush seemed untouched by the ironic setting of the meeting and sought to rewrite the last years of the war in Vietnam. Nothing could prevent American power in the service of freedom from prevailing except a failure of will, he said. Well, asked a reporter, were there any lessons from the Vietnam War debate that applied to Iraq? Yes. "One lesson is," he replied, "is that we tend to want there to be instant success in the world, and the task in Iraq is going to take a while. . . . We'll succeed unless we quit."[30]

It was the Vietnamese who had succeeded, however. Vietnam had long since unified under Communist leadership, had waged post-American wars with China and Cambodia, and was now seeking to find its way into world markets and encouraging Western investments. A strong, unified country presumably had been the objective of American policy in fighting to stay in Saigon. But, despite all the rhetoric about kicking the Vietnam syndrome, the war remained a sore subject in America. Admitting defeat in the first of the neocolonial wars had become a taboo subject, especially as Iraq moved from the giddy days of "Mission Accomplished" to "mission undone." To win in Iraq now made it necessary to refight Vietnam as a virtual war, until America won on all the Playstations, and in all the history books.

Actually, Bush's comment was truer than he might have imagined. Americans were an impatient people, encouraged to be so by their technological know-how and military superiority and the metaphor of progress that, in circular fashion, made them more needy of technological fixes for political dilemmas. Gulf War I had been a cakewalk—and at the same time a misleading desert mirage. There had been all sorts of predictions as Washington readied the nation to finish off Saddam Hus-

sein's evil regime that American soldiers would be welcomed as liberators. Three years later it looked very different. In answer to another
question about how it felt to be in Hanoi, talking to a former enemy, the
president tried to put a spin on the occasion to make it seem as if Vietnam's recent successes were somehow a result of the American war—
which they were, but not in the way he meant:

> Vietnam is an exciting place. It's a place with an enormous future, and
> they obviously have got to work through difficulties like religious free-
> dom, for example, but nevertheless, there's certainly a new hopefulness to
> this country. And so I'm—thought a lot about what it was like, what my
> impressions of Vietnam were growing up, and here I am in this country to-
> day, and I guess my answer is, it's very hopeful.[31]

Bush wanted to celebrate all the distance America had come between
Vietnam and Iraq on the road to Baghdad. But it's best to go back and
look again. When Jimmy Carter first sought to erase bad memories of
Vietnam, with his emphasis on a human rights campaign, his national
security advisor, Zbig Brzezinski, looked instead for a new beginning in
the so-called arc of crisis, and launched the United States headlong into
a new set of uncertainties at the Khyber Pass.

2

ZBIG AT THE KHYBER PASS, OR THE LAST FLIGHT OF THE PERSIAN RUG

Moving up through Central Asia and Afghanistan, if you think about that region just a few years ago, prior to September 11, it really was, as I think it was Zbigniew Brzezinski called it, an "arc of crisis." It's now, in many ways, an arc of opportunity, but we're going to have to work very hard in South Asia, and I expect that to be very important.

—Secretary of State Condoleezza Rice, January 5, 2006

For America, the chief geopolitical prize is Eurasia. For half a millennium, world affairs were dominated by Eurasian powers and peoples who fought with one another for regional domination and reached out for global power. Now a non-Eurasian power is preeminent in Eurasia—and America's global primacy is directly dependent on how long and how effectively its preponderance on the Eurasian continent is sustained.

—Zbignew Brzezinski, *The Grand Chessboard*, 1997

It can be argued that Gulf War II started with the Iranian Revolution of 1979. That is so because the policy of using Iran as a surrogate power to protect American interests in the oil regions ended when the Shah, Reza Pahlavi, fled his country for a second time, and the United States could not put him back in power. Washington had never been completely happy with his pestering and egomania, but for more than twenty-five years after a 1953 CIA countercoup saved his throne, the shah had been the stopper in the bottle. Richard Nixon had vowed in the first months of his presidency that there would be no more Vietnams; henceforth, the United States would rely on regional stabilizers, not American soldiers, to seal off threats to its assets in the far corners of the globe. The shah was thought of in the White House as "our man" in Tehran.

Warning signals were ignored, in part because the shah's arms purchases played an increasingly significant role in helping to deal with a balance-of-payments problem that only seemed to get bigger in the aftermath of our Vietnam excesses. While the shah was anticommunist to the marrow of his bones, he was not above threatening to buy weapons from the Soviets to encourage better treatment from Washington. He dreamed of a Persian renaissance to equal the achievements of Darius the Great. After the 1973 Yom Kippur War and the OPEC shakedown, oil prices soared, convincing the shah that the sky was the limit. Nixon encouraged him with assurances his credit would always be good in the United States, and his requests for the most advanced weapons systems would not go unanswered. Washington hoped he might be a voice for moderation inside OPEC, but he played his leverage to the hilt. National Security Advisor Henry Kissinger once quipped that the shah treated *Aviation Weekly* like a Sears catalog. He suggested to his imperial highness that he might earn more dollars for his toys by going outside OPEC and selling oil to the Pentagon at below cartel prices. But the shah was too savvy to be seduced. There seemed no alternative to going along with the Iranian ruler, but it was always a bumpy ride. Jimmy Carter inherited the policy, and reaped its consequences.

Carter's Dilemma

"I have no new dream to set forth today," Carter said in his brief inaugural speech in 1977. "Even our great nation has its recognized limits . . . We can neither answer all questions nor solve all problems. We cannot afford to do everything." Carter had designed his ceremony to suggest an anti-imperial presidency. Instead of formal attire he wore a $175 three-piece suit picked off the rack back in Americus, Georgia. Rosalynn Carter and Vice President Walter Mondale's wife, Joan, both wore cloth coats. Against the advice of the Secret Service, Carter jumped out of the presidential limousine with Rosalynn in hand—Thomas Jefferson–style— to lead his own inaugural parade down Pennsylvania Avenue.[1]

Conservative columnist William Safire labeled the stroll an inspired stunt that couldn't make up for Carter's uninspired speech. It might rank slightly above Millard Fillmore's, he quipped, but not quite up to Calvin Coolidge's. Where was the recognition that the American dream needed reinflating entering its third century? "Instead, he seemed content to go along with the revolution of sinking expectations."[2]

The sorry end of the Vietnam War and Watergate had punctured the dream, grumbled early critics, and all Carter offered the nation was a patched tire. To make matters worse, during the campaign Carter had lumped Vietnam with other "failures," citing "Cambodia, Chile, Angola" together with "excesses of the CIA" as examples of doing things "that were contrary to our basic character."[3] If he hoped to chase Vietnam out of American politics through repentance, he was praying in the wrong pew.

It was risky, of course, but Carter thought his first task was to reorient disenchantment with Vietnam into a reassertion of American moral influence. Hence the human rights campaign that he hoped would restore American confidence in its sacred metaphor of progress, and at the same time pressure the Soviet Union into changing its attitudes about dissidents. But the harder he tried to disassociate the United States from past errors and turn the page, the more his actions only seemed to add to the sense that Carter had no clear idea where he wanted to go. Expanding on Gerald Ford's limited amnesty for war resisters and deserters, Carter declared a universal amnesty for draft evaders. At Notre Dame University he delivered an address that got far more attention than his inaugural, and gave his political enemies an opportunity to regroup their forces. In the speech he blamed an "inordinate fear" of communism for the Vietnam War. It had led the United States to embrace any dictator out there who wanted American help to stay in power. "I am glad that that is being changed."

> For too many years, we've been willing to adopt the flawed and erroneous principles and tactics of our adversaries, sometimes abandoning our own values for theirs. We've fought fire with fire, never thinking that fire is better quenched with water. This approach failed, with Vietnam the best example of its intellectual and moral poverty. But through failure we have now found our way back to our own principles and values, and we have regained our lost confidence.

Carter had set off headlong for a tangled thicket where all the paths were covered with Cold War roots. Critics never forgave the Notre Dame speech, but it served them well as a rallying point to launch the neoconservative offensive. The real sinners, they argued, were those in the antiwar movement who had allowed the communists to win the war and were now sitting at Carter's side in the White House. Neoconservative

Norman Podhoretz seized on events in Afghanistan, for example, to slash away at Carter's foreign policy. We have indeed succumbed to an inordinate fear of communism, he wrote. "Inordinate not because it exaggerates either the evils or the threat of Communism, but because it breeds the conviction that there is nothing we can do to check the spread of this malignancy over a wider and wider portion of the globe."[4]

Mocked by domestic enemies on the right, Carter's initiatives met with suspicion in the Kremlin as well, a predicament his administration never really overcame. Carter requested increased funding for Radio Free Europe to increase the ability to "penetrate jamming," by Communist censors, and to "encourage a constructive dialogue with the peoples of the U.S.S.R. and Eastern Europe." But Moscow called it an unfriendly act. He abandoned the Nixon-Kissinger SALT (strategic arms limitation talks) approach to arms negotiation, and proposed instead deep cuts in the nuclear arsenals of both powers. But the Kremlin suspected something else was afoot strategically. Soviet premier Leonid Brezhnev called the human rights campaign ideological warfare, hostile to détente. Carter seemed puzzled. "There has been a surprising adverse reaction in the Soviet Union to our stand on human rights. Apparently, that has produced a greater obstacle to other friendly pursuits, common goals, like SALT, than I had anticipated."[5]

But nothing Carter said or did over the next four years could undo the effect of the Notre Dame speech. Critics heckled the human rights campaign as a double-edged failure: It did nothing to change Soviet behavior, they said, and it led to a worse disaster than Vietnam when the shah of Iran was toppled by America's enemies.

Divided Counsels

No one worried more about Carter's mixed signals than his closest adviser on foreign affairs, Zbigniew Brzezinski. Like his predecessor Henry Kissinger, Zbig feared political fallout from Vietnam had left the United States in a confused state, giving the world an impression of weakness and indecisiveness. But maybe there was one way to correct that impression. An emphasis on human rights might become a starting point, but only a starting point, for rejuvenating America's belief in the uniqueness of its mission to the world. "I put stronger emphasis *perhaps* than Carter on the notion that strengthening American power was the necessary point of departure. . . . When a choice between the two had to be made, between projecting U.S. power or enhancing human rights (as for example in Iran), I felt that power had to come first."[6]

Son of a Polish diplomat who sought exile in Canada, Zbig made the Russian Revolution and the Stalinist state his major study at McGill and Harvard. In early 1965 the young academic joined the debate over Vietnam with a letter to the *New York Times* disputing the paper's suggestion that Alexi Kosygin's visit to Hanoi indicated Kremlin concerns about China, and opened up possibilities for a Soviet-American dialogue. He preferred a "more ominous" interpretation: It was more likely that the Soviet leaders had concluded, perhaps even "reluctantly," that Beijing's view of wars of liberation was the surest path to global communism. Keeping Red China from gaining supremacy in Asia, he said in a television debate, was what the war was really about. "A great many Asian nations see a major interest for themselves in an American continued presence in Vietnam as a bulwark."[7]

Three years later, as an adviser to Hubert Humphrey, he had turned "mildly critical" of the war, but more as a harbinger of an isolationist reaction than a policy failure. In 1973, banker David Rockefeller tapped him to direct the staff of the Trilateral Commission, sixty prominent citizens from North America, Europe, and Japan commissioned to plan "the reconstruction of the post-Vietnam world."[8] Brzezinski nominated an obscure governor of Georgia, Jimmy Carter, for membership, over Florida governor Reuben Askew, based on the Georgian's interest in promoting trade between Atlanta businesses and the Common Market and Japan.[9]

"Zbig became my teacher," Carter recalled. In the presidential campaign anything about foreign policy was labeled "Check this with Zbig." No one was surprised, then, when Carter named him national security advisor. When Carter then nominated Cyrus Vance for Secretary of State, however, insiders predicted a struggle for the president's heart and mind. Brzezinski thought Vance was a poor choice to head the State Department. "All in all, in temperament and in training, Vance was representative of an elite that was no longer dominant either in the world or in America. Carter certainly never was part of that America, and it certainly was not easy for me to relate to it either." Cy could not deal "with the thugs of this world. . . . His deep aversion to the use of force was a most significant limitation on his stewardship in an age in which American power was being threatened on a very broad front."[10]

The greatest danger facing America was not Russian nuclear supremacy, he believed, but the Kremlin's ability to spread chaos in the third world. By expanding their role in Africa and the Middle East, the Soviets sustained belief in a historic victory over capitalism, the only fuel left for an aging and increasingly decrepit Marxist engine that sputtered and coughed along, unable to keep up with the West in any other way. "The real problem is not that the Soviet Union is going to establish its domination over Africa or other parts of the world," he explained to a reporter. "The fact is, they don't have the capability, the means of influence, to install their own system in other nations. Their economy is just too weak and their ideology is obsolete. But by stirring up problems as they are in Africa, they can create chaos."[11]

At other times, however, Brzezinski played up the Soviet military threat to encourage a picture of the United States and the Soviet Union as engaged in the final denouement of a much older conflict, "the great game" of Asia played out in the nineteenth century between Great Britain and tsarist Russia. Did not Russian efforts to build a "blue oceans" navy portend an effort to control the Persian Gulf? The Soviets would swarm over Afghanistan down into Iran and control the Persian Gulf states. This new great game would finally be decided in Afghanistan, across the Pamir mountain range known as "the roof of the world." The prize was oil and natural gas. In Tehran, meanwhile, Brzezinski's approach to the Persian Gulf found a ready audience, as the shah was basically delighted with an American policy that promised him more arms. He did all he could to encourage such fears of Russian expansionism in order to increase his bargaining power in Washington. It proved to be a fateful combination—Brzezinski's arc of crisis and Pahlavi's ambition—with consequences that became fully manifest in Gulf War II and its Iranian complications.

Brzezinski fretted that the American people were still too traumatized by the spectacle of helicopters lifting off the roof of the Saigon embassy to respond to the imminent challenges ahead. Every day Zbig asked himself if that image would block out a clear view of the perils looming along an imaginary line stretching from Korea to the Persian Gulf—the arc of crisis. Taking advantage of American distractions, it was argued, Russia had sent advance agents, Cuban troops, into Angola and Ethiopia to pave the way for the pincer move in the Gulf. The game was on in earnest, and Carter's soft advisers like Cy Vance were all bound up in concern over arms treaties to the neglect of geopolitics.

Brzezinski held an advantage, however, in the Washington game of bureaucratic politics. The shifting balance of power in the federal government toward the national security advisor's office and the Pentagon that had begun in the Kennedy years and accelerated under Johnson was sure to continue, whether it was Vance or Al Capone in charge over in Foggy Bottom. But Brzezinski deliberately used his feud with Vance to provide further impetus for the belief that the United States was in danger of falling behind the Soviet Union, and for reliance on the militarization of foreign policy to complete the American mission. Brzezinski redesigned the National Security Council to cement his leading role in policy decisions by persuading Carter to name him chair of the new special coordination committee. To Vance's challenge that making the SCC chair something akin to a royal privy councilor would deprive the president of options he should know about, Brzezinski replied coolly that President Carter intended to be his own crisis manager. He had not "usurped excessive authority," Zbig protested coyly to readers of his memoirs, boasting in the same breath that he now ruled the corridors to the Oval Office. "I would have a major input on our policy toward the Soviet Union, while retention of crisis control meant that in the event of major difficulties I would be in a position to shape the agenda and thus to influence the outcome of our deliberations."[12]

Despite his public condemnations of the Soviets as a predator nation, arguments he relied on to increase his power inside the administration, the calculations that interested Brzezinski most were about the balance of power inside newly independent countries rich in natural resources, and the oil-rich regions of the Middle East. He warned South African ambassador R.F. Botha that if whites in various countries pursued intransigent policies, black/white conflicts would become a red/white contest. Botha countered that the United States did not properly understand South African fears of black domination. That might be so, Brzezinski responded, but "once you begin to see the radicalization of your younger black generations it will be too late." Once an urban working class acquires political consciousness the momentum is too great to stop, and the communists would come on the scene to direct their efforts.[13]

The proof was already there in Angola, a former Portuguese colony, where South Africa had been trying to shore up opponents of Agostinho Neto's Popular Movement for the Liberation of Angola (MPLA). Neto had denounced apartheid, while his opponents had stayed clear of the issue. The United States had joined in the fray via covert CIA aid to opponents of Agostinho Neto, because Henry Kissinger saw the situation as an opportunity to score a cheap victory after Vietnam.[14]

When the Soviet Union sent military advisers to Angola, a scramble for postcolonial Africa seemed well under way, with ideology adding to the nineteenth-century quest for markets and raw materials. Then Cuba started sending troops as well, up to about thirty-six thousand. With that push behind him Neto won the war. Carter had gone into office inclined to ease up on Cuban restrictions, but now he agreed to go this route only if Havana withdrew its troops from Africa. Castro would not be budged. Even so, there appeared to be a mutual interest in damping down tensions. Whatever momentum might be building toward overcoming nearly two decades of hostility came to a quick halt, however, with events in Somalia and Ethiopia near the Horn of Africa. From Brzezinski's point of view, events appeared to be making it less difficult to get Americans excited about foreign affairs again.

Caught on the Horn of Africa

Two weeks after Carter's inauguration the military junta that had overthrown longtime Ethiopian ruler Haile Selassie, whose rule went back to the days of Mussolini's 1935 invasion, turned further to the left. Siad Barre, dictator of neighboring Somalia, then abruptly switched his allegiances, kicked the Russians out of a huge naval base at Berbera they had built for him—a choke point on the Gulf of Aden across from Saudi Arabia—and made ready to attack Ethiopia. Expecting Washington to shower him with good wishes and more tangible forms of aid, in July 1977 Barre moved into the Ogaden desert, an area so sparsely settled it was said one family might have eight to ten miles for grazing camels. But Ethiopia followed Angola's example, and called in the Cubans. Russian leaders were certainly not unhappy with Castro's decision to send troops, as Siad Barre had obviously stirred their ire, but there is no evidence they went at the Kremlin's command.[15]

When American aid did not materialize, Barre's great offensive stalled. The Ethiopians recovered, meanwhile, and were threatening to cross the border into Somalia. Having just gained access to the Berbera base, the U.S. Navy was greatly interested in Somalia's fate. But Brzezinski saw an even greater danger. Failure to respond to Cuban interventions, he warned Carter, would spur accusations of "incompetence as well as weakness." A special emissary Washington sent to Addis Ababa reported back that he had had cordial talks with Ethiopian leaders, however, who assured him that they had no interest in expanding Russia's role in their country. No doubt the Russians would be around for some time, he concluded, but if Washington took up the Ogaden problem diplomatically, the threat would diminish.

That was not what Zbig wanted to hear. He was eager to seize on the "crisis" to encourage third countries such as Saudi Arabia to send military supplies to Somalia, and, more important, an American carrier task force into the gulf. Vance and Defense Secretary Harold Brown argued against a task force as having no specific purpose. It would only have a negative effect. *It did have a specific purpose*, insisted Brzezinski: It would show American determination. During the India-Pakistan war some years earlier, Brown reminded everyone, both sides denounced an American task force. The cases were entirely different, Brzezinski retorted; this task force would oppose the Soviets, nothing else. We would be playing a bluff, countered Vance. If Ethiopia did move across the border the bluff would be exposed for all to see. No one in the Pentagon supported fighting Cubans or Ethiopians, added Brown. "What you want to deter, the Russians," he said to Brzezinski, "do not need to be deterred."

The exchange revealed what Brzezinski really had on his mind, and it was not just options for Ethiopia. If his colleagues did not like that argument, he would supply another: Egypt and Israel would see inaction as weakness, and that could disrupt all-important efforts to get peace talks under way. Besides, Americans would be there only to fight Russians— the Saudis and Iranians would have to fight the Cubans. Brown was incredulous. Saudis and Iranians? What could they put up, singly or together, to match the Cubans? Frustrated at every corner, Brzezinski complained that they were ignoring the consequences of doing nothing. They should be considering steps to influence Moscow's behavior. SALT was the only thing important enough, said one aide. But Zbig had something else in mind: "We might be more flexible on technology transfer to

China." It certainly would "get their attention," agreed Brown, alarmed at where that thinking could lead.[16]

Brzezinski closed the meeting by repeating his warning that American inaction could destabilize three countries: Egypt, Saudi Arabia, and Iran. The lesson they would take away was not to get caught in a tough spot relying on the United States for help. Vance wondered if Brzezinski was not making the situation into a self-fulfilling prophecy with such predictions. Somalia should not be called an ally, and each case ought to be treated on its own, not in the domino thesis worldview that had led to Vietnam. "He would not put any U.S. troops in Africa." Maybe not, Brzezinski conceded, but a way had to be found to "make the Soviets and Cubans bleed."[17]

Brzezinski had other venues for getting his point across. An inspired article in the *New York Times* related frustration felt by policy makers trying to deal with Soviet "maneuverings" in Africa. Brzezinski was said to be busy laying the groundwork for more Congressional aid to African countries. Carter had become worried about Senate "wariness" over a possible strategic arms deal with Russia, the article said, and his aides sensed the need for more "spine," or there would be trouble persuading the Senate to go along with arms treaties. An anonymous White House official told the reporter, "We get the feeling at times that they are testing our manhood." One could guess what official that might be.[18]

"As I have said earlier," Brzezinski argued after leaving office, "SALT was buried in the sands of Ogaden, the sands that divide Somalia from Ethiopia, and eventually led to the Soviet invasion of Afghanistan." But it need not have happened that way. "I would have preferred us to draw the line sooner, and perhaps some of the things that subsequently happened wouldn't have happened."[19]

In the aftermath of that discussion, Brzezinski (with help from a fellow hard-liner, Samuel P. Huntington) laced a speech Carter gave at Wake Forest University with tough language. He wanted to dispel the myth, the president said, that the country "somehow is pulling back from protecting its interests and its friends around the world." American will and determination would be demonstrated "in our actions." It was almost a 180-degree turn from the inaugural speech. Ever since JFK's invocation of the "missile gap," staple Cold War rhetoric declared that the Russians had caught up and were surging ahead in military hardware. Carter now joined the parade. Russia's military spending was increasing, he said, "both in absolute numbers and relative to our own. . . . There has also been an ominous inclination on the part of the Soviet Union to use its military power—to intervene in local conflicts, with advisers, with equipment, and with full logistical support and encouragement to mercenaries from other Communist countries, as we can observe today in Africa." Then he said what really thrilled his co-authors: "If they fail to demonstrate restraint in missile programs and other force levels, or in the projection of Soviet or proxy forces in other lands and continents, then popular support in the United States for such cooperation with the Soviets will certainly erode."[20]

The speech was a good one, wrote Zbig, and "set us on the right course." But it was not enough. He learned, moreover, that Vance's aide, Marshall Shulman, had undercut the speech by assuring the Soviet embassy, without telling the White House, that the speech was intended for domestic consumption, and did not indicate declining interest in a new SALT treaty. Two years later Zbig wrote in his journal about his unhappiness that Carter had sided with Vance and Brown on the question of the task force. "The president backed the others rather than me, we did not react." After that "things began to go genuinely wrong in the U.S.-Soviet relationship."[21]

The Great Wall

Vance had urged finishing arms negotiation with the Soviet Union as a better remedy—before engaging China. But that was just the point for Brzezinski. China should come first. Despite Vance's protests, Brzezinski set out on a trek to the Great Wall with Carter's blessing. The president liked Zbig immensely, noted one analyst, "and relied on him to spin out a broad range of options and analysis—even jokes and wild ideas—that Carter found helpful in forming his judgments." Vance was too much the New Englander to achieve a close relationship with someone "imbued with that southern gene that placed churchgoing virtue alongside an appreciation for mischief."[22]

After Nixon's dramatic 1972 trip to China, Beijing had insisted that full diplomatic relations—and all that promised—depended upon Washington's abandonment of its claim to a right to intervene on Taiwan's behalf. Brzezinski wanted to pick up where that conversation had stalled. In his memoirs he reproduced the instructions he had drafted for a new mission to China, one he planned to carry out himself. These asserted that the United States now saw Beijing as a "central facet" of its global policy. Indeed, the instructions went on, the two countries shared "parallel, long-term strategic concerns. . . . The most important of these is our common opposition to the global or regional hegemony by any single power."[23]

Brzezinski's instructions to himself continued on in a similar vein for several paragraphs, contrasting the possibilities of cooperation with China with the essentially competitive relationship with Russia that was an enduring, deep-seated rivalry, "rooted in different traditions, history, outlooks, interests, and geopolitical priorities." As reflected in these instructions at least, this rivalry went beyond Cold War issues, although they were currently caught in that lens, given Soviet determination to establish its predominance in the third world by exploiting local turbulences. All this was highlighted by Brzezinski's use of the instructions to get around opposition to his scheme for using the Somalia/Ethiopian conflict to project American interests via Chinese aid to Somalia. The instructions concluded, "I also see some Soviet designs pointing towards the Indian Ocean through South Asia, and perhaps to the encirclement of China through Vietnam (and even perhaps someday through Taiwan)."[24]

State Department representatives traveling with Brzezinski were kept out of the talks with Premier Deng Xiaoping, who drove a hard bargain on Taiwan. Brzezinski conceded to Chinese views with scarcely more than expressions of hope that the issue would be settled peacefully, "though we recognize this is your own domestic affair." Exuberant at having persuaded Deng of his bona fides as an ally against the Russians, Brzezinski made tough political statements to the press at almost every stopping point, from the Great Hall to the Great Wall. Joking with Chinese sailors at the Great Wall, he challenged them to a race to the top. The last one there, he shouted, would have to fight the Russians in Ethiopia. They laughed and called him "polar bear tamer." Inside the Great Hall, he gave a comradely toast that one might almost mistake for one coming out of Stalin-Mao era: "Neither of us dispatches international marauders who masquerade as nonaligned to advance big-power ambitions in Africa. Neither of us seeks to enforce the political obedience of our neighbors through military force." Veteran Asian correspondent Fox Butterfield wrote that the Chinese were masters at lavish entertainments that seduced foreigners into making such statements. Brzezinski imagined, however, that he was much more seducer than seduced. He believed he had soothed the Chinese dragon with promises of technological transfers, economic missions, and even intelligence exchanges. He was dealing with no reluctant dragon, however.[25]

During a trip to the United States in 1977, Russian foreign secretary Andrey Gromyko had brought up U.S. policy in the Indian Ocean, half joking that the United States was "still clinging to that rock," the island of Diego Garcia, and "was treading on Soviet toes." Carter had protested that he did not intend to expand the island into a strategic outpost, and indeed favored prohibiting B-52s and other heavy bombers on Diego Garcia, as well as submarine service capabilities. In fact, he said, he was ready to offer to neutralize the whole area of the Indian Ocean where the island was located. That would have meant reversing certain policies already adopted by the United Kingdom, who "owned" the island and who, in 1973, had expelled several hundred of its original inhabitants in order to begin establishing a military base. Such an offer also cut across Pentagon plans to convert the tiny dot in the ocean into a jumping-off place to protect American interests in the Persian Gulf. When Carter changed his mind is not clear, but a year after Gromyko's visit, in the summer of 1978, in the midst of the dispute over Cuban troops in Ethiopia and after Zbig's Beijing "triumph," the neutralization idea was no longer on the agenda.

In an article, "Asia's 'Great Game' Moves With a Vengeance," *Times* reporter Richard Burt detailed the changed perspective. The Soviet Union had lost its best Indian Ocean port at Berbera, but the Ethiopian conflict demonstrated it could still carry out large-scale naval operations near crucial oil-supplying routes. "Accordingly, the United States Navy is moving ahead with the modernization and improvement of its base on the Indian Ocean island of Diego Garcia, which will enable the United States to maintain a carrier task force in the region for prolonged periods."[26]

All this was happening behind the headlines, as the public's attention was focused on Carter's ultimately successful efforts to broker a preliminary peace settlement between Israel and Egypt. Eventually, a peace treaty between Egypt and Israel would be signed, but the fate of the West Bank and Gaza Strip continued to provide the major source of difficulty in resolving the Arab-Israeli imbroglio over the next four decades. The issue of a Palestinian state inevitably became embroiled in questions surrounding American policy toward both Iraq and Iran, despite efforts to keep them separate.

Upon his return from China, Brzezinski rushed into the studios of NBC's *Meet the Press*, a favorite Sunday-morning launching pad for weighty pronouncements. Moscow was violating the "code of détente," he charged, offering as proof a whole list of Soviet misdeeds. These included building up conventional forces, concentrating troops on the Chinese border, maintaining a vitriolic worldwide propaganda campaign against the United States, stirring up racial troubles in Africa, and seeking to encircle the Middle East. To reverse these trends required "demonstrated resolve." Reporter Bernard Gwertzman observed it was "one of the sharpest denunciations of the Soviet Union by a high administration official in years."[27]

State Department aides, UN Ambassador Andrew Young (a former associate of Martin Luther King Jr.), and Russia expert Marshall Shulman tried to counter, but without much success. Young said arguments over Cuban forces in Angola and Ethiopia made too much of the situation, while Shulman reminded reporters that United States activities in the Middle East were equally upsetting to the Russians. The fullest response, however, came from George McGovern, the 1972 Democratic candidate Nixon had crushed. American military power was far and away the greatest in the world, said McGovern, and we had more allies than any country. Even in the Middle East, where Brzezinski saw the Russians encircling the area, the strongest Arab military power, Egypt, had kicked out the Soviets and joined the West. Russia's only reliable ally was "tiny Cuba." Brzezinski had talked fearfully about Russian troop buildups in Europe and on the Chinese border, but, "at a time when Western military outlays are rising, when Mr. Brzezinski treats China as a NATO auxiliary, and global arms spending is on the increase, where else would one expect the Russians to concentrate their forces if not on their common borders with Europe and China?"[28]

Carter tried to insist that Zbig's mission had been misunderstood, "We are not trying, nor will we ever try, to play the Soviets against the People's Republic of China, nor vice versa." There were, however, "worldwide common hopes that we share with the Chinese."[29] All this was going on even as Russian foreign minister Andrey Gromyko met with American officials, including Vance and Carter, to discuss the latest draft of a nuclear arms treaty. He had brought with him important concessions, but the arms talks were sidetracked by the president's insistence on pressing issues of human rights and Cuban activities in Africa. Vance tried to suggest to Gromyko privately that there was an underlying psychological issue—Carter's need to dispel the image of an irresolute and vacillating politician. "Let me tell you straight that there are people close to the president telling him that the latest Soviet actions are a direct challenge to the president, a test of his firmness, and he should show the Russians he is not to be trifled with."[30]

While Brzezinski was in China, Beijing had turned down a Russian offer to negotiate border disputes, and there ensued a series of military skirmishes. And then, in a major speech at the UN, Chinese foreign minister Huang Hua called the Soviet Union the "most dangerous source" of a world war. He also had some harsh words for the United States: "There are some people in the West today who are cowed by Soviet military threats and are afraid of war, or who indulge in a false sense of security and deny the existence of a serious danger of war." They had not awakened and still believe in the Soviet "hoax of détente."[31]

The Road to Kabul

Brzezinski's focus, meanwhile, soon shifted to events in Afghanistan. In April 1978 a successful coup against Mohammed Daoud moved the country to the left, though left and right hardly conveyed the nature of Afghan politics. It was really a fight between rival factions. Iran seemed to be the first big loser, having invested money in Daoud. The new leader in Kabul, Noor Mohammad Taraki, announced he would pursue a proactive neutralist policy, and would not become a satellite of any nation. "Afghanistan has very few highways," wrote one observer, "and not one mile of railway, and most of its people live either as nomads or as impoverished farmers in brown mud villages behind high walls, a life scarcely different from what it was when Alexander the Great passed this way 2,000 years ago. Distressing or pleasing as the change in government may seem to Afghanistan's neighbors, its effect in the country itself may be slight."[32]

Put another way, Bob Hope and Bing Crosby, stars in a famous series of road pictures with Dorothy Lamour, would have had a tough time finding the way to Kabul. Nevertheless, everyone thought there were great stakes involved in the final outcome of Afghan politics. The Soviets had paid out $1.5 billion to equip the Afghan military, which numbered around 100,000. The United States had given Kabul about $500 million in economic aid. Clearly Taraki did not want to lose out on future aid from either side. Far from engineering the coup, Moscow seemed mystified about how to deal with a new government that appeared bent on stirring up religious feelings in a country next to Muslim-populated Soviet republics. But Pakistan used the coup to lobby for more American aid, citing the instability in Afghanistan. And that made India very nervous. And so on.

Taraki's coup also interrupted the shah's plans to draw Kabul into a Tehran-centered regional economic and security center that would include all the states of the Persian Gulf, as well as India and Pakistan. He dreamed of a Persian empire to rival that of Darius the Great. In this, as in all other things, the shah enjoyed American support and covert aid from the CIA. "The shah's secret police, Savak, collaborated with the CIA in establishing ties with radical Islamic groups in Afghanistan, seemingly the first step in a Forward Policy campaign to unsettle Soviet Central Asia."[33]

Brzezinski also wanted to begin covert operations against Taraki immediately, but Carter ordered no direct aid should go to the various groups of insurgents seeking to reinstate a reactionary Islamic theocracy. There was no taboo on indirect aid, however, and Brzezinski encouraged the CIA to work with Pakistan to coordinate aid from China, Saudi Arabia, Egypt, and Kuwait. By February 1979, an article in the *Washington Post* claimed, at least two thousand Afghans were being trained in former Pakistani military bases. "Zbig wasn't worried about provoking the Russians, as some of us were," recalled State Department undersecretary, David Newsom, "because he expected them to take over anyway."[34]

The shah of Iran, always with an eye to the big score, wrote Carter expressing concern about the "recent tragic developments" that made his defense problems much greater. The United States, he said, would have to help him catch up, by buying more oil so that he could purchase the necessary arms to defend the Gulf against the "pressure exerted from certain quarters to push forward to the Indian Ocean." The shah's unquenchable thirst for arms, especially the latest jet fighters, was now seen as indispensable in Washington as a partial solution to the U.S. balance-of-payments deficits. The Iranian ruler estimated that he would be purchasing $4 billion to $6 billion worth of hardware a year—Carter thus found himself in an awkward corner, given his initial impulse to restrict American arms sales abroad. He replied to the shah that he agreed that Soviet domination of Afghanistan would be a development "of great seriousness for the free world."[35]

The shah knew he held the upper hand, and he was right. He used to meet with the head of the CIA station in Tehran every Saturday morning at nine o'clock for two hours, he told an interviewer, Mohamed Heikal, but as he grew more confident, he realized that they needed him more than he needed them. At the end of 1975 the American ambassador in Tehran, former CIA chief Richard Helms, had reported an alarming conversation with the shah. Unless the oil companies purchased more oil, his country would have to give up the idea of extending its influence outward. He would not have the funds to continue purchasing arms and other goods. Military power promoted political leverage, he told the ambassador, but Iran would have to give up the idea of extending its influence outward and become entirely "inward looking." "You and Saudi Arabia can handle the policing of the Indian Ocean."[36]

Sales to Middle Eastern countries raised especially sensitive issues, as Carter undertook peace initiatives to bring a resolution of the Arab-Israeli dispute, but Iran was always an exception. Vance visited Tehran in May 1977 and promised the shah he could buy 160 F-16s. But he needed 300, insisted the shah, to maintain patrols over the Indian Ocean, adding a hint that if he could not get the planes in the United States, he might look elsewhere for comparable aircraft. "I am also looking forward to exchanging thoughts and ideas with you, Mr. President, on subjects affecting the very close collaboration and special relationship between our two countries."[37]

Carter assured him he felt exactly the same way. "I strongly support this relationship and intend, for my part, to preserve and strengthen it." He reminded the shah that he had approved arms and military equipment sales to Iran greater by half than those approved for any other nation in the world. Even so, the new request would be considered sympathetically.[38] Meanwhile, Carter pushed a skeptical Congress to approve the sale of AWACS to Iran, Boeing 707s modified with highly sophisticated thirty-foot-diameter mushroom-like radar systems perched on top. The $1.3 billion sale would boost profits for Boeing and the contract for the seven planes would enable the company to lower its overall costs and produce cheaper planes in the future for the U.S. Air Force. Finally, and perhaps most important, the AWACS represented a vote of confidence in the shah's role as regional influential, as they enabled him to project his power outward in ever greater circles.[39]

In the next few months the friendship between Carter and the shah seemed to grow even stronger. In November the Iranian royal couple stayed at the White House. The president was impressed by the "excellent analysis" his guest offered of the "troubled situation around the Persian Gulf area." For nearly two hours the shah described the Russian pincer movement in Afghanistan and the Horn of Africa designed to surround the oil-producing regions. He also, wrote Carter in his memoirs, detailed the positive changes his "White Revolution" was making in the lives of ordinary citizens. The president knew from "intelligence reports," however, that all was not quite what it seemed in the shah's recounting. In a small room off the Oval Office, Carter raised the issue of human rights. It undermined Iran's world reputation, he began. Was there anything that could be done to "alleviate this problem"? The shah listened attentively, recounted Carter, then replied somewhat sadly. "No, there is nothing I can do. I must enforce the Iranian laws, which are designed to combat communism." Maybe after this serious menace to Iran and Western interests was removed, the laws can be changed, "but that will not be soon."[40]

There had been other warning signals during the visit. Outside on the White House lawn earlier, Carter had hosted a welcoming ceremony complete with the Marine band playing the two national anthems. As the band played on, loud noises from demonstrators across the street in Lafayette Park rose over the protective shield set up by the Park Service police; then wafts of tear gas floated over the White House lawn. "The president and His Imperial Majesty were both photographed wielding handkerchiefs to stanch their weeping."[41]

That night at a White House dinner, Carter played the scene for laughs,

PRESIDENT CARTER: There's one thing I can say about the Shah—he knows how to draw a crowd. [Laughter.]

I really thought today, when the tear gas came across the South Lawn, that the Shah showed a tremendous amount of self-assurance and graciousness and also courage in giving his speech to the people of our country without hesitation, and I deeply appreciate that exhibition of your strength.

SHAH REZA PAHLAVI: Thank you.

PRESIDENT CARTER: This is one time when the news reporters were accurate about me. I saw on the evening television that they said it was one of the briefest speeches I had made. [Laughter.] I was glad to turn the microphone over to the Shah. [Laughter.][42]

The scene played out in Iran, however, as an indication that the United States was ready to dump the shah. How else to explain the willingness of American officialdom to allow such demonstrations to go on? Actually, the reverse had happened. Carter was more determined than ever to support the shah, and apparently had few qualms about Iran's internal situation, other than his concern about Tehran's world reputation. On his way back from a trip to Poland, the president and Rosalynn stopped over in Tehran at New Year's time. In private conversations they reached agreement on a plan for American aid in an Iranian nuclear program "for peaceful purposes."

The United States had been helping Iran since the 1950s with its ambitions for a nuclear program. Early in the 1970s the shah had increased pressure for a special arrangement to permit him to reprocess nuclear fuel, saying that oil would run out one day, and that it should be used to make petro fertilizers, and other products, rather than burned away in big cars. Curiously, the shah's apparent preoccupation with conserving oil fit well with Carter's efforts to stimulate energy conservation in the United States. In any event, the president found himself in agreement with the shah's quest for "most favored nation" treatment in terms of aid for nuclear plants, including the previously taboo question of reprocessing plants for U.S.-origin fuel. Negotiations for Iran's purchase of between six and eight light-water nuclear reactors from the United States were concluded at their meeting—pending approval by the U.S. Congress. The deal collapsed when the shah was overthrown a year later, but Iranian ambitions to dominate the Gulf region and attain status as a nuclear power never flagged under his successor, the Ayatollah Khomeini. American presidents since Eisenhower had pampered the shah beginning with the 1953 CIA-managed counterrevolution that preserved the

Peacock Throne for a generation. Carter paid the heaviest price of them all when it collapsed in a heap. "It was the very confidence the shah had generated among his allies," wrote Barry Rubin, summing up years of self-deception, "that was to contribute to his downfall."[43]

The shah's quest for nuclear energy "for peaceful uses" was a good cover story, but whether he planned to have WMD in the near future, he, like all other nuclear wannabes, saw possession of nuclear arms as the passkey into the inner circle of world powers. He talked constantly (in similar terms as Brzezinski) about the Indian Ocean nexus of power, but it was not merely as a regional influential or subordinate, but as an equal player in international politics, one whose living standards would surpass first Europe and, eventually, even those in the United States. The Iranian air force would be strong enough to protect the whole area, from the Persian Gulf to the Sea of Japan, he boasted to an interviewer. The interviewer, Mohamed Heikal, then asked about nuclear weapons. "For the present I don't have any nuclear weapons," answered the shah. "They are too costly, and we have no delivery system. But one thing I can assure you, and this is that Iran will not be the last in the area to be a nuclear power."[44]

Still, Carter appeared almost enchanted by the shah—incredible as that seems today. The shah staged a dinner for him on December 31, 1977, attended by four hundred guests, with a menu that began with pearls of the Caspian—a kind of caviar reserved only for the shah—and ended with ice cream aflame with cherry sauce. The president then stood up to make his toast. Because of the shah's leadership, he declared, Iran was an island of stability in a very troubled area of the world. The country's progress was a tribute, moreover, to "the admiration and love your people give to you." They shared the "cause" of human rights. "Our talks have been priceless, our friendship is irreplaceable, and my own gratitude is to the Shah, who in his wisdom and with his experience has been so helpful to me, a new leader." Nor was Carter quite finished yet, adding for emphasis, "There is no leader with whom I have a deeper sense of personal gratitude and personal friendship."[45]

The next morning, as Jimmy and Rosalynn were saying fond good-byes, an entire antiaircraft battery, about five hunded soldiers, deserted the Iranian military with their arms. Soon there were disturbances all over the country, stimulated by the exiled Ayatollah Khomeini, who sent his messages into Iran via tape recordings. "For heaven's sake," asked the Empress Farah, "who is this Khomeini?" It might have been Marie Antoinette speaking, wrote the Egyptian journalist Mohamed Heikal.[46]

American policy makers also wondered who Khomeini was. When his name was first mentioned in a Tehran cable to Washington, the State Department had to query the embassy about who this man was. No one thought much about the possibility of a Muslim revolution—there had never been one. Besides, the shah had the SAVAK and the army behind him. The way things had worked in other countries since the beginning of the Cold War, after all, was that national armies were really international forces with loyalties to the American MAAGs, from whence came their modern weapons and snappy uniforms. The shah was so incredulous about Khomeini's army of "ignorant mullahs" being able to organize the demonstrations that he told Henry Kissinger that some other force was behind the trouble—he thought it might be the CIA. Kissinger was stunned. Why would that be? Because, answered the shah, there were those who felt he was too cozy with the Soviet Union, and that a religious government would be more anticommunist than he was![47]

Ambassador William Sullivan returned from Tehran in the summer of 1978 and advised the State Department that the crisis had passed. The shah had found the right way to deal with the mullahs—he paid them off. "They would go back to their mosques and remain quiet." Having delivered this reassuring message, Sullivan departed for a two-month vacation in Mexico. When he got back from leave, things were getting worse—much worse. At a meeting with Brzezinski, the national security advisor told Sullivan that the shah was our man and "we had to stand behind him at whatever cost." There would be no compromise.[48]

In September the shah imposed martial law in an effort to crack down on the huge demonstrations—largely nonviolent—that were spreading to cities all over Iran. Millions of people were on the street. The protests were multifaceted, but certainly the dislocations of the rural population, the growing disparities between rich and poor, the widespread corruption and nepotism that enriched the Pahlavi family beyond all measures of private opulence and arrogance were the strongest ingredients. What the ayatollah offered was a broom to sweep Tehran's streets clean of Western pollutants.

In Washington a debate began over what to tell the shah to do to avoid disaster. A letter Carter sent to the shah repeated American support while urging him to pursue a course of gradual liberalization. Some thought was given to sending an emissary to Khomeini. But at what level? In the end, no one was sent. Vance and Brzezinski waged a private cold war over control of Iranian policy. Working a back channel with Ambassador Ardeshir Zahedi, Zbig sent messages—some of them even unseen by Carter—telling the shah to stand firm. At the same time, the State Department was sending Sullivan messages urging moderation.[49]

On November 9, 1978, the ambassador stunned Washington with a bombshell message, "thinking the unthinkable." The United States should intervene to encourage an orderly transition, and to stand ready to offer economic aid and security. Sullivan hoped that was a recipe to induce the ayatollah to play ball with a post-shah, pro-Western government. But Brzezinski wanted none of it. "He was a Pole," related Henry Precht, the State Department officer on the Iranian desk, "with terrible feelings about the Soviet Union, and he didn't want to see the Iranian part of our containment barrier weakened. That is, the Shah was needed to keep the Soviets from moving towards the Gulf."[50]

On December 2, 1978, Brzezinski wrote a sky-is-falling memorandum to Carter asserting that there were great dangers all along the "arc of crisis," from Iran and Pakistan eastward to India and Bangladesh. Even in Saudi Arabia the political structure was beginning to be "creaky," and Turkey had gone "wobbly." There was no question in his mind, he said, that the situation was as critical as had faced Truman in the late 1940s. Fragile social and political structures were threatened with fragmentation. "The resulting political vacuum might well be filled by elements more sympathetic to the Soviet Union. This is especially likely since there is a pervasive feeling in the area that the U.S. is no longer in a position to offer effective political and military protection."[51]

As the year ended, the mixed messages from Washington got more confused. At a press conference Carter was asked if he thought the shah could survive. The response sounded tepid: "I hope so." Not very strong encouragement there. Sullivan's proposal for sending someone to meet with the ayatollah had been ignored. Instead it was decided to send General Robert Huyser, a man familiar with the Iranian military, to buck up the generals. Stationed in Germany at the time, Huyser learned he was to be sent to Tehran on January 3, 1979, and felt uneasy about what exactly he was supposed to do. At first he was told he would have no written instructions. All he could glean from his orders was that it was essential that Iran continue to have a strong, stable government friendly to the United States. When he protested that he would not go without written instructions, he was first told that he did not understand the level from which the directive had come. "I certainly *did* understand," he wrote of the mission, which was why he insisted on written instructions.[52]

The written instructions finally came, telling him that he must steady the Iranian military so that it supported any civilian government the shah established. That left open the possibility that they should take control themselves. They must understand, the instructions went on, that the U.S. government, from the president down, was strongly behind them: "We are prepared to stick with them. We will maintain our military supply relationship, maintain our establishment and training consistent with their desires." Now Huyser knew why he had had to press so hard for written instructions. "Brzezinski wanted it to convey to the Iranian military a green light to stage a military coup, and considered that it did so. President Carter intended it to convey such a meaning only as a last resort."[53]

Reluctance to provide written instructions indicated something else. Staring the White House in the face was the Vietnam parallel, those long months of summer 1963 when JFK's advisers agonized over what to do about Diem's plight with the Buddhist monks. Kennedy had complained at times that his government was coming apart over Vietnam, but the divisions were nothing like the current fissures. In the event, there was nothing Huyser could do, and after traveling around in a bullet-proof vest, talking to the Iranian generals in endless palaver, he came home. Ambassador Sullivan was appalled at the dysfunctional spectacle the administration was making of itself. The Huyser mission was sure to backfire, and to put the Iranian military in an invidious position with the new government dominated by the ayatollah. Who would doubt, he protested, that the Huyser mission foretold another countercoup like that pulled off by the CIA in 1953 against the Mossadegh regime that had nationalized oil? Certainly not the ayatollah. Certainly not his allies of a less theocratic bent. "I received a telephone call," Sullivan recounted, "relaying a message from Brzezinski, who asked whether I thought I could arrange a military coup against the revolution. . . . I regret the reply I made is unprintable."[54]

"Thus, chaos descended on Iran," Sullivan ended, with a final shot at the national security advisor. He was no prorevolutionary, or believer in the ayatollah's moderation, but he did think American policy played into the hands of extremists who had their own objectives: "The disintegration of the nation is well-advanced and a growing dependence on the Soviet Union has begun." Sullivan and Brzezinski both had that one wrong. While the banned Tudeh Party made some stir on the left, the ayatollah's "remarkable political victory" signaled the beginning of a new era, or, otherwise put, the rebirth of a very old era of presecular Islam.

Giving the Soviets a Vietnam

In a February 2, 1979, report to the president, Brzezinski argued that studies made by people on his staff had led to the conclusion, "*Islamic revivalist movements are not sweeping the Middle East and are not likely to be the wave of the future.*" While that was true, they were particularly suited to attacking "corruption, social injustice, and foreign intervention." They could become a "potent political force for change."[55]

Here was something to think about, nevertheless—using an aroused "revivalist movement" not only to challenge Soviet influence in Afghanistan but also to siphon off Russian energies at various points along the arc of crisis. But the Iranian Revolution posed the immediate threat of an increased menace. A weak Iran, which everyone assumed would be the case, next to a communist Afghanistan? What did that juxtaposition foretell? "I'd have to be blind or Pollyannish," Brzezinski told reporters, "not to recognize there are dark clouds on the horizon."[56] Yet the menace might be reversed. The more Brzezinski thought about it, the more he liked the idea of giving the Soviets their own Vietnam. Leaks from American intelligence sources began finding their way into the popular press, suggesting that the Soviet Union was running short of oil as its economy expanded, and that its moves in the Middle East were driven not by ideology but by the desire to gobble up resources. For some time Brzezinski had found ways like this of getting his ideas out front in the effort to shape the Carter administration's foreign policies.

In March 1979, Brzezinski talked with King Hussein in Amman, Jordan, and told him that the United States was guided by its desire to work with moderates, but not excluding Iraq, a new candidate for his attention: "We see the Islamic resurgence as terribly important. It marks the rebirth of Arab vitality, which is the best bulwark against communism." Over the next decade Washington would play an ambiguous role in the Iran-Iraq War, encouraging one side and then the other—managing to alienate both.[57]

Reviewing the next steps in his plan to use this Islamic resurgence to "delegitimize the Soviet Union," Brzezinski told interviewers years later that his staff had put together a plan in 1978 for covert aid to the non-Russian Soviet republics to destabilize the Soviet Union. The plan was reviewed in March 1979 to see if it was worthwhile to continue trying to suck the Soviets into a Vietnam of their own. In July, Carter signed a formal memorandum authorizing secret aid to opponents of the "pro-Soviet regime" in Kabul. That settled the matter. "And that very day," boasted Brzezinski, "I wrote a note to the president in which I explained to him that in my opinion this aid was going to induce a Soviet military intervention."[58]

At the time Brzezinski made this statement, in 1998, Americans were in the midst of celebrating the end of the Cold War, and everyone wanted to take credit for the downfall of the Soviet Union. Zbig was anxious, obviously, to validate the Carter administration's policies, so roundly criticized by Reaganites and neoconservatives in general. So, asked the questioner as the interview went on, when the Soviets justified their military intervention in Afghanistan in December 1979 as a response to American acts, there was a basis of truth. "You don't regret anything today?"

"Regret what?" Brzezinski shot back. "That secret operation was an excellent idea. It had the effect of drawing the Russians into the Afghan trap and you want me to regret it? The day that the Soviets officially crossed the border [December 25, 1979], I wrote to President Carter, in substance: We now have the opportunity of giving to the USSR its Vietnam war." Indeed, he added, the Afghan imbroglio brought about "the breakup of the Soviet Empire."

QUESTION: And neither do you regret having supported the Islamic fundamentalists, having given arms and advice to future terrorists?

BRZEZINSKI: What is most important to the history of the world? The Taliban or the collapse of the Soviet Empire? Some stirred-up Moslems or the liberation of Central Europe and the end of the cold war?

QUESTION: Some stirred-up Moslems? But it has been said and re-peated, Islamic fundamentalism represents a world menace today.

BRZEZINSKI: Nonsense! . . . That is stupid. There isn't a global Islam. . . .[59]

The covert aid to Taraki's foes may have worried the Kremlin, but for a long time the Russians believed that his major problem was his insistence on pushing through a socialist agenda that alienated too many factions. Moscow attempted to counsel patience, but Taraki remained deaf to their advice to go slow. The Kremlin leadership grew more fearful day by day of what their supposed puppet's behavior would bring down on them all.

Meanwhile, all the headlines in the United States were about "Who lost Iran?" As relations with Tehran continued to deteriorate, the focus narrowed to the exiled shah, and the revelation that he was seriously ill with a form of cancer. A campaign to bring him to the United States for treatment put Carter in a terrific bind. He was perfectly aware of the dangers of yielding to the wishes of the shah's well-wishers, a list that included Henry Kissinger and David Rockefeller, Zbig's patron from Trilateral Commission days. As it happened, however, it was not Brzezinski's call this time, or at least not his alone, because Cy Vance spoke in favor of letting the shah come at a meeting on October 22, 1979, on the grounds of "humanitarian principle."

"What are you guys going to advise me to do," said the president, "if they overrun our embassy and take our people hostage?" Aides checked with the embassy, and it checked with the provisional government of Mehdi Bazargan, and received assurances that while they opposed the move, the embassy would be protected. Carter was right to be worried that these assurances were worthless, but he made the fateful decision to allow the shah entrance for emergency medical care. A week later Brzezinski was in Algeria for a celebration of that country's independence. Also there were Bazargan and Foreign Minister Ebrahim Yazdi.

At the Iranians' suggestion they met to discuss "matters of mutual inter-est." Yazdi was especially anxious to question Brzezinski about the shah's illness. Zbig reacted with indignation. Of course he was ill, he said. Pic-tures of the diplomats shaking hands had appeared in Tehran, and protests against the shah and his American protectors had begun in earnest. "The Americans were obviously looking to make history repeat itself," said one of the student leaders, "and we had to deliver a blow to make them come to their senses."[60]

On November 5, 1979, students stormed the embassy as the much re-duced staff attempted to shred secret documents before they were taken hostage. Thus began more than a year's captivity for fifty-two of the sixty-six diplomats inside the compound (fourteen were released early). When the ayatollah endorsed the take-over Bazargan resigned and the revolution moved into a theocratic stage, where it remained. Thus did American policy makers try to play both sides of the Ping-Pong table, aiding the Islamic militants in Afghanistan while seeking some way to bring about Khomeini's downfall in Iran.

Political pressure on the administration to secure the diplomats' re-lease put all other national questions down the priority list—but it was a long list. The state of the economy as oil prices rose entered into a largely unprecedented period of stagflation, a situation where interest rates and inflation went higher and higher while other indicators showed losses or no gain. Tehran's demands that the shah be returned for trial was the main stumbling block, but there were other issues as well. Carter contributed to the sense of paralysis by his decision not to leave the White House grounds for political campaigning. His frustra-tion played out in a variety of ways, culminating in a desperate attempt to send a special force by helicopter to bring out the diplomats.

The shah's death in Egypt on July 27, 1980, did not help to bring a res-olution of the already prolonged Iranian-American crisis. Meanwhile, Moscow watched these events with a wary eye for its own Muslim "sub-jects" in the Soviet republics that bordered Afghanistan. It was no secret that the ayatollah had great sympathy for the opponents of the Kabul government, and, no less than the shah, imagined a greater role for Iran in Afghanistan's future. The Kremlin did what it could with Taraki, but after his return from one trip to the Soviet Union he suffered the fate of his predecessor. The new ruler was Hafizullah Amin, who turned out to be an even greater burden. Divisions inside the Politburo deepened, as the KGB, which had been funding both men for years, grew tired of Amin's profligacy—he tried to get $400 million from Afghanistan's foreign accounts—and began spreading rumors that he was a CIA agent. It appears that here was a case of blowback, for soon the KGB began believing the story themselves, and reported that Amin was too cozy with Americans, and was seeking to curry favor with the Islamic rebels and Pakistan. KGB chief Yuri Andropov began to fret about the situation, telling his colleagues that the Americans were out to "create a 'New Great Ottoman Empire,' including the southern republics of the Soviet Union."[61]

On Christmas Day 1979, after lengthy debates inside the Politburo, the Soviet Union decided to intervene with military force. Amin was overthrown, and the Russians put Babrak Karmal in the presidential palace. For Carter and Brzezinski the Russian action at least had the clarity of an organizing principle. All the talk about the Soviets not living up to the "code of détente," all the effort to mobilize the country's allies and involve China as an auxiliary of NATO (as George McGovern had put it) now had a focal point.

With considerable hyperbole, Carter called the Soviet incursion "the most serious threat to the peace since the second World War." As he had done from the beginning of his presidency, Jimmy Carter chose words and phrases that put him out on a very weak limb. He placed an embargo on shipments of commodities such as grain and high technology to the Soviet Union, and boycotted the Moscow Olympics during the summer. Nuclear arms talks were suspended. The détente era was over. In the 1980 State of the Union speech he outlined a new Carter doctrine: "Let our position be absolutely clear: An attempt by any outside force to gain control of the Persian Gulf region will be regarded as an assault on the vital interests of the United States of America, and such an assault will be repelled by any means necessary, including military force."[62]

Carter then called for increased defense spending and the creation of a rapid deployment force to boost American capabilities throughout the area. Diego Garcia, once a subject of neutralization talks, became a symbol and substance of the new buildup. When America did launch forces into the Middle East in Gulf Wars I and II, the small island was central as a jumping-off place, or "lily-pad" base. But what was more important over the long run to the Carter doctrine, and its expansion under future presidents, was something the president said in the third paragraph of his speech, passed over at the time but which became a key to understanding events after 9/11. And that was the linking of two disparate challenges into something that could be acted upon as if they were one. During the Reagan years to follow, this connection was not much noticed, but it became the keynote of Gulf War II, as George W. Bush attempted to wage a war on "terror" worldwide by invading Iraq.

At this time in Iran, fifty Americans are still held captive, innocent victims of terrorism and anarchy. Also at this moment, massive Soviet troops are attempting to subjugate the fiercely independent and deeply religious people of Afghanistan. These two acts—one of international terrorism and one of military aggression—present a serious challenge to the United States of America, and indeed to all the nations of the world. Together, we will meet these threats to peace.[63]

Brzezinski's voice came through loud and clear in the speech. Soon he was out rounding up old and new allies, with particular emphasis on closer relations with Pakistan and Saudi Arabia. There had been a certain coolness and distance in relations with Pakistan, he would tell interviewers, but with the Soviet invasion, everything changed: "We collaborated very closely. And I have to pay tribute to the guts of the Pakistanis. . . . We, I am pleased to say, supported them very actively and they had our backing." What that meant, exactly, became clear when Brzezinski went to the Khyber Pass—fabled point in the original great game—and was photographed holding an AK-47 aimed, apparently, down into Afghanistan. "Have the Soviets come up to the border?" he asked. "No," replied a Pakistani general. "Can you hold them here?" "Not really. We'd try to slow them down, down there," he said, pointing to another outpost. Before he could slip away, the national security advisor grabbed him for a photo. "It'll be a historic photo," he said, "Three weeks before the march on Kabul."[64]

There was no march on Kabul, of course, but Brzezinski's words—recorded as jests like his remarks at the Great Wall—were always serious. American aid to the Taliban increased through the eight years under President Reagan, as the Cold War reached its final years. The war in Afghanistan was, as he had hoped it would be, a disaster, and contributed to the downfall of the Russian empire, and the entire Soviet system that had begun with the Bolshevik Revolution in 1917. But it was also the beginning of America's *new* longest war. Yuri Andropov's excuse for invading Afghanistan in 1979 was that the United States sought to create a new Ottoman Empire to capture and hold the Muslim states of the Soviet Union. Five years into a war with no foreseeable end, George W. Bush tried to rally Americans around the idea that "Islamofascists" were bent on creating a new worldwide caliphate with its center in Baghdad. In both cases, the peoples of those countries insisted upon making their own history instead; in both cases, the outcome could not be determined by technological superiority.

3

THE FIRST GULF WAR, IN WHICH THE REALISTS MAKE THEIR LAST STAND

To put it simply, I didn't want Saudi Arabia to become another Iran.
—Ronald Reagan, *An American Life*

I thought when we were facing an imperial Soviet communism that that was the most complicated of times. I don't see it that way [anymore]; more rather than less difficult to lead the world.
—George H.W. Bush, March 11, 1992

I am not interested in seeing one single United States soldier pinned down in some kind of a guerrilla environment. We go in there, we're going to go in there and do what we said we're going to do and get out.
—George H.W. Bush, July 2, 1992

Ronald Reagan was Jimmy Carter's opposite in every way. Where Carter always looked pensive, and acted as if someone was watching his slightest move or gesture, Reagan beamed smiles to every corner of a room he entered, and behaved as if no one could possibly challenge America's frontier spirit and destiny. He had lived it—in the movies—and saw the presidency as his greatest role. Reagan consistently ranks above Carter in all polls by at least ten places in those conducted among scholars of the presidency, and higher in the public at large. The range runs from fifteenth among scholars to as high as second in a few polls, next to Lincoln. In Reagan's second inaugural address he described America's westward expansion as the ever-expanding dream of a nation with a limitless future.

The men of the Alamo call out encouragement to each other; a settler pushes west and sings his song, and the song echoes out forever into the unknowing air.

It is the American sound. It is hopeful, bighearted, idealistic—daring, decent, and fair. That's our heritage, that's our song. We sing it still. For all our problems, our differences, we are together as of old.[1]

The Reagan legend holds that he, personally, won the Cold War, first by his unwavering condemnation of the Soviet Union as the "evil empire" that broke out of the disastrous realpolitik-détente containment straitjacket that had inhibited the power of the true American ideology; and second, by the Strategic Defense Initiative, or "Star Wars," program that broke down the Kremlin's ability to sustain the pace of an accelerated arms race.[2]

Some Reagan observers focus on other aspects of his presidency in the second term, the highly successful negotiations with the last Soviet premier, Mikhail Gorbachev. These produced the first serious nuclear disarmament agreements from the time the Cold War began. A darker side, both in terms of Reagan's reputation and prospects for American policy, however, was revealed in the Iran-Contra scandal, which broke into the nightly newscasts in November 1986, with reports that the United States had sought to trade weapons to Iran for American hostages held in Lebanon and hard cash delivered to Reagan's adoptees, the so-called Nicaraguan freedom fighters, or Contras, seeking to overthrow a leftist regime in Managua. Using *Star Wars*–like language to describe the potential impact of connecting two secret and highly volatile projects, Reagan's close adviser and then attorney general, Edwin Meese, wrote in his memoirs, "The effect for the administration could have been the political equivalent of a nuclear bomb."[3]

The wheels very nearly did come off with the Iran-Contra affair, which involved both some very silly things, like the rumor of Reagan's gift of a chocolate cake in the shape of a key to symbolize an American interest in opening relations with Iran, and some very serious doings, like the effort to circumvent congressional laws against trading weapons for hostages and the Boland amendment prohibiting aid to the Contras by any branch of the government.[4]

What still remains missing in most discussions of Reagan's foreign policy successes and failures is the general question of Washington's effort to find a strategic landing zone in the Middle East to protect its access to, and control over, the Persian Gulf oil fields, and how that effort eventually led to Gulf Wars I and II. What will stand out one day is not George W. Bush's uniqueness but the continuum from the Carter doctrine to "shock and awe" in 2003. Of course oil was not the only American objective, but it was certainly a constant in policy discussions. Still, going to war requires an extra added dimension, and Saddam Hussein finally provided the answer to the puzzle with his 1991 invasion of Kuwait. George H.W. Bush's response recognized the opportunity he had to solve an old question, with his fingers crossed about the future of Iraq. Driving the Iraqi army out of Kuwait proved surprisingly easy. Bush feared that going on to Baghdad might eventually lead to the breakup of Iraq, however, thereby leaving Iran the dominant military force in the region, and perhaps more important, the most militant voice of the Islamic "awakening." Whatever policy makers understood about Middle Eastern politics, and inheriting the role of the British as outside stabilizer, the possibility of touching off an explosion that would splinter Iraq was not something to be taken lightly. Originally a hasty conglomerate of regions put together by the British after World War I to solve *their* Middle Eastern problem in the wake of the breakup of the Ottoman empire, Iraq was held together with weak threads. A drive to Baghdad, Bush and his aides believed, would snip these threads, and only make matters worse.

The Search for a Landing Zone

In remarks at a dinner honoring Richard Nixon just as the first Gulf War ended, President George H.W. Bush said, "Today we are building on RN's roots planted in Tel Aviv and Cairo and Moscow and Beijing. . . . You talk about an exciting story." And it all tied in perfectly, he said, with his policies in the Persian Gulf. "If we had not resisted aggression in the Gulf a year ago, if we had not liberated Kuwait and defeated Iraq's invading army, we would now be facing the economic consequences not of a mild recession but of a deep depression brought on by Saddam Hussein's control over the majority of the world's oil."[5]

There were a lot of assumptions here about what might have happened without American intervention, but they all hinged on the supposed risk to Saudi Arabia, Washington's longtime ally in the Arab world, and its principal supplier of crude. Even if Iraq did not have military designs on Saudi Arabia in the immediate future, its conquest and absorption of Kuwait would threaten the stability of world markets. The loss of Iran was bad enough. Add in an expanded Iraq led by an egocentric and unpredictable dictator, and there would be no safe landing zone.

For twenty-five years after the 1953 countercoup that had restored the monarchy in Iran, the United States believed it could count on two stable regimes to protect its interests in the Gulf area. The 1979 Iranian Revolution disabused policy makers of that notion in a hurry. Its reverberations were felt all the way to the Saudi throne room, when, less than a month after students seized the hostages in the American embassy in Tehran, religious zealots stormed into the Grand Mosque of Mecca. It was the first time in decades that an organized political opposition had openly challenged the royal family on religious terms, and was an unwelcome harbinger of a continuing domestic religious war.[6]

While the royal family responded by putting more money into religious undertakings—a policy that would, in effect, "export" the problem for others to worry about—the major impact of the Iranian Revolution in Saudi Arabia appeared to be an increased fear of a Soviet pincer movement through Afghanistan. The result was a close collaboration between Washington and Riyadh to fund the anti-Russian forces in Afghanistan, the Taliban. "The stage was set for the vast future expansion of outside help," said Robert M. Gates, a future director of the CIA, "all run by CIA."[7]

Given that the aid was going to Taliban fundamentalists, the foreign forces recruited and volunteering to help from Saudi Arabia and other countries were largely composed of like-minded individuals, including one, especially, Osama bin Laden, who would write his name at the top of America's "Most Wanted" list with the 9/11 attacks. It happened this way according to antiterrorist expert Richard Clarke. The United States engaged the Saudis, Egyptians, and others in the fight against the Soviets, thereby overseeing the construction of an Arab army without much thought about what it was composed of or might become after the Russians left.

> The Saudi intelligence chief, Prince Turki, relied upon a man from a wealthy construction family that was close to the Saudi royal family. Turki empowered a son of that family, one Usama Bin Laden, to recruit, move, train, and indoctrinate the Arab volunteers in Afghanistan. Many of those recruited were misfits in their own societies.[8]

According to Clarke, therefore, the CIA had a role (and a pretty large one, even if inadvertent) in creating the al Qaeda terror networks. For

Saudi Arabia, the scheme worked well, for it did indeed export the religious problem. What drove American policy, however, was not simply the desire to give the Soviet Union its own Vietnam in Afghanistan, but the continuing situation in Iran. The Carter administration's failure to overcome a dust storm in a dramatic attempt to rescue the Tehran hostages was both politically and militarily embarrassing. The implications of this failure went far beyond the rescue mission itself, straight to the question of American ability to influence future events in that part of the world—or anyplace else, for that matter.

The hostages were set free, nevertheless, just as Ronald Reagan came into office. What exactly went on in negotiations with Iranian interlocutors behind the scenes in the summer and early fall has never been completely explained. It appears that both Republicans and Democrats were maneuvering around the election clock to work out a deal that would see the return of the hostages in exchange for things the Iranians desperately needed—like spare parts for their American F-4 fighter bombers. The policy of allowing the shah to purchase all those fancy weapons might yet work out to Washington's advantage, at least in the hostage case. Facing diplomatic isolation, Tehran's anxiety had been greatly increased as the result of an Iraqi blitzkrieg attack on September 21, 1980, that began eight years of a bloody conflict that left both countries bleeding and exhausted.[9]

The Reagan negotiators won the battle, because the hostages were not released before the election. The question of why that was so, however, probably depended not on a belief that they would get a better deal from the Republicans, but on Iranian suspicions that the Carter administration had covertly encouraged the Iraqis to begin the war. There were good reasons why the Iranians felt that to be the case.

Iran had engaged in provocative behavior on its border with Iraq in the summer of 1980, feeding suspicions that the ayatollah Khomeini had many of the same ambitions as the late shah in terms of expansion and regional hegemony. There was an added religious dimension as well. The dominant sect in Iran was Shia, and Hussein led a minority Sunni government. The Iraqi leader had traveled to Riyadh in early August, the first Iraqi president ever to visit that capital. Despite their supposed fears of a Soviet pincer movement to surround Saudi Arabia, his hosts looked favorably upon Hussein's Russian-supplied army as a bulwark against Iranian Shiite radicalism. Was the visit an effort to get a green light and promises of aid if he attacked Iran? And if he did, had it been sent over by some courier from Washington? Alexander Haig, Reagan's first secretary of state, reported back after an early visit to Riyadh, "It was also interesting to confirm that President Carter gave the Iraqis a green light to launch the war against Iran through [King] Fahd."[10]

Haig's source may have exaggerated, but it was true that Carter had begun a covert campaign against the mullahs. It accelerated in the Reagan years. Carter had authorized clandestine radio broadcasts into Iran from Egypt at a cost of $20,000 to $30,000 a month calling for Khomeini's overthrow. The Reagan administration then paid $100,000 a month to a group in Paris called the Front for the Liberation of Iran, headed by a man who had presided over the reversion of the country's oil to foreign control after the 1953 coup. Then, in 1986, the CIA pirated Iran's national television network frequency to transmit an eleven-minute address by the shah's son. "I will return," Reza Pahlavi vowed.[11]

At the same time, of course, elsewhere in the U.S. government a CIA intelligence estimate asserted that the "Khomeini regime is faltering. . . . We will soon see a struggle for succession. The U.S. has almost no cards to play. The USSR has many." Denying arms to the regime and denouncing its support for terrorism were not proactive steps and did nothing to prepare for the future. It had become imperative to "think in terms of a bolder—and perhaps slightly riskier policy which will at least ensure [a] greater U.S. voice in the unfolding situation."[12]

The danger that there would be no Americans around to help pick up the pieces when the regime collapsed was the genesis of what became the Iran-Contra scandal. It began with the belief that it was possible to find a way to influence Iranian "moderates" with offers of weapons in exchange for cash, and help in getting hostages held by extremists in Lebanon freed. By the time it was exposed the scheme had already come a cropper. In August and September 1985 the president had authorized the transfer of TOW antitank missiles to Iran through Israel, complicating the picture still further. Israel had been secretly sending weapons to Iran on its own. Now it became a middleman, or, in superspy lingo, a "cutout." Weapons continued to flow to Iran through this channel over the next fourteen months, and some hostages were released. But new ones were seized. When the transactions were revealed Reagan insisted that he had only been trying to open relations with moderates, and denied that he had consciously gone back on his passionate election-year pledges that he would never be intimidated by terrorists, or negotiate with them over the return of hostages.[13]

The revelations seriously damaged the administration, especially when it was also revealed that money from the transactions had been sent to the Contras, contravening the Boland amendments. Iran-Contra was only the tip of the iceberg in terms of the CIA's involvement in the Iran-Iraq War, under the direction of Reagan's close friend, William Casey. No one was quite sure, however, who all the players were or what the ultimate objective was. Casey liked it that way. "This was Eric Ambler land," wrote Gary Sick, a former NSC aide in the Carter administration, "the world of the spy novel, where marginal men pursued their precarious destinies in a haze of ambiguity, uncertain loyalties, and shifting fortunes. Commonly associated with fiction, this world was all too real."[14]

And yet, while the details are almost too complicated to follow except as a spy novel thriller, the best outcome in the war was thought to be a stalemate. The trouble with that position, of course, was that it did not offer any sort of a permanent solution. CIA director Casey was not displeased by a 1981 Israeli bombing attack on Iraq's atomic research facility, but he happily approved sharing spy satellite intelligence with Baghdad. And he sprinkled false intelligence items into the mix just to make things more interesting. As the war went on, the administration tilted more and more toward Iraq, despite the evidence that Saddam Hussein had used poison gas against the Kurds in northern Iraq, an action which triggered an international outcry.[15]

In December 1983, Reagan sent a trusted emissary to Saddam Hussein: Donald Rumsfeld, who had been Gerald Ford's chief of staff and later secretary of defense. His mission was to convey concern about world reactions to the use of poison gas, but also to suggest to Iraqi leaders that closer relations were still possible, and that President Reagan disliked the Iranian regime and its policies just as much as Hussein did. They shook hands cordially, and talked about alternative pipelines for transshipment of oil through safer territory away from possible Iranian actions. The next year Washington resumed diplomatic relations with Baghdad, which had been broken off at the time of the 1967 Six-Day War, and made available a large export credit to enable Iraq to purchase more goods from the United States.[16]

The Reagan administration viewed the chemical weapons issue as primarily a public relations matter, and it in no way took priority over the desire that Iraq should be the instrument to contain Iran's revolutionary regime. How ironic, then, that the CIA's use of clandestine broadcasts and support of supposed exile groups like the Paris-based Front for the Liberation of Iran would be the very techniques the agency employed later, after Gulf War I, to create the illusion of a powerful group, the Iraqi National Congress, in order to sell the American public on the idea that Saddam Hussein's regime would collapse with the slightest push from outside.

Threats and Calculations

The Iran-Iraq War lasted nearly eight years, at a cost of over $150 billion dollars, more money than had been spent on health care in the entire region during that decade. Perhaps a million people were killed in a war marked by extreme brutality on both sides, as Hussein and the Ayatollah threw young men into a struggle that resembled nothing so much as the massed armies that clashed in No Man's Land in World War I. Russia and the Western nations supplied the foes with arms and intelligence. Finally, in August 1988, the Ayatollah accepted a UN peace proposal and the guns fell silent. But the likelihood of a lasting peace was slight—a factor, not incidentally, that convinced the Iraqi dictator to keep secret his military plans and weapons. Saddam faced a serious challenge at home in trying to rebuild his country.

Obviously, Iraq could not, under these circumstances, really play the role of regional stabilizer—the primary objective of American policy. Hussein was all wrong temperamentally for the job; and, besides, the costs of his war with Iran had mounted up over the years, until Iraq was the largest debtor nation in the world. The Iran-Iraq War was the longest war in the twentieth century, barely edging out the American war in Vietnam for that dubious distinction. Khomeini accepted the truce but said it was like taking a cup of poison; Hussein was equally unhappy about the stalemate. The war had enabled him to build up his military forces, but he now had a terrific set of IOUs to settle with his Arab backers. Having fought Iran for their interests as well as his own in blocking radicalism, he looked to them for debt relief. It was not forthcoming.

Kuwait seemed particularly ungenerous in this regard. The oil-rich emirate refused to either lend Iraq $10 billion or write off debts Iraq had incurred during the war. To make matters worse, Kuwait was exceeding the quotas set by the Organization of Petroleum Exporting Countries, which drove down world oil prices and reduced Iraqi oil profits. Hussein tried to invoke the support of other Arab "brothers" to influence the Kuwaitis to see reason (the way *he* saw it), but that was not much more effective in bringing the results he wanted. In response, the Iraqi leader began building a case for war, based on the specific argument that Kuwait was not only undercutting OPEC oil-pricing policies but also using slant drilling into Iraqi territory to steal Iraqi oil, and on the more general argument that Kuwait never should have been independent, as it was really the nineteenth province of Iraq.

Washington watched the dispute grow but did not attempt to insert itself into the argument until the last minute, and then behaved ambiguously, almost like a continuation of the balancing act in the Reagan years. George H.W. Bush had succeeded to the presidency, promising, as is the norm, to continue his predecessor's policies. But there were indications of changed attitudes nevertheless. In Reagan's second term the president had carried on nuclear negotiations with Russian leader Mikhail Gorbachev that made both old conservatives and the rising neoconservatives fairly nervous about whether Ronnie had maybe gone soft on the evil empire.

Bush saw signs of unease in some sections of the Republican Party similar to those Harry Truman confronted at FDR's death, when conservative Democrats were more than ready to jettison liberal New Deal thinking and return to "traditional" issues, including tougher stands on foreign policy. When the Berlin Wall came tumbling down on November 9, 1989, these concerns eased a bit; but a complex combination of nostalgia for the original Reagan, suspicion that Gorbachev was more a con man than true heart, and uncertainty about what would happen with the Cold War lid off made Bush feel that he was vulnerable to attack inside his own party. Probably that accounts for his mantra, "wouldn't be prudent" that fueled Dana Carvey's frequent send-ups on *Saturday Night Live*.

Fully aware that critics were waiting to pounce, Bush did what he could to reassure conservatives that he viewed the world situation and

America's destined role much as they did. This was America's moment, and he would not let it slip away. Asked in July 1989 whether he would meet Gorbachev soon, either in company with other G-7 leaders at an economic summit, or by himself, Bush replied candidly, "There's an awful lot that has to transpire in the Soviet Union, it seems to me, before anything of that nature would be considered. We're talking about free market economies here." Pursued by questioners who wanted know what the main issue was, he replied, "A little more time." Some of his critics, including former president Richard Nixon, thought that he was taking too much time, and the Russian situation might deteriorate to a point where all hell could break loose. Gorbachev said the Cold War was over, queried another reporter, what did he think? "Why do we resort to these code words," Bush shot back, "that send different signals to different people? I'm not going to answer it." Then he elaborated with an insight into the way he saw the world moving. "He can speak for himself in a very eloquent way," the president said of the Russian leader, and it was true the world was changing dramatically. "But if I signal to you there's no Cold War, then it's 'What are you doing with troops in Europe?' I mean, come on."[17]

In his second State of the Union message, in 1990, Bush elaborated on his concerns about Gorbachev, and the possibility that the Russian was trying to do a "Yalta" on him with supposed maneuvers to keep spheres of influence intact. The Yalta Conference in February 1945, he said, had "set the compass points" of the postwar era, dividing East from West unnaturally. But with the fall of the Berlin Wall all that changed. "America stands at the center of a widening circle of freedom—today, tomorrow, and into the next century. . . . This nation, this idea called America, was and always will be a new world—our new world."[18]

Powerful stuff indeed. Yalta had always been a rallying cry for conservatives almost from the very day FDR returned from that long journey and solemnly reported to Congress that the conference had spelled the end to "spheres of influence" with fingers crossed behind his back. Like so many other of Roosevelt's wartime pronouncements, this statement expressed a hope that things would work out over time, not the actual state of affairs. The argument Bush was making by his frequent references to Yalta was that now—after forty-five years—history could pick up from where it should have been, and go on from there. A more dramatic assertion was made by those who contended that with the U.S. victory in the Cold War, history had come to an end. It was something of a play on philosophical ideas about ideologies and how they had evolved, with the contention that liberal capitalism was now the last one standing, à la Bruce Willis. There will be more to say about that in a later chapter.

Bush dealt with the first supposed challenge to the new world order he had proclaimed by invading Central America to oust an old American pal, Panama's Manuel Noriega. Noriega is often called Bush's skeleton-in-chief in a closet somewhat crowded with bones from Iran-Contra, because of Bush's brief stopover in Panama when he was CIA director and the agency was funding the general as an ally against the Sandinistas in Nicaragua. Noriega was a master at playing both sides, cooperating with the American Drug Enforcement Agency while at the same time pimping for the Colombian drug cartel. Given past support, Noriega thought he had a good friend in Washington when Reagan's successor took office, one who could and would deflect growing congressional criticism of his brutal rule. He guessed wrong this time. His offenses made it appear that he was no longer trustworthy loitering around the Canal Zone. These were enough for Bush to want him gone. But the issue went beyond Noriega himself; Washington desired to take down his Panama Defense Force as well. As long as it existed there was the threat that Panama might not be responsive to American wishes. "You had to take down not only Mr. Noriega," said the American commander, General Max Thurman, "but take down elements of his supporting entity—to reduce the PDF to nothing."[19]

The Bush administration gave the invasion the suggestive code name, "Operation Just Cause." Bush offered several reasons why he acted unilaterally to remove Noriega, but they all came down to what he said in issuing the order: "Enough is enough." The president had ignored an opportunity to allow a Panamanian coup to succeed, in part to make the world see that the United States had undertaken to defend the new order against tyrants who got out of line, and in part to secure Bush's personal reputation as a man cut in the mold of great wartime presidents.[20]

The American invasion in December 1989 may have answered all the above needs, but it was widely criticized in international organizations, including the UN General Assembly and the Organization of American States. What is most interesting about Bush's action, in terms of later events in the Middle East, however, is his reliance on a rationale that superseded accepted norms. Chapter II, Article 3(f) of the charter of the Organization of American States provides: "Every State has the right to choose, without external interference, its political, economic, and social system and to organize itself in the way best suited to it, and has the duty to abstain from intervening in the affairs of another State."

This was, on Washington's part, a self-denying pledge, because, of course, most interventions in the twentieth century were carried out, or inspired by, the United States. The 1961 CIA–sponsored attack by Cuban exiles in the Bay of Pigs violated that section of the OAS charter, but when it failed Kennedy did not follow up with an American military intervention. It was still possible, if only barely so, to suggest that there were limits as to how far the United States would go. Castro's connection with Nikita Khrushchev was certainly a provocation, especially the installation of Russian missiles as a deterrent to another invasion. Bush's "Operation Just Cause" asserted a right not simply to go outside the charter of the OAS, but to intervene in the domestic affairs of any nation (at least any post–Cold War *weak* nation) if it did not meet standards set by a superpower or some supranational community, such as, in the ultimate example of Gulf War II, a "Coalition of the Willing." The point to keep in mind is that the rationale for that war had been developing for some time, and was turned into a full-blown theory by Prime Minister Tony Blair, as we saw in Chapter 1, as well as Condoleezza Rice, who often appeared to have the same speechwriter as Blair.

Kicking the Syndrome

On July 25, 1990, Saddam Hussein summoned American ambassador April Glaspie to a late-night meeting. It was the last high-level contact between the two governments before the Iraqi invasion of Kuwait. After the invasion, in late September, the Iraqi Foreign Ministry released a transcript of the meeting. When it was made public, the State Department declined comment on its accuracy, touching off a lasting controversy over whether Ambassador Glaspie had given Hussein a green light, or even an amber light, to go ahead with his plans. It was obvious the Iraqi leadership hoped releasing the transcript would embarrass the Bush administration, if not cause Washington to excuse itself from taking military action. The State Department did not release its own transcript of

Glaspie's cable detailing the conversation until 2003, as the United States prepared to invade Iraq for a second time.

As Baghdad expected, commentators focused on Glaspie's statement midway through the conversation: "We have no opinion on the Arab-Arab conflicts like your border disagreement with Kuwait." Was that a green light, or perhaps even a clever attempt at "entrapment"? Hussein hoped it would appear so. But the conversation had opened with a far more interesting monologue about American policy during the Iran-Iraq War, with the implication that Washington had given a green light for that attack. The decision to reestablish diplomatic relations between the countries that had broken off in 1967, Saddam Hussein said, had been taken in 1980 "two months prior to the war between us and Iran." But it was not accomplished fully until 1984 "to emphasize the fact we are a nonaligned country."

Hussein went on to describe his disappointment at the revelations about American aid to Iran in 1986. "Despite all of that, we accepted the apology, via his envoy, of the American president regarding Irangate, and we wiped the slate clean." But now there were new reasons to "remind us that old mistakes were not just a matter of coincidence." He had evidence, he said, that "certain parties" in the United States with links in the intelligence community had been spreading word among the Arab countries not to aid Iraq. Not only that, but Kuwait and the United Arab Emirates were leading a campaign to drive down the price of oil. Such acts constituted economic war against Iraq, as it struggled with a $40 billion debt as a result of the war. Without Iraq those countries would not have the oil windfall profits they now enjoyed, as Americans knew very well, "and the future of the region would have been entirely different." It was easy for the United States to reach agreements with rich countries whose interests coincide in keeping prices low, "but the starved and the economically deprived cannot reach the same understanding."

He understood America's interest in the free flow of oil, he said, and that it would use its friendship with nations in the area to secure that free flow. But if Washington flexed its muscles Iraq would respond. "If you use pressure, we will deploy pressure and force. We know that you can harm us although we do not threaten you. But we too can harm you. Everyone can cause harm according to their ability and their size. We cannot come all the way to you in the United States, but individual

Arabs may reach you." Unless the United States got out of the way of his efforts to right wrongs done by the Kuwaitis, wrongs that included not only forcing the price of oil down with excess exports beyond OPEC quotas but also slant drilling into Iraqi fields, he was saying, then he would unleash "individual Arabs." But it need not come to that. The United States would make no mistake in having Iraq as its friend, he said. Indeed, President Bush had not made many mistakes, personally, in dealing with the Arab countries, except, of course, for his appeasement of the Zionists, which he hoped was a temporary prelude to a genuine effort to resolve the Arab-Israeli dispute over Palestine.

Glaspie began her reply by assuring him his message had come through clear and strong: "We studied history at school. That taught us to say freedom or death. I think you know well that we as a people have our experience with the colonialists." That was old stuff, of course, but Glaspie branched off to say that, despite what was being said some places in the press, President Bush had expressed his friendship in recent letters. He had rejected any effort to impose trade sanctions on Iraq. Hussein interrupted at that point, "There is nothing left for us to buy from America. Only wheat. Because every time we want to buy something, they say it is forbidden. I am afraid that one day you will say, 'You are going to make gunpowder out of wheat.'"

President Bush was an intelligent man, Glaspie protested, he was not going to declare economic war on Iraq. She had direct instructions to seek better relations with Iraq. It was true, she admitted, that the United States did not want "higher prices for oil," but Iraq should think about the possibility of not "charging too high a price." She had lived in Iraq for years, she said, and admired Saddam Hussein's efforts to rebuild his country. Then came the famous quote. "I know you need funds. We understand that and our opinion is that you should have the opportunity to rebuild your country. But we have no opinion on the Arab-Arab conflicts, like your border disagreement with Kuwait." Washington hoped Hussein could solve the problem through the mediation of someone like Egyptian president Hosni Mubarak. "All that we hope is that these issues are solved quickly."

But, despite later comments, the ambassador did not leave it there. Given all that Hussein had said about Kuwait's transgressions and military preparations, she had been instructed to ask "in the spirit of friendship— not in the spirit of confrontation—regarding your intentions. . . . I do not mean that the situation is a simple situation. But our concern is a simple one." America wanted a peaceful resolution of the disputes. Hussein ended their conversation by asserting that he had invoked various Arab leaders to help with a resolution, but all to no avail. "Now tell us, if the American president found himself in this situation, what would he do?"[21]

Glaspie could not tell Hussein what President Bush would do about an Iraqi invasion—because she did not know. Her second in command, the soon-to-be-famous Joseph Wilson, summed up the confusing situation well. He wrote in his memoirs, *The Politics of Truth*, that while the ambassador's meaning was clear, President Bush himself, in a follow-up letter to the midnight conversation, reasserted Washington's desire for better relations in a manner that may have helped to persuade Saddam Hussein that he would not face anything more than moral censure as a result of action against Kuwait, and certainly not military intervention. In truth, Wilson also wrote, neither Bush's letter nor Glaspie's comments, nor Wilson's own statements to Iraqi ministers after the invasion of Kuwait, threatened "U.S. military action should he fail to heed our entreaties not to invade Kuwait."[22]

Glaspie was later cornered by British journalists brandishing the transcript outside the American embassy in Baghdad. "You knew Saddam was going to invade [Kuwait] but you didn't warn him not to. You didn't tell him America would defend Kuwait. You told him the opposite—that America was not associated with Kuwait." Another chimed in, "You encouraged this aggression—his invasion. What were you thinking?" Her reply added still more to the confusion. "Obviously, I didn't think, and nobody else did, that the Iraqis were going to take all of Kuwait." The journalists chased after her as she entered her limousine. "You thought he was just going to take some of it? But, how could you?" The ambassador said no more as she was whisked away.[23]

The Glaspie Affair did make matters worse for President Bush no matter what he decided to do about the sudden change in the Middle Eastern balance of power. There is something of an urban myth about the whole affair, centered on the role of British prime minister Margaret Thatcher, the Iron Lady. She supposedly wagged her finger at Bush right after the invasion, "Remember, George, this is no time to go wobbly." Actually, what Margaret Thatcher thought about the crisis worried him least. His greatest fear, he would say repeatedly over the next several months, was that there might be some sort of Arab solution proposed and accepted that would exclude a principal role for the United States as the arbiter of all things to do with an act of aggression—or it was clear, a change in the control of oil. With his position enhanced by adding Kuwait's 10 percent of the world's proven oil reserves to Iraq's resources, Saddam Hussein could then become the arbiter of OPEC's policies, and a challenger to American suzerainty. "I worried from day one about the talk of an 'Arab Solution.'"[24]

Kuwaiti leaders were not an easy bunch to feel sorry for. Their attitude toward Iraq's war debts, the border issues, and their undercutting of OPEC made many in the Middle East happy to see them get their come-uppance, though Saddam Hussein's use of poison gas in the recent war with Iran—even on Kurds in his own country—stirred more than a lit-tle uneasiness about what he might be planning elsewhere. Kuwait was not popular with other Arab countries, nor was it an example of a small democratic country struggling to survive like Czechoslovakia at the time of the Munich crisis. Iran and Saudi Arabia also had long-standing un-settled maritime border disputes with Kuwait, whose rulers, the Sabah family, ran a closed oligarchy that exploited its riches for the benefit of a few. Iraq was a brutal dictatorship, but far more advanced in terms of ed-ucation, treatment of women, and social services. Still, the situation had serious implications for the new world order. Kuwait was more than just a very rich oil-producing state in geopolitical terms. Located at the north end or head of the Persian Gulf, the sheikdom enjoyed special prominence not only as an oil producer but also as a stepping stone to vital nearby areas besides Saudi Arabia, including the huge Abadan re-finery in Iran.

As far as the Bush administration was concerned, the invasion posed two immediate challenges: First, would Saddam stop, or go on to invade Saudi Arabia? Second, could Washington use even a threat of an Iraqi invasion to secure a change in Saudi reluctance to host large-scale American forces? The worldwide implications of Iraq's absorption of Kuwait—for America's pretensions as the indispensable nation—seemed tremendous. In the first few days of the crisis, Bush writes in his joint memoir with Brent Scowcroft, he realized full well the perils of call-ing for a military solution. "We had a big job ahead of shaping opinion at home and abroad and could little afford bellicose mistakes at the start."[25]

The administration faced a skeptical Congress, controlled by Democrats, and a deepening economic recession. At the first press conferences after the invasion, Bush allowed reporters to ask leading questions about his intentions toward the "puppet government" the Iraqis had installed in Kuwait, providing only the most general of responses. He did not, at this stage, accuse Iraq of seeking nuclear weapons, or attempt to demonize Saddam Hussein as the reincarnation of Hitler. These charges would come later, when it became clear that simply standing up for Kuwait as a victim would not sell Congress on war. For now Bush was content to tease his questioners, and let them describe possible alternative actions in their queries. His most quotable statement came in a brief press conference on August 5, 1990: "This will not stand. This will not stand, this aggression against Kuwait."[26]

General Colin Powell, Reagan's national security advisor and now chairman of the Joint Chiefs, confided to General Norman Schwarzkopf, "I think we'd go to war over Saudi Arabia, but I doubt we'd go to war over Kuwait." Where he was wrong was in thinking the war would be about Kuwait. It would be about the configuration of the Middle East—and the world. British journalist Martin Walker had it right when he printed a story about a White House speechwriter who quipped that he had his word processor programmed to call up the phrase "new world order" at a single keystroke.[27]

When General Schwarzkopf was asked to brief the National Security Council, Bush asked if he thought there was any chance that Iran would side with Iraq. That was an important clue to the way matters were developing in White House calculations. Reconciliation between two countries so recently at war seemed an unlikely prospect, but any indication of a reshuffling of the deck worried policy makers, who depended on an ability to anticipate and counter untoward combinations, much as had the British empire in the previous century. From the beginning as well, Bush and his aides were aware of the danger of a breakup inside Iraq, and feared the consequences of a radical Shiite regime allied to Iran or a Kurdish independence movement.[28]

Bush's greatest achievement in these first weeks was securing UN resolutions condemning the invasion and demanding an Iraqi withdrawal. Iraq had long counted on the Soviet Union's support, but now Mikhail Gorbachev allied Moscow with the West, at least so far as imposing sanctions. Bush worked the international telephone as well as previous presidents had worked phone lines to Capitol Hill. The Security Council vote condemning the invasion was nearly unanimous, with, however, a key dissent by Yemen, an indication that Bush had yet to convince all the nations of the Arab League that confrontation was the best way to deal with the successful Iraqi invasion.

The next step was to send Secretary of Defense Dick Cheney and General Schwarzkopf, as well as General Powell, to Saudi Arabia to persuade King Fahd to accept a huge American military force on sacred Islamic soil to establish Operation Desert Shield. Fahd's nervousness about accepting the American offer stemmed from several sources, including a long-standing fear of inciting opposition at home that went back all the way to the end of World War II, when the United States secured its first military foothold in the kingdom. President Bush had given the king's favorite nephew and ambassador to the United States, Prince Bandar, a preview, complete with pictures purporting to show an Iraqi force poised to strike Saudi Arabia—but neither he nor King Fahd later was told how many Americans would make up Desert Shield.

General Schwarzkopf was to be the key briefer. He had brought with him all the usual stuff that had always proved so effective with Congress at appropriation time to scare the dickens out of legislators, most of whom were only too glad to vote money for the Department of Defense. As Schwarzkopf developed his presentation, the key pieces of evidence about Iraqi intentions were still the photographs. "I showed the king a series of photos of Iraqi tanks at the Saudi border. Actually, a couple of the photos showed tanks that were *across* the Saudi border. At that point, the king muttered something to Prince Abdullah that [Prince] Bandar didn't translate." Somewhat anomalously, Schwarzkopf then said that he did not know for sure if the Iraqis planned to attack, but that they were "in a strategic pause, busy rearming and reequipping before continuing offensive operations." For the moment this hedge seemed innocuous, but it was more on the order of plausible deniability, a frequent escape clause in diplomacy. As hoped, the briefing accomplished its purpose, and Fahd closed the meeting with a brief OK to the American plan.[29]

Promises had been made that the American soldiers would not stay in Saudi Arabia once the danger was over. There were very tricky issues involved, including the question of whether the soldiers were there only to protect Saudi Arabia, or to use the country as a base for attacking Iraq.

Getting Fahd's approval was, as Cheney told interviewers later, the real breakthrough in establishing the conditions for driving Iraq out of Kuwait: "When King Fahd said that he was prepared to accept our proposition, I was pleased, obviously. That was something that was very important to achieve, but secondly, I also had a sense that this particular decision then triggered a whole sequence of pretty momentous events. Hundreds of thousands of troops going to the desert—[the] U.S. deploying major force halfway round the world—was obviously a significant event."[30]

Fahd's consent did trigger momentous events. For example, it pretty much ruled out what Bush feared most, an Arab solution to the crisis that would leave Saddam Hussein in a powerful position in terms of the world oil market. Even after the first forces started arriving in Saudi Arabia, however, President Bush refused to provide the military with all of his thinking about the next steps. Convincing a skeptical domestic audience was the next step. Powell had a pretty good idea that Desert Shield was only preliminary to the liberation of Kuwait, a decided shift in focus. On several occasions, as he recalled it, he overstepped his assignment, reverting to the sort of questions he had tried to frame while serving as Ronald Reagan's national security advisor. At one White House meeting he had asked "if it was worth going to war to liberate Kuwait. It was a Clausewitzian question which I posed so that the military would know what preparations it might have to make. I detected a chill in the room." Defense Secretary Dick Cheney immediately warned him not to ask such questions, and to stick to military matters.[31]

Despite Schwarzkopf's briefing of Fahd, Powell was in fact convinced that Iraq did not intend to attack Saudi Arabia. And he believed that the effort to liberate Kuwait would inevitably cause huge disruptions in the Middle East, and could create a situation where Iran and Syria came to dominate political affairs in the region—an outcome that *would* endanger American interests. Such views would get him in trouble later, of course, in the Bush II administration, with the same antagonist, Dick Cheney, and earn him the dubious label of "Cassandra," awarded by administration opponents who would not forget or forgive his less-than-absolute loyalty to the cause. But at the time his views were shared by many in Congress.[32]

Powell's semidissent focused attention on the major problem Bush had: How long could the force levels in Saudi Arabia be sustained without causing breaks in the coalition, and even worse, Arab disaffection from the whole project? The U.S. ambassador to Saudi Arabia, Charles Freeman, had been worrying all along about the dangers of cultural clashes. "This will never work," he told a colleague. "All it's going to take is one photo of some GI pissing on the wall of a mosque, and the Saudi government will be overthrown."[33]

In mid-September, Bush reported to Congress that the Iraqis had more than 120,000 troops and over 800 tanks poised on the Saudi Arabian border, but the Pentagon, which upped the number to 250,000, did not show any more photographs of these tanks. In October Bush said he was concerned about the length of time it was taking to get Iraq out of Kuwait with the UN sanctions, but said he had no plans to engage Saddam Hussein in talks. Desert Shield had apparently served its main political purpose: It had provoked the Iraqi dictator into making more bellicose statements. He had reacted to Bush's statements about how the aggression would not stand by attempting to link Kuwait with the Palestinian cause, a ploy he hoped would rally Arab opinion to his side and embarrass the Saudi rulers and others. Instead, it only gave Bush the opportunity to point out that months before the invasion Hussein had said he would "burn Israel to the ground."

The quotation appeared in several forms at the time, was used later to justify Gulf War II, and popped up again in obituaries of Saddam Hussein after he was hanged. Sometimes he was said to be planning only to burn half of Israel, and other times to burn Israel to a crisp. Very seldom is the speech put in context as a response to Israel's warnings that it would launch a new attack if it suspected Iraq of reconstructing the nuclear facilities Israel had destroyed in a 1982 attack. "Iraq, for its part," wrote Scott Ritter, "put Israel on notice that any such attack by Israel would result in an Iraqi counterattack, including the use of chemical weapons that would, according to Saddam Hussein, 'burn half of Israel.' . . . U.S. intelligence data, specifically satellite photographs of western Iraq, had been provided to Israel (via Israeli liaison officers dispatched to Washington, D.C.) to help detect any suspicious Iraqi activity in the deserts of western Iraq."[34]

Bush still worried that he would not have congressional support, even though newspaper polls showed strong popular backing for his actions. On October 17, 1990, he candidly recorded in his diary a conversation with Brent Scowcroft:

A day of churning. Brent Scowcroft, my trusted friend, comes for dinner. We talk about how we get things moving, and what we do about the [question of] provocation [to justify the use of force]. The news is saying some members of Congress feel I might use a minor incident to go to war, and they may be right. We must get this over with. The longer it goes, the longer the erosion. I think we can draw the line in the sand—draw it in the sand in American life.[35]

Important leaders in the Senate, such as Georgia's much respected Sam Nunn, had not been convinced that military action was the best course. Secretary of State James Baker was reminded after the war that some people felt, "Hey, it was just a gas station, and the gas station had changed hands." No, Baker replied, the administration did not see it that way, absolutely not. It had always been American policy to preserve "free access to the oil of the Persian Gulf." Saudi Arabia was not only America's best friend in that regard; it was a guarantor that the price line would always be reasonable. It could not play that role if Iraq controlled Kuwait's reserves as well as its own. "My suggestion that it boiled down to jobs," Baker added, "got a lot of attention and flack, but the fact of the matter is, it would have boiled down to jobs if Saddam Hussein had been able to control the flow of oil from the Persian Gulf, or to, by controlling his own oil and Kuwait's oil, act in a way to influence prices."[36]

As Bush prepared to send the first one hundred fifty thousand troops to the Middle East in the buildup for "Desert Storm," Democrat Dante B. Fascell, chairman of the House Foreign Affairs committee, warned against repeating something like the 1964 Gulf of Tonkin "incident" that Lyndon B. Johnson maneuvered into a grant of powers to wage war and send half a million soldiers to Southeast Asia. "If there is a provocation, it's got to be a real one," said Fascell. "If there's an additional provocation, it can't be two whales passing in the night. It has to be something that can stand the scrutiny of the media, and of the public, and of history." The comment was a reference to LBJ's sardonic admission that American sailors might have been firing at nothing more than whales on that night he turned into a fateful encounter with North Vietnamese torpedo boats.[37]

The problem was that Iraq had given no indication that it would provide the necessary provocation by doing something like attacking Saudi Arabia. It was Kuwait or nothing. Prime Minister Margaret Thatcher cabled Bush that the danger of waiting was very real. "The Iraqis are clearly trying to avoid a provocation," she said. And once the forces are in place, "we should go sooner rather than later. Otherwise we risk losing the support of Arab governments who will not understand delay and come to question our resolve." That was, of course, a statement right out of the book on nineteenth-century imperialism, because the real danger came from the possibility that Saddam Hussein would use new flare-ups in the ongoing Palestinian-Israeli dispute to peel away the Arab cover for the American-led coalition.[38]

Bush agreed with Thatcher that there was not time enough—given the danger of coalition dispersal—to wait for sanctions, but he was anxious to see the UN in accord with his ultimate decision to go to war, especially as he felt he needed the Security Council votes to put pressure on Congress. Even if there had not been such a danger, Bush much preferred to take action that would demonstrate American ability to use military power when necessary to achieve desired political ends. Talking with Senator Robert Byrd, who believed the sanctions were working and would force Iraq to withdraw, and who talked about the impact of mounting casualties, Bush wrote in his diary, "I think he's also underestimating the prestige that would go to the United States for being willing to stand up and support the United Nations resolutions fully, and I think he's underestimating the support we would get from many in the Arab world for getting this brutal dictator."[39]

There remained the problem of a moral equivalent to balance the realpolitik. Encouraged by its American backers, the Kuwaiti government hired the famous public relations firm Hill & Knowlton, complete with its bipartisan stable of famous PR politicos, such as Ron Brown and Frank Mankiewicz, whose liberal credentials stretched from Robert Kennedy to George S. McGovern, to promote the public demonization of Saddam Hussein. Hill and Knowlton then mounted "the largest foreign-funded campaign ever aimed at manipulating American public opinion."[40]

Its greatest feat was the "hearings" held on October 10, 1990, by the self-proclaimed congressional Human Rights caucus. They had all the trappings of a regular congressional committee taking testimony for legislative purposes, but the caucus was in reality only an association of politicians, headed by two representatives who also chaired the Congressional Human Rights Foundation, a separate legal entity that enjoyed free housing in H&K's Washington office. In other words, it was a front organization. The big advantage over regular hearings, of course, was that no testimony was taken under oath and therefore subject to perjury. The star witness that day was a fifteen-year-old girl, Nayirah, who said that she had been a volunteer in a hospital in Kuwait City when Iraqi troops burst in and seized babies in incubators. "They took the babies out of the incubators, took the incubators, and left the babies on the cold floor to die."[41]

Nayirah could not give her last name, it was said, out of fear of reprisals. Had she done so, it would have emerged she was the daughter of the Kuwaiti ambassador to the United States and a member of the ruling Sabah family! Before it could be established that she had been lying not only about her name but about witnessing the incubator raid, the story had become a legend on the order of the undocumented German atrocities in Belgium at the outset of World War I that so inflamed American opinion—when PR started out under the name of propaganda.

Five days after Nayirah's "testimony," President Bush told a fund-raiser for a Texas Republican gubernatorial candidate, "I met with the emir of Kuwait. And I heard horrible tales: newborn babies thrown out of incubators and the incubators then shipped off to Baghdad." He used the story five more times in the next month, embellishing it as he went along. In a speech to troops at Dhahran, he said, "It turns your stomach to listen to the tales of those that have escaped the brutality of Saddam the invader. Mass hangings. Babies pulled from incubators and scattered like firewood across the floor." The story gained immense credibility from a report by the highly respected organization Amnesty International. Alexander Cockburn published the first article disputing the incubator raid in the *Los Angeles Times*, on January 17, 1991. It came too late, wrote John MacArthur, our best authority on how the war was sold—the bombing of Baghdad had begun the night before.[42]

Only three days earlier the *New York Times* had reported on its editorial page an echo of World War II in the current crisis. Apparently there had appeared on Iraqi radio a "Baghdad Betty," who warned the American troops poised to attack that bad things were happening back home: "G.I., you should go home. . . . While you're away, movie stars are taking your women. Robert Redford is dating your girlfriend. Tom Selleck is kissing your lady. . . . Bart Simpson is making love to your wife." President Bush called Iraqi radio ridiculous, and stupid. But the story had not originated with Iraqi radio, or with Hill & Knowlton, rather it was a joke Johnny Carson told on *The Tonight Show* months earlier. It was ridiculous then, but not quite in the way President Bush meant.[43]

Bush had talked about Saddam the invader, a phrase that recalled the legend of Vlad the Impaler, the murderous model for Bram Stoker's vampire, Count Dracula. But the incubator story was quickly supplemented, and then enlarged out of all proportion to become Saddam as Hitler. No person in history was more reviled than Hitler. At one point a reporter challenged Bush's references to Saddam as the new Hitler, asking if the Iraqi dictator had done anything that could possibly be equated with the Holocaust. Bush's reply was a study in equivocation that seemed to suggest that—if anything—Saddam was more evil than the Nazi symbol of pure evil. "I didn't say the Holocaust [compared]," he began, then quickly went on, "I was told—and we've got to check this carefully—that Hitler did not stake people out against potential military targets, and that he did, indeed, respect—not much else, but he did, indeed, respect the legitimacy of the embassies. . . . Go back and take a look at your history, and you'll see why I'm as concerned as I am."[44]

Were reporters stunned at this answer? The embassy reference was to Americans in Kuwait held hostage in the embassy or hiding somewhere in the city away from Hussein's troops. The hostage crisis served Bush's purposes in several ways, both by reminding everyone of the Iranian hostage crisis and his stronger-than-Carter response, and a necessary "provocation" in itself if nothing else happened. The situation was actually more like an American-Iraqi standoff than an international crisis, as other embassies shut down and their nationals left for home. Asked why the United States did not do the same, an administration official replied, "Because we don't want to acquiesce to the annexation of Kuwait." If Iraq refused to allow supplies in, Bush railed, "it would be directly contravening a mandate from the United Nations, and we would view that very seriously."[45]

Saddam backed off, offering passage out of Kuwait to all the Americans in early December, coupled with various invitations to what Baghdad insisted would be serious negotiations—always, of course, to involve the Arab-Israeli question. The hostages were airlifted out, and Bush took up an invitation to have Secretary Baker meet with the Iraqi foreign minister, but only for the purpose of sending a letter to Saddam reiterating the demand contained in UN resolution 678, adopted on November 29, 1990, demanding that Iraq withdraw from Kuwait by January 15, 1991. The administration's unqualified success in the UN, and in building a coalition that even included the old Cold War enemy, the Soviet Union, stood in some contrast to continued concerns about erosion of support at home. These concerns had led the president, as noted, to shift from talk about oil and jobs to portraying Saddam Hussein as a villain among villains, an evildoer on the scale of Adolf Hitler. The shift also included, beginning in November (at the same time he ordered the massive troop buildup), the introduction of Iraq's nuclear weapons program as a reason for military action.[46]

Iraq's nuclear ambitions had been the subject of a recent national intelligence estimate, and of speculation that Saddam Hussein was closer to obtaining a bomb than had been thought previous to the Kuwait invasion. Nevertheless, the existence of the program had not been considered an urgent matter until it was introduced by President Bush as part of his campaign to shore up support for his policies. CIA director William Webster made an odd assertion about the Iraqi threat that attempted to bridge several gaps in strategic thinking. The administration, he said, could have no real confidence the area will ever be secure, unless Saddam were "disassociated from his weapons of mass destruction."[47]

What made this assertion especially problematic was the prewar decision that whatever action was taken to drive Iraq out of Kuwait did not include a march on Baghdad. The mandate under the UN resolution did not call for such a denouement, and the administration had no intention of asking for one. Indeed, quite the opposite, as Bush feared being dragged into a civil war. In his quest for congressional support, Bush finessed a tough situation in the House of Representatives and Senate on January 12, 1991, first securing votes against an antiwar resolution, and then for a war resolution. Bush had held up a vote in December, one that might have gone against him, until after Secretary of State James Baker had met with the Iraqi foreign minister, Tariq Aziz, in Geneva, Switzerland, on January 3, 1991. The Iraqi hard line at the meeting produced the necessary votes. Bush had vowed to go ahead regardless of the outcome of the debate, but he would have had difficulty in keeping that pledge.[48]

At the end of November, on Thanksgiving Day, President Bush had delivered a short speech to the nation that included mention of Iraq's nuclear weapons program. National Security Advisor Brent Scowcroft then linked the possibility of an Iraqi bomb with the fading resolve of the coalition. "This international coalition is a disparate group of people," he said on an ABC news program. "There are all sorts of tensions and pressures one way or another." Defense Secretary Dick Cheney thought the worst-case scenario was that Saddam Hussein might have a bomb within a year. "It couldn't be anything you could deliver from an airplane," he said. "It wouldn't be anything that would be weaponized in the sense we think of a nuclear weapon." But it could produce "some kind of a yield," and could do some damage. The administration seemed to be on the right track here in its campaign, because a *New York Times/ CBS* poll showed that 54 percent of the respondents believed that preventing Iraq from getting nuclear weapons was a good enough reason to take military action.[49]

All along, Bush attempted to walk a very fine line, and here was another indication of the difficulties he faced in selling the war in such dramatic terms. If weapons of mass destruction were the issue, what reason could there be for not removing Saddam Hussein from power? The leading American historian of the Manhattan Project and its consequences down through the years, Richard Rhodes, took sharp issue with the administration's case for war. Forty-five years of postwar history, he wrote, had demonstrated that acquiring such weapons in a nuclear-armed world was "inescapably self-deterring." Nuclear proliferation was not good, obviously, and having another power with such weapons was destabilizing, whether it was Iraq or any other nation. But an embargo on potential weapons material was a first step, not war, followed by serious attention to an overall Middle East settlement, and finally general nuclear disarmament.[50]

Such recommendations were unlikely to get much attention in a White House not given, as Bush had said, "to underestimating the prestige that would go to the United States for being willing to stand up" to Hussein's presumed threat. The UN resolution had given Iraq until January 15, 1991, to comply with its demand that Kuwait be restored. Arab nations that had sought a compromise—Bush's worst fear, remember—were frustrated when the Baghdad dictator announced that he was making the sheikdom the nineteenth province of Iraq. On January 16, the president addressed the nation to announce the beginning of bombing operations that would continue for five weeks before ground forces were introduced into combat. In the speech he rehearsed every one of the charges against Saddam Hussein:

> While the world waited, Saddam Hussein systematically raped, pillaged, and plundered a tiny nation, no threat to his own. He subjected the people of Kuwait to unspeakable atrocities—and among those maimed and murdered, innocent children.
>
> While the world waited, Saddam sought to add to the chemical weapons arsenal he now possesses, an infinitely more dangerous weapon of mass destruction—a nuclear weapon.[51]

He finished the talk with the recent innovation of citing the common man's opinions as his inspiration, in this case a master sergeant, J.P. Kendall of the 82nd Airborne. "We're here for more than just the price of a gallon of gas. What we're doing is going to chart the future of the world for the next one hundred years. It's better to deal with this guy now than five years from now."

The war was going to wipe the slate clean of the Vietnam debacle. "I've told the American people before that this will not be another Vietnam, and I repeat this here tonight. Our troops will have the best possible support in the entire world, and they will not be asked to fight with one hand tied behind their back." Bush's promise to undo the harm Vietnam had inflicted on the world's impression of America—tied down in Vietnam, and handicapped by faulty leadership in Washington—was part of the mantra of the rising neoconservative movement, but it was also one of the enduring myths of American exceptionalism, and the metaphor of progress. Thus, "America never lost a war. . . ." But he needed to be wary of the backside of that myth: ". . . or won the peace." This last part of the old saying was a favorite of unilateralists, who would not be happy when Bush refused to march on Baghdad for realist reasons.

The president tried to protect himself from that charge by ordering the American troops into the war to ensure Hussein's "military might was diminished or destroyed. . . . This was behind my concern that he might withdraw from Kuwait before we had managed to grind down his armor and heavy equipment, and it underscored the need to launch a ground campaign to finish the job—and sooner rather than later." The ground campaign lasted barely one hundred hours, however, and it became a rout, as American planes strafed retreating Iraqi soldiers on what became known as the "highway of death."[52]

Bad Vibes

Almost immediately, nevertheless, this ending for the war became less of a celebration of the new world order than a burden for Bush to try to explain away. The administration had hoped that Saddam Hussein would be overthrown from within, but when that did not happen, and when the dictator suppressed rebelling Kurds and Shiites, the humanitarian argument went the other way. In later years Bush provided many answers to questions about why coalition forces did not go to Baghdad once the war started in January 1991 to "disassociate" Saddam Hussein from his weapons of mass destruction. Talking to veterans of the one-hundred-hour war in 1999, the former president said about the questions, "It burns me up." He was not in the business of second-guessing his military commanders, who, he said, told him the mission was accomplished when the Iraqi army surrendered. "I don't believe in mission creep," he added. He could have been in Baghdad in another forty-eight hours, but what then? "Which sergeant, which private, whose life would be at stake in perhaps a fruitless hunt in an urban guerrilla war to find the most-secure dictator in the world?" America would be an occupying power in an Arab land, with no allies. "It would have been disastrous."[53]

Colin Powell, whose role in both Gulf wars remains the subject of great interest as a tragic figure exploited by the second President Bush, told a PBS interviewer five years after Gulf War I that demonizing Saddam Hussein had already had consequences. "When you demonize an enemy such as the president tended to do with Saddam Hussein, and others did—and, frankly, I did it from time to time, because it was useful putting a face on this crisis—but, in so demonizing him, by the president and the rest of us, you raised expectations that you would do something about him at the end of the day."[54]

The air war was viewed from within Baghdad by CNN reporters, whose cameras showed the sky lit up like a Fourth of July fireworks display night after night. Psychiatrist Robert Lifton quoted one pilot, who declared that the assault on the retreating Iraqis "'was close to Armageddon. . . .' Our hi-tech weapons eased the process by enabling us to remain numbed to it and disassociated from it. This war psychology required us to view our soldiers as noble heroes toward whom opposition to the war would represent betrayal." In that sense, Gulf War I did reverse the antimilitary psychology of the Vietnam War and its immediate aftermath. There, certainly, and with American casualties in the hundreds rather than thousands, Bush succeeded.[55]

Less commented upon after the war was the manipulation of intelligence that produced Saudi acquiescence in the stationing of American forces in that country. The photographs showing Iraqi tanks near the border, and massed troops—the evidence Schwarzkopf had presented to King Fahd—became the subject of intense controversy. A justly renowned investigative reporter for the St. Petersburg Times, Jean Heller, who had twice been runner-up for a Pulitzer Prize, managed to obtain satellite photos taken by a Russian commercial company, Soyuz Karta, of Kuwait and the Saudi border. These showed no signs of an Iraqi buildup, said by the administration in the months before the war to number more than 265,000 men and fifteen hundred tanks. She took the photos to an expert, former Defense Department analyst Peter Zimmerman of George Washington University. He agreed that there was no sign of the troops, and the road where the troops were supposed to have traveled was covered over with sand.[56]

Heller then made an effort to secure a comment from the Pentagon, asking Defense Secretary Cheney to confirm America's position or refute the satellite photos she had obtained, before she printed an article with her evidence. The only response she got was, "Trust us." So she went ahead with the article on January 6, 1991, commenting later, "It's time to draft Agatha Christie for duty in the Middle East. Call it, 'The Case of the Vanishing Enemy.'"[57]

Gulf War I ended without a resolution of the question of a safe landing place for American interests. A Pentagon Strategic Assessment document written in 1999 took note of the parallel to pre–World War II problems facing the British, "where control over territory was seen as essential to ensuring resource supplies." President George H.W. Bush did not pursue Saddam Hussein's army back to Baghdad, out of fear of completely losing control in the ensuing chaos. Obviously, things did not work out as he hoped they would, with the overthrow of Saddam in a palace coup that would leave the status quo untouched in other ways. But he had already undermined his position if such a coup did not occur by demonizing the Iraqi leader, and, more important, raising the issue of

Saddam's quest for atomic weapons without then following the presumed imperative of "disassociating" him from the capability of producing such a fearful arsenal. Indeed, the introduction of the nuclear issue seemed little more than a last-minute supplement to an indictment that began dubiously with the "testimony" of a supposed teenage eyewitness to the pillaging of Kuwait City hospital maternity wards.[58]

These efforts to manipulate public opinion provided a precedent for much more ambitious efforts to persuade Congress and the public before Gulf War II. In this regard, the unresolved matter of the "Vanishing Enemy" tanks deserves a special note for revealing the nearly nonchalant attitude Defense Secretary Cheney displayed in facing questions of evidence in the aftermath of a short, and apparently successful in all regards, ground war that lasted only one hundred hours. President Bush averred that he had kicked the Vietnam syndrome. Part of that syndrome, of course, was the credibility gap that Lyndon Johnson tumbled into headlong when that war turned into a long-term affair with no end in sight. The credibility gap reappeared, wider and deeper than ever, when Gulf War II lasted long enough to permit troubling questions about the failure to find WMD to arise, and then for "Mission Accomplished" to become a bad joke or a multitrillion-dollar ticket to witness (and participate in) an imperial sunset.

THE END(S) OF HISTORY, IN WHICH THE THEORY AND PRACTICE CONFLICT

But what defines this nation? What makes us America is not our ties to a piece of territory or bonds of blood; what makes us American is our allegiance to an idea that all people everywhere must be free.
—George H.W. Bush, April 13, 1991

If we have to use force, it is because we are America! We are the indispensable nation. We stand tall, and we see further into the future.
—Secretary of State Madeleine Albright, February 19, 1998

We should have no misgivings about our ability to destroy tyrannies. It is what we do best. It comes naturally to us, for we are the one truly revolutionary country in the world, as we have been for more than 200 years.
—Michael Ledeen, "Creative Destruction," September 20, 2001

Victory in Gulf War I brought forth a torrent of self-congratulatory statements about the inevitability of American global leadership and the marriage of the nation's military power to its nobility of spirit. Technology alone is insufficient, said President Bush in a speech shortly after the war ended. "A warrior's heart must burn with the will to fight. And if he fights but does not believe, no technology in the world can save him."[1]

Infused with the rhythm of biblical verse, the speech was filled with assurances that America was not only an exceptionalist state; it was *the* exceptionalist state. "Never before has the world looked more to the American example. Never before have so many millions drawn hope from the American idea. And the reason is simple: Unlike any other nation in the world, as Americans we enjoy profound and mysterious bonds of affection and idealism." Yet it was also a speech in which Bush gave perhaps his fullest expression to the practical meaning of the new world order. In the first place, he did not intend for anyone to think that in saving Kuwait—and by implication, future victims of aggression—he had become a bleeding heart neglecting American interests. It was not a sneaky liberal fantasy. "The new world order does not mean surrendering our national sovereignty or forfeiting our interests," he said. It was really a way of working with other nations to achieve stability and deter aggression.

Second, and related to this first point, Bush still wanted no part of a civil war in Iraq. That was why he had not gone to Baghdad. "I want our troops out of Iraq and back home as soon as possible. . . . I do not want one single soldier or airman shoved into a civil war in Iraq that's been going on for ages. And I'm not going to have that." He intended to treat Iraq as a pariah nation until its leaders abandoned the "brutality and repression that is destroying their country." He called for Saddam Hussein's overthrow, while still fearing that he would spark a revolution in the process. The message he hoped to send was to disgruntled Iraqi military figures who, he hoped, might be willing to take matters into their own hands and come up with a new leader. It was a gamble either way, of course, but he did not want to destroy Iraq's fragile political structure and open the way to Iranian or Syrian dominance.

We must build on the momentum of Desert Storm, he argued, to encourage European nations to "shoulder a large share of this responsibility," especially when it came to reintegrating the "eastern half" of Europe, so long under the former Soviet Union's malign control. He had been focusing on "free trade" as well as the Gulf, he said, including the North American Free Trade Agreement, and obtaining congressional approval for fast-track trade agreements—a difficult hurdle for all presidents, particularly during a recession. Bush had been delighted with Mikhail Gorbachev's cooperation in the months leading up to Gulf War I, but kept a close eye on any attempt to perpetuate Russian influence in the former satellites. In 1992, after the demise of the Soviet Union, the White House embraced Boris Yeltsin, the man who replaced Gorbachev as Russia's leader, and offered some financial aid. But it was a potential vacuum in Eastern Europe that Bush was most concerned about filling. "I am determined that American business be given the chance to invest and trade with the new states." He talked about "significant new trade relationships [that can] create jobs right here in this country," but his primary concern centered on preventing a resurgent Russia from again dividing Europe, Yalta fashion, and placing a large area outside the new world order. As had always been the case, separating out economic and political factors in American policy was beside the point.[2]

A strategic researcher and teacher at the Naval War College, Thomas P.M. Barnett, later described Bush's quest as defining the ongoing struggle between globalizing forces and preglobalized states, or connectivity and disconnectivity, the latter being the source of the greatest danger to the United States and the capitalist world order it was always destined to lead.

> When Vladimir Lenin wanted to create the world's first socialist state in defiance of the capitalist world system, he ended up in Russia, a nation whose economic development was significantly retarded—or precapitalist. Correspondingly, when [Osama] bin Laden and al Qaeda sought to launch their worldwide resistance to the United States–led globalization process, they invariably settled in a nation whose economic connectivity to the outside world was severely retarded—or preglobalized.[3]

Barnett's read on Osama bin Laden highlights the difficulty ahead in adopting the Taliban to combat the Soviet Union in Afghanistan. A Saudi with ties to the royal family, bin Laden had fought alongside the Taliban, enjoying American support as well. But he was fighting a different war—he was fighting a holy war that included opposition to Western policies and thought, as well as to Soviet imperialism and communist ideology. On his own, bin Laden had raised an army of volunteers to fight in Afghanistan, many from South Yemen, a self-described Marxist state that had disenfranchised large property owners. He persuaded sons of former landowners to join him there in the struggle against the hated Russians. His supporters in Saudi Arabia admired—and somewhat feared—his success as a kind of freebooting military adventurer, whose ultimate aims even about his homeland were far from clear. Keeping him at a safe distance, preferably outside the kingdom, was the best option, lest his popularity splash over like boiling water into Saudi politics.[4]

The Iraqi invasion of Kuwait provided him with a perfect opportunity to expand his horizons, and at the same time project a challenge to the Saudi hierarchy. When the Americans—Dick Cheney, Colin Powell, and Norman Schwarzkopf—came to Riyadh to persuade King Fahd to accept an immense foreign army on the sacred soil of Islam, bin Laden was ready with a counteroffer. "Inspired by his Afghan jihad experience, Osama arrived with maps and detailed diagrams. In keeping with the Prophet's injunction, he insisted that no nonbeliever army be allowed to sully the sacred land of the two holy mosques."[5]

Here was something more than a bid to undertake the defense of Saudi Arabia. What bin Laden really desired was to sever the long political relationship with the United States that had begun with the 1945 meeting between President Franklin D. Roosevelt and King Ibn Saud that led to the construction of the first American airbase. The relationship had grown year by year, as billions of dollars in arms came to Saudi Arabia, while the regime provided Americans with a steady supply of reasonably priced oil. Rebuffed, bin Laden reportedly stormed out of the palace hurling threats that he would be heard from again soon enough.

Most likely, he had never expected his offer to be taken up. And he no doubt enjoyed Saudi explanations that he had been transformed into an uncontrollable menace by the rejection—for that gave him more credibility in certain places for recruiting adherents to his cause. In the first Gulf War, Saddam Hussein had fired Scud missiles at the Prince Sultan base in Saudi Arabia without much effect. The continuing American presence in bases along an extended archipelago from Kuwait, through Bahrain and Qatar to Oman and Saudi Arabia, was justified by both Bush and his successor, Bill Clinton, as required to contain Saddam Hussein. But in June 1996 a bomb went off at the high-rise barracks on the airbase, killing nineteen American servicemen. Osama bin Laden, not Saddam Hussein, claimed credit, though United States and Saudi officials concluded Iran was behind the attack, a political conclusion more than an intelligence one. However that might be, in the run-up to Gulf War II, the argument was made that removing Saddam—and installing bases in Iraq—would open the way to evacuating the increasingly problematic bases in Saudi Arabia. It was by no means agreed, however, that simply clearing Iraq of the troublemaker would alleviate America's concern about a permanent solution. An American diplomat noted that the oil-rich emirates were practically defenseless against any regional power; even if Saddam were to disappear the bases would remain essential. "Think Iran, think Iraq," he said, "The Saudis and other smaller oil emirates live in a nasty neighborhood."[6]

The 1990s saw the Bush and Clinton administrations attempt to deal with these problems, though Barnett's later focus on bin Laden was not the central concern of contemporary critics, who looked at the victory in Gulf War I as less than complete. One of the most trenchant critiques came from conservative pundit George F. Will, who wrote that the "burst of triumphalism" at the end of the Gulf War was self-refuting. "If that war, in which the United States and a largely rented coalition of allies smashed a nation with the GNP of Kentucky, could make America 'feel good about itself,' then America should not feel good about itself. Twelve months later, it doesn't."[7]

Will's indictment cut both ways. By invoking the United Nations as the authorizing authority, Will said, Bush was storing up trouble for future presidents who might find out that the grand coalition would not be quite so grand come another challenge to American interests, and gaining Security Council approval prove impossible. On the other hand, Will charged, he had treated Congress in a cavalier fashion. Bush came close, he wrote, "to amending the Constitution unilaterally by stripping from Congress all right to involvement in the making of war." As things played out, he was proved right on both counts. Then there were the series of rationales that Bush had given, starting with the defense of Saudi Arabia, and the restoration of Kuwaiti sovereignty, as well as the Hitler analogy, and keeping Saddam from developing nuclear weapons. "Each rationale was better than the impression Bush gave of improvising rationales."

When the recession did not lift in time for the 1992 election, and Bush blew a presidential debate against Bill Clinton, the man who could feel everyone's pain, by looking at his wristwatch impatiently, as if this trifling ritual of American democracy was beneath a Skull and Bones brother, the campaign fell off the stage with a soft thud. Still bitter about the election years later, when speaking at a Texas A&M conference on the end of the Cold War, Bush complained to the audience. What had been his reward? He got the "order of the boot." Clinton's victory made it so much easier for the rising neocon faction to launch its campaign against a Democrat instead of a Republican incumbent. The war against Saddam Hussein had not been a success, the neocon authors of the Project for the New American Century claimed, and the uncertain outcome had kept the Middle East in turmoil.

Planning for the End of History

In December 1990, National Security Advisor Brent Scowcroft told *U.S. News & World Report*, "This is a defining moment in world history. The cold war is over." Iraq was obviously to be the test case of whether the "incipient cooperation" of the permanent five would become something lasting, working through the United Nations. If that were to be the case, he said, a lot of people would be dissuaded from using force to solve problems. "And the next time, all it may take is a single U.N. resolution to solve the problem and not deployment of massive armed forces."[8]

These were bold statements that sounded more of a Wilsonian note than an earthbound realist assessment. Perhaps they were only a result of the euphoria the administration felt at having assembled the coalition that would march together in Gulf War I, but there was something else in play here. Scowcroft anticipated that the end of the Cold War would bring about an essential agreement that there was no rival to liberal capitalism. It was the last ideology left standing. As Scowcroft saw it, Saddam Hussein did not represent something that would later be called "Islamofascism"; he was an unruly thug like Manuel Noriega, who could be dealt with as the Panama dictator had been. The complication in the Middle East was how to handle the matter so as not to empower rival Iran.

The increasing number of "terrorist" attacks against American targets in the years after Gulf War I made Scowcroft's suggestion about preempting the use of force by a single UN resolution look like wishful thinking. He had not anticipated the power of nonstate actors. Americans had been given to the idea—almost an obsession—during the Cold War that revolutions were always the result of agents, or subversive forces, operating from Kremlin central. With the disappearance of the Soviet Union, there had to be some rethinking, obviously, about that interpretation of post-1917 international history. Still, even the worldview that sought to replace Cold War containment began with Scowcroft's idea of the defining moment in world history.

A year after the Gulf War, Scowcroft gave another interview, to *New Perspectives Quarterly*, and faced questions about the new world order and events in Bosnia, where Serbian aggression had gone unchecked as the United States and Europe had stood by without lifting a hand. There would be failures, Scowcroft admitted, but the United States had secured a UN resolution imposing tougher sanctions on Serbia than anything seen since the Gulf War. It had been easy to forge a coalition to force Iraq out of Kuwait, but the strife in the countries torn out of the former Yugoslavia were much more difficult to deal with in the same fashion. But did he think it was impossible? It was a matter of will. The United States had to have the will to shape the new world order, for it could not turn "wholly inward and let the pieces fall where they may."[9]

If the American people did that, there could be a return to the world of the 1930s, when closed trading blocs caused a global depression. "The U.S., being the most powerful country in the world for decades, has trading interests all over the planet. Protectionism is not in our self-interest." The United States could not be a "globocop," but there was no other nation to mobilize the industrial powers to work together in the interests of "a world of law and order and decent behavior." Balance-of-power thinking, or realpolitik, might have been appropriate for a certain historical era, but it no longer applied. "Rather, I think we should try to have a shifting coalition of the industrial democracies all pursuing the same general goals: pluralism, open markets, and security from aggression." The United States was the only nation that could operate such a system, "a shifting set of coalitions given the circumstances that arise—which one simply can't know in the abstract." Scowcroft had obviously amended his position, without completely abandoning the hope that a single UN resolution could suffice to forestall the use of force. Scowcroft's dilemma would become Colin Powell's nightmare when the question of going to the United Nations for authorization became a critical issue before Gulf War II.

At the time Scowcroft gave his 1992 interview, a much tougher version of "shifting coalitions" appeared in a Pentagon draft of a new defense planning guidance (DPG). Authored mainly by rising neoconservative figures Paul Wolfowitz, Defense Department deputy secretary for policy, and his protégé Zalmay Khalilzad, it began:

Our first objective is to prevent the re-emergence of a new rival. This is a dominant consideration underlying the new regional defense strategy and requires that we endeavor to prevent any hostile power from dominating a region whose resources would, under consolidated control, be sufficient to generate global power. These regions include Western Europe, East Asia, the territory of the former Soviet Union, and Southeast Asia.[10]

The best way to do this, said the draft, was to convince potential competitors that "they need not aspire to a greater role or pursue a more aggressive posture to protect their interests." But if that failed, "we must maintain the mechanisms for deterring potential competitors from even aspiring to a larger regional or global role." A conflict could arise over "access to vital raw materials, primarily Persian Gulf oil; proliferation of weapons of mass destruction and ballistic missiles, threats to U.S. citizens from terrorism or regional or local conflict, and threats to U.S. society from narcotics trafficking." Scowcroft might be saying that the United States had no desire to be a globocop, but the draft DPG almost looked to mean that even a sparrow's fall would cause a raised eyebrow or two in the Pentagon.

Khalilzad, a naturalized American citizen from Afghanistan, held a PhD from the University of Chicago, where many of the neocons had studied (including Wolfowitz) with philosopher Leo Strauss—a godfather of sorts to the neocon intellectuals. Author James Mann, whose highly praised book *Rise of the Vulcans* traces George W. Bush's war cabinet, calls the 1992 draft defense planning guidance "one of the most significant foreign policy documents of the past half-century." But when it was leaked to the press, the White House quickly disavowed it—as written—lest assertions of America's Olympian prerogatives cause distress to members of the grand coalition who had rallied to Bush's call, and not incidentally, paid most of the bill to oust Iraqi forces from Kuwait in Gulf War I. Various members of the allied coalition had, in fact, reimbursed the United States for 88 percent ($54 billion) of the total amount of $61 billion, "so the actual cost to the [U.S.] taxpayer was only about $7 billion, roughly the same as for the Spanish-American War, and on a per capita basis only $26.92, arguably the least expensive war in the nation's history."[11]

While such figures suggested real dollar value in the coalition, Khalilzad's draft argued that it was not likely to be repeated. Future coalitions were more likely "to be ad hoc assemblies" formed to deal with a particular crisis, disbanded when the crisis was over. They could not be the determining factor in whether or how the nation responded to one of the challenges listed in the DPG. "The United States should be postured to act independently when collective action cannot be orchestrated." Washington could not always be sure it would have partners, or desire them, but must always be sure it had freedom of action. Most tellingly, there was no mention in the draft about taking action through the United Nations.

One supposed lesson from Vietnam would not be repeated: the bitter experience of disappearing allies, as when America's formal allies in SEATO (Southeast Asia Treaty Organization) jumped ship, or perhaps better put, never got on board, as had been the case of French president Charles de Gaulle. The SEATO experience was recalled, obviously, when the United States fashioned the "coalition of the willing," again over Paris's objection, to wage a second war in Iraq.

The authors of the 1992 DPG returned to the Pentagon nine years later to help with an even stronger statement of American prerogatives, entitled the National Defense Strategy, issued on September 17, 2002, this time as a White House document outlining defense strategy for the future, with a covering letter written by President George W. Bush. "Our forces will be strong enough to dissuade potential adversaries," the 2002 version reiterated, "from pursuing a military buildup in hopes of surpassing, or equaling, the power of the United States." Yet it was far more than an update of the 1992 document, setting forth positions on every major foreign policy question facing the nation, from AIDS in Africa to American refusal to submit its soldiers to investigations, inquiry, or prosecution by the International Criminal Court. No such court could judge Americans, it asserted, because the nation stood apart and above all others in terms of its global responsibilities. "In exercising our leadership, we will respect the values, judgment, and interests of our friends and partners. Still, we will be prepared to act apart when our interests and unique responsibilities require." Should disagreements with friends and allies arise "on particulars," these will not be allowed to obscure "our shared fundamental interests and values." The best wordsmiths in the administration had obviously worked over the language into the late hours of the night to satisfy the minimal requirements of diplomacy. Their task, difficult as it was, would have been impossible in the pre-9/11 world; but now the administration and its supporters had fashioned out of the tragedy what they sometimes called a new posthistorical world.

In this new world, Washington asserted the right of preemption to protect against future terrorist attacks, but there was something of a disconnect between the assertion and the reality of how terrorists actually operated from their bases. Bush tried to cover that omission in his cover letter, explaining that the danger emanated from "weak states," as Afghanistan had demonstrated. "The events of September 11, 2001, taught us that weak states, like Afghanistan, can pose as great a danger to our national interests as strong states. *Poverty does not make poor people into terrorists and murderers. Yet poverty, weak institutions, and corruption can make weak states vulnerable to terrorist networks and drug cartels within their borders.*"[12]

These reflections Bush voiced in his cover letter to the 2002 White House–issued exposition of National Defense Strategy are worthy of special consideration. They are, to start with, updated riffs on a classic conservative assessment that stresses the immutability of the flawed nature of the human condition—sometimes put in biblical terms, "In Adam's fall . . ." In addition, the reflections have special relevance to the cultural assumptions of the war on terror. Poverty is invoked not as a cause of terrorism but as a cause of a weakened state, unable, in other words, to manage affairs to keep order—a situation Thomas Hobbes portrayed as the natural state of humans in *Leviathan*. One might even argue that *Leviathan* is the dark side of Walt Rostow's view that such conditions can usually be remedied by an outside force. It is an interesting connection to ponder.

The assumptions in Bush's letter, finally, were brought out clearly during a White House meeting with a leading American evangelist. Journalist Ron Suskind discusses the president's encounter with a religious leader, Jim Wallis of *Sojourners* magazine, in the White House on February 1, 2002. The president seemed eager to greet Wallis to discuss the latter's book *Faith Works*, but the conversation quickly turned in a direction Bush did not like or understand. Wallis said he told Bush, "Unless we drain the swamp of injustice in which the mosquitoes of terrorism breed, we'll never defeat the threat of terrorism." Bush looked quizzically at the minister. "They never spoke again after that." Wallis recounted the episode for Suskind, and then told him, "When I was first with Bush in Austin, what I saw was a self-help Methodist, very open, seeking. What I started to see at this point was . . . a messianic American Calvinist. He doesn't want to hear from anyone who doubts him." Suskind wondered, on the other hand, if a president trying to rally a country crying out for leadership in a crisis had time to entertain doubters. Still, Wallis's comments and fears had to do less with the immediate needs to respond to the nation's agony in the aftermath of 9/11 than with evidence of underlying assumptions and longer-term policies.[13]

Posthistory

The unfolding story of the DPG and the 2002 National Defense Strategy ran parallel to the rise of a theoretical justification that attempted to do for the new world order what George Frost Kennan had done in 1947 with what came to be known by his pseudonym as his "X" article, "The Sources of Soviet Conduct" for the Cold War—provide a theoretical basis for American foreign policy. As the Soviet Union began to implode, an argument was made that history itself had come to an end. Grasping what that really meant depended upon double entendre, just the sort of wordplay the rising neoconservative movement delighted in as the twentieth century closed. Of course there would still be plenty of events to fill the pages of Foreign Affairs, quipped Francis Fukuyama, its first and most famous publicist, but the central historical issue of the modern era had been resolved. The sudden collapse of the evil empire took everyone by surprise, and had produced an intellectual shock wave that Fukuyama and his followers rode like surfboarders at Big Sur. All viable systematic alternatives to Western liberalism had disappeared, he declared. What we may be witnessing was not just the end of the Cold War, "but the end of history as such: that is, the end point of mankind's ideological evolution and the universalization of Western liberal democracy as the final form of human government."[14]

This statement left open, however, whether there were any possible variants to "Western liberal democracy," or whether humankind's ideological evolution rode along a narrow track. It also shoved aside the matter of American intervention, or what Scowcroft had called the "nudging" power of world leadership. Like all bold pronouncements, of course, Fukuyama's essay was often taken too literally to mean that he imagined an end to conflicts between nations. Comparisons with Kennan's famous "X" article were inevitable. Kennan had headed the State Department's policy planning staff when he wrote the anonymous article that became the theoretical underpinning for the Cold War policy of isolating the Soviet bloc. Fukuyama was deputy director of the policy planning staff when he wrote his piece dividing the globe into historical and posthistorical societies. Kennan's article dominated theory and action for a generation, a period when the White House and Congress generally operated from a liberal-centrist agenda at home and abroad; Fukuyama's essay fit into the conservative era that had begun with Ronald Reagan's election in 1980.

Kennan had portrayed the Soviet regime as a product of Russian historical experience overlaid with a paranoid Leninist Marxism that could survive only by perpetuating a sense of permanent crisis. Even at the end of World War II, with its old enemies crushed, he argued, Moscow could never loosen its grip on Eastern Europe, or its absolute control at home, without destroying the only rationale for its continued repression of basic human rights, and, indeed, its very existence. Marxist ideology was a rotting fig leaf of respectability it employed to cover its perpetual sins. Despite his condemnation of the Soviet system, however, Kennan counseled patience, and argued that containment would promote the mellowing or even the breakup of Soviet power. Pursuing such a policy would impose terrific strains on his nation, he recognized, not least in the area of confidence in American ideals and institutions.

Understood as a commentary on containment, Fukuyama's argument tried to explain why Kennan's realist code of operations was no longer relevant and should be abandoned, lest it corrupt American ability to think clearly about its interests in the post–Cold War era. Indeed, it was argued, realism had started to lose its value years earlier when Kissinger and Nixon reformulated containment as détente, in the wake of the Vietnam War, in order to obtain questionable arms control agreements that did little to improve American security and, in fact, helped to sustain (and legitimize) a decrepit regime that had fallen behind in every area but missile throw weight. Détente, so the argument went, underestimated Soviet military strength even as it overestimated the stability of the Soviet political position at home and worldwide. Ronald Reagan's frontal assault on the evil empire as lacking any legitimacy startled realists who had accepted the permanence of the Cold War, and left them theory-less when the Soviet Union collapsed in a heap of unfulfilled promises and shredded dogma.

Actually, while not using the term "evil empire," American leaders had been saying very much the same thing since the beginning of the Cold War. Kennan had said it in the "X" article, after all, but he had been a critic of military bluster and building the H-bomb. Reagan's supposed achievements encouraged what some called a "muscular Wilsonianism," and sent realists scurrying here and there after some alternative explanation to the end of the Cold War—and an operational code for the future. But Fukuyama-style arguments implied there would no longer be a need for theory, any theory. Unfortunately, cultural lag explained the failure to recognize containment's irrelevance and prevented a proper understanding of America's unique position in the world until 9/11. Thus, the argument continued, the first Gulf War a decade earlier had ended inconclusively because President George H.W. Bush refused to push on to Baghdad to remove the tyrant Saddam Hussein. Realist arguments for restraint at the banks of the Euphrates appeared to neoconservatives unworthy of Reagan's promise to restore America in the Puritan image of a city on the hill—but not only unworthy, positively dangerous in a world where, as his son president George W. Bush admonished audiences after 9/11, terrorists had access to weapons of mass destruction.

Fukuyama's arguments had appeal not only to neoconservatives, at least in terms of the rejection of George Kennan's worldview. Among those who thought Kennan's suspicion of human rights diplomacy outdated was Richard Holbrooke, an adviser to Bill Clinton. Holbrooke attended a dinner where the ninety-two-year-old Kennan brutally attacked the policy of expanding NATO into Eastern Europe. "Kennan's warning that enlarging NATO would destabilize Europe—'an enormous and historic strategic error'—carried the dinner audience with its eloquence and sense of history. Events, of course, proved Bill Clinton right, and Kennan—and the bulk of the liberal intellectual community—wrong."[15]

Even more than NATO enlargement, Kennan opposed the promotion of human rights and democracy as "a terrible, morally arrogant mistake." He favored a deal with Moscow over American troops in Europe. "He had accurately predicted, at the end of the Cold War, the outbreak of ethnic violence in Yugoslavia, but he did not understand the need for American involvement in the problem, let alone the use of military force to end the Balkan wars. "Why should we try to stop ancient ethnic hatreds?"[16]

Kennan's innate conservatism (which included a cluster of attitudes about women, blacks, immigrants, etc.) made him an easy target for both neoliberals like Holbrooke and neoconservatives, who had an alliance of sorts to use the "C" word as a synonym for inaction. End of history theorists believed that because of American actions, the world was changing its form every time the planet made its circle around the sun. During the summer of 2002, when the new defense strategy document was being written, Ron Suskind met with a Bush aide, probably Karl Rove, who expressed displeasure about an article he had written on another aide, Karen Hughes, and let Suskind know what he thought of his kind of journalism:

> The aide said that guys like me were "in what we call the reality-based community," which he defined as people who "believe that solutions emerge from your judicious study of discernible reality." I nodded and murmured something about enlightenment principles and empiricism. He cut me off. "That's not the way the world really works anymore," he continued. "We're an empire now, and when we act, we create our own reality. And while you're studying that reality—judiciously, as you will— we'll act again, creating other new realities, which you can study too, and that's how things will sort out. We're history's actors . . . and you, all of you, will be left to just study what we do."[17]

The Mission

To his harshest critics, the elder Bush had indicted himself for his failure to carry through the mission with a comment to the American Society of Newspaper Editors on April 9, 1992: "With the passing of the Cold War, a new order has yet to take its place. The opportunities, tremendous, they're great. But so, too, are the dangers. And so, we stand at history's hinge point. A new world beckons while the ghost of history stands in the shadows."

History's ghost, asserted the critics, stood behind Saddam Hussein, blocking the path to the future. The brutal tyrant might have been driven back from Kuwait, but he had been close to developing a nuclear weapon, readying himself to strike again at those foolish enough to leave him in power. Even as criticism of Bush I continued, measures he had set in motion helped to produce the climate for a second war with Iraq. In a sense, the policy Washington followed was the Cold War agent theory of revolution in reverse: While the United States had blamed revolutions in the third world on Kremlin manipulations, President George H.W. Bush signed a document in May 1991 directing the Central Intelligence Agency to create the conditions for Hussein's removal.

The first major initiative the agency undertook was the creation of an exile group, the Iraqi National Congress (INC), by supplying a private contractor, the Rendon Group, a public relations firm headed by John Rendon, with $23 million to launch it. Using a U.S. government transmitter in Kuwait, and even a station inside the Kurdish area of Iraq, the INC broadcast its message for more than eleven hours every day. Efforts were made to contact Iraqi generals, to encourage a coup d'état, and to take advantage of no-fly zones to rally opposition and prepare for an invasion.[18]

The INC's most famous spokesperson became Ahmed Chalabi, who initially found great favor in the CIA, and then later in the Department of Defense. Chalabi's background included an indictment for banking fraud in Jordan, but he seemed to have no trouble maintaining his credibility with those in high U.S. places. And his "intelligence" sources convinced many who wanted to see Iraq as a country rotten to a point that a simple push would do to get rid of the tyrant, so that a free country could emerge. But serious analysts began to have doubts about him, and his sources, causing a split between the intelligence professionals and the true believers. The central headquarters of the true believers was the Project for the New American Century, which lobbied the Clinton administration on an almost daily basis. The manifesto of the PNAC was signed by a group of former policy makers and like-minded intellectuals who declared that the object of American foreign policy was to gain absolute dominance in the Middle East.

> The United States has for decades sought to play a more permanent role in Gulf regional security. While the unresolved conflict with Iraq provides the immediate justification, the need for a substantial American force presence in the Gulf transcends the issue of the regime of Saddam Hussein.

Most worrisome to the PNAC (as well as to many others), the primary military base in the area was located in Saudi Arabia, where, it was feared, the presence of American military personnel caused the Saudi royal family headaches stemming from threats uttered by the strange man who seemed to have a private army, Osama bin Laden and al Qaeda. The PNAC's focus centered, however, on Iraq, not on bin Laden.

Blaming Saddam

In 1993 a small group of radicals led by Sheikh Omar Abdel Rahman carried out an attack on the World Trade Center, using a truck loaded with explosives in the underground parking garage. The blast did not bring down the towers, but six people died and hundreds of others were injured. One conspirator escaped and was captured later in Pakistan, after his computer was found in a hotel room in the Philippines. In the computer were details of a plan to blow up several jet airliners simultaneously. Messages found on the computer revealed his identity, or at least the alias he used, Ramzi Yousef. He had come to the United States from Pakistan in 1992, and had ties to a Brooklyn group known as the Afghan Refugee Service, the American arm of a larger organization founded by Osama bin Laden that would later evolve into al Qaeda.[19]

There was no tie-in yet with Saddam Hussein. But one would emerge in the arguments of a Harvard PhD, Laurie Mylroie, who quickly became a favorite of neoconservative hawks Richard Perle and Paul Wolfowitz. Mylroie, who was a Clinton adviser in the 1992 campaign, had once been a supporter of Saddam Hussein as a force for stability. The Gulf War had changed her mind, and now she would see him pulling strings behind nearly every terrorist attack, including the 1995 Oklahoma City bombings. She claimed that Ramzi Yousef was, in fact, an Iraqi intelligence officer who had taken the name of Abdul Basit, after stealing his passport. Her proof was that Yousef and Basit were four inches apart in height. Against her view, all the intelligence pointed instead to the conclusion that they were one and the same man, and that Yousef was part of al Qaeda, not a Saddam henchman.

Despite the total blank drawn by intelligence agencies, from those in New York City to the FBI and the CIA, Mylroie continued to argue her ever more bizarre case that all these attacks were revenge for Gulf War I. Writing in the *National Interest* after Yousef's arrest, and while he was awaiting trial, she said that the reason his true identity as an Iraqi agent had not been exposed was lack of cooperation between the U.S. Justice Department and national security agencies. "Once that process [the indictment] is under way, the Justice Department typically denies information to the national security bureaucracies, taking the position that passing on information might 'taint the evidence' and affect prospects for obtaining convictions."[20]

This article was a forerunner of her book *Study of Revenge: Saddam Hussein's Unfinished War Against America*, published in 2000 by the conservative think tank the American Enterprise Institute. The main blurb on the back cover was written by Paul Wolfowitz, who declared, "[Her] provocative and disturbing book argues that . . . Ramzi Yousef, was in fact an agent of Iraqi intelligence. If so, what would that tell us about the extent of Saddam Hussein's ambitions? How would it change our view of Iraq's continuing efforts to retain weapons of mass destruction and to acquire new ones? How would it affect our judgments about the collapse of U.S. policy toward Iraq and the need for a fundamentally new policy?"[21]

In January 1998 PNAC sent an open letter to President Bill Clinton urging him to seize the opportunity of Iraqi resistance to UN inspections to enunciate a new strategy to protect U.S. interests and those of the country's allies around the world. Above all, the strategy should aim at the removal of Saddam Hussein's regime from power. It was a perfect moment for such an appeal, because the Iraq imbroglio had reached one of its many crisis points over inspections and sanctions. "The policy of 'containment' of Saddam Hussein," read the letter, "has been steadily eroding over the past several months. . . . [W]e can no longer depend on our partners in the Gulf War coalition to continue to uphold the sanctions or to punish Saddam when he evades UN inspections." The letter signers included Francis Fukuyama, Paul Wolfowitz, and Donald Rumsfeld, and asserted that existing UN resolutions provided authority to take the necessary steps to protect the nation's vital interests. "In any case, American policy cannot continue to be crippled by a misguided insistence on unanimity in the Security Council." The ideas, and many of the words, came right out of the 1992 draft defense planning guidance. The letter's primary purpose was to ban the word "containment" forever from national security shorthand. Once that was accomplished, the rest would be easy.[22]

A month later there was a second letter signed by an even larger number of former Republican policy makers, including some who had signed the first PNAC letter, and with the addition of a few Carter administration figures to lend a bipartisan gloss to what was essentially a neoconservative project. One signer was Reagan secretary of defense Caspar Weinberger, who had struck a relatively cautious note on the use of American military policy in those years. This second missive zeroed in on Hussein's supposed arsenal of biological and chemical weapons and his alleged past use of poison gas in the Iran-Iraq War. "It is clear that this danger cannot be eliminated as long as our objective is simply 'containment,' and the means of achieving it are limited to sanctions and exhortations." Only a program to effect regime change in Baghdad would bring the crisis to a satisfactory solution. While the first letter described the task as a difficult one, the second suggested that, although that might be so, Iraq was actually "ripe for a broad-based insurrection. We must exploit this opportunity."

The letter ended with a set of recommendations apparently drawn from Ahmed Chalabi's Iraqi National Congress. Chalabi was convinced, and convinced others, that regime change was merely a matter of setting up a "provisional government" in the south of Iraq near Basra, and supporting it with minimal armed forces until a "rolling" coup could get under way, rumble onward to Baghdad, and bowl over Hussein. CIA analysts who had heard Chalabi's rantings on the subject thought his plan was more likely to produce a Bay of Goats than a new government. The letter recommended, nevertheless, recognition of a "provisional government of Iraq based on the principles and leaders of the Iraqi National Congress (INC) that is representative of all the peoples of Iraq." But that was only the beginning. From there the next step would be to establish a safe area where it could function and expand its authority over more and more territory. To ensure its success would require little more than air strikes against Hussein's elite Republican Guard divisions that "prop him up."[23]

Chalabi's pipe dreams were a poor basis for designing a policy that went beyond profound ignorance about Iraqi political and cultural realities, as would become so painfully apparent in the months after March 2003. But those had never been major considerations anyway for the founders of PNAC. The issue had been, and would continue to be, finding a way to flatten out Middle Eastern politics to secure a safe landing zone for American interests: oil and the protection of its ally Israel. Bill Clinton had endorsed regime change, but by most accounts he had serious reservations about the efficacy of outside aid to install an Iraqi National Congress operation. In 1993, acting upon somewhat dubious evidence, Clinton had sent Tomahawk missiles against Hussein's national intelligence center in retaliation for a supposed assassination attempt on former president George H.W. Bush, who was visiting Kuwait in something of a victory lap. The attack came at night, when presumably few people would be inside the building, and succeeded in killing no important political figures, but at least one major Iraqi artist when a Tomahawk missed its target.[24]

"We could not and have not let such action against our nation go unanswered," Clinton said in his televised address. "From the first days of our revolution, America's security has depended on the clarity of this message: Don't tread on us." Such statements gave a measure of credence, of course, to those who argued that Saddam Hussein was in fact pulling the strings of terrorist attacks everywhere. The intelligence on the assassination plot came from "confessions" to American FBI agents in Kuwait City, and through examination of bomb-making materials that supposedly originated in Iraq. It remains an open question whether Saddam ordered the assassination attempt.

In early 1998, Clinton insisted that Iraq readmit the UN weapons inspectors. "If we fail to respond today, Saddam and all those who would follow in his footsteps will be emboldened tomorrow." The stakes could not be higher. "Some day, some way, I guarantee you, he'll use the arsenal." The Iraqi leader finally agreed to allow the inspections to resume, but insisted that the Gulf War sanctions imposed on his country had to come to an end. American and British planes had enforced no-fly zones over Iraq ever since the Gulf War, and the UN had imposed other military and economic sanctions that had created intense hardships. But Saddam remained in power. The longer he did so, the more infuriating the situation became, especially to those who wanted a template resolution of the Iraq "situation."[25]

"We have to defend our future from these predators of the twenty-first century," said Clinton. "They will be all the more lethal if we allow them to build arsenals of nuclear, chemical, and biological weapons, and the missiles to deliver them. We simply cannot allow that to happen. There is no more clear example of this threat than Saddam Hussein."

The president then sent Secretary of State Madeleine Albright, Defense Secretary William Cohen, and National Security Advisor Sandy Berger on a strange mission to the American heartland, Ohio State University's St. John Arena, where the Buckeyes played basketball, to make a case, apparently, to launch a military strike against Iraq. A funny thing happened on the way to this forum, however, when the three advocates ran into a hailstorm of opposition from many in the crowd of six thousand attending the convocation. Albright was nearly drowned out by chanters opposing military action. Others in the crowd insisted that if it were going to be done, this time it should be to remove Saddam Hussein. Cohen answered such complaints by saying, "We've spent seven years containing him at no loss to U.S. lives." An attack would reduce the threat of chemical and biological weapons "that will pose a threat to your children and grandchildren for the future." Such answers only provided a puzzle about why, if the threat was so great, merely containing it from year to year had gone on for so long?

But there were others who challenged that position. Why was the United States obsessed with Saddam Hussein above all other dictators? "No one has done what Saddam Hussein has done, or is thinking of doing," replied Secretary Albright. "He is producing weapons of mass destruction, and he is qualitatively and quantitatively different from other dictators." Those were bold assertions, but they did not stop the questioning. The forum was proving a difficult time for administration figures—a lesson the second Bush administration would not forget when it came time for them to sell a war. When one heckler got to the microphone and, referring to the sanctions, argued that the way to deal with Saddam was not with the blood of the Iraqi people, Albright fell back on American exceptionalism.

> What we are doing is so that you all can sleep at night. I am very proud of what we are doing. We are the greatest nation in the world [here she was interrupted by applause] . . . and what we are doing is being the indispensable nation, *willing to make the world safe for our children and grandchildren, and for nations who follow the rules.*[26] [Italics added.]

Republican representative John Boehner called it an Oprah Winfrey show. In her memoir, Albright admitted that it was her worst day in office. She had not yet learned how to deal with protestors. "Ohio State" became a code word for a screwup in communications. Yet the very next day, she repeated the claims in even more strident terms.

> If we have to use force, it is because we are America! We are the indispensable nation. We stand tall, and we see further into the future.[27]

Her memoir was published in 2003, however, too soon for her to admit that such assertions made that day at Ohio State about Hussein's weapons programs were simply not the case.[28] She was also wrong about that day being her worst day. On August 20, 1998, the United States launched cruise missiles against a suspected Osama bin Laden hideout in Pakistan, and at a factory where it was thought biological weapons were being made in the Sudan. Instead of worldwide praise, however, the response was muted, and Albright noted that there were no calls for follow-up military actions. She blamed this on the *Wag the Dog* syndrome, stemming from a movie in which the White House stages a war to distract attention from a sex scandal. These allegations were groundless, she said, but contributed to an atmosphere of distrust. The entire year of 1998 was taken up, she acknowledged, with the Monica Lewinsky story and the effort to impeach the president.[29]

But that was not why the administration had to backpedal on its assertions about the factory in the Sudan. Press reports abroad, mainly in England and in Germany, shredded administration arguments that the factory had ties to Osama bin Laden, or that it was in the business of producing chemical or biological weapons. At the Ohio State forum, Defense Secretary Cohen had admitted that strikes against individuals or singular targets posed problems, and inadvertently lent strength to the argument for, as his successor Don Rumsfeld would put it, going massive and sweeping everything up. On October 31, 1998, Clinton signed the Iraq Liberation Act, which declared, "It should be the policy of the United States to support efforts to remove the regime headed by Saddam Hussein from power in Iraq and to promote the emergence of a democratic government to replace that regime." It authorized only about $100 million for this effort, however, and still stopped short of a full, all-out authorization for military action, counting on the Iraqi dictator to provide an excuse for it. That same day, Saddam Hussein ordered a halt to the inspections, but reversed himself on threat of attack in mid-November. The inspectors returned and carried out over three hundred inspections. From that point on things become very murky. A report to the United Nations on Iraqi compliance was shaped "at the margins" during discussions at the American UN mission in New York. And even before that, Clinton had issued secret orders to the Pentagon to launch the air attacks that bore the curiously memorable code name Desert Fox.[30]

Beginning on December 16, 1998, American and British planes began four days of attacks on Iraq that continued even as the Security Council discussed the reshaped report submitted by Richard Butler, the Aus-

tralian diplomat who headed the WMD inspection team. It was clear
that no authorizing resolution could have been secured at that point,
because of opposition from France, Russia, and China. Desert Fox thus
became an appropriate code name in Washington for avoiding any
commitment to UN-sanctioned collective action, anticipating policy
decisions five years later.

The onset of prowar thinking was well under way, despite Clinton's
apparent reluctance to go that route. In a speech at Georgetown University Secretary of State Albright even picked up on a clichéd criticism of
President George H.W. Bush's supposed initial reluctance to confront
the Iraqi leader when he invaded Kuwait. She began by repeating that
Americans had "a vital interest in the security of the region's oil supplies," and for that reason had forged strong friendships with nations
that respected international law in all its aspects. Then she zeroed in on
Iraq, saying, "We recognize that stability is not an import; it must be
homegrown. But we also know that circumstances may arise in which
active American leadership and power are required."

This was one of her favorite themes, of course. In 1996 Lesley Stahl
had said to Albright that she had "heard" that more than half a million
children had died because of American sanctions. "I think this is a very
hard choice, but the price—we think the price is worth it." In Albright's
memoir, she said that of course she did not mean to justify the death of
innocent children; rather that Saddam Hussein could have ended the
sanctions by cooperating with the inspection regimes.[31]

But whether that was so seems doubtful. Having made the link between American interest in Gulf oil and respect for international law,
Albright then reeled off in her Georgetown speech all the things Iraq
must do before sanctions could be lifted, including being willing to "end
support for terrorism and stop brutalizing its people." These were deliberately vague requirements, but they made it clear destruction of weapons and weapons programs was not enough; Iraq had to comply with a
list that seemed to grow longer with each reading by an American official. Hussein's inability to meet all these demands was taken as a given:
"Is it possible to conceive of such a government under Saddam Hussein?
When I was a professor, I taught that you have to consider all possibilities. As secretary of state, I have to deal in the realm of reality and prob-
ability. And the evidence is overwhelming that Saddam Hussein's
intentions will never be peaceful."

Lest anyone miss her point, she added, "We do not agree with the nations who argue that if Iraq complies with its obligations concerning weapons of mass destruction, sanctions should be lifted." Then she closed with a flourish, "This is not, to borrow Margaret Thatcher's phrase, the time to go wobbly towards Iraq." These were the very words, of course, that Bush I's neoconservative critics had seized upon throughout the Clinton years to suggest that it had taken Thatcher's prodding to get him to act, and that he had not lived up to the prime minister's challenge in the months and years since Desert Storm.[32]

In the days after Desert Fox, Clinton's National Security Advisor, Sandy Berger, seemed anxious to find a middle way for dealing with Saddam Hussein. Responding to the incessant arguments that containment had not ended the Cold War and was even more inappropriate in dealing with Iraq, Berger insisted in a speech to the National Press Club on December 23, 1998, that the policy had been a success, especially when mixed with occasional bombing raids to degrade Hussein's weapons production. Berger boasted that it was possible to use airpower to "damage the systems Saddam needs to deliver his weapons of mass destruction." That seemed an oddly insufficient, even mealy-mouthed, claim when stacked against the alarmist PNAC letters or Madeleine Albright's strident rhetoric. Berger did not deny he had such weapons; rather, he treated them as fact, arguing instead that airpower was really the best way to contain Saddam Hussein, while the alternative would be to send hundreds of thousands of troops.

In the speech Berger even conceded contentious points that would provide George W. Bush with almost all the ammunition he would need to launch his invasion of Iraq less than five years later. One of the key arguments after 9/11 was that Saddam had ready stocks of deadly anthrax to unleash on his neighbors and around the world. Berger said, "We destroyed a number of unmanned 'drone' aircraft we believe were fitted to spray anthrax." Secretary of State Colin Powell's worst moment, he would say later, came when he repeated similar charges before the United Nations Security Council, holding up vials of a powdered substance as he talked about mobile labs and drone aircraft in the final run-up to the war. Whatever stocks of anthrax Saddam Hussein might have had at the time of Gulf War I, these later images did not reveal what they purported to prove. Also said Berger, even more illogically from his perspective of trying to describe a middle way,

Disarmament does not promise perfect results. But then, neither did disarmament by inspections. Even at its most effective, UNSCOM never had it in its power to uncover every act of deception in every nook and cranny of Baghdad. And for much of the last year, the Iraqis have only been allowing UNSCOM to look where Iraq knows there was nothing to be found.[33]

Whatever his listeners that day thought about Berger's remarks, they were little different than the arguments later used by Vice President Dick Cheney and Defense Secretary Donald Rumsfeld to discredit the idea of UN inspections as a way of discovering what Saddam Hussein supposedly had in store for the world, concealed until he was ready to act in places no one could find. Berger had left no real options except to wait for Saddam to die of natural causes or be overthrown. Cheney and Rumsfeld were convinced it would not take long, and certainly not hundreds of thousands of troops.

AXIS OF EVIL, IN WHICH THE NATION'S ENEMIES ARE REVEALED

I fully believe we're making great progress. I told the American people many times, and I've told the press corps many times that this is a struggle that's going to take a while, that it's not one of these Kodak moments.
                    —President George W. Bush, November 7, 2001

We are at the beginning of our efforts in Afghanistan, and Afghanistan is only the beginning of our efforts in the world. No group or nation should mistake Americans' intentions.
                    —President George W. Bush, November 8, 2001

Our fight against terror will uphold the doctrine, "Either you're with us or against us," and any nation that thwarts our ability to rout terror out where it exists will be held to account, one way or the other.
                    —President George W. Bush, January 15, 2002

Our response to the September 11 attacks has proved even more momentous than it seemed at the time. That is because we could have chosen security as the battleground. But we did not. We chose values.
                    —Prime Minister Tony Blair, "A Battle for Values," 2007

In the aftermath of the attacks on the World Trade Center and the Pentagon, President Bush's speechwriters searched for a way to answer the question: If you were to say that we are extending our definition of the war beyond simply al Qaeda, how would you say it? They looked closely at Franklin D. Roosevelt's speech after Pearl Harbor, and tossed around various phrases such as "acts of hatred." But no one thought it hit the right note. "Well," said Michael Gerson, "the president has been calling the terrorists evildoers," based on his favorite psalm, the 27th Psalm.

"And so tinker, tinker, tinker," recalled fellow wordsmith, David Frum, "'acts of hatred' becomes 'axis of evil.'" Frum felt sure it would resonate.[1]

It certainly did with their boss. His January 29, 2002, State of the Union message will always be remembered as the "axis of evil" speech. The regimes in Iran, Iraq, and North Korea, he said, formed an axis of evil. "States like these and their terrorist allies constitute an axis of evil, arming to threaten the peace of the world. By seeking weapons of mass destruction, these regimes pose a grave and growing danger. They could provide these arms to terrorists, giving them the means to match their hatred. They could attack our allies or attempt to blackmail the United States. In any of these cases, the price of indifference would be catastrophic."

Bush's speechwriters soon fell to arguing among themselves—and in public—about which of them deserved the most credit for a phrase that recalled the lineup in World War II. Stirring memories of Pearl Harbor was a very useful thing for the White House. True, there were no treaty ties between Iran, Iraq, and North Korea, as had been the case with Italy, Germany, and Japan. Also true, in the early weeks after 9/11, Iran had been cooperative in the effort to establish a new government in Afghanistan once American forces defeated the Taliban. Thousands had turned out in the streets of Tehran to show support for America after the 9/11 attacks, and there was a moment when things seemed to be moving in a positive direction away from the impasse that had begun with the 1979 revolution and the hostage crisis. But it quickly passed.

The State of the Union message was a big surprise, said Iran's ambassador to the United Nations, Javad Zarif, given his country's cooperation in Afghanistan. "We were all shocked by the fact that the U.S. had such a short memory and was so ungrateful about what had happened just a month ago." "But the hardliners in Washington," said the *Guardian*, "had been bolstered by Israel's discovery just a few weeks before the speech of a consignment of arms alleged to be heading from Iran to Palestinian groups."[2]

The abrupt turnabout suggested more, however, than irritation at an arms shipment. The axis of evil supplied a rationale for a rolling list of enemies that could be expanded to include Syria, for example, and that continuing favorite, Castro's Cuba. It also put doubters in the audience on the defensive. From the beginning of the administration, hard-liners like Vice President Dick Cheney and Defense Secretary Donald Rums-feld, old colleagues and friends since the Ford years, had been allied against Secretary of State Colin Powell, in what was fast becoming a one-sided fight for the president's heart and mind. Don Rumsfeld had been pushing his thesis, for example, that the terrorist-supporting coun-tries were forging networks parallel to the process of globalization, so the absence of formal treaty relationships meant nothing. With Powell and his aides sitting motionless, the 2002 State of the Union Speech pretty much settled the outcome of debate within the inner circle by asserting—if still obliquely—that there existed *a* connection between 9/11 and Iraq. The key sentence in this regard read, "*They* could provide these arms to terrorists, giving them the means to match their hatred." Iraq's possession of WMD is simply assumed here, and its desire to dis-tribute them to terrorists is placed in the conditional, they *could* if they so chose, do just that.

The 2002 State of the Union speech thus completed the shift in focus from terrorist groups like al Qaeda to state actors, who, it implied, would be the enablers of any future attacks on the United States—with far more devastating results than what the hijackers had wrought using only box cutters and mace to turn jetliners into incendiary rockets. It began in earnest the selling of the war on Iraq as an integral component of a successful war on terror. If it still seemed difficult for many to imagine how an atomic attack could be launched by al Qaeda acting with Bagh-dad's support, there was something else to think about—the mysterious anthrax-laden letters sent to Capitol Hill and news offices. These letters killed fewer than ten people, but somehow they loomed larger as a future threat than a repeat of the attacks that killed three thousand and brought down the World Trade Center in a roaring tumult of twisted steel and shattered concrete. This was so because they revived an old fear of subversion and infiltration along the lines of the famous sci-fi film classic *Invasion of the Body Snatchers*.

As the film begins, someone tried to warn the town; at first glance, everything looked the same.

It wasn't.

Something evil had taken possession of the town.

Bush alluded to the inseparable nature of the threats the country faced in a press conference on November 2, 2001.

What I've been saying all along is, we're in a new day here in America. We're fighting a two-front war, and I believe most Americans understand that now. . . .

I think that the American people ought to conclude that our enemy [country?] is fighting an army not only overseas but at home, that the enemy is being hunted down abroad and at home. We've detained over a thousand people here in America.

In such comments the president made clear his contention that there was a national enemy behind both the attacks on the World Trade Center and the anthrax letters, and its name needed to be said—Iraq.

"We do not yet know who sent the anthrax," Bush said the next day, "whether it was the same terrorists who committed the attacks on September the eleventh or whether it was the—other international or domestic terrorists." The pause, as is often the case with President Bush, was significant, just enough to indicate that the government did have an idea that the same ones were behind both assaults. Saddam Hussein had been known to have stockpiles of anthrax, so he was very likely connected to the letters. "We will solve these crimes, and we will punish those responsible." From the perspective of a war on terror, however, Bush misspoke by calling the anthrax letters a "crime." He would not make such mistakes after the State of the Union speech. "The world changed on September the eleventh," he said on another occasion, "And since that day, we have changed the world."

Before 9/11

The 2000 election had finally ended with a five-to-four vote on the Supreme Court that stopped a Florida recount and awarded the presidency to George W. Bush. The new president joked with newspaper editors about the elongated election not being settled until the Supreme Court ruling. You often get criticism as president, he said, but he believed he took it pretty well. "In the spirit of constructive criticism, I thought I'd make some suggestions to you as to some of the headlines I'd like to see in the future. 'Cheney Cloned—[laughter]—President Has Nothing to Do at All Now.' [Laughter.]"[3]

There were stories that Dick Cheney had been put on the ticket by grown-ups in the Republican Party to watch over the Oval Office until the dauphin learned the ropes. The president never denied their unusual relationship, as, for example, when he discussed their joint appearance before the 9/11 Commission investigating the failure to prevent the attacks. He had insisted they appear together to answer questions. "If we had something to hide," Bush quipped to reporters, "we wouldn't have met with them in the first place." He wanted commission members to "see our body language—how we work together."[4]

Dick Cheney had yearned for a major role in rescuing the imperial presidency from its post-Vietnam trauma, ever since he served as Gerald Ford's chief of staff. "Over the years, he got tired of suffering fools," said a longtime friend. "He thinks it's all BS." The BS was the 1973 War Powers Act imposed on Richard Nixon in an attempt to prevent future wars waged without specific authorization. When Cheney made a great deal of money as chief executive of Halliburton, the friend added, he came to believe "that he didn't have to care what people in Washington thought." He wanted to be independent of all obligations, except on his own terms. With George Bush he reached that position.[5]

In 1987 during the Iran-Contra hearings, then representative Dick Cheney of Wyoming defended Reagan's disregard for congressional bans on aid to the Contras by invoking the "history" of presidential initiatives. It was a perfect irony. The House Foreign Affairs Committee had published a list of these interventions in 1973 to demonstrate why the War Powers Act was needed. Cheney seized on the list for his own purposes. "Of the 199 listed actions," he said, "only 81 could be said under any stretch of the imagination to have been initiated under prior legislative authority. . . . That leaves an extremely conservative number of 118 other occasions without prior legislative authorization." If anyone missed his point, he would spell it out. "In short, presidents exercised a broad range of foreign policy powers for which they neither sought nor received congressional sanction through statute. This history speaks volumes."[6]

It certainly spoke volumes about Dick Cheney's view of presidential powers. Cheney had once thought about making a run for the presidency himself—but quickly abandoned the plan when not enough political supporters showed up for the announcement party. He had credentials. He also had a bad heart. A protégé of Donald Rumsfeld, he became at thirty-four Gerry Ford's White House chief of staff and learned where the levers of power were located and how to use them. He then served several terms in the House of Representatives, but cared little for Capitol Hill, preferring the view from the White House, or across the river from the Pentagon.

James Baker, who would become Ronald Reagan's chief of staff, once asked Cheney for advice about what he would do if he had that job again. Cheney obliged Baker, who took good notes. "1. Restore power & auth to Exec. Branch—Need strong ldr'ship. Get rid of War Powers Act—restore independent rights. (6 Asterisks) Central theme we ought to push."[7]

In 1989 George H.W. Bush named Cheney secretary of defense. It was more than a giant step up the power ladder. In the geopolitics of Washington, D.C., the heartland had become the Pentagon. He who controlled the Department of Defense controlled the government. Power had steadily gravitated to the Pentagon during the Cold War, as the number of American overseas bases grew, training missions integrated the American military with elites from other countries, and responsibility for strategic planning shifted from other places in government, especially the Department of State—the military's only real rival. The Department of Defense's global network of bases—excluding those added in Iraq—numbered over seven hundred in thirty-eight countries in 2004. It refers to itself as "one of the world's largest 'landlords.'" In the United States, the Department of Defense owns or leases more than 75 percent of all federal buildings.[8]

In 1992 Cheney successfully fought against the creation of an intelligence "czar," arguing that competition was the best way to insure that the president received the most effective reporting possible. In fact, however, far from protecting a free market for intelligence sources, he was protecting the Defense Department's near monopoly, with 80 percent of the intelligence budget. After 9/11 it became impossible to hold back pressure for a national director of intelligence, in part, ironically, because of Vice President Cheney's attacks on the performance of the CIA, but what emerged was a much weaker director of national intelligence who would not ever become a rival to the secretary of defense.

At the end of Gulf War I, however, Cheney had publicly opposed pushing on to Baghdad. "If you're going to go in and try to topple Saddam Hussein, you have to go to Baghdad," he replied to critics. "Once you've got Baghdad, it's not clear what you do with it. It's not clear what kind of government you would put in place of the one that's currently there now." And that would be only the beginning. "How much credibility is that government going to have if it's set up by the United States military when it's there? How long does the United States military have to stay to protect the people that sign on for that government, and what happens to it once we leave?"[9]

Cheney's perspective changed rapidly after he left office and became CEO of Halliburton Industries, known modestly as a "global oil services company." In a few short years he made a fortune for himself and huge profits for the company. "Dick gives us a level of access that I doubt anyone in the oil sector can duplicate," Halliburton president David Lesar told *BusinessWeek*. Cheney was determined, the magazine reported, to put Halliburton in the center of the scramble for oil concessions in former Soviet republics along the Caspian Sea. "This is where I expect to spend the rest of my career."[10]

Cheney thought big. His ultimate goal was to lock in the Caspian as the future oil and energy reserve for the United States, and that would continue to be his mission when back in office. Meanwhile, he lamented that Washington seemed stuck with a "dual containment" policy of balancing Iraq and Iran, an approach that could not bring an end to the long period of regional instability that began with the 1979 Revolution, and continued with the Iran-Iraq War, right on through to the invasion of Kuwait. In a 1998 speech to the Cato Institute he offered his solution. He began by asserting the need "to understand that the drive of American firms to be involved in and shape and direct the global economy is a strategic asset that serves the national interest of the United States."

As matters stood, American interests were hamstrung by the government-imposed sanctions on Iran. "The nation that's isolated in terms of our sanctions policy in that part of the globe is not Iran. It is the United States." The effort to enforce UN resolutions on Iraq, he went on, had not succeeded because of the Iran boycott, a policy that had "raised doubts in the minds of many of our friends about the overall wisdom and judgment of U.S. policy in the area." There was another alternative to ending sanctions on Iran, however, and Cheney as vice president refocused on Iraq as a way to break out of the stalemate.[11]

Right after he took the oath of office, Cheney received a visitor, Bush I's vice president, Dan Quayle, who had dropped in to offer advice about the job. "Dick, you know, you're going to be doing a lot of this international traveling, you're going to be doing all this political fundraising . . . you'll be going to the funerals." That was what vice presidents do, he told him. Cheney "got that little smile," Quayle said, and replied, "I have a different understanding with the president." He would be, Quayle recalled him saying, a "surrogate chief of staff."[12]

The vice president was a deductive thinker, i.e., he worked back from conclusions to find supporting evidence. He formulated the "one percent doctrine" on that basis, but not as a response to Saddam Hussein, simply as a general approach to problems. "If there's a one percent chance that Pakistani scientists are helping al Qaeda build or develop a nuclear weapon, we have to treat it as a certainty in terms of our response," he said during a meeting of Bush advisers. "It's not about our analysis, or finding a preponderance of evidence. It's about our response."[13]

Cheney was immediately put in charge of formulating a new national energy policy. Documents released in July 2003 under the Freedom of Information Act were heavily blacked out and sketchy about the Cheney commission's deliberations and who was brought in to offer advice; but there was much discussion of Iraq's oil fields and potential suitors for the oil-field contracts once the UN sanctions ended. In a speech to the Associated Press explaining the purpose of the commission, the vice president declared, "During our campaign, then governor Bush and I spoke of energy as a storm cloud forming over the economy."[14]

A dark cloud hung over Iraq, certainly, a country headed by a ruthless tyrant who had not only managed to offend world opinion but also, by his oil policies, held back private exploration of vast areas. In the mid-1990s rumors that the Iraqi leader planned to open up his oil fields to foreign competitors of American companies such as France's Total and Russia's Lukoil once UN sanctions collapsed had sent shivers through the *Wall Street Journal*'s editorial board. Antagonism between Washington and Baghdad, the newspaper said, would leave us out, and "the companies that win the rights to develop Iraqi fields could be on the road to becoming the most powerful multinationals of the next century." An April 2001 report by the Council on Foreign Relations that Cheney commissioned asserted, "Iraq remains a destabilizing influence to . . . the flow of oil to international markets from the Middle East." And "Saddam Hussein has also demonstrated a willingness to threaten to use the oil

weapon and to use his own export program to manipulate oil markets."
The report recommended that the United States review all its options in
regard to Iraq, including possible military options.[15]

The review process had already begun at the first meeting of the Bush
National Security Council on January 30, 2001. During a brief exchange
on the Israeli-Palestinian question, Bush startled Secretary of State
Colin Powell by suggesting that in such conflicts, "Sometimes a show of
strength by one side can really clarify things." The president then turned
to National Security Advisor Rice, "So, Condi, what are we going to
talk about today? What's on the agenda?"

"How Iraq is destabilizing the region, Mr. President."

As he watched the discussion develop, Treasury Secretary Paul
O'Neill got the feeling that the exchange had been scripted, especially
when Rice noted that Iraq might be the key to reshaping the entire region.[16] She turned the meeting over to CIA director George Tenet, who
pulled out a long scroll the size of an architectural blueprint and flat-
tened it on the table. It was a grainy photograph taken by surveillance
planes. The agency believed it might be a plant, Tenet said, "that pro-
duces either chemical or biological materials for weapons manufactures."
Tenet elaborated with a pointer: "Here are the railroad tracks coming
in . . . here are the trucks lined up over here. . . . They're bringing it in
here and bringing it out there." What it was was not explained. But Vice
President Cheney was eager for everyone to see the layout up close. He
motioned to the backbenchers lining the wall. "'Come on up,' he said
with uncharacteristic excitement, waving his arm. 'You have to take a
look at this.'"[17]

O'Neill interjected that he had seen a lot of factories around the
world that looked like this. What intelligence was there that stamped
these as WMD facilities? Tenet agreed that there was no confirming intelligence about what was going on inside, but then proceeded to roll out
more scrolls on top of the first that showed an airstrip on which a destroyed Iraqi plane sat, and fortifications Saddam Hussein had put in
place around Baghdad. Tenet concluded by mentioning that the CIA
had received information that Saddam was paying rewards to the fami-
lies of suicide bombers. "He was also selling underpriced oil to Jordan
and Syria, creating a web of interdependency and support among neighboring countries." Bush nodded: "We need to know more about this, and
also his destructive weapons."[18]

The president turned to Powell. Devise a new sanctions regime, he ordered, one that would really work. The Pentagon, meanwhile, should look into ways of using American forces to support dissident groups inside Iraq. Powell knew what he was up against—and who would prove to be his unwavering opponent. Throughout their careers Powell had always been one step below Cheney. Bush chronicler Bob Woodward wrote of the impending clash, "Powell detected a kind of fever in Cheney. . . . The vice president was beyond hell-bent for action against Saddam. It was as if nothing else existed."[19]

The secretary of state had one advantage. He was far more popular than Cheney, or, indeed, than President Bush, at least up until 9/11. When the meeting ended Powell began thinking about how to reformulate the Iraq sanctions in hopes of diverting the forces inside the administration driving the war party. If he could get the Arab nations to agree with him on a plan to stiffen the ban on strategic items, while easing controls on civilian supplies, he might have the beginnings of a coalition. He knew that whatever he did would infuriate the hard-liners. It will be charged that the plan weakens the sanctions, Powell told reporters after a trip to the Middle East, where he had negotiated the changes. But the message he had heard from the countries he visited was that the old sanctions gave Saddam a propaganda tool to use "against us—and really is not weakening him." Under his plan Hussein "would not be able to arm his nation with weapons of mass destruction." He also let it be known through interviews that he opposed arming opposition groups. Reporters listening to the secretary of state did not miss these clues as to what was going on. Powell was lining up his allies for the showdown. Diplomats from the countries he visited were lavish in praising their old comrade in arms from Gulf War I. He was received as a "secretary of state plus," said one. Another added, "He is the only one who can say, 'I have been out there.'" Unlike his predecessor, Madeleine Albright, wrote a *Times* reporter, "General Powell talked frequently on the record to reporters traveling with him."[20]

Even before Powell returned from the Middle East, however, Bush launched his first military attack on Iraq, and a preemptive political attack on the secretary of state. According to newspaper accounts, Bush had "consented" to an attack on Iraqi radar installations that had been used to "harass the British and American planes" enforcing the no-fly zones put in place at the end of Gulf War I. There had been no change of policy, the president insisted, but he wanted to put down a marker. This sounded a lot like LBJ and the Gulf of Tonkin beginnings of the Vietnam War. "We're going to watch very carefully as to whether or not he develops weapons of mass destruction," he told reporters. "And if we catch him doing so, we'll take appropriate action." He went on to talk about big themes, free trade in the Americas, and extensive cooperation in energy production. "Ours is going to be an active foreign policy. It's going to be consistent and firm."[21]

Both Powell and Condi Rice had frequently expressed the opinion that Saddam Hussein's regime had been put in a box by American policies. In his Cairo press conference on February 24, 2001, Powell did not waver in his criticism of Saddam Hussein's regime, and he urged that the sanctions be updated for better effect, but, he said, "they have worked. . . . He has not developed any significant capability with respect to weapons of mass destruction." Several times over in testimony before Congress on May 15, 2001, Powell used the C word—containment—concluding with: "The Iraqi regime militarily remains fairly weak. It doesn't have the capacity it had ten or twelve years ago. It has been contained."

But Bush told Bob Woodward that 9/11 changed all that. "Keeping Saddam in a box looked less and less feasible to me." He was a "madman" who had used weapons of mass destruction in the past. *"He has created incredible instability in the neighborhood"* (emphasis added). Therein was the real problem. "The options in Iraq were relatively limited when you are playing the containment game."[22]

Go Massive

Powell's other cabinet foe was Don Rumsfeld. He was a signer of the open letters to President Clinton in 1998 demanding that regime change be the policy of the United States government, and he had chaired a bipartisan commission appointed by House speaker Newt Gingrich to study the need for an antiballistic missile system. Not surprisingly, Rumsfeld's report cast a jaundiced eye on the inadequacies of the Central Intelligence Agency. There was no time to lose in building a "rudimentary shield" to protect the nation against Iran or North Korea, or Libya, it warned, any one of whom might build a weapon, or even buy one, so as "to get the drop on us." Conservative columnist William

Safire championed the report as authored by nine men "with command experience [who] had the advantage denied to compartmented C.I.A. analysts."[23]

All these attitudes resurfaced after 9/11; the disdain for the capabilities of the intelligence community (outside of the Department of Defense), and the assumption that a rogue nation could "get the drop on us." Donald Rumsfeld's worldview posited the irrationality of foreign leaders, who would commit nuclear suicide by launching a missile against the United States, along with the untrustworthiness of allies or "coalitions," and the doubtful accuracy of the liberal-infested Central Intelligence Agency. Constructing a missile shield was the only way to reassure America's allies that we would always be there, willing to perform our special role as guarantor of world order, because alone of all the world's nations we could not be held in check by a rogue state or group brandishing a nuke! The world had been enjoying great prosperity since the Cold War, he told Congress on June 21, 2001, as the free-market system spread into all corners of the world. To hesitate now in building an antimissile system, was to choose "intentional vulnerability," and risk everything gained thus far, putting future economic expansion in jeopardy.

> At present we are enjoying the benefits of the unprecedented global economic expansion—an expansion driven by information technology, innovative entrepreneurs, the spread of democracy, free economic systems, and the growth of societies that respect individual liberty and reward individual initiative. . . .
>
> In the event of a hostile threat by one of these [rogue] states, we would have three unpleasant choices: acquiesce and allow it to invade its neighbors (as Iraq invaded Kuwait); oppose the threat and put Western population centers at risk; or be forced to take preemptive action.
>
> Intentional vulnerability could make building coalitions against aggression next to impossible. At worst, it could lead to a rise in isolationism—something that would surely damage economic progress in our still dangerous world.[24]

Building a shield would be a form of preemptive war against terrorism. He jumped the gun on the axis of evil speech, identifying North Korea, Iraq, and Iran as the most likely to attempt such a ploy. Unlike Soviet leaders in the Cold War, he said, who had to answer to the Politburo at least, Saddam Hussein and Kim Jong-il had unbridled power to do as they pleased. "These are very different regimes." Yet they were coming together. "Just as we see growing interdependence within the free world, there is also a growing interdependence among the world's rogue states. Those states are sharing information, technology, weapons material, and know-how at a rapid pace."

When the third hijacked plane smashed into the Pentagon on the morning of 9/11, it solved Rumsfeld's problems. In his recent presentation to Congress on a missile shield, he had used the Cold War expression "free world," which, as it had in those years, demanded an equivalent enemy "evil empire." Now he had proof that it was out there, in the form of Islamic extremists directed by rogue states. Despite no evidence that Saddam Hussein had ordered the attack, decided Rumsfeld, it was impossible to believe otherwise. In his very first meetings with Pentagon aides on the day of the attacks, Rumsfeld had made up his mind about the proper response. The third plane had hit the Pentagon at just after 9:30 in the morning. At 2:40 in the afternoon, the defense secretary called for a quick review of all the intelligence data: "Judge whether good enough hit S.H. at the same time," an aide wrote in his notes. "Not only UBL [initials used for Osama bin Laden]." It apparently mattered little whether Hussein was involved in the actual attacks or not. "Go massive. Sweep it all up. Things related and not."[25]

At the next day's meeting with the National Security Council in the conference room of a Cold War–era bunker known as the Presidential Emergency Operations Center, Bush announced, "We have made the decision to punish whoever harbors terrorists, not just the perpetrators." That afternoon, over a secure phone from Air Force One, the president told Rumsfeld he would be responsible for organizing the war. "We'll clean up the mess," he told the defense secretary, "and then the ball will be in your court."[26]

Bush was with Rumsfeld all the way on the fundamental question of who to blame. Like the defense secretary, he demanded aides produce intelligence to expose Saddam Hussein as the man behind the attack and related events from years past. "I want you, as soon as you can," the president ordered the head of counterterrorism, Richard A. Clarke, "to go back over everything, everything. See if Saddam did this. See if he's linked in any way." Clarke was stunned. "But Mr. President, al Qaeda did this." "I know, I know, but . . . see if Saddam was involved. Just look. I want to know any shred." Rumsfeld even suggested at one of the early strategy sessions that there were better targets in Iraq than in Afghanistan, where the Taliban regime sheltered Osama bin Laden and his al Qaeda minions. Clarke thought he must be joking. But Rumsfeld was never more serious. He made clear that his objective was "getting Iraq." Bush listened, but for the moment Colin Powell's objections carried the day, and the focus would be on al Qaeda. When the meeting broke up, Clarke hastened to thank Powell for his support. Powell shook his head. "It's not over yet."[27]

Indeed, it was not. Paul Wolfowitz, Rumsfeld's point man on Iraq, had argued that there was a 10 to 50 percent chance that Saddam Hussein was behind the attacks. His source, apparently, was Laurie Mylroie's book on Saddam, *Study of Revenge*. At these early meetings Bush told Wolfowitz to back off—but not because he disagreed. Cheney also laid back on that one. You couldn't do that—at least not right away— because that would give up our place as the good guy. Powell was even more adamant. Other nations would jump off the bandwagon. "They'll view it as bait and switch."[28]

Dick Cheney was Bush's *chef de cabinet*, with an office down the hall. More powerful than a gatekeeper, as some presidential aides had been known, Cheney was the last person the president talked to before a decision was announced. His first opportunity to define the war on terror came in a *Meet the Press* broadcast on September 16, 2001, only five days after the tragedy. He had just come from an NSC meeting that had been going on for thirty-six hours. Waiting outside at a special studio set up at Camp David as Cheney emerged from the deliberations was TV anchorman Tim Russert, who introduced him in somber tones. "What can you share with the American people this morning?" Well, he began, this was not going to be like Desert Storm in Gulf War I. Terrorism was a different problem, and it was likely to last for years. "The focus has to be not just on any one individual." With the nation still traumatized no one noticed that he had admitted at the outset that selling a war to get Saddam Hussein was going to be a tough proposition. Even though it might be a hard sell, there were reasons why a war on al Qaeda alone was an insufficient platform for developing plans to use 9/11 like Pearl Harbor to secure national mobilization on a number of fronts. A war against just Saddam Hussein would not do nearly enough to supply a rationale for something as drastic as the USA Patriot Act and all the other long-term plans that called for secret wiretaps, special prisons for suspected terrorists, and the expansion of military bases into the oil-rich former Soviet republics on the Caspian. The anthrax scare would do much to help provide a solution by blending threats around the core idea that Saddam Hussein would happily use terrorists to do his bidding. Indeed, the major figure in the administration that would push the connection between Iraq and the anthrax attacks—not surprisingly, given these concerns— was Vice President Cheney.[29]

Russert moved on. Did the war on terror mean a massive call-up of reserves? No, Cheney didn't think so. The task was to root out cells at various places around the world. But he brought Saddam into the picture, however blurred the image. "What's changed in terms of U.S. policy is the president's determination to also go after those nations and organizations and people that lend support to these terrorist operators." Cheney said he was not going to talk about operational matters involving the military. "We also have to work, though, sort of on the dark side, if you will. . . . A lot of what needs to be done here will have to be done quietly, without any discussion, using sources and methods that are available to our intelligence agencies." He did not need to spell out what he meant by methods available to the intelligence agencies.

But would we have any reluctance going after Saddam Hussein, pressed Russert? And, for emphasis, he quoted the Iraqi dictator on 9/11: "The American cowboy is reaping the fruits of crime against humanity." The question gave Cheney the opportunity to respond instead of initiating the idea, exactly the sort of position he preferred. No, said Cheney, there would be no reluctance. Then he made this remarkable comment, almost as if he lost the thread for a moment. "But at this stage, you know, the focus is over here on al Qaeda and the most recent events in New York. Saddam Hussein's bottled up, at this point, but clearly, we continue to have a fairly tough policy where the Iraqis are concerned."[30]

Rumsfeld helped to fill in the gaps that still needed filling before the axis of evil speech. Various accounts suggest that the idea for a war on terrorism came from the secretary of defense. Biographer Rowan Scarborough has Rumsfeld tell the president, "This is not a criminal action. This is war." It meant more than going after al Qaeda in Afghanistan. After the defense secretary used the term, Bush picked up the theme and declared he wanted "retaliation . . . That was really a breakthrough strategically and intellectually," Undersecretary of Defense Douglas Feith told Scarborough. "Viewing the 9-11 attacks as a war that required a war strategy was a very big thought and a lot flowed from that."[31]

Most of it flowed between the Defense Department and the office of the vice president. The OVP was operational headquarters for a network of Cheney "agents" throughout the administration, especially in the Pentagon. The head of day-to-day operations was Cheney's chief of staff, I. Lewis "Scooter" Libby. He was assisted by legal counsel David Addington (who had provided Cheney with arguments for expanded presidential power since the days of the Iran-Contra minority report), and about a dozen others, the largest staff dealing with foreign affairs ever assembled by a vice president. Close to Libby in the Pentagon were Deputy Secretary of Defense Paul Wolfowitz; Douglas Feith, undersecretary of defense for policy; and William Luti, the head of the tiny Office of Special Plans—a secretive group that sifted through raw intelligence for evidence to convict Saddam Hussein of conspiring with al Qaeda to launch the 9/11 attacks and commit other terrorist crimes. While the DOD had its own Defense Intelligence Agency and other ways of evaluating intelligence, OSP went its own way—using a direct channel to Cheney's office to bypass both Pentagon analysts and the Central Intelligence Agency. Lieutenant Colonel Karen Kwiatkowski was assigned to Luti's staff, and quickly learned to her distress that the paper flow sailed across the Potomac to the OVP, where it became accepted truth. Time and again she was told to make sure a document got to Scooter right away. Luti had been Cheney's naval aide when the vice president was secretary of defense in the first Bush administration. He also served as an adviser to Newt Gingrich when the congressman was majority leader, and who now served on Rumsfeld's Defense Policy Board (DPB), along with Richard Perle and Princeton Middle East historian Bernard Lewis.[32]

Douglas Feith would be assigned to head the new Office of Special Plans. Its purpose was to review intelligence on Iraq's illicit weapons program, with the objective of demonstrating that CIA estimates and other intelligence products (even those of the Defense Intelligence Agency) had it all wrong. The OSP and the civilian Defense Policy Board, chaired by Richard Perle (until he was forced to resign because of conflict of interests), brought into the Pentagon Iraqi exiles, and bought into their stories of Saddam's weapons programs. "We did not think it was wise," Feith admitted to the BBC, "to create a brand-new office and label it an office of Iraq policy."[33]

Feith thus established his own laboratory for second-guessing raw intelligence files. One particular day in August 2002, Feith drove over from the Pentagon to CIA headquarters in Langley, Virginia. He brought with him his own analysts for a showdown meeting with top CIA people. Their mission was to suggest that the CIA had gone about the Iraq business from the wrong end. Instead of building a hypothesis from scattered pieces of information, the proper way to do it was to "build a hypothesis, and then see if the data supported the hypothesis." This was Cheney's deductive logic at work. As Feith defended the practice to a sympathetic reporter, "If you take thirty movie reviewers and show them the same movie, they will understand its meaning in thirty different ways, and they will even understand the plot in different ways, and I'm not talking about watching 'Rashomon.'"[34]

To influence opinion outside the government, Rumsfeld had another idea that came a cropper when a big story broke in the *New York Times* on February 19, 2002. Shortly after the 9/11 attacks the Pentagon had created an Office of Strategic Influence, with the mission of influencing public opinion abroad, especially in Islamic countries. The idea was to plant stories with foreign media organizations through outside concerns that might not have obvious connections with the Department of Defense. Its commander, Brigadier General Simon Worden, envisioned a broad campaign that would use disinformation and covert activities. "It goes from the blackest of the black programs to the whitest of white," a senior Pentagon official said.[35]

But that was not the most interesting part of the story. The reporters revealed that the Pentagon had hired an international consulting firm based in Washington, the Rendon Group, "to help the new office." Headed by John Rendon Jr., who liked to describe himself as an "information warrior," the firm was most famous for its work with the Kuwaiti royal family to publicize supposed Iraqi atrocities to influence Congress before Gulf War I, but it had also worked with the Central Intelligence Agency to create the Iraqi National Congress, the exile group dedicated to the overthrow of Saddam Hussein.

The *Times* story caused a furor in the White House, wrote a reporter for the *Washington Post*. There would be no change in the administration's "strict policy of providing reporters with the facts," promised Karen Hughes, a close adviser to President Bush. "The president is a plainspoken, truthful man," protested another White House aide, "and he expects that same high standard from every public affairs spokesperson in the government." Whoever leaked the story about the OSI, said a third official, did the president "a tremendous disservice." That left the door ajar to a question: Was it the existence of the OSI that did the president a disservice, or the leak?[36]

Rumsfeld hinted that it had been the revelation that the OSI existed, rather than what it did, that caused the trouble. Answering questions at a news briefing, Rumsfeld complained that some of the negative editorial comment and political cartoons had been off the mark. "But that's life. We get up in the morning and we live with the world like we find it. Therefore, the office is done. It's over. What do you want, blood?! [Laughter.][37]

Stiffing the CIA

Rumsfield's hints that he had special intelligence about the links between al Qaeda and Saddam Hussein, given what had appeared to be serious doubts elsewhere, led to some probing questions at a news conference about an article that claimed a special Defense Department team was sifting through intelligence separate from the CIA and the Defense Intelligence Agency (DIA). "I asked about this," he began, as if somewhat surprised to learn about it himself, "and I'm told [!] that after September eleventh a small group—I think two, to start with, and maybe four now, or some number close to less than a handful of people—in the policy shop were asked to begin poring over this mountain of information. . . . It is not—any suggestion that it's an intelligence-gathering activity or an intelligence unit of some sort, I think, would be a misunderstanding of it." For once there was a significant follow-up question. The suggestion in the article, said the questioner, was that he was unhappy with the intelligence that he was getting about the link between al Qaeda and Iraq. "Why would I be unhappy?" quipped Rumsfeld. "The intelligence is what intelligence is. It says their best estimates."[38]

It was a disingenuous answer. Rumsfeld had chafed at intelligence that he did not control, and the Office of Special Plans in Undersecretary

Douglas Feith's office had been engaged for more than a year in an exercise to make the intelligence fit the policy. "They are politicizing intelligence, no question about it," a former CIA counterterrorism chief, Vincent M. Cannistraro, told *Washington Post* reporters. "And they are undertaking a campaign to get George Tenet [the director of central intelligence] fired because they can't get him to say what they want on Iraq."[39]

Rumsfeld replied to such comments by insisting that he and "George," couldn't have a "closer relationship." The secretary of defense actually found George Tenet's conversations of little use to his purpose, as the director tried to impress him with spy tales. "Tenet was trying to impress him," an aide said, but without success. But even if he had found Tenet a keen reporter on questions that mattered to him, Rumsfeld had set out not only to reform the military but also to extend its control over all intelligence. This became clear very early on after 9/11 when former national security advisor Brent Scowcroft presented a draft memorandum to Rumsfeld and Vice President Dick Cheney detailing his own ideas for intelligence reform. It centered on creating an "intelligence library," a central location that would bring all resources together, but what especially stood out was his plan for putting the CIA in charge of everything. Rumsfeld strongly disagreed, and Scowcroft went to Cheney, who simply said he ought to take it to the president. Scowcroft looked forward to future discussions, but that was the last time he was ever to see the inside of the vice president's office.[40]

Perhaps the best way to circumvent the regular intelligence channels reporting on Iraq came with the anthrax letter scares that began but a few weeks after 9/11. Cheney and Paul Wolfowitz both made serious headway with doubters when those deadly missives showed up on Capitol Hill. The anthrax, sent by means of a white powder in letters, killed five people. One of the victims was an elderly woman, while others were postal workers. The letters were mailed to media figures and to the offices of two United States senators, Tom Daschle and Patrick Leahy—both of whom had voiced reservations about the Bush administration's Patriot Act, submitted to Congress after the 9/11 attacks. Almost immediately, spokespersons for the administration went into action to make a four-way link between Osama bin Laden, the putative author of the 9/11 attacks; the anthrax letters that were sent just a week afterward; Mohammed Atta, the key planner of the attacks; and Iraq. The nexus of the whole plot was supposed to be an April 2001 meeting between Atta and an Iraqi intelligence agent in Prague. It all fit together—except that it didn't when the CIA discovered that Atta was actually in the United States at the time of the supposed meeting. Instead of discrediting the rumor, administration officials used it to cast still more doubts on the intelligence agency.

Thwarted by CIA resistance to the Atta connection, Cheney still found the anthrax threat useful. Indeed, he introduced the idea of a connection with a foreign entity as early as October 2001 in a speech to the Republican Governors Association. "We do not yet know who has been sending the anthrax, nor at this point do we have evidence linking these incidents to the terror network responsible for the attacks of September 11." He promised reliable information would be provided "as soon as it's available." Instead, there was a heavy campaign of insinuation that culminated in Bush's State of the Union speech: "The Iraqi regime has plotted to develop anthrax, and nerve gas, and nuclear weapons for over a decade."[41]

The vice president did not even need to volunteer a strong opinion on the anthrax scare and who was responsible. His questioners, like PBS's highly regarded Jim Lehrer, did that for him. When the focus was on bin Laden, it was easy for Cheney to point to him as the culprit: "We have copies of the manuals that they've [al Qaeda] actually used to train people with respect to how to deploy and use these kinds of substances. So, you start to piece it altogether." At this point Cheney launched into a complicated set of statements to Lehrer designed to show that, rather than a plot directed by Osama bin Laden, the facilitator was Saddam Hussein. "I must say I'm a skeptic," where it came to al Qaeda acting on its own, he told the broadcaster. Later, after the defeat of the Taliban in Afghanistan—but without the capture of bin Laden, who had operated out of the country—Cheney discussed anthrax several times with Tim Russert, who supplied him with "evidence" cited by former CIA director James Woolsey, a signer of PNAC manifestos and the favorite Democrat of Iraq War boosters. "We know," Woolsey was quoted by Russert, "that at Salman Park, in the southern edge of Baghdad five different eyewitnesses—three Iraqi defectors and two American UN inspectors—have said, and now there are aerial photographs to show it, a Boeing 707 that was used for training of hijackers, including non-Iraqi hijackers, trained very secretly to take over airplanes with knives."

"And we have photographs," said Russert, displaying one for the camera. "As you can see that little white speck, and there it is. . . . If they're harboring terrorists, why not go in and get them?"[42]

The anthrax scare was a powerful selling tool for the administration, no matter who was behind it. No one was more ingenious at spreading the rumor that the anthrax came from Baghdad than Vice President Cheney, who always avoided a direct accusation, but in this series of television appearances promoted the idea that the hijackers were part of a larger terrorist group that had distributed the letters, and were linked to Atta, leaving viewers to draw their own conclusions. And it lost none of its potency even when the FBI reported that the anthrax's origins were purely domestic. Within a few weeks of the attacks it was determined that the two strains of anthrax found in the letters had originated in the United States, and could in no way be traced to Iraq. The timing of the anthrax letters—whose author(s) are still unknown—made it appear that there was a connection with the hijackers, even when suspicion fell on an American scientist working at a Defense Department laboratory. The perpetrator, said the agency, was probably an adult male who would refer to the 9/11 attacks in his notes only as a decoy. He could have enough scientific information even as a lab technician, with equipment costing no more than $2,500. A psychological profile indicated he was a loner, rational, and methodical, but someone who lacked "the personal skills necessary to confront others."[43]

For Cheney, nevertheless, none of this exonerated Saddam Hussein. In an interview with Tim Russert near the first anniversary of the attacks on the twin towers, this exchange took place on Saddam's possible use of a nuclear weapon.

TIM RUSSERT: But if he ever did that, would we not wipe him off the face of the Earth?

VICE PRESIDENT CHENEY: Who did the anthrax attack last fall, Tim? We don't know.

TIM RUSSERT: Could it have been Saddam?

VICE PRESIDENT CHENEY: I don't know. I don't know who did it. I'm not here today to speculate on or to suggest that he did. My point is that it's the nature of terrorist attacks, of these unconventional warfare methods, that it's very hard sometimes to identify who's responsible.[44]

The anthrax question became a complicated issue—with overtones of conspiracy arising as the FBI failed to find the culprit(s)—but it served the administration's purposes very well indeed. Deputy Secretary Wolfowitz even figured out a way to get the anthrax question out from under Mohammed Atta, where it didn't fit well. In an interview with the BBC, as the war against the Taliban was going on, Wolfowitz talked first about asymmetric warfare, then played down whether it was really necessary to catch Osama bin Laden. "One could imagine dismantling the entire structure under him and having him live as a fugitive somewhere in the mountains of Central Asia, and say we've [won]. So I don't think one has to say that it's essential, but obviously of all the people we'd like to catch, he's number one on our list." But it would not be sufficient. "It's quite clear," he went on, from before September 11, that al Qaeda would have "the capacity to carry out a monstrous act of terrorism even if bin Laden had been captured. Whoever is mailing anthrax around now has the capacity to do enormous damage. No matter what we do to bin Laden. This is a network that has penetrated into some sixty countries, including very definitely our own, and it's got to be rooted out everywhere, and particularly in the countries where they (inaudible) [sic] do damage."[45]

Other anonymous aides filled in remaining gaps by talking about Saddam Hussein as a virus infecting the world that had to be eliminated, like the source of a global epidemic. But the success of the campaign was perhaps best caught in the words of a Selma, Alabama, firefighter who expressed his firm belief that no one knew for sure who was already in the United States waiting to attack. What did that have to do with Iraq? he was asked. "They're all in it together—all of them hate this country." The reason? America's "prosperity."[46]

It was little short of amazing how easily the American public became used to the idea that catching up with Osama had fallen completely off the agenda. Rumsfeld's attitude toward the effort to locate Osama bin Laden, and to bring him to justice as President Bush promised the nation in Old West style in the days immediately after 9/11, shifted behind his clever ripostes at the podium as the effort began to impinge upon larger objectives of the key players in the administration. In an interview broadcast on the CBS program *Face the Nation* on September 23, the first question asked was whether the Taliban should be believed when they said that they really did not know where Osama was? Rumsfeld was blunt: "Of course not. They know where he is." The implication was that the posse was ready to mount up and go after their man in the badlands. Only a week later, however, he started to back away from the idea that a ground force could find the evildoer. This time, on NBC's *Meet the Press*, the questioner was Tim Russert, who recalled the Russian experience in trying to subdue the Afghan resistance. Rumsfeld agreed. "I think the idea of thinking that a conventional ground effort in that country, when what you're looking for are needles in a haystack, I think that . . . those kinds of comments need to be given careful attention."[47]

When the first air attacks were launched against Afghan targets in early October 2001, Rumsfeld debated with Colin Powell, who had been arguing that the United States could not just go into Afghanistan and then leave it a vacuum, as had happened when the Russians withdrew a decade earlier. That had produced the Taliban regime. God knew what would happen this time. But Rumsfeld wanted to minimize American involvement. When the attacks began he issued a fifteen-page directive to his generals reminding them the president had ordered a global war on terrorism, not just on the al Qaeda network or Afghanistan. It was clear as clear could be that he did not want a prolonged search for Osama bin Laden if that meant a distraction from dealing with Saddam Hussein. On October 24, this time talking to the editorial board of *USA Today*, he amplified what he had told the generals in his policy guidance directive. Do you need to get bin Laden to succeed? "My attitude is, if he were gone tomorrow the same problem would exist. He's got a whole bunch of lieutenants that have been trained, and they've got bank accounts all over, and they've got cells in fifty or sixty countries." Of course that was true, as subsequent events would show, but whether the answer was attacking Iraq should have led to other questions. It did not. Instead Rumsfeld left the impression of a man determined to bypass bin Laden to get to the real trouble. "I don't get up every morning and say that's the end, the goal and the end point, of this thing. I think that would be a big mistake."[48]

At about the same time, President Bush was in New York City for a rally near Ground Zero and a private meeting with business leaders about rebuilding the city. "I truly believe," he told them, "that out of this will come more order in the world—real progress to peace in the Middle

East, stability with oil-producing regions." As for the possibility of preventing new attacks, he was less confident. "I can't tell you whether the bastards will strike again."[49]

Some weeks later, Bill Keller interviewed Wolfowitz for an article in the *New York Times*:

> "There's an awful lot we don't know, an awful lot that we may never know, and we've got to think differently about standards of proof here," Wolfowitz tells me. "In fact, there's no way you can prove that something's going to happen three years from now or six years from now. But these people have made absolutely clear what their intentions are, and we know a lot about their capabilities. I suppose I hadn't thought of it quite this way, but intentions and capabilities are the way you think about warfare. *Proof beyond a reasonable doubt is the way you think about law enforcement. And I think we're much closer to being in a state of war than being in a judicial proceeding.*"[50] [Emphasis added.]

The only thing missing in Wolfowitz's rendition of the logic of the Bush administration was an acknowledgment of the role that news anchors had played after 9/11, as substitute intelligence analysts, providing Bush people with the right leading questions.

Two of a Kind

Condi Rice and British prime minister Tony Blair provided Bush with what some liked to call a "neoliberal" approach to the post-9/11 world. Bush was earthier in private. "F_____ Saddam," he told a group of senators discussing the UN route to solving the problem with National Security Advisor Condoleezza Rice. "We're taking him out." Bush wasn't interested in any of these ideas. He waved his hand dismissively and left the meeting.[51]

Rice was not entirely at ease with neoconservatism as a description of Bush's foreign policy, preferring the term neoliberalism. "It is, indeed, possible to see age-old problems in a new light," she said remarking on what 9/11 had wrought. "And, as an academic, may I suggest, to put aside age-old distinctions between realism and neoliberalism in thinking about the task ahead." Realists downplayed the importance of values and the internal structures of states, she went on, emphasizing instead the balance of power as the key to stability and peace. "Neoliberals empha-size the primacy of values, such as freedom and democracy and human rights and institutions, in ensuring that a just political order is obtained." This was an interesting twist on the battle for control of linguistics.[52]

The president then outlined his Bush Doctrine to the 2002 graduating class at West Point, beginning with a new battle cry for American ex-ceptionalism: "You will wear the uniform of a great and unique country." America had been attacked and knew what it must do to eliminate the threat.

> Our security will require the best intelligence, to reveal threats hidden in caves and growing in laboratories. Our security will require modernizing domestic agencies such as the FBI, so they're prepared to act, and act quickly, against danger. Our security will require transforming the military you will lead—a military that must be ready to strike at a moment's notice in any dark corner of the world. And our security will require all Ameri-cans to be forward looking and resolute, to be ready for preemptive ac-tion when necessary to defend our liberty and to defend our lives. [Applause.][53]

The Bush doctrine, Rice said, was simply a belated recognition of what the nation faced. "The fall of the Berlin Wall and the fall of the World Trade Center were the bookends of a long transition period. Dur-ing that period those of us who think about foreign policy for a living searched for an overarching, explanatory theory or framework that would describe the new threats and the proper response to them." Now we knew the answer, and what the answer required. There could be no doubt that "America faces an existential threat to our security—a threat as great as any we faced during the Civil War, the so-called 'good war,' or the Cold War."[54]

The threat was so great, indeed, that preemptive action was only a matter of common sense. "'If there is a rattlesnake in the yard,'" she quoted former secretary of state George Shultz, "'you don't wait for it to strike before you take action in self-defense.'" A rattlesnake did not quite add up to something on the scale of Gettysburg, but she insisted that 9/11 had introduced an existential crisis as great as the Civil War. In that conflict Lincoln suspended the right of habeas corpus. With this comment about rattlesnakes in the backyard, Rice had completed her metamorphosis from realist theorist to transformationist thinker, and, given the Civil War analogy, one now close to Dick Cheney's views about operations on the dark side. Again, the Civil War analogy was very familiar to those who recalled how safeguards for American civil liberties had been breached. With the West Point "Bush Doctrine" and Rice's exegesis, the shift to war rhetoric was almost complete. Preemption as national policy, had it been debated in a calmer atmosphere, would have raised far more questions than it did less than a year after the jets smashed into the World Trade towers.

The only moment when a halfway serious debate on the road to war in Iraq took place was during August and September 2002. The most dramatic utterance came from National Security Advisor Rice in an "anniversary" edition of CNN's *Late Edition* on September 8, 2002, with Wolf Blitzer presiding. Throughout the program Rice kept tying 9/11 to Iraq's supposed WMD program. "Given what we have experienced on September 11," she began, "I don't think anyone wants to wait for the one hundred percent surety that he has a weapon of mass destruction that can reach the United States." Blitzer asked again and again—how close was Saddam to getting a weapon? He had set up the questions with video-clip denials from Tariq Aziz, Hussein's deputy prime minister, and former UN arms inspector Scott Ritter. She brushed them aside as hardly worth comment. "The problem here is that there will always be some uncertainty about how quickly he can acquire nuclear weapons. *But we don't want the smoking gun to be a mushroom cloud.*"[55]

Rice's comment was also a stinging rebuke to Colin Powell, who had recently told British newscaster David Frost that it would be wrong to move without the cover UN inspections would provide. American newspapers carried early excerpts from the BBC interview, noting that Powell "tread carefully" because of "possible disagreements" with other administration officials. The story said Powell was breaking his silence because of Dick Cheney's recent speeches, in which the vice president had asserted that the idea of more weapons inspections was "dangerous" in that they "would provide false comfort."[56]

Aiding in the campaign against the supposed passive containment holdovers was Prime Minister Tony Blair, who came to Camp David and was introduced to the press by an ebulliently grateful President George W. Bush: "It's awfully thoughtful of Tony to come over here . . . because he's an important ally, an important friend." Blair provided assurance that war on Iraq would not endanger relations with Europe—especially if he could act as go-between with continental Europe and bring those traditional allies along as well. Blair had his price, however, and it was somewhat higher than Bush really wanted to pay. The prime minister insisted that they must go back to the UN for his sake, to control Labor dissidents who might hold up the military convoy to Baghdad before it got started. Blair's debating skills were on full display for the American press: "This is an issue for the whole of the international community. But the UN has got to be the way of dealing with this issue, not the way of avoiding dealing with it. Now, of course, we want the broadest possible international support, but it's got to be on the basis of actually making sure that the threat we've outlined is properly adhered to."[57]

Blair's appearance at Camp David would demonstrate that diplomacy had not yet been exhausted, that Saddam would have a last chance to come clean. It was like a visit to Caesar's camp on the Rubicon. Blair knew very well from his own intelligence chief, Sir Richard Dearlove, that the decision for war had already been made. Sir Richard had reported back on Washington conversations in July.

> Military action was now seen as inevitable. Bush wanted to remove Saddam, through military action, justified by the conjunction of terrorism and WMD. But the intelligence and facts were being fixed around the policy. The NSC had no patience with the UN route, and no enthusiasm for publishing material on the Iraqi regime's record. There was little discussion in Washington of the aftermath after military action.[58]

Blair led off their joint press conference at Camp David by declaring that the purpose of their meeting was to work out the right strategy for dealing with the Iraqi threat, "because deal with it we must." When the inevitable question came, asking what new evidence there was to justify such a crisis mentality, Bush leaped in to say that Tony had cited a new report that very morning on work at old nuclear weapons sites. "I would remind you that when the inspectors first went into Iraq and were denied—finally denied access—a report came out of the IAEA that they were six months away from developing a weapon. I don't know what more evidence we need." Parsing this sentence is a true challenge. The first thing to say is that Bush misrepresented the situation after the first Gulf War. There was obstructionism and a decided lack of cooperation,

but the inspectors did gain access and did oversee the destruction of potential nuclear weapons facilities. Later, after Gulf War II, Iraqi government officials explained that Saddam Hussein had been afraid of letting
Iran know about the state of his programs, but when Bush said, "What
more evidence do we need?" he was talking about the state of play after
1991, not what intelligence said in 2002.[59]

Blair's countryman Lewis Carroll would have delighted in the prime
minister's Cheshire-cat grin as Bush answered for him. But a reporter's
next question cut through the murky grammar: "What is your actual target in Iraq? Is it weapons of mass destruction or Saddam Hussein?" Bush
again intercepted the question. Regime change had been stated policy
since 1998. Saddam Hussein had had more than a decade to keep his
promise to get rid of weapons of mass destruction, and "we're going to
talk about what to do about it."

When they were alone, Bush told Blair that his wish had been
granted; Bush would go back to the UN for one last time to get a resolution that would provide cover for his ally. The prime minister agreed for
his part to take the lead in producing a fifty-page intelligence dossier for
Parliament to read with alarm that contained an assertion Saddam Hussein had the capacity to strike Britain within forty-five minutes of his orders! It also included a reassertion of the CIA-discredited claim that
Saddam had purchased uranium in Niger. Pressed by the CIA to drop
the claim, Blair's people insisted that they had alternative sources to the
forged letters that had first appeared a year and more earlier.[60]

Last Words

Dick Cheney began the final round of warm-up speeches for war. First came
his speech to Veterans of Foreign Wars on August 26, in Nashville. The
vice president opened with the well-worn theme that the terrorists were
waiting to strike again. "There is no doubt they wish to strike again, and
that they are working to acquire the deadliest of all weapons."[61]

The Taliban, he went on, had learned the lesson of what it meant to
harbor terrorists, but that was only the beginning of a lengthy campaign.
Iraq was the central issue now: how to deal with "the case of Saddam
Hussein, a sworn enemy of our country." Cheney recited the discovery in
1991 that he had been closer to obtaining a nuclear weapon than anyone thought. From there it was merely a hop, skip, and jump to: "Many

of us are convinced that Saddam will acquire nuclear weapons fairly soon." Just how soon was impossible to gauge, because "intelligence" was an uncertain business. "We often learned more as a result of defections than we learned from the inspection regime itself." Indeed, sending inspectors back into Iraq would not produce reliable results—but would only encourage a false sense of security. By the time he finished, Cheney had made "intelligence" seem like a dirty word, something a medieval church leader would put on the proscribed list of things undermining the faith.

It was in this speech also that the vice president tried out the we-will-be-greeted-as-liberators theme, citing an expert, Professor Fouad Ajami, who would become the administration's favorite Arab pundit, saying that the streets in Basra and Baghdad were sure "to erupt in joy in the same way the throngs in Kabul greeted the Americans." Once again, as in the axis of evil speech, the language conjured up something like the liberation of Paris from the Nazis. But Cheney had a different image in mind as well, not connected to World War II but to the PNAC agenda. "Extremists in the region would have to rethink their strategy of jihad. Moderates throughout the region would take heart. And our ability to advance the Israeli-Palestinian peace process would be enhanced, just as it was following the liberation of Kuwait." On taking office, of course, George W. Bush had washed his hands of any new efforts to achieve such a settlement. But that was only a detail for Cheney.

The VFW speech glowed with total faith in an easy war and the multiple benefits that would follow an American invasion. But, once again, Powell played spoilsport, by contradicting Cheney on inspections and telling a BBC interviewer that the first step in dealing with Iraq should, in fact, be to get the inspectors readmitted. Interestingly, then White House chief of staff Andy Card followed that up with a statement that the president had not authorized Cheney's language on inspections. Other "administration sources" said that Mr. Cheney had failed to check the facts behind his allegations against Iraq with the CIA, and that the State Department had never seen the final text.[62]

President Jacques Chirac of France, in another warning sign that not everything would go smoothly, called the emerging Bush doctrine of preemptive military action in the war against terrorists "extraordinarily dangerous." Chirac said that there were other voices in the administration, especially that of Secretary Powell. "What Mr. Cheney says does not interest me. What interests me is what Mr. Bush says. Because I hear Mr. Cheney saying one thing: I hear Mr. Powell saying another." He would not have to wait long.

Cheney's role had apparently been to deliver a punch to the solar plexus, leaving it to the president for the knockout. Bush appeared before the United Nations on September 12, 2002, and began by saying, "We must choose between a world of fear and a world of progress. We cannot stand by while dangers gather." Recalling the fate of the League of Nations, he challenged UN members to cooperate with the American policy toward Iraq now so clearly indicated as regime change.[63]

The UN speech kept his promise to Blair that he would seek further resolutions before undertaking military action against Saddam Hussein. In trial-prosecutor fashion he recited Iraq's record of broken promises, its expulsion of UN weapons inspectors, and other sins, all the while staring directly at the Baghdad delegation. But the speech did not go over well. The only applause came when he announced that the United States would rejoin UNESCO, after several years of boycotting it on the grounds that it was prejudiced against Israel on human rights questions. "For a guy who's used to clapping and cheering," he mused later, "dead silence is interesting."[64]

With the UN speech and Tony Blair's invaluable support, Congress became easy pickings. On October 2, 2002, the Senate approved a resolution, 77–23, authorizing the use of force. Its key section read:

SEC. 3. AUTHORIZATION FOR USE OF UNITED STATES ARMED FORCES.
(a) AUTHORIZATION. The president is authorized to use the Armed Forces of the United States as he determines to be necessary and appropriate in order to
(1) defend the national security of the United States against the continuing threat posed by Iraq; and
(2) enforce all relevant United Nations Security Council resolutions regarding Iraq.

In one of the many "whereas" clauses that followed, an assertion was made without a shred of evidence that "members of al-Qaida, an organization bearing responsibility for attacks on the United States, its citizens, and interests, including the attacks that occurred on September 11,

2001, are known to be in Iraq." It had been impossible to get any intelligence confirmation for such an implication that Iraq and al Qaeda were allied, but it slipped into the official rationale for war with no comment at all. Congress was doing Cheney's work for him. Senator Chuck Hagel, who voted for the resolution, later recalled that when the original resolution came over to the Senate, it was in a very different form. It talked about the whole region. "It was astounding. . . . It was anything they wanted. It was *literally anything. No boundaries. No restrictions.*" Hagel and two other senators, Richard Lugar and Joe Biden, stripped it back down to Iraq. "But I was told by the president—we all were—that he would exhaust every diplomatic effort."[65]

Memories of the various congressional resolutions from the time of the 1947 Truman doctrine, Eisenhower's Asian and Middle East doctrines, and, of course, the 1964 Gulf of Tonkin resolution should have warned Hagel to be even more careful about giving the president such blanket authority. Perhaps some were uneasy, but 9/11 still mesmerized congressional leaders. This resolution was unique, however, in that for the first time, the American homeland had been attacked, and the rhetoric of WMD seemed at least plausible. It was also unique, despite Hagel's efforts to water it down, in opening the way to the Cheney agenda, both in terms of remaking the presidency and the Middle East. The acerbic *New York Times* columnist Maureen Dowd—one of the very few in the press who were not part of the gullible majority—used a Swiftian rapier to skewer the Bush administration's pretensions. "Saddam can admit a legion of inspectors," she wrote, "but that may not stop Mr. Bush from wriggling out of the U.N. restraints and declaring the despot's compliance a sham." And behind it all:

> Karl Rove is building a Republican empire. Richard Perle, Paul Wolfowitz and Scooter Libby are building an ideological empire. Dick Cheney is building a unilateral empire. And Donald Rumsfeld is building a military empire.[66]

After the UN speech a rapid series of speeches attempted to nail Saddam with 9/11. In Cincinnati, on October 7, 2002, before an invited audience of Republican faithful, Bush began by taking on all those who still claimed the Iraqi threat was neither imminent nor unique. These questions had been fully debated inside the administration, he said, and he was ready to give the answers. All other matters aside, he said, it came down to one point: the nature of the regime.

> Some citizens wonder, after eleven years of living with this problem, why do we need to confront it now? And there's a reason. We've experienced the horror of September the eleventh. We have seen that those who hate America are willing to crash airplanes into buildings full of innocent people. Our enemies would be no less willing, in fact, they would be eager, to use biological or chemical or a nuclear weapon.
>
> Knowing these realities, America must not ignore the threat gathering against us. Facing clear evidence of peril, we cannot wait for the final proof—the smoking gun—that could come in the form of a mushroom cloud. As President Kennedy said in October of 1962, "Neither the United States of America, nor the world community of nations can tolerate deliberate deception and offensive threats on the part of any nation, large or small. We no longer live in a world," he said, "where only the actual firing of weapons represents a sufficient challenge to a nation's security to constitute maximum peril."
>
> Understanding the threats of our time, knowing the designs and deceptions of the Iraqi regime, we have every reason to assume the worst, and we have an urgent duty to prevent the worst from occurring.

The link with al Qaeda had never been proved, but the campaign to convince the nation it existed had made a lot of headway; all that was needed to feel comfortable about going to war. As with "axis of evil," the speechwriters had turned the mushroom cloud into a potent image that resonated with a large majority of Americans and blotted out lingering doubts. After the speech he received a two-minute standing ovation, in contrast to the treatment he had endured at the UN. Bush had claimed all the issues had been fully debated. It was a very old claim, but in this instance, Cheney, Rice, and Bush had all repudiated the professional intelligence analysis they had heard, and seized upon speechwriter Michael Gerson's image of a mushroom cloud as proof of the danger.[67]

Bush had still not said war was inevitable—a line that gave several Democratic senators, including a future presidential candidate, Hillary Clinton, the ability to claim that when she voted for the resolution authorizing the president to use military action, she had voted to support strong diplomacy. But he had carefully sketched out all the supposed ways the Iraq threat had been approached and failed: economic sanctions, no-fly zones, limited military strikes—all under the rubric of containment. And that was the key clue, or, better put, the flashing red light at a railroad crossing. Containment was no longer the policy; liberation was. "The time for denying, deceiving, and delaying has come to an end. Saddam Hussein must disarm himself—or, for the sake of peace, we will lead a coalition to disarm him."

6

SHOCK AND AWE, IN WHICH WE LEARN HOW SOME DEMOCRACIES GO TO WAR

You'll see simultaneous attacks of hundreds of warheads, maybe thousands, so that very suddenly the Iraqi senior leadership, or much of it, will be eviscerated. . . . The pressure will continue until we run out of targets.
—Harlan Ullman, self-declared father of the
"shock and awe" tactic, January 30, 2003

Yet, the longer-run strategic meaning transcends the essentially three-week war itself. The outcome will alter the strategic—and psychological—map of the Middle East.
—James Schlesinger, former CIA director, secretary of defense,
and secretary of energy, "Political Shock and Awe,"
Wall Street Journal, April 17, 2003

What we would like to see is a greater understanding of power, of the democratic system, the open-market economic system, the rights of men and women to achieve their destiny as God has directed them to do if they are willing to work for it. And we really do not wish to go to war with people. But, by God, we will have the strongest military around. And that's not a bad thing to have. It encourages and champions our friends that are weak, and it chills the ambitions of the evil. . . . The reason for that is that no other nation, with a few exceptions, is yet as well grounded politically in the democratic system as we are, or to be trusted with the kind of military power we have.
—Secretary of State Colin Powell, August 2, 2004

In the weeks after Bush's mushroom cloud speech in Cincinnati on October 7, 2002, the White House Iraq Group (WHIG) consolidated its strategy for taking the country to war. There was still work to be done because, as late as February 5, 2003, when Secretary of State Colin Powell held up a small vial filled with white powder he claimed (falsely) to be dry anthrax in a dramatic speech at the United Nations, polls showed that more than half of the nation still doubted whether it was necessary to use military force. "Less than a teaspoon of dry anthrax, a little bit—about this amount," he intoned, "shut down the United States Senate in the fall of 2001."[1]

The connection between 9/11 and Saddam Hussein had never been established, nor any link to the anthrax attacks, and Powell did not attempt that again, though others would when they apparently thought the public memory had run short. No, the argument he now made was that the Iraqi dictator had mobile labs and military airplanes that could develop anthrax bombs and deliver them against his enemies far and wide. After the speech the number supporting military action rose 7 points, to 57 percent. Using Colin Powell in this way was considered essential to the WHIG faction (which included everyone within shouting distance of the Oval Office) to sell the war. If the poll numbers went up for war, Vice President Dick Cheney had argued, Powell's popularity might suffer a loss of 10 points—a double bonus for those who wanted to take the secretary of state down a peg or two. One has to wonder, therefore, if the vice president expected untoward developments despite his assurances to the contrary.

Even if Cheney did fear some trouble along the way, and wanted Powell preempted, he fully expected, as did others in the administration, that the war would be short-lived. By the time it was discovered that Saddam Hussein had no WMD—if that proved to be the case—the war would be over. And who would care then?

The WHIG Campaign

Karl Rove, as Bush's chief political counselor, saw the WHIG campaign as essential to the creation of a new Republican era, featuring strong presidents with a determination to reshape the world. He believed that the nation had reached a point where an unlikely hero, someone like his favorite, William McKinley, who launched the "splendid little war" with Spain, would ensure the nation would not turn away from its world responsibilities. McKinley was known as a deeply religious man who prayed for guidance about what to do with the Philippine islands he liberated from Madrid's tyrannical rule. Bush was also guided by prayer, he told chronicler Bob Woodward.

"Can you tell me what the gist of those prayers were?"

"I prayed that our troops be safe, be protected by the Almighty, that there be a minimal loss of life," President Bush said.

He continued, "Going into this period, I was praying for strength to do the Lord's will. . . . I'm surely not going to justify war based upon God. Understand that. Nevertheless, in my case I pray that I be as good a messenger of His will as possible. And then, of course, I pray for personal strength and for forgiveness."

The most interesting thing, perhaps, about these prayers was that a third party, National Security Advisor, Condoleezza Rice, who was supposedly not present as Bush engaged God in this dialogue while walking outside the White House meditating on his duty, reviewed the transcript of the Woodward interviews and instructed the journalist that he had missed something important.

About a month after these interviews, Condi Rice, then the national security adviser, called to say that she had reviewed a transcript of the interviews with Bush and she had discussed the March 19, 2003, prayers with the president. She said he also prayed that morning for all those who were to go into harm's way and for the country. So I added such a line to the book.[2]

Condi's correction fit in better, obviously, with the images that preceded shock and awe, and the tenor of the WHIG campaign. On September 7, 2002, *New York Times* reporter Elisabeth Bumiller had written a story about the administration's strategy for selling the war. In what became the most famous statement about that campaign, she quoted White House chief of staff Andrew Card, who was coordinating the WHIG effort: "From a marketing point of view," said Card, "you don't introduce new products in August." The highlight of the whole shebang would be President Bush's September 11 speech on Ellis Island, "where the Statue of Liberty will be seen aglow behind Mr. Bush." Karl Rove, the chief political adviser to the president, told the reporter that it was a day when the nation would want to hear from their leader. It will also be a time, said Rove, "to seize the moment to make clear what lies ahead." The next day the president was to address the UN. The goal was to secure a congressional resolution authorizing the use of force. "In the end it will be difficult for someone to vote against it."[3]

The next day another story on the selling of the war appeared in the *Times*. This one referred to "aluminum tubes" Iraq had supposedly sought in order to construct a centrifuge to convert low-grade uranium into weapons-quality, highly enriched uranium. Buried in the story, however, was a phrase that would soon become famous, first when Condi Rice used it, and then President Bush. Hard-liners were concerned that waiting for analysts to confirm what defectors had told the Pentagon and other sympathetic listeners was an unacceptable risk. "The first sign of a 'smoking gun,' they argue, may be a mushroom cloud." Then this marvelous Orwellian turnabout, "Still, even though hard-liners complain that intelligence about Iraq's program is often spotty, they plan to declassify some of it to make their case in coming weeks." It almost sounded as if serious matters of war and peace were being decided by carnival operators of a peep show.[4]

Certainly Vice President Cheney played a game by suggesting, in a television interview with his favorite media outlet, Tim Russert, that the *Times* had broken a top-secret piece of intelligence. Russert had asked about the things Hussein would need to build nuclear weapons. There was a vague discussion of what later became the uranium "yellowcake" hoax that the administration relied on in the end to sell the war, but in this instance Cheney concentrated on the aluminum tubes claim. "There's a story in the *New York Times* this morning—this is—I don't—and I want to attribute the *Times*. I don't want to talk about, obviously, specific intelligence sources, but it's now public that, in fact, he has been seeking to acquire, and we have been able to intercept and prevent him from acquiring through this particular channel, the kinds of tubes that are necessary to build a centrifuge."

Cheney purposefully appeared to stumble over the source of the *Times* story all the more to imply by his ruminating manner that it was based on solid intelligence broken in the press without the help of anyone in the administration. Both his manner and his statement were false. Not only was the story a plant, it was one that had been orchestrated by the office of the vice president, if not directly then by hints and guidance. But the major specific information that the tubes were destined for Hussein's nuclear program was also the view of only one strident voice, whose insistence that the tubes were to be used in that way, and only could be used that way, was shared by no one else with any expertise. And it turned out, of course, that there was nothing to the accusation.[5]

Cheney was not happy about Bush's decision to go to the UN to seek further resolutions that would enable the United States to take matters into its own hands with a coalition of the willing. But if it must be, to satisfy Tony Blair—but for no other reason—then he wanted something else included in the speech. Cheney and his aides wanted to insert a paragraph about secret intelligence that said that Iraq had attempted to acquire five hundred tons of uranium yellowcake from the state of Niger in Africa. This plan was thwarted at the last minute by CIA objections that the documents proving the contract existed were forgeries, and very crude ones at that.[6]

The idea that Saddam Hussein had sought to purchase uranium from Niger was a substitute for the unsatisfactory public response to the supposed Mohammed Atta–Prague link to Saddam Hussein (with or without the anthrax ingredient), though Vice President Cheney kept dancing around that subject, changing a word here and there in an effort to say that the meeting had not been disproved, until finally in 2004 he said, "I have not suggested there is a connection between Iraq and 9/11." Of course he had sought to make the connection all along—for that was the only way to sell the war. And he had done a good job, especially in dealing with Congress in the fall of 2002, in response to demands from Senator Bob Graham for a national intelligence estimate. Prepared in a hurry, the NIE hedged on important questions, but it nevertheless supported what the administration argued, and became a key lever to secure the votes needed for a resolution to empower the president to take action against Iraq. The yellowcake question was set forth in the NIE (for those who read it carefully) as nothing more, however, than a "report" from a foreign government, enabling the CIA to issue a disclaimer later, as it in fact did.

Iraq has about 550 metric tons of yellowcake and low-enriched uranium at Tuwaitha, which is inspected annually by the IAEA. Iraq also began vigorously trying to procure uranium ore and yellowcake; acquiring either would shorten the time Baghdad needs to produce nuclear weapons.

A foreign government service reported that as of early 2001, Niger planned to send several tons of "pure uranium" (probably yellowcake) to Iraq. As of early 2001, Niger and Iraq reportedly were still working out arrangements for this deal, which would be for up to 500 tons of yellowcake. We do not know the status of this arrangement.

Reports indicate that Iraq also has sought uranium ore from Somalia and possibly the Democratic Republic of the Congo.[7]

Now came time for the quid pro quo from Tony Blair, who announced in Parliament that his government had additional evidence of Saddam's efforts to obtain yellowcake, and again, in what became known as the "dodgy dossier," that Iraq could launch WMD within a notice of forty-five minutes. Blair laid out the case for war, declaring that as a result of intelligence, he judged that Iraq had "sought significant quantities of uranium from Africa, despite having no active civil nuclear power programme that could require it."[8]

Around this time, Russian defense minister Sergei Ivanov arrived for talks with Rumsfeld at the Pentagon. With the American secretary of defense standing close by, Ivanov said he believed that UN weapons inspectors could settle the issue without undue difficulty. We have had experience in that sort of business—both Americans and Russians—said Ivanov, a pointed reference to Reagan's famous "trust but verify" mantra during START negotiations. "I think we can easily establish [whether] there exist or not weapons of mass destruction technology."[9]

Rumsfeld did not interrupt Ivanov, but he told the House Armed Services Committee that Congress must act on Bush's recommendation before the UN Security Council took up an American-sponsored resolution on Iraq authorizing the use of force. "Delaying a vote in the Congress would send a message that the U.S. may be unprepared to take a stand, just as we are asking the international community to take a stand." This was the classic Cold War White House ploy to put Congress over a barrel, first used with the 1947 Truman doctrine. Bush had added even more pointed friendly words of advice for congressional incumbents seeking reelection. "If I were running for office, I'm not sure how I'd explain to the American people—say, vote for me, and, oh, by the way, on a matter of national security, I think I'm going to wait for some-body else to act."[10]

And not too long a wait, either. Bush vowed there would be deadlines within the resolution being proposed at the UN. "Our chief negotiator for the United States, our secretary of state, understands that we must have deadlines. And we're talking days and weeks, not months and years." It was a dual message, or even a triple one—to the UN, to Con-gress, and to Colin Powell. There was always the fear that while Powell would never defect, he would somehow come up with a backdoor ma-neuver to rely on the inspectors. Rumsfeld tried to preempt such a move by setting forth a novel distinction between weapons inspectors and weapons discoverers. UN inspectors could never get anywhere, he insisted, unless they were dealing with a cooperative regime; nobody could, for it would be asking the impossible with such a huge territory to cover. And yet, after the war began, Rumsfeld would insist that he could practically pinpoint the locations of the hidden WMD—with hardly a concern for matters of consistency.[11]

Such assertions, it will be remembered, had already been voiced by Clinton's national security advisor, Sandy Berger, who had declared it was impossible for inspectors to search in every nook and cranny in Baghdad, or to outwit someone who was determined to steer them into blind alleys. At the end of September 2002, Rumsfeld put his final gloss on the case for war, declaring he had "bulletproof" evidence of Iraq's links to al Qaeda. Newly declassified intelligence reports revealed senior members of al Qaeda had been in Baghdad in "recent periods," he said. He could not give out details without jeopardizing the lives of spies and drying up sources of information, but these reports were "factual" and "exactly accurate." Nothing could be proven beyond a reasonable doubt, he conceded, and even he admitted his information was probably not strong enough to stand up in an American court. But Cheney and Rice had already dealt with that problem. This was about war, not prosecuto-rial error.[12]

Yet Bush still worried that what the NIE had to offer might not be quite enough for "Joe Public." Did the CIA have anything more to offer, he asked George Tenet? Tenet responded, according to administration sources, by waving his arms in the air as if he were at a Georgetown bas-ketball game cheering a "slam dunk." Tenet denies waving his arms and questions whether he actually said "slam dunk." Little wonder. When the administration saw its case for Iraq's WMD go bad, seriously bad, the director's "slam dunk" phrase was cited by Bush defenders to prove that either the CIA was out to get the president or the agency was incompetent. No one was better at that than Dick Cheney, who used TV interviews to put the blame on Tenet for slam dunks that caromed off the rim.

In his memoir the former CIA director tried to answer the charge that his agency had been derelict in not stopping Bush from going out on a limb in his January 28, 2003, State of the Union message, which had contained the notorious "sixteen words," without really saying it was false. (What Bush had said was "The British government has learned that Saddam Hussein recently sought significant quantities of uranium from Africa.") Tenet wrote in a somewhat rueful mood that an old friend had cautioned him not to stay on for more than six months in a new administration. "Be careful," he was warned, "you are not one of the inner circle going back to the campaign. It doesn't matter how the president may feel; if it suits that group, they will throw you overboard." As he watched Cheney slam-dunk him on national television, he mouthed some bitter thoughts, "As if you needed *me* to say 'slam-dunk' to convince *you* to go to war with Iraq."[13]

Cheney did need Powell to say some strong words at the UN, however, to introduce the resolution that would bring the Security Council into line, or demonstrate why America had to form a "coalition of the willing." The vice president saw himself in a win-win situation. If the resolution route worked, fine, but if it did not, also fine, maybe better, because that would show that Powell's magic did not work when it came down to the nitty-gritty of a war-peace vote, and, the biggest bonus of all, the principle of independent action would have been preserved forevermore. Henry Cabot Lodge Sr., Woodrow Wilson's chief antagonist in the League of Nations fight, would have been delighted at this ploy. When Powell balked at presenting evidence to the UN that the vice president's aides, Scooter Libby and John Hannah, had assembled to link the Iraqi dictator directly to terrorists, Cheney confronted him outside the Oval Office. "Your poll numbers are in the seventies," the vice president declared. "You can afford to lose a few points." Only moments before he was to begin his speech, Scooter Libby tried to telephone Powell in an attempt to slip the Prague connection back into the text. Powell refused to take the call.[14]

But despite his protests that much of what he was sent from the OVP was "bullshit!" Powell delivered a speech he would regret ever after. "It's a blot," he told Barbara Walters. "I'm the one who presented it to the world, and [it] will always be a part of my record. It was painful. It is painful now." Still, even as he backed further and further away from how the war was sold, Powell justified his support for Bush's war on the argument that Saddam Hussein had to be removed by force because he had ignored UN resolutions over the years. He was glad he was gone. When Walters persisted in asking about the aftermath, Powell fell back on the common rationalization former Bush officials and liberal hawks gave: "Who knew what the whole mess was going to be like?"[15]

"He sure likes to be popular," Cheney quipped later at a gathering of "mission accomplished" celebrators. Paul Wolfowitz interjected that once Powell saw what the president wanted, and delivered the UN speech, he became a good loyal member of the team. No, the vice president shook his head, Powell remained a problem. "Colin always had major reservations about what we were trying to do."[16]

Councils of War

As Powell tore up drafts of his UN speech to take out the most egregious assertions of the OVP cadre, the president was telling Tony Blair in an almost offhand manner that he "intended to invade whether or not there was a second UN resolution and even if UN inspectors found no evidence of a banned Iraqi weapons programme." At one point Bush suggested "flying U2 reconnaissance aircraft planes with fighter cover over Iraq, painted in UN colours," in hopes of provoking Saddam to shoot at them, providing a casus belli. The Iraqi army would "fold very quickly," said Bush, and the elite Republican Guard would be "decimated by the bombing." They envisioned a quick victory and a smooth transition to a new Iraqi government. Bush predicted it was "unlikely there would be internecine warfare between the different religious and ethnic groups." Blair thought he was right.[17]

Bush's second favorite ally, Spanish prime minister José Maria Aznar, was not so sure. Aznar met with the American president at his ranch in Crawford, Texas, on February 22, 2003. Their conversation was perhaps the most revealing of all the prewar exchanges Bush had with foreign leaders, and included the president's wish to punish smaller nations—

and even Vladimir Putin's Russia—if they stood out against the United States in the final vote on a second United Nations resolution. At this moment Bush felt confident that he would obtain at least a majority on the Security Council on a useful resolution that could be used to make it appear that the world body had authorized military action. "We will see that the resolution is written so that it does not contain obligatory steps [for Iraq]," he told Aznar, "that it does not mention the use of force, and that it states that Saddam Hussein has been unable to fulfill his obligations."[18]

During the conversation the president made it clear that he had gone back to the UN for another resolution only to serve the purposes of public diplomacy, and to satisfy the few dissenters in his own administration, primarily Secretary of State Colin Powell. In other words, such a resolution, which did not mention military force, was a cover story, nothing more. Yet he still showed some anxiety about the outcome of the vote. "From now on I will try to tone down the rhetoric as much as possible." The conversation had begun with Bush informing Aznar that he wanted a vote as soon as possible. "Saddam Hussein will not change and will continue playing games. The moment has come to be rid of him. That's the way it is." Bush repeats this thought several times during the conversation, suggesting—indeed, more than suggesting—that the president had turned the conflict into a blood feud, leading him, as he does in this conversation, to underestimate the consequences and aftermath of shock and awe.

"We have to take him right now. We have shown an incredible degree of patience so far. There are two weeks left. In two weeks we will be militarily ready." It became clear, as Bush went on, that what he meant was not patience with Saddam Hussein's tactics, but patience with those nations who wished for more evidence of Iraq's WMD before acting. "We have the three African members [Cameroon, Angola, and Guinea], the Chileans, and the Mexicans. I will speak with all of them, also with Putin, naturally. We will be in Baghdad at the end of March."

> We would like to act with the mandate of the UN. If we act militarily, we'll do it with great precision and focus on our targets to as high a degree as possible. We'll decimate the loyal troops, and the regular army will quickly know what it's all about. We sent a very clear message to Saddam Hussein's generals: we will treat them as war criminals. We know they

have stocked big amounts of dynamite to blow up the bridges and other infrastructure, and the oil wells. We are planning to take control of those wells very soon. Also, the Saudis will help us by putting as much oil as necessary on the market. We are developing a very strong aid package. We can win without destruction. We are already working on the post-Saddam Iraq, and I think there's a basis for a better future. Iraq has a good bureaucracy and a relatively strong civil society. It could be organized as a federation. Meanwhile we're doing all we can to fulfill the political needs of our friends and allies.

The description Bush offers here of shock and awe, which juxtaposes decimating loyal troops and yet winning without destruction, is a fascinating example of the American faith in techno-war as something that leaves in place what one wishes to preserve and erases what one is determined to eliminate. As for the world reaction, it also would fall into categories that fit American presuppositions. French President Jacques Chirac, for example, simply misread the Arab mood. "The problem is that Chirac thinks he is Mister Arab, but in fact he is making their lives impossible." And they were for the Americans: "The Arabs are sending Chirac a very clear message: Saddam Hussein must go."

There was only one hitch. Condoleezza Rice reported to Bush and Aznar about what to expect from the latest report by the UN arms inspectors. She seemed pleased that it would not likely produce a lengthy exchange with those who had actually been on the ground, even though there would be an appearance by the group. "As with the previous ones, it will be a mixed picture. I have the impression that [Hans] Blix will now be more negative than he was before, with regard to the Iraqis' intentions." She expected the vote on the resolution would follow within a week. While the Iraqis may try to explain that they were fulfilling their obligations, and announce the destruction of some missiles, "it won't be sufficient."

Bush came back to the charge after she finished her planned rebuttal to the arms report. And the conversation became animated:

PRESIDENT BUSH: This is like Chinese water torture. We must put an end to it.

PRIME MINISTER AZNAR: I agree, but it would be good to have the maximum possible number of people. Have a little patience.

PRESIDENT BUSH: My patience is exhausted. I don't intend to wait longer than the middle of March.

PRIME MINISTER AZNAR: I do not request that you have infinite patience. Simply that you do everything possible so that it all works out.

PRESIDENT BUSH: Countries like Mexico, Chile, Angola, and Cameroon must realize that what's at stake is the security of the United States, and they should act with a sense of friendship toward us. [Chilean president Ricardo] Lagos should know that the free trade accord with Chile is awaiting Senate confirmation, and a negative attitude about this could put ratification in danger. Angola is receiving Millennium Account funds [to help alleviate poverty], and that could be jeopardized also if he's not supportive. And Putin must know that his attitude is putting in danger the relations of Russia with the United States.

Aznar remarked that Tony Blair, America's most faithful ally, would also like a few more days to rally the Labour Party. But Bush was not willing to delay even for Blair.

"I prefer the tenth. This is like a game of bad cop, good cop. I don't mind being the bad cop, and Blair can be the good one."

Aznar tried another tack. Was there a possibility that Saddam Hussein would go into exile?

"The possibility exists, including that he will be assassinated." There had been some sort of information from Egyptian president Hosni Mubarak that Hussein would leave for $1 billion and the right to take documents about WMD with him. The second half of this proposed deal is not easy to fathom, but it apparently referred not to an admission that he once had such weapons, but to information about America's past role in aiding his chemical weapons industry. What will eventually be known about this supposed offer is far from clear, but Bush wanted to go in and catch him. Saddam thought he had escaped justice, said Bush. He thought that the worldwide demonstrations against the expected invasion had saved him. "And he thinks that I am very weak. But the people around him know that things are otherwise. They know his future is in exile or a coffin."

At this point Aznar gave up. "The only thing that worries me about you is your optimism." Bush replied, "I am optimistic, because I believe that I am in the right. I am at peace with myself." He was irritated that the Europeans were not sympathetic to those who had suffered so long from Saddam Hussein's cruelty and wars. He must believe that "perhaps because he is brown-skinned, far away, and Muslim, many Europeans think that everything is all right." He was mistaken. "The more the Europeans attack me, the stronger I am in the United States."

Rice's prediction about what Hans Blix would say was way off the mark. When he began his report to the UN on March 7, 2003, it was at once clear that she had misread the auguries. "Some practical matters," he said, "have been resolved at meetings, which we have had in Baghdad. Initial difficulties raised by the Iraqi side about helicopters and aerial surveillance planes operating in the no-fly zones were overcome. This is not to say that the operation of inspections is free from frictions, but at this juncture we are able to perform professional no-notice inspections all over Iraq and to increase aerial surveillance."

Blix's report was indeed mixed, portraying an Iraqi regime that was not always immediately forthcoming, but which eventually yielded to the inspectors' demands. Blix said he needed more time—but not an indefinite period.

> How much time would it take to resolve the key remaining disarmament tasks? While cooperation can . . . and is to be immediate, disarmament, and at any rate verification of it, cannot be instant. Even with a proactive Iraqi attitude induced by continued outside pressure, it will still take some time to verify sites and items, analyze documents, interview relevant persons, and draw conclusions. It will not take years, nor weeks, but months.
>
> Neither governments nor inspectors would want disarmament inspection to go on forever. However, it must be remembered that in accordance with the governing resolutions, a sustained inspection and monitoring system is to remain in place after verified disarmament to give confidence and to strike an alarm if signs were seen of the revival of any proscribed weapons programs.[19]

Blix would admit later that while he, like many others, had actually believed at one time that Saddam Hussein had WMD, in the middle of the inspection process he became convinced that they did not exist, and that the momentum whipped up by the United States had produced a "witch hunt." Iraqi "prickliness" about some questions from the inspectors, Blix wrote in his memoir of the failed search, was reasonable, given the past connections between some members of UNSCOM and American intelligence agencies. Baghdad suspected, not unreasonably, that some questions they had posed referred to "conventional defense."[20]

The WHIG campaign had continued up until the moment Condoleezza Rice came to New York to talk with Blix about his crucial report to the Security Council. The inspector told her that Iraq had been more forthcoming, but that questions remained to be answered. When an account of the meeting appeared in the *Washington Post*, however, Blix read that she had been sent to press him "to acknowledge" that Iraq had failed to scrap its weapons program. Her mission had been carefully designed to underscore concern that his report might "not be decisive enough to persuade wavering Security Council members to support an immediate move to war."[21]

That, at least, was accurate. The resolution Washington hoped would be adopted was never brought to a vote, nor were any other compromise resolutions offering a benchmark step-by-step approach presented to the Security Council. France, Germany, Russia, and China all opposed the American attempt to shut off the inspections until they had had more time to demonstrate conclusively the presence or absence of WMD. Once the war began, Blix did not hold his fire against those he believed had smeared the inspection team. "There are people in this [U.S.] administration who say they don't care if the UN sinks under the East River, and other crude things." In September 2003, he added another bitter thrust: "We know that advertisers will advertise a refrigerator in terms they do not quite believe in, but you expect governments to be more serious and have more credibility." And, in March 2004, "The witches exist; you are appointed to deal with these witches; testing whether there are witches is only a dilution of the witch hunt."[22]

Removing Saddam Hussein

In the first days after the invasion, nevertheless, some wanted Blix to return to Iraq to complete the unfinished work. The White House was not interested. "For the time being, and for the foreseeable future," said the

American ambassador to the United Nations, John Negroponte, "we see it as a coalition activity." The only inspectors tabbed for the assignment were those from the United States, Britain, and Australia. A report in the *Guardian* noted that these were the same countries that had propagated the falsehood that Iraq had sought uranium yellowcake in Niger. Asked to comment, a Whitehall representative responded only that while it might be true the documents that it had given to the inspectors were forgeries, there were other sources for the alleged purchases. He offered no evidence for his claim.[23]

But did it matter? The war had supposedly come to an end with the fall of Baghdad. There had been a hope at the very beginning that a bombing strike had killed Saddam Hussein and two of his sons. A quick decapitation of the Iraqi regime would surely guarantee what Bush most needed. As his advisers openly acknowledged, he was "gambling his political future on a quick victory." If that gamble succeeded, all those troublesome questions about WMD would blow away—like chaff in the wind. If it did not, there would be another campaign to sell the war, of course, but it could be much more difficult.[24]

Invading American forces would be welcomed as liberators, said Vice President Cheney. And they would trigger changes all over the Middle East. Even more remarkably, he assured an interviewer on the eve of the attack, such firmness "would go a long way, frankly, towards calming things in that part of the world." Take out Saddam Hussein and the grateful Iraqis would rush to take advantage of their freedom. "People who are moderate, people *who want to believe in the United States, and want to support us, will be willing to stand up, because the United States is going to stand with them and not pull back and disappear when the going gets tough.*"[25] (Emphasis added.)

This none too subtle reference to what had happened in Gulf War I, when American forces halted south of Baghdad, was intended to demonstrate that, yes, the second Bush administration had completed the work of the first, and the presidency had been restored to its full potency. When army chief of staff general Eric Shinseki had dared to contradict the Pentagon hierarchy, saying it would take three hundred thousand soldiers—nearly three times the number Rumsfeld had approved—to secure the victory, Paul Wolfowitz, deputy secretary of defense, who had served under both Cheney and Rumsfeld, promised Congress it would not take a large force to do the job. Wolfowitz called the general's con-clusion wildly off the mark, and disputed claims that the war would cost as much as $90 billion in the first fiscal year. It would be a quick war, he asserted, with no real obstacles to a rapid recovery. Why should there be? There was no history of ethnic strife in Iraq, he insisted, as there was in Bosnia or Kosovo. Looking abroad, he had nothing but contempt for America's erstwhile allies, those who had lined up to help in Gulf War I but who were now shuffling their feet, refusing to accept their role as Washington's loyal seconds—ready to provide moral support and, not incidentally, promising to pony up with financial contributions as in the earlier conflict. This time around, he said, it seemed the administration was dealing with "countries that are quite frightened of their own shad-ows." Even countries like France, however, he said would soon enough rediscover their strong interest in assisting Iraq's recovery.[26]

The Race to Baghdad

The Rumsfeld plan for victory envisioned even greater use of airpower than the unprecedented campaign in Desert Storm, said the *Christian Science Monitor*, quoting shock and awe theorist Harlan Ullman, an an-alyst at the Center for Strategic and International Studies. The bombing would be followed by ground forces to protect the oil fields and "make the situation look very hopeless for Saddam Hussein and the leader-ship. . . . The pressure will continue until we run out of targets." This time around, however, the idea would be to keep the Iraqi military intact so that it can turn on Saddam Hussein. "The Japanese quit because they couldn't appreciate the fact that one bomb could do what five hundred planes did in a night. That was shock," said Ullman. "Now, can you take that level of shock and apply it with conventional weapons? We thought you could."[27]

Ullman, a retired Navy commander, had a team at the National De-fense University work on his theory, and they produced a book, *Shock and Awe: Achieving Rapid Dominance*, that appealed to Pentagon savants and Rumsfeld as the very antithesis of Vietnam. Winning a war, said the authors, depended upon shocking and awing civilian populations into submission. Ullman cited Hiroshima and the German blitzkrieg as ap-propriate strategies for victory. The book also criticized—in terms Rums-feld would appreciate—Gulf War I as an example of a "decisive force" strategy that required time and concentrated on force-on-force warfare. Shock and awe, on the other hand, would concentrate on changing the whole environment. "The target is the adversary's will, perception, and understanding."

> Total mastery achieved at extraordinary speed and across tactical, strategic, and political levels will destroy the will to resist. With Rapid Dominance, the goal is to use our power with such compellance that even the strongest of wills will be awed.

But wouldn't this be warfare against civilian populations? The book nodded slightly in the direction of acknowledging what was obvious.

> Rapid Dominance will strive to achieve a dominance that is so complete and victory is so swift, that an adversary's losses in both manpower and material could be relatively light, and yet the message is so unmistakable that resistance would be seen as futile.[28]

So the adversary's losses "could" be relatively light, but the example the book used was Hiroshima! As Pentagon planners worked on the "force sizing" needed to mount a shock and awe campaign against Iraq, Secretary Rumsfeld had seized the political initiative by adding his own conditions to what the UN had previously required of Saddam Hussein to avoid war. Security Council Resolution 1441, adopted on November 8, 2002, had found Iraq in "material breach" of its obligations under previous resolutions concerning UN inspections, and demanded Baghdad permit the inspections to resume. As Secretary General Kofi Annan put it, "If Iraq's defiance continues . . . the Security Council must face its responsibilities." The resolution gave Iraq forty-five days to comply. When Iraq did readmit the inspectors in 2003, Secretary Rumsfeld hastened to tell reporters what the *United States*—not the UN—required of Iraq. Inspections were essentially useless poking around in the desert. "The burden of proof is not on the United States or the United Nations to prove that Iraq has these weapons. We know they do." Unless Saddam Hussein first came clean and admitted that he had the WMD, the inspectors were just so many tourists with special escorts. Since Bush and Rumsfeld had already called the Iraqi regime a bunch of liars and deceivers, owning up to having the weapons would have no value in validating their destruction. The only alternative to war "would be for Saddam Hussein to leave."[29]

The American media was already in awe of Pentagon boasts about what was in store for Iraq if Saddam Hussein stayed in Baghdad. Author Harlan Ullman explained the plan in quite open terms in a newspaper interview: "We want them to quit, not to fight, so that you have this simultaneous effect—rather like the nuclear weapons at Hiroshima—not taking days or weeks but minutes." Even if such talk was only meant to scare Hussein into leaving, it appeared to dismiss any protests from other nations or domestic critics that it was premature to think about the horrors of unleashing such a war, or the precedent of such threats. "You're sitting in Baghdad and, all of a sudden," continued this Dr. Strangelove-like interview, "you're the general and 30 of your division headquarters have been wiped out. You also take the city down. By that I mean you get rid of their power and water. In two, three, four, five days they are physically, emotionally and psychologically exhausted."[30]

Amid all this talk, someone at the Pentagon noticed that the Air Force bragging about its new twenty-thousand-pound bomb that would create its own mushroom cloud, without saying where it would be used, might not be a good fit with political statements about molding Iraq into a democracy. "The Pentagon," wrote veteran journalist Mary McGrory, "is torn between bragging about what it can do and boasting about what it won't do as we liberate Iraq." General Tommy Franks, who would command the ground forces, did not want to be drawn into the middle. He was making no promises, he said. War is war.[31]

With all the talk about shock and awe, twenty-thousand-pound bombs, and such, the White House began to worry that its projections of easy victory and postwar joy might be overshadowed by fears of the cost in human lives. At one point just two days before the bombing began, the president announced on television that he was giving Saddam Hussein and his sons forty-eight hours to leave Iraq. "The danger is clear: Using chemical, biological, or, one day, nuclear weapons obtained with the help of Iraq, the terrorists could fulfill their stated ambitions and kill thousands or hundreds of thousands of innocent people in our country or any other," Bush said. But an Arab League ambassador cautioned in response to the president's ultimatum, "It's a very grave day. This is the day that international law has been shoveled away. War will not solve this problem. Unfortunately, those who are going to war will find it will be very difficult to get out of it."[32]

Bush still hoped it would be over in a trice. Early in the afternoon of March 19, 2003, CIA director George Tenet arrived at the White House with a stunning tip from an Iraqi spy working for the Americans: Saddam Hussein would be in a bunker in southern Baghdad that night. It meant jumping the gun by a few hours, but if Saddam was killed the risks would be worth it. "It had huge possibilities," said one of Tenet's listeners. "You know, huge, positive outcomes." Most of all, it could bring about victory in an even shorter time than Gulf War I. Perhaps the illusion of such a victory by decapitation was responsible for the absence of serious thought (in the White House) concerning how to go about decontaminating the Iraqi army and ministries.

As the discussion went on, some doubts crept in around the edges. One participant warned that the Iraqis might "do the baby-milk factory thing again," a reference to a moment in Gulf War I when reporters were taken to see casualties at a supposed civilian location. Bush worried that there would be accusations "you struck women and children." Condi Rice then reminded the group that "Iraqis" (significantly she did not say Saddam Hussein) "love to propagandize and lie about what's just taken place." Here, pinpointed nicely by Rice, was the central assumption that guided the war makers: it was not just getting rid of Hussein that mattered, but ruling over Iraq to change the way business was done in that part of the world.[33]

However that may be, the prewar attack on the bunker did not get Saddam. Bush kept urging on his aides the need for a PR effort to match the military successes that followed rapidly upon the opening of air and ground attacks. On the telephone the president told Tony Blair that Iraqi soldiers by the thousands were just taking off their uniforms and going home.

"Yes, they are just melting away," said Blair.

"Just melting away," Bush echoed.

The president turned his attention to the propaganda battle, telling Rumsfeld, "We need to remind people why we are here . . . remind the world of who we are fighting." Later he asked at a NSC meeting, "How does this look to the average Iraqi?" He was not happy with the answers he got. The broadcasts from three giant, four-engine transport planes—

flying TV and radio stations—were not enough. "You have to calibrate it. You have to market programs. People don't turn on television if there's nothing to watch." Still later, on April 4, 2003, someone mentioned at an NSC meeting that the electricity had been turned off in Baghdad. Who turned out the lights, Bush asked? General Franks responded that it was most probably the regime. "But we don't know for sure."

"Well, then, if it's the regime, put the word out that we didn't do it."[34]

PSYOPS

Don Rumsfeld was enjoying the war more than anybody else in the administration. He was the man at the Pentagon podium almost every day, deflecting questions with sardonic wit and condescension. He was the anti-Clinton, anti–Brad Pitt symbol of post-9/11 American masculinity, declared a delighted writer in National Review, the personality who had retrieved the media spotlight from liberal icons.

> Reports have it that people gather round to watch Rumsfeld press conferences the way they do Oprah.
> One Hollywood grande dame, hostess of a prized post-Oscar party, says to another Hollywood grande dame, "I'll call you in the morning." The second dame replies, "Okay, but be careful: Rumsfeld's on at 9:45."[35]

"The images of thousands of cheering Iraqis, celebrating and embracing coalition forces," declared Rumsfeld on April 11, 2003, "are being broadcast throughout the world, including the Arab world." They gave the lie to reports that Iraqis were ambivalent or opposed to the coalition's arrival in their country. "I think it's important that that message be seen, for America is a friend of the Arab people. And now, finally, Arab people are hearing the same message, not from U.S. officials, but from their fellow Arabs, the liberated people of Iraq."[36]

In the middle of this celebratory news conference, however, came a series of inconvenient questions that Rumsfeld answered with a soon famous comment—"Stuff happens"—a quip that would shadow him wherever he went all the rest of his years in office. Picking up on the theme of cheering Iraqis, a questioner asked about other pictures of raucous Iraqis carrying out antiquities looted from Baghdad museums, along with similar scenes across the country. Rumsfeld tried to make light of the tele-vision images. "The images you are seeing on television you are seeing over, and over, and over, and it's the same picture of some person walk-ing out of some building with a vase, and you see it twenty times, and you think, 'My goodness, were there that many vases?' [Laughter.] 'Is it possible that there were that many vases in the whole country?'"

But the questions kept coming. Did he think, then, that words like "anarchy" and "lawlessness" were ill chosen? "Absolutely. I picked up a newspaper today and I couldn't believe it. I read eight headlines that talked about chaos, violence, unrest. And it was just Henny Penny—'The sky is falling.' I've never seen anything like it!" Here was a country being liberated from a vicious dictator, and all this newspaper could do was to show a single bleeding civilian and call it chaos. But there were more questions. And an obviously irritated Rumsfeld finally declared that you could take a television camera into any American city in recent years and film riots and looting. "Stuff happens!" It happened every-where. "It is a fundamental misunderstanding to see those images over, and over, and over again of some boy walking out with a vase and say, 'Oh, my goodness, you didn't have a plan.' That's nonsense."[37]

The single most impressive image of the opening days of Gulf War II was the scene at Firdos Square in Baghdad on April 9, when, according to Fox News, jubilant Iraqi citizens in the heart of the city pulled down a twenty-foot-tall statue of Saddam Hussein. A group of Iraqi men dragged the head of the statue, taking turns riding on it, while bystanders slapped it with their shoes—"a gross insult in the Arab world." Ameri-cans were, in other words, watching (and maybe helping a little bit) as the Iraqis tore down the biggest symbol of an unimaginably repressive regime. The message was that the cultural gulf had been breached in Iraq, and there was no reason why it could not be in other places in the Mid-dle East where people yearned for the freedoms enjoyed in the West.[38]

In London, the Telegraph added more ornamentation to the first ac-counts of the statue razing: "Thousands of ecstatic Iraqis gave U.S. forces a tumultuous welcome in the capital before turning on the symbols of the regime that had lasted for 24 years, tearing down statues and pictures of the old dictator, pelting them with rocks and smashing them to pieces." The paper quoted—who else?—Donald Rumsfeld, who said the scene was "breathtaking. . . . Watching them, one cannot help but think of the fall of the Berlin Wall and the collapse of the Iron Curtain."

American power and goodness went hand in hand in such accounts, and Iraq was a natural consequence of victory in the Cold War, which foretold a future secured by the wise policies the Republicans had reinstalled after the Clinton hiatus.[39]

In the White House George Bush was delighted at the spontaneous demonstration that appeared before his eyes on an Oval Office television set. "They got it down!" he exclaimed. It wasn't the end yet, but he could see the beginning of the end. A few days later he delivered a message to the Iraqi people: "You're free! And freedom is beautiful." In this euphoric state he even ventured to criticize—however obliquely—his father's realist restraint in not marching to Baghdad. The second Bush administration could be trusted to finish the job. These were people who had been betrayed in the past "and then were absolutely hammered by the Iraqi regime." Little wonder they had been skeptical. "Now they believe, they're beginning to understand we're real and true."[40]

Perhaps someone told Bush that the statue scene was not quite what he had imagined, for he ruminated a bit at a press conference, "You know, it's amazing. The statue comes down on Wednesday and the headlines start to read, 'Oh, there's disorder.'" "Well, no kidding," he went on. "It is a situation that is chaotic because Saddam Hussein created the conditions for chaos. He created conditions of fear and hatred. And it's going to take a while to stabilize the country."[41]

Bush still seemed not totally aware that the statue scene had been staged. A marine colonel had had the idea to topple the statue, not joyous Iraqi civilians. Quick thinking by an army psychological warfare (PSYOP) team made it appear to be a spontaneous Iraqi undertaking. The colonel selected the statue as a "target of opportunity," and had the PSYOP team use loudspeakers to round up a crowd. At the last minute there was a bit of a gaffe, as the marines draped an American flag over the statue's face. The flag was supposedly the one flying over the Pentagon on 9/11, sent over for some appropriate occasion to sustain the idea that Saddam Hussein was behind the attacks. PSYOP probably did not think that one up by itself. But it was a bad idea, and a sergeant quickly replaced it with a pre-Saddam Iraqi flag. "We didn't want to look like an occupation force."[42]

There were not thousands present that day as the first reports indicated, but a few hundred at most, as the square had been shut off by

American military vehicles, and snipers sat on rooftops to make sure that nothing untoward happened. Even so, several shots were fired at the marines as they prepared to topple the statue, sending them scrambling for nearby armored personnel carriers. But the danger lasted only a few minutes, and soon the soldiers were back at work bringing Saddam down to earth.[43]

Among those present in the square that day was Ahmed Chalabi, once the darling of the Pentagon and considered the front-runner to head the new government. But there had been a decided cooling off toward the head of the Iraqi National Congress. The process of creating a new government was going to be from the ground up, said a State Department spokesman, Richard Boucher, starting with a series of regional conferences, culminating in a Baghdad conference to create an "interim authority." The simmering feud between the Pentagon and the State Department continued unabated, however, and it was Rumsfeld who set the goals—at least for the near future—and these included at the top of the agenda securing the oil fields and discovering the hiding places of the WMD. "We need help," the secretary of defense announced, indicating a willingness to pay substantial sums to those who cooperated. "We need people to come forward and volunteer that information," he said. "And we're at a point now where they need not fear—if they're in one of the liberated areas, they need not fear this regime."[44]

The Missing WMD

Rumsfeld's offer was either disingenuous or an example of self-delusion. It made good reading in the American press, as purporting to show that only *after* a war could there be any chance of securing the truth. It also fit in comfortably with Condi Rice's suggestion that Iraqis were not to be trusted (except when paid off), even now that Saddam was gone, until the society's values had been overhauled according to American standards. Rumsfeld, who had once been so sure the WMD existed, and could even pinpoint the locations, now began to allow little drops of doubt to trickle down around the sides of his optimism. Defense officials said, for example, that they had set up roadblocks on main highways between Iraq and Syria, but admitted that those "seals" had remained imperfect, and several trails remained open—a suggestion that maybe

Saddam Hussein had gotten them out of the country in the nick of time. This naturally brought up the question of whether that might mean another country could be next in American sights. It was, Rumsfeld said, "not a question I can answer."[45]

Eleven days into the war, on March 30, 2003, when the first flickers of doubt about the WMD began to sneak into the mainstream media, Secretary Rumsfeld answered a question posed by ABC News. "We know where they are. They're in the area around Tikrit and Baghdad and east, west, south, and north somewhat." Rumsfeld later conceded that he might have overreached just a bit about the location of the hidden WMD. "I should have said, 'I believe they're in that area. Our intelligence tells us they're in that area,' and that was our best judgment."[46]

The search for WMD was a costly affair, in terms of cash—but the real issue was ending the war. If it could be brought to a quick conclusion, no one would really care all that much, because a tyrant had been removed, and now there was a real opening for a new era in Middle Eastern politics. Deputy Defense Secretary Paul Wolfowitz elaborated on the advantages of getting rid of Saddam Hussein in an interview on May 9, 2003, but in doing so, he seemed to suggest that WMD were only a "bureaucratic" device for providing a rallying cry inside the administration—and by extension, national opinion:

> The truth is that, for reasons that have a lot to do with the U.S. government bureaucracy, we settled on the one issue that everyone could agree on, which was weapons of mass destruction as the core reason, but—hold on one second . . . —there have always been three fundamental concerns. One is weapons of mass destruction, the second is support for terrorism, the third is the criminal treatment of the Iraqi people. Actually, I guess you could say there's a fourth overriding one, which is the connection between the first two.[47]

It was hardly surprising that when the first part of this statement was published it made dramatic headlines, especially as the search for WMD proved futile. Wolfowitz had gone on during the interview to talk about the opportunity to remove American forces from Saudi Arabia, and to make a new beginning on the Arab-Israeli problem. The war had been sold on the issue of Saddam's threat to the world, but shock and awe had always had a political objective. Immediately after the interview it was announced that the United States was sending fourteen hundred searchers to Iraq to ferret out the missing WMD, and the administration initiated a "holding pattern," apparently in the hopes that at least something would be found while they formulated explanations to explain their absence.

Then major general Keith Dayton, who headed the Iraq Survey Group, said his team would shift its focus away from areas identified as suspicious sites before the war to areas where documents, interviews with Iraqis, and other new clues suggested biological or chemical weapons could be hidden. A top official in the Defense Intelligence Agency, Dayton said he did not know why no chemical or biological weapons had been found yet, but he remained convinced they would be. "These things could have been taken and buried. They could have been transferred. They could have been destroyed," Dayton told reporters at the Pentagon. "That doesn't mean they weren't there in the first place."[48]

Reporters caught up with Tony Blair in Poland to ask what he thought about the search. Blair insisted he was certain concrete evidence of banned weapons would be found. "Have a little patience," he said in Warsaw, Poland. "I have absolutely no doubt at all that we will present the full evidence after we have investigated all the sites, after we've interviewed all the scientists and experts, and this will take place in the coming weeks and months."[49]

On May 1, 2003, Bush landed on the aircraft carrier USS *Abraham Lincoln* and stepped out of the cockpit of an S-3B Viking in full flying gear. It was called the war's Paul Newman moment. Lincoln was the favorite president by far in the Bush White House, thus completing another symbolic circle. Bush had written a brief autobiography, *A Promise to Keep*, a title that 9/11 had supposedly made into a prophetic vision akin to Lincoln's passage from Springfield, Illinois, to the White House on the eve of the Civil War. Bush's life, it was now argued, paralleled Lincoln's growth as a man who looked heavenward for guidance.

It is not surprising that the modern religious right has highlighted Lincoln's example. Thomas M. Frieling's collection of Bush statements on God and country begins with a reference to Lincoln, and to the strikingly similar ways Bush expresses his reliance on the Almighty. Neoconservatives hold the same admiration for Lincoln, not as the Great

Emancipator, but for his willingness to suspend the Constitution to defend the state, specifically the right of habeas corpus. Lincoln was an au-
tocrat, in this view, in defense of democracy.[50]

Bush spoke in front of a banner that in red, white, and blue proclaimed,
"Mission Accomplished." The idea for the banner had not been hatched
in the White House, but otherwise the preparations for his speech on
the *Lincoln* off the coast of San Diego was scripted down to "the variance of the sunlight, the glare off the ocean, and how these would be
factored in to the choreography of the ship's inalterable schedule."[51]

The speech began with high praise for the incomparable American
military.

> Operation Iraqi Freedom was carried out with a combination of precision
> and speed and boldness the enemy did not expect, and the world had not
> seen before. From distant bases or ships at sea, we sent planes and missiles
> that could destroy an enemy division, or strike a single bunker. Marines
> and soldiers charged to Baghdad across 350 miles of hostile ground, in one
> of the swiftest advances of heavy arms in history. You have shown the
> world the skill and the might of the American Armed Forces.

From there he went on to recall the scene in Baghdad of Iraqis pulling
down Saddam Hussein's statue.

> In the images of falling statues, we have witnessed the arrival of a new era.
> For a hundred of years of war, culminating in the nuclear age, military
> technology was designed and deployed to inflict casualties on an ever-
> growing scale. In defeating Nazi Germany and Imperial Japan, Allied
> forces destroyed entire cities, while enemy leaders who started the conflict
> were safe until the final days. Military power was used to end a regime by
> breaking a nation.
>
> Today, we have the greater power to free a nation by breaking a danger-
> ous and aggressive regime. With new tactics and precision weapons, we
> can achieve military objectives without directing violence against civil-
> ians. No device of man can remove the tragedy from war; yet it is a great
> moral advance when the guilty have far more to fear from war than the in-
> nocent. [Applause.]

Whether intended or not, Bush's remarks updated President Truman's
celebration of what American scientific know-how and engineering had

wrought in developing and delivering the atomic bombs at the end of World War II. Now, he said, hundreds of years of warfare had ended not in a bomb that destroyed cities killing everyone, innocent and guilty, but with the latest technological advance—a.k.a. shock and awe—that was used "to end a regime by breaking a nation" in a way that was "a great moral advance."

> In the images of celebrating Iraqis, we have also seen the ageless appeal of human freedom. Decades of lies and intimidation could not make the Iraqi people love their oppressors or desire their own enslavement. Men and women in every culture need liberty like they need food and water and air. Everywhere that freedom arrives, humanity rejoices; and everywhere that freedom stirs, let tyrants fear. [Applause.]

After assuring the crew and the world that the hunt for WMD would continue until all the secrets were uncovered, Bush made yet another assertion about what the mission had accomplished.

> The liberation of Iraq is a crucial advance in the campaign against terror. We've removed an ally of al Qaeda, and cut off a source of terrorist funding. And this much is certain: No terrorist network will gain weapons of mass destruction from the Iraqi regime, because the regime is no more. [Applause.][52]

Shock and awe had done its work, or so it seemed for this brief period in the history of American efforts in the Bush administration to reshape the world. What was most arresting in this speech was the terrible feeling one got that the president believed every word he spoke. The Iraq War had opened a new era in human experience, the statue razing had been a spontaneous act of newly liberated Iraqis, Saddam Hussein had been an ally of al Qaeda—all of it. The next day, indeed, he repeated the list in a shorter, less formal speech to workers at a factory that made new armored vehicles:

> One of the things that people learned about your company, as well, is how useful the Hercules tank recovery system can be. [Applause.] The guy with the sledgehammer on the statue needed a little help. [Laughter.] Thankfully, there was a Hercules close by. [Laughter.] A Hercules, which pulled that statue of Saddam Hussein to the ground.

That meant more to the Iraqi people than you can possibly imagine. It was a symbol of their future. A future based upon something that we hold dear to our hearts; a future based upon something that is not America's gift to the world but the Almighty God's gift to each and every individual— a future based upon freedom. [Applause.][53]

Back in Washington, Vice President Dick Cheney had watched from his West Wing office as Bush landed on the *Lincoln.* "He watched with a big smile," a Cheney aide said.[54]

THE OCCUPATION, IN WHICH WE LEARN WHAT FOLLOWED SHOCK AND AWE

There was no occupation until the insurgency created one. Before then, if we went into a town it was probably to rebuild a school. It was only in response to the insurgents that we had to act like an army of occupation.
> —senior White House adviser, June 29, 2004

There is going to be skepticism among Iraqis. Some will surely see the new government as stooges. I hope they will see we are changing the way we deal with them. There will no longer be Americans telling them what the daily agenda is.
> —Francis J. Ricciardone, State Department planner, June 29, 2004

On June 30, the Coalition Provisional Authority will cease to exist, and will not be replaced. The occupation will end. . . . Our embassy in Baghdad will have the same purpose as any other American embassy, to assure good relations with a sovereign nation.
> —President George W. Bush, May 24, 2004

What kind of embassy is it when everybody lives inside and it's blast-proof, and people are running around with helmets and crouching behind sandbags?
> —Edward Peck, former top diplomat in Iraq, May 19, 2007

Deputy Secretary of Defense Paul Wolfowitz seemed oblivious in late April 2004 to the actual number of American soldiers killed in the first year of the occupation. "It's approximately 500," he told a House appropriations subcommittee, "of which—I can get the exact numbers—approximately 350 are combat deaths." The real numbers were 722—521 of them from combat. "He misspoke," said a Defense Department spokesman, shrugging it off. "That's all."[1]

It was not all, of course. April 2004 had been the deadliest month of the war, with more than one hundred killed and nine hundred wounded. The most dramatic action took place at Fallujah, a city of two hundred fifty thousand that even Saddam Hussein had pretty much left alone. The trouble began when the Marines took responsibility for establishing control of the city. They had a different view of the assignment than the Army, which, following the orders of General John Abizaid, had trod lightly around the outskirts, not wanting to make the city a flash point. Fallujah had a mayor, a police force, all the trimmings, said a determined Marine commander. "But it had termites." And he wanted to stir them up, get them out in the open to step on them.[2]

Marine operations to root out the termites had just gotten under way when two SUVs carrying Blackwater security contractors bypassed a military checkpoint and drove into the city on unspecified business. They ran straight into a deadly ambush set up a day earlier—the result, said a senior intelligence official, of a leak from the heavily guarded Green Zone, the American command center and site of the future embassy. The four men were dragged from the cars, beaten, and dismembered. Two bodies were hung from the girders of a bridge over the Euphrates, then taken down and set afire on a pile of tires while crowds cheered and danced around the flames.[3]

It was a chilling scene. The first reaction in Iraq by the head of the Coalition Provisional Authority (CPA), L. Paul Bremer, was to hold off a bit on a retaliatory attack. But word came back from Washington that President Bush wanted action within a few days. "We still face thugs and terrorists in Iraq who would rather go on killing the innocent," he said at a political fundraiser the night of the killings, "than accept the advance of liberty." But during a series of videoconferences with Bremer and General Abizaid, the president began to calm down and settled for leaving the city under siege—at least temporarily. "At least they're inside there," he said.[4]

Multiple political considerations shaped the decision not to go all out with a retaliatory attack, and then to abandon the siege. Warnings came from inside Iraq that progress toward a credible postwar government would be put in danger, but there was also the American political campaign and White House fears of domestic repercussions if an attack spread turmoil all across the country. After Bush was reelected in November, the political considerations ran the other way. It was full speed ahead. Defense Secretary Donald Rumsfeld declared: "One part of the country cannot remain under the rule of assassins . . . and the remnants of [former Iraqi president] Saddam Hussein. . . . You can't have a country if you have a safe haven for people who chop people's heads off. These folks are determined. They're killers. They chop people's heads off. They're getting money from around the world. They're getting recruits."[5]

When it was all over, Operation Fallujah II, or "Phantom Fury" (later renamed "New Dawn"), had nearly leveled Fallujah. Some postop reports called it a "city of ghosts." The Pentagon claimed twelve hundred insurgents were killed, but an informal body count numbered less than one hundred. One key target, Abu Musab al-Zarqawi, escaped, as apparently did most of the insurgents, who slipped out of the surrounded city. Yet Iraqi and Arab world reactions were somewhat muted, in part because of the recent death of Palestinian leader Yasir Arafat, and in part because of the brutality insurgents had shown to captives. Final political judgments on the battle—the largest military engagement since Vietnam—were tentative. Washington cheered the outcome as a victory that made the January 2005 Iraqi elections possible. An Army colonel argued that the battle had undercut the insurgents' ability to launch attacks to block the election. "The coalition fought its way to the elections," he said. That was likely accurate, wrote Thomas Ricks, "but if major military operations were necessary preambles to political movement, it likely meant that the U.S. was in for a very long war." By January 2007, and the adoption of the "surge strategy," that prophecy had been more than borne out.[6]

Bring 'Em On!

The insurgency had begun to gel by midsummer of the first year of the occupation. It was the beginning, wrote a longtime opponent of Saddam and his Ba'athist Party, Ali A. Allawi, of an "infrastructure war." Various insurgent groups sprung up around the country with names like the Party of Return and the Army of Omar. The Islamic Army of Iraq specialized in what became the deadliest weapons against the occupation, the improvised explosive devices (IED) that targeted coalition forces and police officers. The CPA remained in a state of denial for a long time. "Underlying this smug indifference was a misplaced confidence in the ability of the Coalition to contain and defeat what were still thought of as the desperate acts of the remnants of a defunct regime."[7]

The infrastructure war was aimed at oil refineries and pipelines and electric power grids, key elements of sustaining the Iraqi economy and its viability. Until those essentials were brought back, the country would remain crippled, no matter what collection of interest groups argued among themselves over power inside the Green Zone. Iraq quickly became a pseudostate. The interim government, as it was called, was rife with corruption and simple incompetence. The Ministry of Electricity, for example, was run by an Iraqi American who, prior to his appointment by the CPA, had managed an electricity consulting and recruitment company in Illinois. It failed to meet any of its self-proclaimed targets for supplying electricity to the country. Auditors found that the ministry was unable to provide justification or even documentation for nearly $500 million in contract awards. When the transitional national government replaced the interim government after the January 2005 elections, a number of the ministers of the previous regime fled the country, as arrest warrants were being prepared against them.[8]

At a brief press conference on July 2, 2003, President Bush was asked whether the "posse of small nations, like Ukraine and Poland," would be enough to keep the peace in Iraq. With casualty rates rising, wouldn't he need some of the bigger powers to pitch in, like France and Germany and Russia? Bush was obviously irritated by the premise of the question. We'll put together a force structure to meet the threats, he replied. "And we got a lot of forces there ourselves. . . . Anybody who wants to harm American troops will be found and brought to justice." Those who thought they could drive the Americans out "prematurely . . . don't understand what they're talking about." Bush was riled up, and it showed in his resort to tough-guy language.

> There are some who feel like that, you, the conditions are such that they can attack us there. My answer is, bring them on. We got the force necessary to deal with the security situation.
>
> Of course we want other countries to help us. Great Britain is there. Poland is there. Ukraine is there, you mentioned. Anybody who wants to

help, we'll welcome to help. But we got plenty tough force there right now to make sure the situation is secure.[9]

Once he finished with that question, the president made a brief nod in the direction of understanding that the targeted destruction of electricity lines was more than simple criminal activity. They weren't really hurting Americans, he said, they were hurting Iraqis. "But we will deal with them harshly as well." Even so, the whole tenor of his remarks established nothing so much as his belief that the insurgents were little more than a temporary nuisance—as even the questioner himself implied with the word "posse" to describe the White House attitude.

Another questioner asked if, after the few months of looking for them, it was fair to say that there was a "discrepancy between what the intelligence community, and you and your top officials, described as the threat from Saddam Hussein was actually there on the ground?" Bush replied with the first fallback position of many to come: Hussein had had a program once. "Remember he used them—he used chemical weapons on his own people." It was just a matter of time, said Bush, until he would have had a new one. "See, we've been there for—what?—I mean, how many days? You're counting the days since we've been there, because I'm not—eighty, ninety. Frankly, it wasn't all that long ago that we started military operations. And we got rid of him; much faster than a lot of people thought. And so, we're bringing some order to the country, and we're beginning to learn the truth."

It was a somewhat odd summary of developments, but it accurately reflected the dilemma that was developing, because the quick war had not led to a rapid reconstruction. Secretary of Defense Donald Rumsfeld was distressed because he had imagined that by summer's end troop levels could be cut in half, to sixty thousand, or maybe even by three quarters, to thirty thousand, by that time. But it wasn't happening. Instead the insurgency kept picking up momentum. In early September Pentagon officials told Congress that American forces were straining to meet the security requirements in Iraq. "We are looking for work-arounds," the chair of the Joint Chiefs, General Richard Myers, warned the Senate Armed Services Committee. "But we also have to realize we are a nation at war, and we have to do what it takes in this case to win."[10]

This testimony came as the Army announced that the tours of twenty thousand reservists and National Guard troops in Iraq and Kuwait would be extended by as much as a year, months beyond what the soldiers had expected. In the offing as well was a new budget request of $87 billion for postwar needs in Iraq and Afghanistan. Pentagon officials had scoffed at those who warned that the prewar estimates for the war would far exceed the initial DOD figures of less than $50 billion; now it was clear that doubling or even tripling that figure was not too much to expect.

"We have no desire to own this problem, or to control it," Deputy Secretary Paul Wolfowitz told the committee. "The more other countries are prepared to contribute, the more they're absolutely entitled to share and control over how resources are used." A few months later, however, the Pentagon announced a flat-out policy of denying countries that had opposed the American war to bid for reconstruction contracts. Wolfowitz explained that the ruling was necessary to protect "essential security interests." He then elaborated what was a tough-love approach. "Limiting competition for prime contracts," he averred, "will encourage the expansion of international cooperation." He hoped that private companies in those countries would pressure their governments to adopt a more cooperative attitude in Iraq. As matters stood, the two largest contracts for Iraq's reconstruction had been given to Bechtel, the American construction firm where former secretary of state George Shultz had once served as CEO, and Kellogg Brown & Root, a subsidiary of Vice President Dick Cheney's old company, Halliburton.[11]

Wolfowitz's pronouncement caught both the State Department and the White House off guard at the very moment the president had requested former secretary of state James A. Baker—who had also been the kingmaker in the 2000 election—to go to Europe to convince the leaders of France, Germany, and Russia to forgive Iraq's debts. Wolfowitz's diktat even excluded Canada, America's closest neighbor, which had already given $190 million for reconstruction. Asked about the ruling, Deputy Prime Minister John Manley replied sharply that "it would be difficult" now to add to that sum.[12]

The White House may have been exaggerating its discomfort a little bit, however, for while State and Defense had no end of an argument going over Iraq—every phase of the conflict from before the war—officials near the end of the day "hinted" that in exchange for writing down Iraq's debts, those countries might yet claim a piece of the action. The Pentagon quickly picked up the theme. "This is not a fixed, closed list," said a spokesman for Secretary Rumsfeld, "This is meant to be forward looking and potentially expansive."[13]

Rumsfeld, meanwhile, had continued to argue that sending more troops to Iraq would not answer the problem of the insurgency, which now stood at about fifteen attacks a day on American troops. His idea of the American military in post–Cold War conflicts arising in what used to be called third world countries was one that could strike with lightning swiftness and leave next to no footprint. That thesis was under challenge. Sending more troops, he said in a speech on September 11, 2003, was no solution, and would only hold back reconstruction and the development of Iraqi security forces. More troops meant more support, more protection, and were no substitute for the "ramping up of their own security capabilities."[14]

A fierce debate had already been launched about the decision to disband the Iraqi army, a decision apparently made by L. Paul Bremer, head of the CPA, in the first days of the occupation—but even that was in dispute. However it was made, whether on orders from Washington or on his own initiative, Bremer's decision had proved a serious hindrance in combating the insurgency, not simply because the army was disbanded, but also because many of those who had been in the military had gone over to the insurgents.

While the secretary of defense said that he opposed sending more American troops, anonymous commanders in the field were quoted as saying that it was "crucial" to have a third foreign-led division of ten to fifteen thousand "peacekeepers" in place within a few months to avoid further strains on the Army or force the Pentagon to send marines, who were not normally assigned to such duties. Rumsfeld reiterated his position, nevertheless, that it was the responsibility of Iraqis to take over the political, economic, and security levers of power as soon as possible.

"I don't believe it's our job to reconstruct the country," he insisted, apparently not taking into account, said the New York Times, the $13 billion Bush had requested to restore electricity and running water in Iraq. They would have to restore their country over time, Rumsfeld still insisted in reply, adding that oil revenue would not be enough to rebuild Iraq's decrepit infrastructure. They would have to have a plan to develop industries, "like tourism, that would benefit from national and historic treasures like the ruins of the ancient city of Babylon."[15]

This reference to Iraq's historical treasures as a foundation for its future prosperity sounded a little bit funny coming from the same man who had reacted with avuncular nonchalance at the looting of museums and cultural sites as hardly anything more than the naughty exuberance of newly liberated men. Secretary of State Colin Powell on a quick drop by in Baghdad assured friendly questioners that more progress was being made than had been reported in the press.

> There is just a great deal that is happening in this country, whether it's the formation of PTAs in local schools, whether it's our brigade commanders giving $500 to each school in their district as long as that school comes up with a PTA, something unheard-of here before, and uses that PTA to determine how the money will be spent. That's grassroots democracy in action.[16]

European powers were said to have given their colonies roads and schools. Powell added PTAs as the American contribution. But for the time being, at least, he could not see those PTAs in operation, as he could not move outside the tight security cordon that whisked him in and out of Baghdad. Reporters attending his press conference had to walk a quarter of a mile through barbed-wire fences and encounter four checkpoints, including three body searches. Overhead Apache helicopters circled the conference center, and Bradley fighting vehicles sat outside guarding all entrances.

Inside the Green Zone Powell assured listeners that the Americans came not as colonialists, but "under a legal term having to do with occupation under international law. . . . We came as liberators. We have experience being liberators. Our history over the last fifty, sixty years is quite clear. We have liberated a number of countries, and we do not own one square foot of any of those countries, except where we bury our dead."

Progress was being made. No doubt of it. "We're not hanging on for the sake of hanging on." Everyone had to understand that it would still take time to expunge elements of the old system, along with criminal elements, and foreign terrorists, in order to give Iraq the fresh start it deserved. One questioner dared to ask if the secretary was basing his conclusion about progress being made on official reports—a veiled reference to the "five o'clock follies" in Vietnam. Powell bristled at that. "I thínk I've been around long enough to understand the things I'm being told, and to see behind the things I'm being told."

The reference to what had happened in Vietnam was especially painful for Powell, a platoon commander in that war. Every day in Saigon during the war, official briefers gave their interpretation of what was going on in the countryside. It was so at variance with what was actually happening that reporters began calling the sessions the "five o'clock follies." The questions also were painful because Powell himself had been known as one of the skeptics about how Gulf War II would end—or not end.

In a separate interview with CNN's Wolf Blitzer, still a media cheerleader for the war, Powell dismissed critics who had started to whisper Vietnam as using "rather bizarre historical allusions." That ought to stop. The nation needed to concentrate on the facts on the ground. America's job was to help the Iraqi people "put together a government that they can be proud of, a government that will never again be called a dictatorship, but rather a government that can be a model for this region and the rest of the world."[17]

Liberators and Bases

As noted in chapter 6, Paul Wolfowitz set off a big debate over U.S. military intentions in a democratized Iraq, telling an interviewer that, while Saddam's supposed WMD were the main bureaucratic reason for the war—meaning that everyone could rally around that cause—there were also important subsidiary reasons for the decision to oust the dictator. "I'm not blind to the uncertainties of this situation," he told Sam Tanenhaus, "but they [critics] just seem to be blind to the instability that that son of a bitch was causing."

> There are a lot of things that are different now, and one that has gone by almost unnoticed—but it's huge—is that by complete mutual agreement between the U.S. and the Saudi government we can now remove almost all of our forces from Saudi Arabia. Their presence there over the last 12 years has been a source of enormous difficulty for a friendly government. It's been a huge recruiting device for al Qaeda. In fact if you look at bin Laden, one of his principle grievances was the presence of so-called crusader forces on the holy land, Mecca and Medina. I think just lifting that

burden from the Saudis is itself going to open the door to other positive things.[18]

The question that arose immediately from this and other similar comments by Wolfowitz was where, then, would American forces in the Middle East be based in order to protect the oil? Nobody, least of all Wolfowitz's boss Secretary Rumsfeld, wanted to talk about permanent bases in Iraq. We were liberators, was the constant DOD mantra. "You have shown that America is, in fact, a land of liberators, not a land of occupiers," Rumsfeld told American soldiers in Iraq in early 2005, adding that the recent national election was "a stunning blow" to the insurgency, and proved Iraqis want freedom.[19]

From the beginning of the occupation Rumsfeld had been obliged to fend off questions, stemming in part from his deputy's assertion that Middle Eastern stability would be improved by Hussein's removal and the proposed scale-down of American bases and forces in Saudi Arabia. A discordant note struck in the early moments of celebration after the fall of Baghdad came from retired lieutenant general Jay Garner, the designated first head of the CPA, who gave out some indiscreet interviews making a less favored comparison than to the usual liberation theme. Asked about future military bases in Iraq, Garner compared the situation to the result of the Spanish-American War in the Philippines, when the United States established naval bases that exist today, a hundred years later. Those bases, said Garner, allowed the United States to maintain a "great presence in the Pacific." "To me," Garner continued, "that's what Iraq is for the next few decades. We ought to have something there . . . that gives us great presence in the Middle East. I think that's going to be necessary."[20]

The general explained that bases did not mean a large troop establishment in Iraq, and like President Bush predicted that as Iraqi forces were trained, the number of American troops needed would go down. Some U.S. military units would need to be stationed nearby as a "little 9-1-1 force for the guys you put on the street," while others would serve as advisers, training and developing national security forces. In subsequent interviews, Garner used a slightly different analogy, comparing proposed bases in Iraq to coaling stations from the era of colonial rivalries and the race for sea mastery in the Age of Imperialism. Although Garner's comments were actually in line with Secretary Rumsfeld's strategic notions of how the American military would fulfill its missions in the twenty-first century, they caused considerable alarm in civilian offices at the Pentagon. The base issue was a delicate one, a question of how much to let out of the bag.

Undersecretary of defense Douglas Feith would explain to the House Armed Services Committee, for example, that Rumsfeld's plans envisioned the most thorough restructuring of U.S. military forces since the end of the Korean War in 1953. This was necessary, he said, to ensure the nation's ability to "deploy powerful capabilities rapidly anywhere in the world, [while] lightening our footprint [and] eliminating unnecessary irritations." The twenty-first-century military had to be prepared to go anywhere, into, for example, "ungoverned and under-governed areas within states, which can serve as breeding grounds and sanctuaries for terrorists" to answer the "asymmetric warfare that adversaries will use to counter U.S. conventional military superiority. . . . We no longer expect our forces to fight in place; our forces need to be able to project power into theaters that may be far from where they are based." Feith's testimony came nearly a year and a half after the coalition of the willing attacked Iraq to end Saddam Hussein's reign in Baghdad. And he was now ready to explain how the United States expected the Rumsfeld reorganization to work out in the post-Saddam years. "In the Middle East, we propose to maintain what we call 'warm' facilities for rotational forces and contingency purposes, building on cooperation and access provided by host nations during Operations Enduring Freedom [Afghanistan] and Iraqi Freedom."[21]

The objective, noted two commentators in Foreign Affairs, the magazine where policy makers and future policy makers often explore alternatives, was to diversify access points to crises and station troops in nations more likely to agree with U.S. policies. "The Bush administration is now proposing to shift virtually every aspect of [the nation's] armed presence in a sort of military 'big bang.'" In other words, to reduce the presence of American forces in places like Germany and Japan and South Korea, and build up facilities in what Rumsfeld would call "New Europe," as well as in the new nations made out of the old Soviet Union tiered along the ancient trade routes through Central Asia, now valuable for their proximity to huge stores of petroleum and natural gas.[22]

Iraq was expected to be part of the shift—a leader in the transformationist project, not just an isolated piece of sandy real estate—especially in terms of moving American forces to less volatile locations in the Middle East. But it was to be a quiet transformation. On other occasions Pentagon officials described the strategy as lily-pad basing, a network of jumping-off points around the world. Many of these would be aimed at the Middle East, for example, Diego Garcia in the Indian Ocean. This base had already proved useful in Gulf War II, as a refueling point for American planes flying from Subic Bay in the Philippines, one of several reminders of the long-term outcome of the Spanish-American War. The history of the American presence in Diego Garcia went back to 1965, when the United States subsidized the building of facilities on this British-owned dot in the middle of nowhere. Various schemes were used to secure Diego Garcia, including price breaks on sales of American submarines to a cash-short Great Britain. In the years that followed the original contracts, the base kept getting bigger and bigger, until, indeed, there was no space for the local inhabitants, who were removed on orders of the U.S. government. As noted earlier, President Carter had at one point touched the brake pedal with a suggestion to the Russians for neutralizing the Indian Ocean, but after the 1979 Iranian Revolution work speeded up to complete runways and support facilities.

General Garner's comments on the uses of Iraq were essentially nothing more than a repetition of agreed-upon strategy at the highest levels. But they got him fired. Well, not those comments alone, but also because Garner wanted to turn over the government to Iraqis sooner than Washington thought wise, before the landscape work was finished on the new-looking Iraq. Sensitive to charges that the coalition of the willing was a cover story, Secretary Rumsfeld reacted to the general's statements immediately, calling them "enormously unhelpful." There had been "zero discussion" among senior administration officials about such a possibility, he went on, although he allowed it was true that the United States was reevaluating its "military footprint" in the area, and this would take place "over an orderly period of time." Deny it as he might, there were simply too many accounts of American military planning for the future that confirmed a determination to maintain at least four military bases in Iraq. Some parodied the administration's chosen name for the Afghan war, Enduring Freedom, as "Enduring Bases." After all, the new installations had concrete foundations, and equally important, American culture signatures all over them—just as in Cold War days. The deeper you dig, quipped one commentator, the harder it is to get out.

Enduring Bases, it turned out, was not a term the Pentagon necessarily objected to, because it conveyed, apparently, not a commitment to permanent bases but something somewhere in between tent cities and reinforced concrete. The idea was—if the insurgency could be put down—that the plan for quick access could be carried out, and American forces in "old Europe" could be dramatically reduced. "Who needs Germany," said John Pike, director of GlobalSecurity.org, "when you have Iraq?" Plans were going ahead for four megabases in Iraq, bases that would easily accommodate the number of Americans who had been located in South Korea for over a half century. Then White House press secretary Tony Snow did a sleight-of-hand turn parsing out the issue of "permanent." "U.S. bases in Iraq," he said, "would not necessarily be permanent, because they would be there at the invitation of the host government, and the person who has done the invitation has the right to withdraw the invitation."[23]

In spring 2004, Brigadier General Robert Pollman, chief engineer in charge of bases in Iraq, strayed into the same territory that had landed Garner in trouble, telling the *Chicago Tribune* that the bases were indeed intended as a "swap" for those in Saudi Arabia. Air Force lieutenant colonel Karen Kwiatowski, a staunch conservative who resigned after experiencing life in Douglas Feith's Office of Special Plans, noted that the Pentagon went into the war determined to negotiate a status-of-forces agreement like those signed with Japan and Korea. Such an agreement, as former CPA adviser Larry Diamond has written, was one of the highly contentious issues with Iraqi leaders. The Bush administration was trying to maintain the fiction that its occupation forces were there by invitation, but after surveying the situation, decided against pursuing a status-of-forces-like agreement—as too limiting on American movements. Observed Kwiatkowski, "We're pouring concrete. We're building little fiefdoms with security, moats, and walls. . . . Eighty percent of Iraqis will grouse, but they have no political power. We'll stay whether they want us to or not."[24]

Congress authorized emergency supplemental funds for these bases, to a total of nearly $1 billion—not a trivial sum, even in these days when oil costs more than $110 a barrel and is going higher, and indeed, a not unrelated cost. Speaking at the University of California, Los Angeles, law school on February 7, 2005, Larry Diamond, who believed in the original mission, if not the way it was carried out, declared that one way

to reverse the downward spiral of the American presence and the growing insurgency would have been to declare that the United States was
not seeking permanent bases. It was not necessary to set a deadline of
2006 or 2007 to remove all troops, but it was to pledge not to maintain
military bases, which, of course, become centers or little islands of the
American way of life, as well as constant reminders that a country is—as
Garner said—useful. As Diamond put it:

> Number one, we could declare, and I urged the administration to declare
> when I left Iraq in April of 2004, that we have no permanent military de-
> signs on Iraq, and we will not seek permanent military bases in Iraq. This
> one statement would do an enormous amount to undermine the suspicion
> that we have permanent imperial intentions in Iraq. We aren't going to
> do that. And the reason we're not going to do that is because we are build-
> ing permanent military bases in Iraq.[25]

New bases in Iraq are only part of the war story, however. They would
be, by themselves, of limited usefulness, except to keep order in the immediate environs. The containment of Iran is an essential part of the
history of Iraqi-American relations from 1979 to the present day. With
the end of the Cold War, the opportunity emerged to exploit opportunities in the old defunct Warsaw Pact countries, and in former Soviet Republics bordering on the Caspian Sea, a goal that Vice President Dick
Cheney had pursued throughout both his public and private careers. But
it was 9/11 that provided the real spark to base securing in Azerbaijan,
Uzbekistan, and Kazakhstan—all having serious oil- and natural gas–
producing potential, as well as strategic significance for the Middle East.

In Baku, site of an old Soviet oil center and the capital of Azerbaijan,
Ambassador Reno Harnish commented, "Only recently have we started
to see that we need both of them," referring to building up the maritime
capabilities of Azerbaijan and Kazakhstan. "This is an unpredictable region." In addition to naval bases, the United States is renovating radar
sites in Azerbaijan near the Iranian border, atop a mountain just south of
Russia's post-Soviet borders. The Azerbaijan government, meanwhile,
remains "tight-lipped" about American military assistance.[26]

In Kyrgyzstan, another former Soviet republic, the United States
moved swiftly after 9/11 to secure rights at Manas Air Field, a place with
tall weeds, collapsed and rusted light towers, and an aircraft graveyard

that includes old wooden Russian biplanes. But it had also a fourteen-thousand-foot runway that was soon packed with Air Force KC-135 refueling jets and C-135 transport planes. By 2004 the tent city first thrown up had already given way to hard-walled structures. "It looks permanent," said the vice commander of the base, Colonel Mike Sumida, "but it could be unbolted and unwelded if we felt like it." There were no indications that his superiors in Washington would feel like it very soon. Nor did it seem likely that Kyrgyzstan would feel like asking the Americans to leave very soon, as the dollars—$52 million annually—pouring into the base and environs represented about 5 percent of the country's gross national product. Reporter Ann Scott Tyson, who toured Manas International Airport, added, "More than one hundred local residents work in the base dining hall alone, serving items ranging from crab cakes to seasoned steaks. Other workers clean offices and occasionally perform traditional Kyrgyz dances as entertainment."[27]

If Iraq no longer greeted the Americans with such open arms, such scenes in the former Soviet republics made up a little for the disappointment, and promised a lot for the future of American access to oil and natural gas. The development of regional strong points passed under the radar of the national media, as the administration's shifting rationale for war attracted much more attention. More moviegoers, such as those who bought tickets for James Bonds's recent adventure in the Caspian taking on oil buccaneers, *The World is Not Enough*, than newspaper readers who read about the war, got some idea about what was going on.

Meanwhile, as President Bush still celebrated the toppling of Saddam's Hussein's statue, he made an oblique reference to the base issue in an October 2003 speech in the Philippines. He compared the American experience in leading that former colony to freedom with what was then occurring in Iraq. When Americans boast of having never taken a foot of foreign territory, they always return to the Philippines as proof of their anti-imperialism in theory and action. There were those who said that the culture of the Middle East would not sustain "the institutions of democracy," Bush began, but they had not looked at the history of the Philippines, now a favored example as well to replace outlandish comparisons to postwar Germany or Japan. "You have earned your freedom," he declared. "America is proud of its part in the great story of the Filipino people. Together our soldiers liberated the Philippines from colonial rule." The Philippines had achieved their independence nearly six decades earlier—but Bush did not comment on the nearly five decades of tutelage, not the sort of thing, apparently, to say about the prospects for Iraq, or the base at Subic Bay.[28]

Bush lavished praise on the Philippines as a partner in the war against terrorism, and in a "vibrant" trans-Pacific commerce. "Our countries are joined by more than a market, even more than an alliance. . . . We believe in free enterprise, disciplined by humanity and compassion." In a seemingly deliberate echo of the 1947 Truman doctrine, the president declared, "Every nation in Asia and across the world now faces a choice. Nations that choose to support terror are complicit in a war against civilization." Some readers of this speech might note that one of the original issues connected to the Truman doctrine was the problematic nature of internal subversion, as opposed to military aggression; i.e., how did one tell the difference? In this case, Bush was setting up the dominos for a different game, in effect inverting Truman's words about the communist "threat" to portray a threat arising inside countries, and then projected outward to the new "free world" bloc—or, as he put it here, "civilization." Under such a rubric, intervention can be justified, as Douglas Feith had put it, to suppress would-be terrorists in "ungoverned and under-governed areas within states." That Bush chose to reiterate his new take on the Truman doctrine so strongly in the Philippines, where, in fact, an Islamic resistance movement has grown in power, only underlined the base issue.

In this speech, delivered while he yet basked in the sunshine of victory, the president was still claiming to have discovered evidence of an ongoing WMD program. A less favored parallel ignored by the president and his advisers was with the aftermath of the three-month war against Spain in 1898. Madrid yielded quickly to the new power in the world lineup, but Washington's plans for an equally quick start to reconstructing the islands were put in check by a very difficult pacification. The Philippine insurrection lasted for three-and-a-half years, costing the army 4,234 deaths, with nearly 3,000 wounded. Filipino deaths numbered 69,000 combatants and nearly 200,000 civilians. "The American war effort," noted Fred Kaplan, "was marked by much burning, pillaging, and torturing, and the commanders finally achieved victory through a strategy of isolating the guerrillas."[29]

But there are still other comparisons, with the postwar situations in Cuba and the Philippines, that need some comment. Bush talked about the Philippines's adherence to free-market ideals, one of the key aspects, he reminds us, of the true path to democracy. The transformation of Asia was supposed to begin with the Philippines after the war of 1898, and produce a new day in nearby China. The original Garner figure in Cuba after the war was General Leonard Wood, a medical doctor who rode with Teddy Roosevelt up San Juan Hill and into the governor general-ship of the island between 1899 and 1902. In 1900, he wrote to President McKinley, "When people ask me what I mean by stable government, I tell them money at six percent." Wood's reign in Cuba was noted for its efforts to improve the basic infrastructure of the island after the years of insurrection against Spain. Between 1897 and 1917, American trade with Cuba flourished, noted historian Walter LaFeber, skyrocketing from $27 million in 1897 to over $300 million by 1917.[30]

Wood left Cuba in 1902 for a new command in the Philippine Islands, lamenting the lack of good Cuban candidates for political office.

Cuba has remained a political problem for the United States for more than a hundred years. Both there and in the Philippines, however, Washington has held on to useful military bases. The Cuban base at Guantánamo Bay has served a variety of purposes over the years, most recently as a holding pen for suspected al Qaeda terrorists who pose a contentious issue involving questions about the treatment of such cap-tives, from the way they became prisoners to a proper forum for trying them and determining their guilt for presumed crimes. The interroga-tions at Guantánamo employed methods that were linked to techniques used at Abu Ghraib, a notorious prison in Baghdad and the scene of practices that involved extreme psychological humiliation and physical abuse made public in pictures taken by some of the jailers.

Only low-ranking enlisted men and women were charged with crimes at Abu Ghraib, but their defense attorneys have argued that the tactics were those recommended by Major General Geoffrey D. Miller, who commanded at Guantánamo, and was sent to Iraq to improve interroga-tion techniques there, including hooding and the use of dogs.[31]

Disappearing Act

Wolfowitz, who in some ways initiated the discussion of bases by his re-marks about the side benefits of the war in terms of removing forces from

Saudi Arabia, also seemed to become the point man on the question of Iraq's missing WMD. His comment to Tanenhaus, that the possible presence of WMD was a bureaucratic convenience to line up the ducks, caused a storm of comments. He did not say, as some critics eagerly insisted, that the WMD were never there in the first place, but the continuing failure to find any stockpiles of weapons put the administration on the defensive.

President Bush fell back one step on the issue, arguing that Hussein had had WMD at the time of Gulf War I, and that he had used them in the Iran-Iraq War. If left to his own devices, the argument went, he would have reacquired them at some not-too-distant date in the future, and then the whole world would be put at risk. Perhaps it was true that he would not dare to use the weapons, but there was always the possibility that he would supply terrorists with deadly anthrax powder, or nerve gas, or even a nuclear weapon. His villainy knew no bounds, so why believe he would not do that? Bush had sent David Kay as his discoverer in chief to find where the weapons were, or where they had gone. Kay, a fellow Texan with a PhD in international relations from Columbia University, had been the chief weapons inspector after Gulf War I. His experience in uncovering Saddam Hussein's progress toward a nuclear weapon inclined him toward the belief that the Iraqi dictator did indeed have a flourishing WMD program.

Before Gulf War II, the administration used Kay as a counter to Hans Blix, who was not following the favored course. Without being involved in the UN search, a virtue in the eyes of the Bush White House, Kay issued authoritative-sounding statements about Iraq's violation of international orders to "rid itself of these weapons." He went to Iraq convinced he would find them. But he didn't on the first go-round—and never would. Kay returned to Washington in midsummer 2003 to report that he needed George Tenet's CIA stations to report on whether WMD might have been smuggled out to Syria when the war began. At a White House briefing he suggested that a big mistake had been made to allow all the looting and lawlessness in the first weeks of the occupation. Iraq was a mess, and that made his job vastly more difficult. Did Kay imagine that looters had tucked canisters of nerve gas into their swags along with ancient pottery bowls? He then suggested that perhaps the Iraqis had a way of fooling everyone. "Some of this evidence is beginning to shape up as if they had a just-in-time policy," he said, with the equipment and facilities available to make weapons on short notice. But he didn't really believe that explanation either. "We have not found large stockpiles. You can't rule them out. We haven't come to the conclusion that they're not there, but they're sure not any place obvious."[32]

Another account of this briefing has Kay openly admitting that the mobile weapons labs Colin Powell had pictured for the UN Security Council never existed, and all the intelligence that said they did had been based on the fabrications of one man, known to German intelligence as "Curveball," an exile from Iraq with ties to Ahmed Chalabi's Iraqi National Congress. "The United States had gone to war to chase a mirage," Kay feared. Bush showed no reaction. "He asked no follow-up questions. Bush already knew about Curveball, Kay realized."[33]

As long as this "secret" was kept inside the White House, the damage could be contained. The continuing resistance inside Iraq had spoiled the first line of defense about missing WMD—that a quick victory would render the issue politically harmless. The situation was now being called an insurgency, and no one could say with confidence when it would end. Accordingly, the administration took up its next line of defense—that Iraq was the central front in the war against terrorism. Osama bin Laden might still be at large somewhere in the mountains between Afghanistan and Pakistan, but he had agents inside Iraq who would turn the country into a stronghold if Americans left before their mission was complete. Asked about the continuing violence and deaths of American soldiers, Paul Wolfowitz sought to establish the theme in an interview with a friendly Fox News commentator, that their "sacrifice" was going to "make our children and our grandchildren safer because, Brit [Hume], the battle to win the peace in Iraq now is a central battle in the war on terrorism."[34]

Wolfowitz was also given an assignment by Cheney and Rumsfeld to help out with a potentially devastating op-ed piece by former ambassador Joseph Wilson that had appeared in the July 6, 2003, *New York Times*. Wilson's expose concerned the yellowcake uranium that both President Bush and Prime Minister Blair had claimed Iraq had sought to purchase from Niger in Africa. The op-ed piece, "What I Didn't Find in Africa," detailed his mission to Niger in 2002 to discover if documents originating in Italy about the attempted purchases had any validity. He had reported back that the documents were forgeries, but the accusation turned up again in Bush's 2003 State of the Union address in the famous sixteen words, about how Iraq had pursued Niger's yellowcake to feed its nuclear program. The repeated insistence on the story as proving the case for war disturbed Wilson, who set out on a crusade of his own. "It was disinformation. It had never occurred to me to keep quiet about this. Until the issue was addressed seriously, I felt obliged to keep raising it."[35]

Wilson's bombshell piece put the White House into full crisis-management mode in an effort to discredit the former ambassador's accusations. Once again Vice President Cheney took charge, the kind of work he always relished as the administration's enforcer-in-chief. He operated this time through Wolfowitz but also his close aide, I. Lewis "Scooter" Libby, instructing the latter to plant leaks in the press about Wilson's wife's identity as an undercover CIA agent. The operation was not so much on the dark side as the murky side, for it remains unclear precisely what the leaks were supposed to accomplish. The idea apparently was to suggest that the intelligence agency had some sort of vendetta against Bush, or that it wanted to cover up its own mistakes with a tardy denial of the yellowcake story and how it had been misrepresented. Cheney, meanwhile, had portions of the October 2002 NIE declassified, and instructed Libby to use them to say to the press that "a key judgment of the NIE held that Iraq was 'vigorously trying to procure' uranium." All this was done to bolster the argument that if anyone had misled the country it was the CIA. So here was where the situation stood after Cheney's maneuvers: Before the war the OVP had damned the CIA for failing to report the true story about Saddam's dangerous path to obtaining nuclear weapons; now, with the anti-Wilson campaign, Cheney reversed course for a tactical assault to argue that the CIA had given out exaggerated estimates of his capabilities.[36]

It was a tactical switch only, of course, for Cheney realized that this was a shaky position for the administration to adopt, imperiling still further the argument for war. Hence the deliberate murkiness. Wolfowitz, meanwhile, was to play messenger, delivering to the *Wall Street Journal* selected still-classified portions of the October 2002 NIE, as well as to provide the paper with talking points to demonstrate that the CIA continued to believe the yellowcake indictment against Saddam Hussein after Wilson's mission. Thus the point would be made that only after the first search for WMD had failed to turn up anything did the CIA back off its conclusion. It had now come time to throw CIA director George

Tenet off the train, despite all his past efforts to tailor the NIE to suit what the White House had wanted to hear.[37]

Press secretary Ari Fleischer was having his own tough time with the Wilson op-ed piece. All the reporters were missing the "bigger picture," he insisted. The case for war was not based on the specific yellowcake issue, but on Saddam Hussein's record of concealment, and his undoubted possession of WMD: "In 1991, everybody in the world underestimated how close he was to getting a nuclear weapon." But Wilson never claimed that was false, said a reporter; he had made the case that there was no basis for the yellowcake accusation. No, no, insisted Fleischer; Wilson only reported that Niger denied the sale. What else would you expect them to do? That was not what Wilson had reported, but Fleischer continued to insist that revelations about the forged documents only became apparent later, and he scampered back to what he thought was safe ground. "But again, 1991, the world underestimated how close Iraq was to obtaining nuclear weapons. There is a bigger picture here that is just as valid today as it was the day of the [2003 State of the Union] speech."

The questions kept coming, until finally Fleischer was forced into a corner. His final statement was a classic dodge reserved for when all else fails.

> I think the burden is on those people who think he didn't have weapons of mass destruction to tell the world where they are. We know he had them in the nineties; he used them. So just because they haven't been found doesn't mean they didn't exist. *The burden is on the critics to explain where the weapons of mass destruction are.*[38] (Emphasis added.)

But the Wilson story would not go away. Suddenly the former ambassador was everywhere, even displacing Dick Cheney on *Meet the Press*, where the vice president had reigned supreme since right after 9/11. The White House finally seemed to back away from the Niger connection, releasing a statement that the sixteen words did "not rise to the level that we would put in a presidential speech." This grudging admission that somehow the words got slipped in when nobody was looking put the blame, as Cheney hoped, on George Tenet, who promptly fell on his sword, received a medal for good behavior, and exited stage right, shaking his head about the "dumbest" two words he ever said: "slam dunk."[39]

Almost as soon as the White House issued this statement, however, it began to have regrets about telling the truth. *Washington Post* columnist Walter Pincus, who had written articles before the op-ed piece that drew on Wilson's experience, told the ambassador that one official even said that owning up that way "was the biggest mistake the administration made."

If Wilson's op-ed piece continued to go unchallenged and unpunished, moreover, others might be tempted to give their opinions, and the whole fabric of the WMD rationale could come flying apart in short order. "I think this just hit a nerve," said one of Libby's associates. Uranium might be a side issue—Iraq's own supply was under the control of the IAEA—but to admit that the Niger story was disinformation could be "the beginning of the unraveling of the big story."

Following orders, Libby met with *Times* reporter Judith Miller, who had been an outlet for the scary story about aluminum tubes that also bordered on deliberate disinformation, and attempted to plant more information about Wilson's wife's role. She took notes, misidentifying Plame as Valerie Flame—as if she had escaped from Marvel Comics—but never wrote the story.[40]

It was actually Deputy Secretary of State Richard Armitage who leaked the information to columnist Robert Novak, who then wrote the story revealing Plame's identity. At least three people were involved in trying to plant stories with media outlets—Libby, Armitage, and Bush's top political adviser, Karl Rove. Rove told one of his contacts that Wilson had given money to John Kerry and was a Democrat. Wasn't that plain enough?[41]

Thus far, however, the Wilson caper had not touched on possible illegal activities by the leakers. That changed when *Nation* correspondent and well-known author David Corn wrote a column that asked whether the leak had been a violation of the Intelligence Identities Protection Act, a 1982 law that specified a heavy fine—$50,000—and up to ten years' prison time for revealing identities of covert agents. Ironically, it had been passed as a response to the outing of more than a thousand CIA operatives by a case officer turned vehement critic of the agency's covert activities, Philip Agee.[42]

On September 26, 2003, the FBI launched an inquiry into the leak. President Bush seemed almost nonchalant about it all. "I don't know if we are going to find the senior administration official," he said. "Now,

this is a large administration, and there's a lot of senior officials." Behind
the scenes, however, Libby was getting squeezed. He told the FBI that he
had gotten the name of Valerie Plame from Tim Russert, and then passed
it on as gossip to Matt Cooper of *Time*. He also said he had not discussed
Plame at all with Judy Miller, when they had met on July 8. Perhaps
Libby believed that the investigation would go nowhere, as Bush had
suggested, or more probably, he understood that the White House could
not back away from a campaign that challenged Wilson's honesty in a
hasty fashion. If he told the truth about how the campaign had been orchestrated to put Wilson in the worst light, he would in a certain sense
be abandoning the vice president.[43]

Libby was the only one ever indicted, and ultimately convicted, of
perjury, for saying that it was Tim Russert who told him about Plame's
identity. When Libby's trial got under way, the jury heard testimony that
Cheney had indeed orchestrated the campaign against Joe Wilson by
outing his wife to discredit a critic who he believed was making him look
foolish. The testimony came from Cheney's former press aide, Cathie
Martin, who told the court that Cheney had even dictated what Libby
should say to the reporters to rebut Wilson, although she offered no
proof that the vice president had instructed Scooter specifically to identify Plame. That mystery remained. The Libby trial, despite Special
Prosecutor Patrick Fitzgerald's repeated demurs, put the Iraq War on
trial—precisely what the administration did not want to see.[44]

Dodge Ball

Throughout the summer of 2003, and even after as the occupation
stretched on toward a date that seemed to recede with each step the administration labeled as progress, Paul Wolfowitz continued to hold out
hope the WMD would be found. In an interview with a friendly newspaper, the *Jerusalem Post*, Rumsfeld's deputy introduced a new Saddam
Hussein horror to explain the failure to locate the weapons. "Iraq is what
the intelligence people call an extremely hard target, and it's a kind
of a[n] antiseptic, technical way of saying it's a place where people's
tongues were cut out if they talked when they weren't supposed to, [but]
we have very good people working on it, and I assume we'll get to the
bottom of the thing, but it will take time."[45]

In the process of getting to the bottom of the thing, Wolfowitz became a master of the non sequitur. On CBS's *Face the Nation*, Bob Schieffer raised the question of the administration's prewar claims about connections between Saddam Hussein and al Qaeda. Have you found any new evidence to support that claim, asked Schieffer? Wolfowitz responded as if he had been asked again about WMD, saying it was hard to break the veil of secrecy.

> You fly over Baghdad, I don't know my geography perfectly, I'm told it's the size of Los Angeles. It is just huge. You look at house after house after house. You say, every one of those houses is big enough to have a lethal quantity of anthrax in the basement. You're not going to find it by house-to-house searches. You're only going to find it when people talk.
> An illustration of that, we visited the police academy, because some terrific training is going on to build a new police force. . . . What they didn't know, but was discovered a couple of days before I got there, was that they had subsequently discovered that behind the police academy was a torture chamber, where this woman who was reported in the press last week as having been tied to a tree, and they did unspeakable things to her. . . . We're going to be unveiling secrets in Iraq day after day after day.[46]

Schieffer tried one more time. "But have you found at this point any new connections to al Qaeda that you didn't know about?" And once again Wolfowitz appeared not to hear him right—or something: "Bob, this is in the very capable hands of the CIA, led out there by David Kay." Schieffer tried a new approach, asking if one of the justifications for war had been because Osama bin Laden had escaped capture. Finally Wolfowitz gave an answer of sorts: "Information about terrorism is inevitably murky, because terrorists hide, and because you get an awful lot of information that's simply not true." At that point Schieffer gave up. "I wish we had more time; unfortunately we don't. Thank you very much."

Cheney also believed he had no choice but to continue to assert the arguments for Saddam Hussein's WMD program, even as the special teams sent into Iraq to find the missing weapons kept coming up empty-handed. On September 14, 2003, the vice president was back once again on one of Tim Russert's news shows, previously friendly territory. But this time Russert opened the program with a videotape of Cheney's appearance on the eve of the war, when he claimed that American troops would be greeted as liberators. Who convinced the administration of that? Ahmed Chalabi and all those other Iraqis who briefed the White House? Russert asked. No, Cheney answered. They were all anxious to liberate Iraq from one of the worst dictatorships of the twentieth century, but, he said, shifting, the spotlight, he had received, "evidence on a fairly regular basis" that showed the Iraqi people were with the Americans. "I mean, if you go out and look at what's happening on the ground, you'll find there is widespread support."[47]

Evidence no one else has access to remains the escape hatch of government officials backed into a corner. This time, however, Russert did not just watch him squeeze by, and he moved on to another piece of videotape, this one featuring Cheney's prewar contention that Saddam Hussein had developed chemical and biological weapons and was in hot pursuit of nuclear weapons. Where are they, Russert asked? The jury was still out on that one, Cheney responded; but the NIE that he had based his comments on in March "wasn't an idea cooked up overnight by a handful of people." In fact, the NIE of October 2002 *was* indeed a rush job inspired by the need to meet congressional complaints about a lack of the evidence to justify a vote authorizing the president to use military action. Many of its arguments—including the yellowcake fantasy—had been pushed by a handful of people from the OVP during Cheney's and Libby's many visits to CIA headquarters.

Cheney rambled on, nevertheless, talking about Saddam's programs since the 1980s. The new chief inspector, David Kay, was a good man, said Cheney, and as he was able to talk with people who were no longer afraid to come forward, we would learn that "he had a robust plan, had previously worked on it and would work on it again." No one had expected to drive into Baghdad and find someone pointing, "Hey, there's the building over there where all of our WMDs [are] stored." That's not the way the system worked.

Well, Russert came back, what about Joe Wilson? "Were you briefed on his findings in February, March of 2002?" "I don't know Joe Wilson," replied Cheney. "I've never met Joe Wilson." The whole thing, he said, started with a question about Iraq's effort to purchase uranium in Niger. "I get a daily brief on my own each day before I meet with the president to go through the intel [sic]. And I ask lots of questions." It was another revealing moment, both about the relationship between the two men and Cheney's technique of pressuring the CIA and other intel agencies to conform to the OVP view. In this case, he said, the CIA had commented that there was "'a lot we don't know,' end of statement. And Joe Wilson—I don't know who sent Joe Wilson. He never submitted a report that I ever saw when he came back."

Cheney thus hoped he could leave the impression with Russert and his audience that there never had been a full "report" and the op-ed piece was a post facto effort to plant a false statement—black propaganda, in other words. "The committee of the British Parliament" that spent ninety days investigating all this," Cheney went on, "revalidated their British claim that Saddam was, in fact, trying to acquire uranium in Africa." And that assurance was in the State of the Union speech and the original British white papers. "So there may be a difference of opinion there. I don't know what the truth is on the ground. . . . Like I say, I don't know Mr. Wilson. I probably shouldn't judge him." All these comments belonged under the label "plausible deniability," for Cheney might not have met Mr. Wilson, but he had carried out a vendetta against him. As for *the* British committee, it was once again Tony Blair riding in on horseback to the rescue when his American partner needed help in the worst way.

Russert, surprisingly perhaps, still did not back down, and continued with more questions about the failure to uncover WMD. Cheney fell back to the by now familiar position that Saddam had had "robust" programs in the past. "As I say, the British just revalidated their claim. So I'm not sure what the argument is about here. I think in the final analysis, we will find that the Iraqis did have a robust program. . . . So I say I'm not willing at all at this point to buy the proposition that somehow Saddam Hussein was innocent, and he had no WMD, and some guy out at the CIA, because I called him, cooked up a report saying he did."

Cheney even revived the long discredited Prague connection in this interview to move into the new rationale for the war: that, even if no WMD were ever found, Iraq was now the central front in the war on terrorism. "With respect to 9/11, of course, we've had the story that's been public out there. The Czechs alleged that Mohammed Atta, the lead attacker, met in Prague with a senior Iraqi intelligence official five months before the attack, but we've never been able to develop any more of that yet, either in terms of confirming it or discrediting it."

Russert did not pursue the matter, but other reporters did, querying the OVP about the Atta in Prague story. They got no response. But Mary Matalin, a former aide to Cheney, would talk to *Washington Post* reporters

Dana Priest and Glenn Kessler, who asked her about the evidence Cheney said he had. The vice president did not base his opinions on "one piece of data," she said, but he had access to information that if made public would harm national security or compromise sources. "His job is to connect the dots in a way to prevent the worst possible case from happening"; but in public, "he has to tiptoe through landmines of what's sayable and not sayable."[48]

The image of Cheney tiptoeing around anything is something to contemplate. He certainly did not back off the idea that Iraq and the war on terror were synonymous, especially as the 2004 presidential campaign got under way in earnest. Bush eased into the idea by saying that Hussein "had ties to terrorist organizations," but did not persist with an argument that there was any specific tie to al Qaeda or 9/11. That remained Cheney's job. But now, in addition to Tim Russert, there were public challenges from David Kay, the man the vice president had declared was the best person possible for turning up the missing WMD. In an interview Kay tried to put the question to rest once and for all. "At various times al Qaeda people came through Baghdad and in some cases resided there," he said. "But we simply did not find any evidence of extensive links with al Qaeda, or for that matter, any real links at all." But what about Cheney's claim that there was "overwhelming evidence" of an ongoing connection? Kay scoffed at the idea. "Cheney's speech is evidence-free. It is an assertion, but [he] doesn't say why we should believe this now."[49]

David Kay's comments were supported by the 9/11 Commission, which found no connection between Saddam Hussein and the attacks. President Bush tried to span the gap, claiming the administration had never said the attacks were orchestrated with Iraqi help, but rather that there were "numerous contacts" with al Qaeda. Cheney was still in full-throated pursuit of a lasting connection. "There clearly was a relationship. It's been testified to. The evidence is overwhelming." All the commission said, he insisted, was that they could not find evidence of involvement in the attack. "We had one report, which is a famous report on the Czech intelligence service, and we've never been able to confirm it or knock it down." Asked if he knew information that the 9/11 Commission did not know, Cheney replied, "Probably."[50]

ABC reporter Diane Sawyer interviewed the president on December 16, 2003, three days after Saddam Hussein was flushed from his spider hole near his home in northern Iraq. Was this the best day of his presidency, she asked? No, not the best, but he had talked to his dad, the elder president Bush, and could tell that his father's voice was filled with pride. "It was a touching moment." Much later in the interview, Sawyer turned to the mounting criticism that there was no hard evidence that Saddam Hussein had WMD when the war began. Bush struggled with what to reply, his answers suddenly filled with vocalized pauses. "What—I, I—made my decision based upon enough intelligence to tell me that this country was threatened with Saddam Hussein in power." What would it take to convince him, asked Sawyer, that Hussein didn't have weapons of mass destruction? It didn't make any difference whether he had them or only aspired to them, Bush replied. "Diane, you can keep asking the question. I'm telling you—I made the right decision."[51]

At the Radio and Television Correspondents' Association dinner, March 24, 2004, the president showed slides depicting what a satirist might say—standard operating procedure for these dinners, where presidents were expected to roast themselves. At one point Bush showed a photo of himself looking for something out a window in the Oval Office, and he said, "Those weapons of mass destruction have got to be somewhere."

"The audience laughed," reported David Corn. "I grimaced. But that wasn't the end of it. After a few more slides, there was a shot of Bush looking under furniture in the Oval Office. 'Nope,' he said. 'No weapons over there.' More laughter. Then another picture of Bush searching in his office: 'Maybe under here.' Laughter again."[52]

Making Iraq Safe for Democracy

Bush's pantomimed search for WMD at the March 24 dinner came only a few days before the Fallujah ambush of Blackwater security guards. It was a sobering scene.

> Men with scarves over their faces hurled bricks into the blazing vehicles. A group of boys yanked a smoldering body into the street and ripped it apart. Someone tied a chunk of flesh to a rock and tossed it over a telephone wire.
>
> "Viva mujahedeen!" shouted Said Khalaf, a taxi driver. "Long live the resistance!"

Nearby, a boy no older than 10 ground his heel into a burned head. "Where is Bush?" the boy yelled. "Let him come here and see this!"

Masked men gathered around him, punching their fists into the air. The streets filled with hundreds of people. "Falluja is the graveyard of Americans!" they chanted.[53]

It was never supposed to be this way. The administration never imagined there would be an "occupation." Yes, Colin Powell had warned that Pottery Barn rules applied, "You break it, you own it," and, on another occasion that Iraq was like a crystal goblet that would shatter into myriad slivers, but he continued to be the odd man out in the policy-making circle.

When the Pentagon called upon retired general Jay Garner to head the Office of Reconstruction and Humanitarian Aid (ORHA), the name itself suggested something on the order of a Red Cross relief mission. He was told to expect to be in Iraq for no more than three months—if that long. The State Department had prepared lengthy position papers on the next steps in Iraq, after the military stage was completed, but Secretary Rumsfeld had little use for any of these, or for the people State wished to accompany Garner on his mission.

Expectations of a foreshortened rule by military authority before a transfer of "sovereignty" to Iraqi exile leaders did not appear contradictory, so it seemed, to Pentagon assumptions about a lasting military relationship and large bases in Iraq, though why that should be so remains mystifying. Garner's loose talk about prospective bases helped to get him fired long before his ninety days were up, but the larger question of his failed tenure had to do with the general's relationship with Ahmed Chalabi, the sixty-year-old leader of the Iraqi National Congress, who had returned from exile expecting to head the new government.

Chalabi had long been the Pentagon's favorite, although the CIA, which had funded the Iraqi National Congress, had grown wary of its would-be man in Baghdad. Chalabi had been the discoverer of Curveball, the alcoholic cousin of one of his aides who had provided more than one hundred "reports" on WMD to German intelligence, none of which turned out to be true. As early as 2001, when the reports were first challenged, German officials warned the CIA that Curveball was out of control. Those who challenged his bona fides were discounted, nevertheless, and analysts who made the accusations were forced to leave the unit examining his claims. One of those skeptics was Robert Baer, who later said, "Chalabi was scamming the U.S. because the U.S. wanted to be scammed."[54]

Chalabi's Pentagon allies, however, especially Paul Wolfowitz and Douglas Feith, felt he was being hustled off the scene in Iraq because of continuing CIA and State Department resentments at being excluded, like those who would supposedly account for Joe Wilson's op-ed attack on the Niger uranium yellowcake story. His fate is central to the unfolding American debacle in Iraq, however, because it provides a clear view of the self-delusions that fueled the entire project for turning Iraq into the first Arab democracy.

When L. Paul Bremer replaced General Garner he selected twenty-five notables for an interim governing council (IGC), and let everyone know that he was not interested in an early transfer of power to any truly independent regime. At his behest, for example, the IGC adopted Order 17, which exempted all foreign personnel in the Coalition Provisional Authority from "local criminal, civil and administrative jurisdiction and from any form of arrest or detention other than by persons acting on behalf of their parent states." Supposedly a temporary measure, Order 17 remains in force more than three years after the United States returned "sovereignty" to an Iraqi government on June 30, 2004. General Richard B. Myers, chairman of the Joint Chiefs, asserted in congressional testimony that the immunity order could not be repealed by the interim government—and, it became clear, could not be repealed by its successor without causing a crisis in Iraqi-American relations. "There are hundreds of orders that the C.P.A. issued that are going to continue in force," said one Washington official. "They may not be the law of the land, but they are part of the architecture of Iraq." Still, he allowed, "if the new government wants, they can change them."[55]

At the height of the colonial era in the late nineteenth century such rules were imposed on semi-independent countries, China being the prime example, under the rubric of "extraterritoriality." European diplomats raised the key question of whether the new caretaker government would have the right to object to American orders from American officers sending Iraqi soldiers into combat against other Iraqis? An anonymous senior Bush administration official said such a demand was unnecessary. It was self-evident that no one could order Iraqi troops to take action against their will. "Are we going to send them into battle at the point of a gun?"[56]

It was not so easy to brush off such questions, however, in the wake of the battle for Fallujah. There was little doubt in either Washington or Baghdad that the bloody scenes from that city had changed the course of the occupation. Fallujah was the culmination of the first stage of the occupation. Ever since Bremer arrived he had exhibited little inclination to hasten along the political process, and that brought him into conflict with several factions, including those loyal to Chalabi. The exile's return had been less than triumphant. He brought with him a security guard, and made himself highly visible at the toppling of Saddam Hussein's statue. But there his popularity seemed to peak. Many in the IGC were suspicious of Chalabi's ambitions, as were a growing number in Washington, even in the Pentagon, his principal sponsor. The failure to find the WMD and the first Curveball revelations had put Chalabi under much closer scrutiny. It was a real shock to Chalabi's neocon allies when an Ohio congressman asked Air Force general Richard Myers, chairman of the Joint Chiefs, if he thought the United States was "duped by a con man" into going to war, and Myers responded: "I think that remains to be seen. Probably. But I just don't know."[57]

Deputy Secretary Wolfowitz, once one of Chalabi's strongest supporters, was also asked to comment on the exile's role in providing false intelligence. The best he could summon up in Chalabi's defense was an equivocation: "Nothing in Iraq is black and white." On another occasion Wolfowitz said that the idea that the Pentagon had groomed Chalabi for the number-one spot in Iraq was just "a bit of street legend." Vice President Cheney added that Chalabi was but one of several Iraqi wanna-bes. But documents from the Pentagon's Office of Special Plans, overseen by Douglas Feith, indicated a preference for Chalabi and other Iraqi National Congress (INC) figures.[58]

Chalabi blamed Wolfowitz for his shunning. "The real culprit in all this is Wolfowitz," he told a *Times* feature writer. "They chickened out. The Pentagon guys chickened out." In an interview with London's *Daily Telegraph*, Chalabi made some comments the White House could not forgive, because they touched on a forbidden truth. He declared that the failure to find WMD was of no importance. "As far as we're concerned, we've been entirely successful. That tyrant Saddam is gone and the

Americans are in Baghdad. What was said before is not important. The Bush administration is looking for a scapegoat. We're ready to fall on our swords if he wants."

"We are heroes in error."[59]

Such statements did not go over well, not only in antiwar circles, but at the highest level, especially with their implication that all along Chalabi had been the man designated by Americans to lead the new Iraq. They made the Pentagon's slogan "Operation Enduring Freedom" end with a question mark. And that would never do. The Defense Department ended the INC's monthly subsidy of $325,000 on May 8, 2004. Twelve days later, on May 20, 2004, Iraqi and American forces carried out a raid on Chalabi's office and home, carrying off a family Koran, smashing a portrait of his father, and destroying family heirlooms as well as computers. His name had not appeared on the warrant signed by an Iraqi judge, and the policemen who carried out the raid with the Americans did not know they were to target the INC leader. They apologized. But the Americans who ordered the raid claimed to have intelligence information that Chalabi was in contact with Iranian officials, and had given them classified information.[60]

Whether the intelligence information was accurate or not—Chalabi, of course, denied the charge—he had become persona non grata. Only four months earlier, at Bush's 2004 State of the Union speech, Chalabi had been seated in the gallery in a place of honor directly behind Laura Bush. At a meeting with the president, Chalabi had warned against allowing a UN emissary, Lakhdar Brahimi, to give former Ba'athists a role in the interim government. "If there is anything you don't have to worry about," Chalabi claimed Bush assured him, "it's that." The United States had actually encouraged the UN to pass a resolution empowering occupation officials to proceed with the creation of a provisional government, and welcomed Brahimi's mission to oversee the process. Chalabi was already aware that that meant Washington no longer had any use for him.[61]

If there was any doubt about that, Bush made it clear that Chalabi was history, and, less truthfully, that he never really had been in the picture. On June 1, 2004, the president announced that after consultations with the IGC and other Iraqis, Brahimi had selected Iyad Allawi to be the prime minister in an interim government, pending elections in January 2005. Allawi, a former Ba'athist Party member, had spent years in Saddam Hussein's prisons, and had become another exile leader with close ties to both the CIA and British intelligence. Power would be turned over to the new government on June 30, 2004. Reporters asked Bush if he thought it was possible other nations would come forward with offers of troops for Iraq. Bush hedged. "I don't know if there will be a major commitment of new troops, but I think there will be a major focus on helping Iraq to become a free country." In other words, the United States did not want troops from countries that had opposed the war; it wanted their support in other ways. Then he was asked if, given that many in the new government had received money from the United States in the past, would other countries see this as a puppet government—and, given that criticism, could he state what role, if any, he had in the selection of Allawi and others? "I had no role. I mean, occasionally, somebody said, this person may be interested, or that—but I had no role in picking, zero."

A little later came an inevitable question about Ahmed Chalabi:

REPORTER: Mr. President, Mr. Chalabi is an Iraqi leader that's fallen out of favor within your administration. I'm wondering if he provided any false information, or are you particularly—

PRESIDENT BUSH: Chalabi?

REPORTER: Yes, with Chalabi.

PRESIDENT BUSH: My meetings with him were very brief. I mean, I think I met with him at the State of the Union, and just kind of working through the rope line, and he might have come with a group of leaders. But I haven't had any extensive conversations with him. Mr. Brahimi made the decision on Chalabi, not the United States. Mr. Brahimi was the person that put together the group. . . . I don't remember anybody walking into my office saying, Chalabi says this is the way it's going to be in Iraq.

Having ignored the question about the administration's susceptibility to false information about WMD, and placed the responsibility for dealing with both Chalabi and Allawi on Brahimi's shoulders, Bush came back to the one consistent theme, or, better put, warning that would continue to define the administration's response to all criticisms throughout the war.

However, I just want to remind you that the mission of the enemy is to get us to retreat from Iraq. Is to say, well, it's been tough enough, now it's time to go home—which we are not going to do. We will stand with this Iraqi government.[62]

There was very little doubt, nevertheless, that the key player in the se-lection of Iyad Allawi had been Robert Blackwill, a career diplomat sent by Bush to Iraq to manage the whole process. Bremer and Blackwill had closely questioned the "candidate" about whether he was fully commit-ted to early elections to move the process on from a provisional govern-ment to a more permanent solution to Iraq's future—and to give the United States some distance from the day-to-day running of the coun-try's affairs, in the hope that the post-Fallujah insurgency would die down. Bremer—a new convert to a rapid turnover—stressed that the president wanted that assurance. "Iraq can't be secure without American help," Bremer told him. "Americans are idealistic people. Most Ameri-cans will support our continued involvement if they're convinced that Iraq is moving toward democracy." For a moment the room was quiet. "Allawi shrugged. I'd left him no way out. 'But . . .' he began, and then took a deep breath. 'Of course, you're right.'"[63]

These confidential discussions essentially left Brahimi out of the loop. The UN negotiator and the Americans agreed on one thing, how-ever: Chalabi was not to be considered under any circumstances. After Fallujah—and the Abu Ghraib scandal—it was absolutely essential to have a government in place that could deflect some of the anti-American out-bursts that were already burgeoning into a widespread insurgency. With the American presidential election looming, said a top State Depart-ment official, the White House was so eager to turn the Iraq mess over to the UN that Brahimi "could hand us a Safeway list, and we'd give it to him."[64]

It was certainly true that congressional Republicans were nervous about the election, but it was not at all so that the administration wished to turn over the Iraq mess to the UN. At the time of the changeover from the Coalition Provisional Authority to the Allawi interim govern-ment, the president said, "The struggle is, first and foremost, an Iraqi struggle." And he was "hoping that if we get out of the way of the Iraqi people, they will have an incentive to make it work." Defense Secretary Rumsfeld, however, had a momentary vision of a darker future. He compared the insurgency to the Tet offensive, a battle the North Vietnamese and Vietcong ended up "winning psychologically." The insurgents in Iraq had studied the history of that earlier war, and were hoping to use the twenty-four-hour news cycle to launch their blows timed to obliterate the news of an Iraq struggling to its feet. "Will it work?" Rumsfeld asked. "I think not."[65]

The Vietnam analogy had crept back into the political debate, and it would not be chased out easily. Even many neoconservatives who had played the role of war hawks to the hilt were beginning to have second thoughts. Some, like Richard Perle, were bitter over the way Chalabi had been dismissed, and saw in his downfall a prelude to a wider failure in Iraq. Others began calling for Rumsfeld himself to resign for having botched the crucial postwar period, thereby leaving Iraq in a state of near chaos. Paul Wolfowitz seemed unfazed, however. Saddam's murderers and torturers had abused the Iraqi people, and were now proving to be a tough enemy, he said. "But no one should have expected a cakewalk, and that's no reason to go wobbly now. I spend most of my time with officers and soldiers, and they're not defeatists—not even the ones who suffered terrible wounds in Iraq."[66]

One heard an echo here of Margaret Thatcher's supposed admonition (repeated later by Madeleine Albright) as Wolfowitz sought to stir the spirits of wavering souls while visions of joyous Iraqis welcoming American GIs disappeared from the streets of Fallujah and Baghdad's Sadr City. The new hope was Iyad Allawi, the head of the Iraq National Accord, a counterpoint to Chalabi. Allawi had once been the CIA's chosen instrument to launch a bombing campaign against Saddam's regime. The campaign wasn't particularly effective, said one former agency official: "[B]ombs were going off to no great effect." After being named prime minister, Allawi said his first priority would be to stop the bombings and insurgent attacks—a promise several former agents found "ironic."[67]

But there seemed no one else at the moment to deflect the threat of retribution at the polls for all that had gone wrong. Senator John Kerry proved an inept challenger, but the president was also helped at the last minute by a taunting message from Osama bin Laden that gave a brief boost to the administration's claims that the war in Iraq was indeed what it claimed it to be: a central front in the war against terror. "Despite entering the fourth year after September 11," bin Laden jeered, "Bush is still deceiving you and hiding the truth from you, and therefore the rea-

sons are still there to repeat what happened." Whether the tape reelected George Bush or not, Americans bitterly resented both the timing and the message, no matter what they thought about the intelligence
fiasco, or whether they harbored darker thoughts about the war's origins.

Allawi's tenure proved less secure. It was believed, said one Western
diplomat in Baghad, that he was more acceptable to the Iraqi people.
"Though whenever I see him, I have to force myself not to think of Tony
Soprano." *The Sopranos* ran on HBO for many seasons, as Tony struggled
with the FBI and rival gangs, but Iyad lost out in an election in January
2005. His major sponsor, Robert Blackwill, now a partner in the Republican lobbying firm of Barbour Griffith & Rogers, hid his disappointment
well, if he was disappointed, and called the election a triumph for Bush's
foreign policy, as voters defied death threats to turn out in large numbers
to help get the wagons of democracy rolling in the Middle East. Allawi,
he said, might still emerge as a compromise candidate for prime minister,
having received over a million votes. He did not, and the job went instead to Nouri al-Maliki. But Blackwill, known as "the Shadow" back in
2004 when he promoted Allawi, was right on another count. "I see no
evidence," he said in an interview, that the new government "will want
to have a timetable for a U.S. troop withdrawal from Iraq."[68]

American discontent with Maliki would smolder along for the next
two years and more, but who else was there? In the summer of 2007
Allawi made news again by paying Blackwill's agency $300,000 to pro-
vide him with "strategic counsel and representation." Other former Bush
officials, such as Secretary of State Condi Rice's longtime trusted aide
Philip Zelikow, now worked at Barbour Griffith, and were outspoken
about Maliki's failures. Time was running out for Maliki, said Zelikow in
an interview. "I can confidently guess that our government is quietly
speculating about a lot of different options, knowing how much concern
Iraqis have about their leadership."[69]

Making Iraq safe for democracy, after four years of occupation, was
still tricky business.

THE DREAM DIES HARD, IN WHICH THE ADMINISTRATION LOSES THE MANDATE OF THE PEOPLE

SECRETARY RUMSFELD: *We're so impatient, you know, as a people.*

SEAN HANNITY: *It's a big part of it, isn't it?*

SECRETARY RUMSFELD: *Impatience is a good thing in the sense that it makes people want to get things in hand, it can be—it can lead you to wrong decisions, because if there's any—think of the Cold War. That took persistence. That took successive administrations, both political parties—*

SEAN HANNITY: *And Ronald Reagan.*

SECRETARY RUMSFELD: *You bet. Harry Truman, as well.*

SEAN HANNITY: *Absolutely.*
> —Exchange between Sean Hannity of FOX News and Secretary of
> Defense Donald Rumsfeld, October 27, 2006

We've had to do some difficult things. We've had to make clear that the war on terrorism has to be fought, has to be fought on the offense. While people may not always agree with our policy, they love the United States. This is still a beacon of hope for the world.
> —Secretary of State Condoleezza Rice, September 19, 2006

President Bush declared his reelection a mandate on the war. "We had an accountability moment," he told interviewers, "and that's called the 2004 elections." Aboard Air Force One at the head of a long table, Bush was relaxed as he discussed his second-term plans. "The American people listened to different assessments made about what was taking place in Iraq, and they looked at the two candidates, and chose me."[1]

His inaugural speech would focus on his vision for spreading democracy around the world; he sounded almost like Jimmy Carter when he launched his human rights presidency. But he also expected to ask Congress to appropriate $100 billion for "emergency spending" on the Iraq war. "Sometimes the unexpected will happen," he explained, "both good and bad." The American people needed to show some patience as Iraq moved toward a democracy after so many years suffering under a dictatorship. "If we are not diligent and firm, there will be parts of the world that become pockets for terrorists to find safe haven, and to train. And we have a duty to disrupt that."

But what about the most notorious terrorist of them all, Osama bin Laden? Why hadn't he been found? Bush quipped, "Because he's hiding." But he was isolated, and someday he would be brought to justice. "I think he will be." Asked then about America's diminished standing "in some parts of the world," Bush allowed that there were problems on that front. "There's no question we've got to continue to do a better job of explaining what America is all about."

Osama isolated—but not caught—was actually useful to George Bush, strange as that may sound. In that position he helped the president maintain his knife-edge balance between claiming credit for no new terrorist outrages on American soil, and warnings that the slightest letup in the war would surely unleash untold horrors far beyond what had happened on 9/11. Iraq was now the central front, he kept repeating, in the war on terror. The World War II era was the favorite reference point for the administration, starting with the Pearl Harbor analogy and continuing into the beginning of the Cold War. The twenty-first-century ideological battle for world supremacy with Islamic radicals was just like those struggles, it was argued, with fascism and communism—and the stakes were once again winner takes all.

What Would It Take?

During the above interview with *Washington Post* reporters, the president refused to say if there could be a significant troop reduction in Iraq before the end of his second term in January 2009. "The sooner the Iraqis are . . . better prepared, better equipped to fight, the sooner our troops can start coming home." The mantra—we will stand down when they stand up—became the most familiar nonestimate over next two

years about what it would take, culminating, of course, in the announcement of the "surge" in January 2007 that brought troop strength to over
one hundred sixty thousand as the president entered the last quarter of
his presidency. Bush's frequent vows to hold the home front steady until
his commanders in Iraq, from generals George W. Casey to David Petraeus, told him the enemy had been vanquished, and soldiers could start
coming home, made it seem as if, unlike LBJ, he would listen to the generals. For some attuned to other aspects of the late Bush presidency, it
sounded like the president had abandoned Harry Truman's famous motto
"The buck stops here."

The January 2005 election made Nouri al-Maliki the new prime minister, but the insurgency showed no signs of abating. After a bombing attack shattered the golden dome on a famous Shiite shrine in Samarra on
February 22, 2006, the violence exploded into a nationwide outpouring
of rage. "Shiite militia members flooded the streets of Baghdad," reported the New York Times, "firing rocket-propelled grenades and machine guns at Sunni mosques as Iraqi Army soldiers—called out to stop
the violence—stood helpless nearby. By the day's end, mobs had struck
27 Sunni mosques in the capital, killing three imams and kidnapping a
fourth."[2]

On July 26, 2006, Maliki addressed Congress, as public support for the
war continued to diminish, and the administration's faith in the prime
minister's ability to do much about the violence began to ebb as well. "I
know that some of you here question whether Iraq is part of the war on
terror," he said, and went on to describe his country as the scene of a battle going on between "true Islam . . . and terrorism, which wraps itself in
a fake Islamic cloak." Iraq, he said, was in the "vanguard for defending
the values of humanity. . . . The fate of our country and yours is tied.
Should democracy be allowed to fail in Iraq and terror permitted to triumph, then the war on terror will never be won elsewhere."

Maliki's stout-hearted rhetoric was exactly the sort of thing the Bush
administration wanted to hear, but from the beginning policy makers
had their doubts about his ability to turn things around. There might be
an ambassador sitting in the Green Zone now instead of a viceroy, but
L. Paul Bremer's Order 17 was still in force, with its extraterritorial-style
exemptions of foreign personnel from prosecution, and the new Iraqi intelligence service was organized, and paid for, by the CIA. The head of
the new Iraqi National Intelligence Service (INIS), Mohammed Abdul-

lah Shahwani, was a longtime opponent of Saddam Hussein, and had attempted a coup against the dictator. In retaliation Saddam executed three of his sons. Before that, however, Shahwani had been a high-level officer in the Iraq-Iran War, and his reputation as a fighter made him stand out as another possible asset for the postwar era, alongside Chalabi and Allawi, the other two contenders funded for years by the agency.

In the aftermath of the initial phase of the war, the CIA sent more than five hundred operatives to Iraq, more than were in Vietnam at the height of that conflict, and Shahwani was installed as the head of INIS. It was hoped that he could create a "neutral" agency that would give the new government good intelligence, whoever wound up in charge. His closest ally became Allawi, during the brief period from July to December 2004 that the latter led the provisional government. During all this time, nevertheless, he continued to report to the CIA. When Maliki came to power, U.S. forces "stashed the sensitive national intelligence archives of the past year inside American headquarters in Baghdad in order to keep them off-limits to the new government."[3]

It was not much of a vote of confidence in Maliki, but American officials feared that his government would turn over files to Iranian agents, who, it was believed, might well have special ways of getting inside information from his supposedly pro-Tehran administration. Maliki decided to create a second intelligence agency operating out of the ministry for national security. "It's a ministry I created," complained Allawi, "but things have been spun around." The prime minister continued spinning things around, charging Shahwani with corruption. Allawi suggested that such charges were really an attack on American intelligence.

The outcome of the shadow struggle between Maliki and Allawi continued to remain in doubt; but however much the prime minister echoed President Bush's words about Iraq as the central front in the war on terror, the distrust between Washington and Baghdad continued to grow. While Maliki stayed on message in public, declaring that American troops would have to remain until the security of the nation was beyond question, Bush officials wondered if, in the end, they were not helping to establish a pro-Iranian government. As Washington focused more and more on the argument that Iraq was the central front in the war on terrorism, it opened itself up to other complications. Thus Maliki was able to project himself as the key figure, by declaring, as he did in his appear-

ance before Congress, that the objectives of the United States and Iraq
were identical. "Should democracy be allowed to fail in Iraq," he had
said, "and terror permitted to triumph, then the war on terror will never
be won elsewhere."

But the complications were not limited to Iraq. Bush would find himself in a quandary in a few months about how to deal with General (or
president, depending upon the day) Pervez Musharraf, Pakistan's dicta-
torial leader, who reaped billions from Washington in the post-9/11 war
on terror. He was determined not to relinquish any power to the opposition headed by an American favorite, former prime minister Benazir
Bhutto, whose return from years in exile had been managed by Secretary
of State Rice in an effort to preempt a political upheaval. The second
Bhutto set foot in Pakistan the troubles began. The administration's
scheme for dealing with increasing Pakistani discontent was to have
Musharraf continue to head up the army while Bhutto would attract the
loyalty of the democrats. But Musharraf made it clear that he was having
none of it by declaring a state of emergency and arresting dozens of opposition leaders. The constitution was suspended, and future elections
put in doubt. The Bhutto alternative was a risky one, since she was now
seen as an American pawn whose previous tenure as prime minister had
brought charges of corruption and led to her exile.

Bush's desire to spread democracy in the Middle East was also suspended, as Washington's reaction to these events was—"muted." Rice
said the situation was under review, but it was necessary to remember
that President Bush's first concern was "to protect America and protect
American citizens by continuing to fight against terrorists." There was
no move to curtail American aid as the crisis developed, only a plea from
the White House that Musharraf restore democracy in a timely fashion
by holding scheduled elections. While critics of Washington's policy
might question where much of the $10 billion Pakistan had received had
been spent, an aide to Musharraf pinpointed the predicament created by
rhetoric the administration had used to rally flagging support for the Iraq
War. "If your agenda is to save attacks in the U.S. and eliminate al
Qaeda, only the Pakistani Army can do that," said the aide. "For that,
you will have to forget about elections in Pakistan for maybe two to
three years."[4]

The Bhutto gambit had gone awry. Moreover, she raised exactly the wrong questions about American Middle East policies in a *New York Times* op-ed piece ironically titled, "Musharraf's Martial Plan." "Let us be perfectly clear," she wrote, "Pakistan is a military dictatorship." No one knew exactly where the $10 billion from America had gone, she noted, but clearly it had not led to the defeat of the Taliban and al Qaeda, nor to the capture of Osama bin Laden and suppression of the opium trade. "It certainly has not succeeded in improving the quality of life of the children and families of Pakistan. . . . I recall the words of President Bush in his second Inaugural address when he said: 'All who live in tyranny and hopelessness can know: the United States will not ignore your oppression, or excuse your oppressors. When you stand for liberty, we will stand with you.'"[5]

The question of whether Bhutto was a pro-American plant designed to move Pakistani politics in a somewhat different direction was made moot by her assassination on December 27, 2007. The murky circumstances of her death and the ensuing trial of two men (one a teenager), described by the government as pro-Taliban fanatics, raised more speculation about the long-term value of Washington's investment in Musharraf. Her party won parliamentary elections, but it remained unclear how much would change. When Robert Gates, Bush's second defense secretary, hinted in January 2008 that the United States would be willing to send a limited number of American troops to Pakistan to fight al Qaeda and Taliban guerrillas near the Afghan borders, Musharraf rejected the offer out of hand.

The Army You Have

A sarcastic quip went the rounds that only in comparison to Pakistan did the outlook for Iraqi democracy look good. In Iraq, after deposing a murderous dictator, the United States had, in Lincoln's famous phrase, created a house divided against itself. The ensuing effort to deflect criticism and shape reality more in consonance with presumptions led policy makers back to Cold War themes. Thus Washington stressed the role of "foreign agents" operating against the Iraqi government and American troops. On August 4, 2005, Pentagon and intelligence officials leaked a story to NBC and CBS that American troops had intercepted dozens of shaped charges (special IEDs with enhanced penetrative powers) smuggled into Iraq from Iran. The leaks coincided with Defense Secretary

Donald Rumsfeld's accusations that the shaped charges were "clearly, unambiguously from Iran." The accusation was soon picked up by other policy makers, who had no really firsthand experience with the intelligence, and who fell back to assertions. "I think there is plenty of evidence that there is Iranian involvement with these networks that are making high-explosive IEDs," said Secretary Rice, echoing her mushroom cloud alerts, "that are endangering our troops, and that's going to be dealt with."[6]

The accusations served several purposes. They provided additional reasons to explain the inability to bring the Iraqi "situation" under control, and they focused attention on Iran as a dangerous rogue state led by fanatics who, if permitted to go ahead with their nuclear program, would use atomic threats to intimidate neighbors, and even the world. Finding evidence to back up the accusations was quite another matter, however. Despite show-and-tell briefings in Baghdad, the administration failed to make its case. Nevertheless, in an atmosphere of increasing Iran-America tensions, they served to keep the pressure on wavering congressional support for the war.

At the outset of Gulf War II, Donald Rumsfeld had stood tall at the Pentagon podium deflecting potentially embarrassing questions with the greatest of ease. Then, on December 8, 2004, at what was labeled a "town hall" meeting in Kuwait, the secretary of defense began by reminding his audience of soldiers that it was the sixty-third anniversary plus one day of the Japanese attack on Pearl Harbor, December 7, 1941. As it was then, a new generation of Americans had been called forth to defend freedom. There was no finer legacy, he went on, than to be part of "the world's forward strategy for freedom," and the nation was deeply grateful to them for all that they were doing. With those salutations, he promised to answer all the tough questions they might have, to the best of his knowledge.

At first the questions gave him no trouble. Then came one about the lack of armor for the vehicles that would carry them north into Iraq. "Why do we soldiers have to dig through local landfills for pieces of scrap metal and compromise ballistic glass to up-armor our vehicles, and why don't we have those resources readily available to us?" The transcript records at this point, "[Applause]." Rumsfeld said he was aware of the problem. Vehicles from all over the world were being taken to assembly points and rearmored at a rate of about four hundred a month, he began, then realized that talking about failures to anticipate the weapons Iraqi insurgents would use against American forces offered critics an opening. So he attempted to elaborate—and made things worse for himself and the administration:

> As you know, you go to war with the Army you have. They're not the Army you might want or wish to have at a later time. Since the Iraq conflict began, the Army has been pressing ahead to produce the armor necessary at a rate that they believe—it's a greatly expanded rate from what existed previously, but a rate that they believe is the rate that is all that can be accomplished at this moment.[7]

Rumsfeld may have meant to say "you go to war with the *armor* you have," but it came out sounding like a very strange answer to a question about inadequate equipment. What had happened to the post-Vietnam Army if it was not yet what "you might want or wish to have"? Rumsfeld and his immediate predecessors had taken great pride in rebuilding the army on an entirely new basis since the last days of the Vietnam War. But not only that, his answer admitted that there was continuing inability to keep up with the requirements for armored vehicles, as the insurgency deepened and IEDs became the leading cause of American deaths.

That question and answer was followed by more hostile questions about logistics, and about differences in equipment between regular forces and National Guard troops—who would make up large numbers of the forces in Iraq—and about the "all-volunteer" army that had replaced the draftee army of the Vietnam years. "My husband and myself," began a staff sergeant from North Carolina, "we both joined a volunteer army. Currently, I'm serving under the stop-loss program. I would like to know how much longer do you foresee the military using this program?" The stop-loss program revealed the hidden weakness of the Pentagon's reliance on an all-volunteer force in any situation like Gulf War II. Invoking it in June 2004 to prevent thousands of enlistees from leaving the army by adding months to duty tours beyond contracted terms not only lowered morale but also was a bad advertisement for future recruiting. Obviously, Rumsfeld replied, it was something you prefer not to use, but, except in a perfect world, sometimes it was necessary to protect unit cohesion. "My guess is that it will continue to be used as little as possible, but that it will continue to be used."

On that ambiguous note, Rumsfeld brought the town meeting to an end. Both questions and their less-than-responsive answers made newspaper headlines the next day. "Rumsfeld Gets Earful From Troops" was the title of Thomas Ricks's article in the *Washington Post*. Democrats on Capitol Hill were the harshest critics, labeling Rumsfeld's comments "callous" and "contemptuous." But one retired four-star general who spoke on condition of anonymity said senior officers and sergeants were worried that "we are breaking a small, great professional force." And a former civilian at the Pentagon added that Rumsfeld acts less like a head coach and more like the owner of the football team. "For this reason, he doesn't do well at 'win one for the Gipper'–type speeches."[8]

These responses to Rumsfeld's performance indicated several things, not just about the secretary's performance at the podium, or the management of America's huge investment in defense since the beginning of Gulf War II, but about the conception of the nation's role in world leadership itself. The media in general continued to support the fiction that, yes, this war was a continuation of themes begun in World War II that Rumsfeld had invoked as "the world's forward strategy for freedom," even down to the repeated error of calling the soldiers GIs in articles on military actions in Afghanistan and Iraq. Few even remembered that GI meant General Inductee, someone who had been drafted to serve in the armed forces, the last so serving in Vietnam.

The "new" Army Rumsfeld had pushed to create had several precedents in the "foreign legions" of the European colonial powers and, more recently, as the result of failure in Operation Eagle Claw, Jimmy Carter's failed attempt to rescue hostages at the American embassy in Iran in 1980 that contributed to Ronald Reagan's victory. The Special Operations Command (SOCOM) was created in 1987 to provide what was thought to have been missing in Eagle Claw—close coordination among all the services to carry out missions within states where American interests were endangered in some way. In 2003, at a change-of-command ceremony, Rumsfeld praised SOCOM's role in defending the nation in the war on terror. "It is an honor to be here among these warriors who are, paradoxically, both the best, and probably the least-known, in the world."[9]

SOCOM was a successor, in some ways, to the Green Berets, but with a much more ambitious agenda, as a semiclandestine force with an aura of the cavalry riding to the rescue in a Saturday afternoon matinee. Their role was pivotal, said Rumsfeld, "in this global fight to preserve our freedom." By boasting about their secret role the secretary added that spoonful of mystery always so essential to the notion that the government—and only the government—knew enough about the enemy to fight the evil, and with what weapons. Here is how Rumsfeld described how ordinary people should understand SOCOM as their first line of defense in a world threatened by the forces of darkness.

> When the war began, our commander in chief, President George Bush, said it would require many battles, seen and unseen, with victories that are "secret even in success," and you, of course, are fighting that unseen war on terror. And though most Americans know little about your truly remarkable exploits, they do take comfort in knowing that you're in the fight.

SOCOM by itself could not fight the war in Iraq, of course. And the new Army would also rely heavily on new techniques to secure volunteers, as well as National Guard resources and reservists. In addition, private subcontractors and individual firms doing reconstruction work would replace large numbers of soldiers who had performed such tasks in previous conflicts, both abroad and at home. All these innovations were predicated on short wars won quickly, through shock and awe and high-tech weapons.

Rumsfeld's Secret Army

SOCOM offered an operational solution to the problem of the character of places that had never entered the posthistorical world, like Afghanistan—but presumably anywhere, for example in Africa or Latin America. In Ronald Reagan's administration, CIA director William Casey had yearned for an off-the-shelf capacity to carry out covert missions that would never come under congressional scrutiny. His experiment in that area ended up as the Iran-Contra scandal. Vice President Dick Cheney had done his best to reverse the restrictions of the War Powers Act, but with 9/11 Rumsfeld gained a free running to make SOCOM into that clandestine force. At the 2003 change-of-command ceremony, he put it as plain as it possibly could be:

The war on terror is not a war that we asked for. But it is a war that we must fight, and we must win. There is no safe, easy middle ground. Either we take this war to the terrorists and fight them where they are, or we will have to deal with them here at home. All over the world people long for what we have, for what you, the men and women in uniform standing before us and their associates, defend: liberty, democracy, and a future without fear. That is why we must prevail.[10]

Like his answer to the soldier in Kuwait, Rumsfeld's language was ambiguous. The comment could be read to mean that the rest of the world wished it could have a SOCOM force, but only America did, and that that justified its moral position. In the run-up to the invasion of Iraq, Rumsfeld protested that the war about to begin was not about oil, as critics charged. "Nonsense," he said in November 2002. "It just isn't. There are certain things like that, myths, that are floating around. I'm glad you asked. It has nothing to do with oil, literally nothing to do with oil." After the invasion, however, he dealt with critics and the oil question from a different perspective.

The fact of the matter is—if Saddam Hussein were still in power in Iraq, he would be rolling in petro dollars. Think of the price of oil today. He would have so much money. And he would be seeing the Iranians interested in a nuclear program, he would be seeing the North Koreans developing a nuclear program, and he'd say, well why shouldn't he—and he would. So we're fortunate that he's gone.[11]

Rumsfeld would argue that both statements were accurate. The war was not about oil, but about what America's enemies could do with oil. It is much too simple to argue that the war was fought to establish either a "new" Army, or an imperial presidency, and it is not being argued here that that was the case, but for many years Cheney and Rumsfeld had dreamed of just such an opportunity to achieve just these ends. Now it had happened. You fight with the army you have, Rumsfeld had told the soldier, and you use the circumstances you have to shape that army.

The central theme argued throughout this book was perfectly expressed in this statement by Secretary Rumsfeld. From the time of the Iranian Revolution the United States sought a way and a place to change

Middle Eastern politics. Iraq was going to be both, it now seemed clear, but not in the direction Washington desired.

For years other branches of the executive had been losing out to the Pentagon, without too much of a fight, whether it was in terms of the intelligence budget or the dominant voice in foreign affairs. In a series of articles, the *Washington Post* detailed Rumsfeld's vision for SOCOM (it was about the only media source to do so), and outlined what they implied for the civil-military relationship. In January 2004 the *Post* reported, "Under Rumsfeld's direction, secret commando units known as hunter-killer teams have been ordered to 'kick down the doors,' as the generals put it, all over the world in search of al Qaeda members and their sympathizers." A year later the *Post* followed up on Rumsfeld's "new espionage arm," the secret Strategic Support Branch, created because the defense secretary wished to end his "near total dependence on CIA" for human intelligence (HUMINT). Rumsfeld sought to be able to employ a range of methods, from interrogation of prisoners to the recruitment of foreign spies, including "notorious figures" whose links to the U.S. government might prove embarrassing if disclosed. But the espionage missions were also cover, the article disclosed, for other activities. Assistant Secretary of Defense Thomas O'Connell, who oversaw SOCOM, asserted that his boss had discarded the "hide-bound way of thinking" and "risk-averse mentalities" of previous Pentagon officials "under every president since Gerald R. Ford."[12]

Watergate and Iran-Contra were nowhere as fraught with perils to the Constitution as what Pentagon officials called Rumsfeld's "secret Army of northern Virginia." Asked to describe a scenario where the Strategic Support Branch might play a role, Secretary O'Connell happily obliged. "A hostile country close to our borders suddenly changes leadership. . . . We would want to make sure the successor is not hostile."[13] Within a few weeks it emerged, in yet another *Post* article, that Rumsfeld wanted his special operations forces to be able to enter a country and conduct operations without explicit concurrence from the U.S. ambassador: "In Pentagon policy circles, questions about chief-of-mission authority are viewed as part of a broad reassessment of how to organize the U.S. government optimally to fight terrorism. In this view, alternative models of U.S. military, diplomatic and intelligence authority—possibly tailored to specific countries and situations—should be considered." The Pentagon view was that the war against terror requires similar freedom to prosecute as the war in Iraq. The State Department finally felt it had to make a stand against these incursions. Chief-of-mission authority was a pillar of presidential authority overseas, said an official familiar with the struggle between State and Defense. "When you start eroding that, it can have repercussions that are . . . risky." Colin Powell's chief aide, Deputy Secretary of State Richard Armitage, instructed his counterterrorism coordinator, J. Cofer Black, to act as point man to thwart the Pentagon's initiative. "I gave Cofer specific instructions to dismount, kill the horses, and fight on foot—this is not going to happen."[14]

At first, Powell's successor, Condi Rice, stood up against encroachment on chief-of-mission authority, but the erosions continued. In 2004 Rumsfeld first won approval from Bush for putting SOCOM in charge of the global war on terrorism, and in a privileged position vis-à-vis State and the CIA. Its budget grew accordingly, to $8 billion in fiscal 2007.[15] And finally Rumsfeld got the executive order he wanted, wrote Ann Scott Tyson, who had first pursued the question of SOCOM's challenge to chief-of-mission authority. "In a subtle but important shift contained in a classified order last year," she wrote on April 23, 2006, "the Pentagon gained the leeway to inform—rather than gain the approval of—the U.S. ambassador before conducting military operations in a foreign country. . . . 'We do not need ambassador-level approval,' said one defense official familiar with the order."[16]

The Real Army

Whatever the consequences of these decisions, it is certain that traditional boundaries have broken down. The regular Army, meanwhile, tried to fill recruiting quotas by paying large bonuses, and providing a fast track to citizenship for immigrants, among other methods of recruitment. But it was not enough, as despite increasing age limits, accepting high-school dropouts, lowering passable grades on standard tests, and increasing immigrant access to citizenship still saw some goals go unmet.

The regular Army remained a safety valve for a variety of recruits, on the other hand, not only from poverty-blighted communities, but especially from far-flung areas. Army recruiters turned to U.S. territories in the Pacific, stretching from Pago Pago in American Samoa to Yap in Micronesia, four thousand miles to the west, and found a small bonanza. Army salaries have no difficulty competing with the average income in such places. "'You can't beat recruiting here in the Marianas, in Micronesia,' said First Sergeant Olympio Magofna, who grew up on Saipan and oversees Pacific recruiting for the Army from his base in Guam. 'In the states, they are really hurting,' he said. 'But over here, I can afford [to] go play golf every other day.'"[17]

The overall numbers from such areas are small, and little more than a finger in the dike. By the end of 2006 the Army faced serious shortfalls in funding. "It's kind of like the old rancher saying 'I'm going to size the herd to the amount of hay that I have,'" said the Army's top budget official. "[He] can't size the herd to the size of the amount of hay that he has because he's got to maintain the herd to meet the current operating environment."[18]

Army chief of staff General Peter Schoomaker took the dramatic step of withholding a required budget plan for 2008, after protesting to Rumsfeld that the service could not maintain its current level of activity in Iraq and its other commitments without billions in additional funding. All the services had relied on supplemental appropriations to cover war costs, but perpetual uncertainties over such funding, which were not part of the budget cycle, hit the Army the hardest, as the service most heavily involved in Iraq.

The Army had a backlog of thousands of pieces of equipment awaiting repair, reported Schoomaker, because there was not enough money to pay for the repairs more quickly. At the Red River Army Depot in Texas, for example, nearly fifteen hundred humvees, Bradley Fighting Vehicles, and trucks awaited repairs; another five hundred M1 tanks and hundreds of other tracked vehicles were backlogged at Anniston Army Depot in northeastern Alabama. The ongoing rotations of troops in and out of Iraq, along with increased wear and tear on equipment, created what Schoomaker called, "a slope of diminishing returns."[19]

There were other American forces in Iraq, however, and these continued to grow steadily. Counting both security guards such as Blackwater and civilian contractors, this force rose from 10,000 in September 2003 to more than 160,000 by 2008. General Shinseki did not have these auxiliaries in mind when he testified that it would take hundreds of thousands of soldiers more than Rumsfeld had decided were necessary. Given that they did many jobs previously assigned to uniformed personnel in other wars, one might argue he had actually underestimated the real totals needed to reconstruct Iraq. "The private sector is so firmly embedded in combat, occupation, and peacekeeping duties that the phenomenon may have reached the point of no return: the U.S. military would struggle to wage war without it."[20]

Eager mercenaries, who could earn thousands of dollars a month, were recruited from many countries, especially in Eastern Europe and Latin America. Blackwater found Chile a particularly good recruiting ground for commandos, who had received their military training in the days of dictator Augusto Pinochet. El Salvador, to take another example, had sent three hundred regular soldiers to stand in the ranks of the coalition of the willing, but twice that number worked for private security companies doing everything from KP duty to guarding oil installations and senior personnel. They came from faraway Fiji, the Philippines, and India. By March 2005 their numbers had doubled to twenty thousand—more than twice the British contingent.[21]

Anne Garrels, a reporter in Iraq for National Public Radio, discussed the contrasting lifestyle of the private army from the interior of the Green Zone, the four-square-mile redoubt in the center of Baghdad that houses the Iraqi government and the American and British embassies, as well as thousands of employees dedicated to building the new Iraq. After securing the seven different security badges one must obtain to travel around through the various offices, the PX, and the McDonald's restaurant, Garrels was taken to the Bunker Bar, where the ceiling is covered with parachutes and the walls hung with automatic weapons. The manager or owner told her that army grunts are not allowed in the bar, which was filled with security men hired by the contractors. These men, the owner went on, have a once-in-a-lifetime (maybe) opportunity to earn a lot of money, $15,000 to $20,000 a month. They come from the United States, from Sri Lanka, from Fiji—from all over the world. Garrels noted that they all looked like "Yul Brynner on steroids." Indeed, she went on, steroids seem to be the drug of choice in Iraq.[22]

Quite aside from the Yul Brynner types, who serve as models for the computer games that rule the lives of teenage Americans (of all ages), the second Iraq war has seen the war service industry expand and become a permanent fixture in the larger Pentagon order of battle. The outsourcing of supplies and support to huge megacompanies like Halliburton and its subsidiary Kellogg Brown & Root has created a host of new problems for the military, as well as serious legal and constitutional questions about how possible it is to hold contractors to account who fail to perform in combat zones out of an unwillingness to take risks.

Within contractor ranks, moreover, were divisions of labor and pay scale, with TCNs (third-country nationals) on the lower end. Many of these were from Asian countries, where average annual incomes were around $4,000, or less. To them a salary that doubled that figure offered a good living. Their pay came out of the $24 billion that the U.S. government had let to private American contractors, and was the principal argument for why private enterprise could supposedly do the job less expensively. Poor living conditions, substandard food, and delayed paychecks were often the lot of the TCNs, who were the opposites of the semiglamorous, sunglassed sentinels hired by the State Department to guard diplomatic convoys. Those from the poorer countries were available at almost bargain-basement prices, $15,000 a year compared to the salaries Americans got, up to $150,000. Promises were made—and often broken—about American citizenship for veterans of these armies. Secretary Rice, whose diplomats are protected by Blackwater USA guards, was bullish on the program. "If it's well managed," she said, "and we look at it very, very closely—then I'm quite sure we're going to continue to make use of contract security."[23]

Authors Dina Razor and Robert Bauman, with years of experience in investigative journalism and fraud in DOD contracts, concluded:

> Whether or not contractors will ultimately be subject to military law, it remains [that] the contractors' emphasis on profit over all else clashes sharply with the priorities of the Army. Capitalism simply does not mesh with the way the Army operates on the battlefield. Business and the military operate on different value systems and rules of employment. Army personnel take a strict oath and give up some of their rights in order to fight effectively as a unit. The contractor and its employees, no matter how patriotic they may feel, have their own self-interest as their number one priority.[24]

No matter how such questions are resolved, moreover, the authors argue that the war service industry—in its infancy when Rumsfeld took over the reins at the Pentagon—has now become a crucial sector of the nation's defense structure. What form will it take in the future? The premise was that logistics support and certain security duties could be done more efficiently and cheaply by private enterprise, thereby "freeing up more troops to be trigger pullers. That was the theory. In reality, however, privatization has had a negative impact on the troops in war zones."[25]

Without the ability to force contractors to enter a war zone, or to provide other critical support functions, military units and individual soldiers are left scrambling to carry out their missions. Often their equipment is inferior to that of the contractors. And there have been accusations that weapons brought in by the contractors wind up being sold to insurgents. Such concerns appeared to have little impact on the administration's attitude about outsourcing. The value of all contracts signed by the federal government since 2000 had doubled in the Gulf War era, to $412 billion a year, with the Defense Department by far the biggest awarder. The latest Pentagon department to increase its outsourcing was the Defense Intelligence Agency (DIA), which in 2007 announced that it would award contracts totaling more than $1 billion to private firms. Before the war began, of course, government intelligence agencies had been under attack by the Office of the Vice President, so, it could be argued, the private analysts might indeed offer better analysis, since they would not be reporting to highly motivated political overseers. Perhaps. But it was equally—or more—likely that the record of the private concerns would offer little more, as they competed with one another on performance contracts. What would happen, moreover, asked retired general Anthony Zinni, when these contractors got into the business of planning intelligence operations, a breach in chain of command and control?[26]

"We have almost 300 million Americans who are being protected by 2.4 [million] volunteer active, Guard, and reserve members," the chair of the Joint Chiefs, General Peter Pace, said on January 5, 2006. "We must recruit to that force." He was responding in this particular instance to remarks by Representative John P. Murtha, who had originally supported the war, but now opposed it. He would not volunteer if he were a young man today, Murtha had declared, nor ask others to do so. Pace was upset by the defection. "When a respected leader like Mr. Murtha, who has spent thirty-seven extremely honorable years as a Marine, fought in two wars, has served the country extremely well in the Congress of the United States, when a respected individual like that says what he said,

and eighteen- and nineteen-year-olds look to their leadership to determine how they are expected to act, they can get the wrong message."
Young people should be encouraged to join, not shun, the military, "especially when we're in a war, where our enemy has [the] stated intention
of destroying our way of life."

Pace recycled here yet another variation on the Pearl Harbor, World
War II, "greatest generation" theme, but Murtha was not intimidated.

> The military had no problem recruiting directly after 9/11, because
> everyone understood that we had been attacked. But now the military's
> ability to attract recruits is being hampered by the prospect of prolonged,
> extended, and repeated deployments; inadequate equipment; shortened
> home stays; the lack of any connection between Iraq and the brutal at-
> tacks of 9/11; and—most importantly—the administration's constantly
> changing, undefined, open-ended military mission in Iraq.[27]

Tugs of War

A Cold War Democrat with a history of cooperating with Republicans
on military matters, including Dick Cheney in past years, and a fervent
supporter of Gulf War I, Murtha's defection was a big shock, and it generated ugly rebuttals. Cheney led the assault, which was picked up by
White House press secretary Scott McClellan, who compared the congressman to antiwar filmmaker Michael Moore. McClellan said it was
"baffling that [Murtha] is endorsing the policy positions of Michael
Moore and the extreme liberal wing of the Democratic party." Finally,
President Bush stepped in, as if to calm down his loyalists, who were be-
having as if Murtha *was* Moore, or even Benedict Arnold. He understood, he said, "that the decision to call for an immediate withdrawal of
our troops by Congressman Murtha was done in a careful and thoughtful
way. I disagree with his position. . . . Congressman Murtha is a fine man,
a good man, who served our country with honor and distinction as a Marine in Vietnam and as a U.S. congressman." But Rumsfeld carried on
the administration's attack anyway. As was usual before such verbal
maulings, the defense secretary allowed that it was a free country, and
that everyone had a right to say whatever he wished, but, "put yourself
in the shoes of the enemy. The enemy hears a big debate in the United
States, and they have to wonder, maybe all we have to do is wait, and

we'll win. We can't win militarily. They know that. The battle is here in the United States."[28]

It would be Vietnam all over again, he implied, the war lost on the home front because of a failure of will on the part of the American people. But other hawks had lost feathers as well in scraps over Iraq. Representative Walter Jones, Republican of North Carolina, whose district included the military installations at Camp Lejeune and Cherry Point, had claimed a small place on network news hours with a successful effort in March 2003 to have the House dining hall change the name of its "french fries" to "freedom fries" to show contempt for French behavior at the UN when "America's oldest ally" led the charge against a resolution specifically authorizing military action. At the time most neoconservatives cheered, because now it would be clear that the UN had become, as Bush suggested it would, irrelevant to American policy. Two years later, however, after hearing from several war widows, Walter Jones had some long second thoughts about "freedom fries" and those who had cooked up the war. Laying his cheek in his left hand during a congressional hearing, he sighed, "I wish it had never happened." The nation had gone to war "with no justification," Jones charged, and he demanded an apology from Richard Perle during testimony before the House Armed Services Committee. Perle would not oblige him, of course, and fell back to blaming bad intelligence. Perle even claimed that the nation had been sucked into war by "double agents planted by the regime," who succeeded because of the "appalling incompetence" of the CIA. Jones was left gaping at the absurdity of Perle's pirouette around the truth: "I am just incensed with this statement."[29]

Richard A. Viguerie, the veteran conservative direct-mail consultant, startled fellow Republicans even more than Walter Jones did with his statement that Mr. Bush had "turned the volume up on his megaphone about as high as it could go to try to tie the war in Iraq to the war on terrorism" before the 2004 election. "I just don't think it washes after all these years." In a category all by itself in terms of conservative commentary was the novel by Caspar Weinberger and Peter Schweizer, *Chain of Command: A Thriller*, published in June 2005. In this work of fiction a sitting vice president executes a coup d'etat by first eliminating the president, so that he can fight the war on terror with extralegal methods, beginning with the Freedom From Fear Act, which would take away most of the first ten amendments. Among its political heroes, the novel features a southern senator very much like Sam Ervin of Watergate fame, or more pointedly, Robert Byrd, Bush's sometimes lonely opponent on the floor of the Senate. The novel does not downplay the terrorist menace, but is a cautionary tale about the misuse of foreign threats to achieve perfect "security."[30]

Weinberger, a former secretary of defense in the Reagan administration, now seemed worlds apart from Donald Rumsfeld, who might have stepped out of his novel when he announced that the Pentagon would initiate a special commemoration on the fourth anniversary in 2005 of 9/11. "This year the Department of Defense will initiate an America Supports You Freedom Walk." The line of march will begin at the Pentagon, he said, and end at the National Mall. Participants in this tribute would be invited to a special performance by country singer Clint Black. At the same time there appeared a startling new commentary from Francis Fukuyama, who had signed one of the 1998 letters to Clinton sent by the Project for the New American Century urging action against Iraq. Fukuyama now joined the side of all those late-blooming critics who were arguing that the president ignored choices "in keeping with American foreign policy traditions"—the very sorts of containment policies the neoconservatives abominated as belonging to the historical era. "We do not know what outcome we will face in Iraq. We do know that four years after 9/11 our whole foreign policy seems destined to rise or fall on the outcome of a war only marginally related to the source of what befell us on that day. There was nothing inevitable about this. There is everything to be regretted about it."[31]

Fortress Bush

As public support for their policies dwindled, Bush and Cheney strapped the Pearl Harbor analogy tight to their chests like a bulletproof vest. Cheney stood the main watch on the fortress towers. Thus, when all his predictions about the war had been proven wrong, the vice president went to Camp Lejeune, North Carolina, in early October 2005 to introduce the latest variation on the analogy. "It is tough and it is dangerous to fight enemies who dwell in the shadows," he told Marines who had just returned from Iraq. "Sounds like you're glad to be home." Unfortunately, many of them would have to go back for another tour. There was hard slogging ahead, he knew, but eventually the "terrible threat will be removed from the lives of our children and grandchildren." The threat arose, he now argued, because both Republican and Democratic administrations had failed to retaliate decisively to terrorist attacks stretching back to the 1983 bombing of a Marine barracks in Beirut, and down to the suicide bombing of the USS *Cole* in 2000. The 9/11 tragedy happened because "the terrorists came to believe that they could strike America without paying any price."[32]

The Pearl Harbor analogy could not stand up to careful scrutiny, of course, unless Saddam Hussein was linked directly to 9/11, and after his capture on December 13, 2003, only if al Qaeda could be said to be in control of the insurgency. Otherwise, there was nothing in Cheney's speech to explain why the Marines would have to go back to Iraq to win the war on terrorism. The argument made sense only if it was supposed that American actions had pinned down the terrorists in Iraq, leaving them no place else to go. As the resurgence of the Taliban in Afghanistan dramatically demonstrated, that was not a valid assumption. Cheney and Bush had tried again and again to connect Saddam Hussein with 9/11, finally settling on the vision of a mushroom cloud rather than evidence. In June 2007 and again on the Fourth of July 2007, Bush took Cheney's Lejuene argument to its logical end. Where the vice president had blamed dereliction of duty in the pre-9/11 decades, the president now insisted that Iraq had become the central front in a war to eradicate the sponsors of all the attacks up to and including the ones on American soil. Forget about the idea that Hussein yearned to use WMD; it had always been a war against al Qaeda. "Al Qaeda is the main enemy for Shia, Sunni and Kurds alike," he asserted in a speech at the Naval War College. "Al Qaeda's responsible for the most sensational killings in Iraq. They're responsible for the sensational killings on U.S. soil."[33]

At the end of his Camp Lejeune speech, however, the vice president did give his audience another reason why the Marines would be sent back. "In the broader Middle East and beyond, America will continue to encourage free markets, democracy, and tolerance." Iraq was now the center of the battle for the whole world, just as the war against the World War II axis of evil had made America the leader of the free world.

After the 2004 election, Cheney and other members of the administration oscillated between describing the Iraq War as an existential struggle that would test American will even more than Vietnam had ever done, to celebrating a supposed successful reconstruction on the order of postwar Germany or Japan. The vice president insisted over and over that the insurrection was in its last throes. In June 2005, Wolf Blitzer asked if he wanted to amend that statement. Not at all, said Cheney, but he would explain a bit what "last throes" meant. It no longer meant an immediate end to the violence in this new version, but outlasting the enemy. But there had been free elections, and the establishment of a government. "We will, in fact, succeed in getting a democracy established in Iraq. And I think when we do that will be the end of the insurgency."[34]

The furor about the WMD errors would then blow away, leaving not a trace of recrimination behind. Cheney even expressed sympathy for the intelligence agencies that made the exaggerated reports. "I think the [intelligence] community did, in fact, miss the exact status of the stockpiles at the time. But I don't think there was any question about his intent, or about what he'd done in the past, or the fact that the world is better off without Saddam Hussein." Blitzer shifted to the forgotten man, Osama bin Laden. The new head of the CIA had said he had an excellent idea where bin Laden was hiding out. "Do you?" asked Blitzer. Cheney's response sounded cavalier. "We've got a pretty good idea of a general area that he's in, but I—I don't have the street address." Well, was there some hope he would be found soon, or even not so soon? "What," Cheney retorted, "do you expect me to say, three weeks from next Tuesday? [Laughter.]"

Of course, with bin Laden still at large, it was considerably easier to sell the public on continuing the war on terror, given all the criticisms that had come up not only about the insurrection in Iraq, but also about the domestic measures the administration had persuaded a very willing Congress to enact, beginning with the Patriot Act, and measures it had not informed Congress about as well, such as the wiretaps the National Security Agency had placed on international calls, or the establishment of Guantánamo as a prison "outside" the United States to house terrorist suspects without worrying about American laws protecting the rights of defendants, or the interrogation methods used on suspects at Abu Ghraib prison in Baghdad. In each of these Cheney had played a key role either in the origins of the policies, or in defending them from critics.

By totally conflating al Qaeda in Mesopotamia/Iraq with bin Laden's

9/11 plotters, Cheney and Bush had succeeded in making real at least one of their war claims—that the United States would be fighting bin Laden in Iraq—in a circular fashion. A few months after 9/11, to go back for a moment, Cheney had appeared in the Oval Office with an executive order that would give the president the right to hold suspects indefinitely at the Guantánamo naval base in Cuba, outside the official borders of the United States. Powell had not been told about the decision. He exploded. "What the hell just happened?" What had happened, of course, was that he had been outmaneuvered. Two years later Wolf Blitzer asked Cheney if the "reputation" of Guantánamo was such that it should be shut down. "No," Cheney thundered. "Because?" Blitzer asked. "Because it's a vital facility." Why not move them to Fort Leavenworth? Blitzer persisted, someplace like that. Cheney was incredulous that anyone should think the Guantánamo prisoners were maltreated: "They're very well treated down there. They're living in the tropics. They're well fed. They've got everything they could possibly want. There isn't any other nation in the world that would treat people who were determined to kill Americans the way we're treating these people." Blitzer gave up at that point, pausing only to note a new poll by the Pew Charitable Trust suggested that China had a more favorable image in much of the world than did the United States. "I, frankly, don't spend a lot of time, Wolf, reading polls."[35]

A year and a half after this interview, Cheney faced questions from another reporter, Terry Moran, on an ABC News *Nightline* broadcast. "We don't engage in torture," he insisted. Moran asked about evidence that more than one hundred people in U.S. custody had died, twenty-six of them being investigated as criminal homicide. "No, I won't accept your numbers, Terry. But I guess one of the things I'm concerned about is that as we get farther and farther away from 9/11, and there have been no further attacks against the U.S., there seems to be less and less concern about doing what's necessary in order to defend the country."[36]

In other words, people who questioned interrogation methods were less than patriotic citizens. From such interviews, and his defense of waterboarding as a "no-brainer," Cheney began to be called things like "Darth Vader" and the "vice president in charge of torture." He bristled only at the latter description. Two days after talking with Terry Moran, Cheney again spoke with reporters, who questioned him this time about revelations in the *New York Times* detailing the secret wiretapping program. He thought it was unfortunate that the *Times* had decided to print the report. The paper had held back for a year. "I think it damages national security." But wasn't he concerned about a possible backlash that could end up restricting the president's freedom of action? No, he said, the American people understood that the reason we haven't been hit in four years was because of what the government was doing. "Either we're serious about fighting the war on terrorism or we're not."

> But if there's anything improper in that [the wiretapping and other measures], my guess is that the vast majority of the American people support that, support what we're doing. They believe we ought to be doing it, and so if there's a backlash pending, I think the backlash is going to be against those who are suggesting somehow that we shouldn't take these steps in order to protect the country.[37]

Here was the ultimate justification—the posited general will of the American people, a frightening echo from prewar Europe—even if the measures were improper, or, indeed, in violation of either national or international law. Or, finally, even if at some indeterminate point, there appeared to be a temporary majority against the administration. Here is Cheney speaking on that point as the 2006 congressional elections neared, suggesting that Democrats would thwart that sacred compact between the president and the people, the general will, if they took control. "Unfortunately, at this stage, I think there's some jeopardy, depending on how the election comes out, as to whether or not we'll be able to continue those policies," he told a Fox News Channel reporter. After the election, again on Fox News, Cheney resurrected the arc of crisis image first popularized by Zbig Brzezinski in the Carter administration. "Iraq is just part of the larger war—it is, in fact, a global war that stretches from Pakistan all the way around to North Africa." For the United States to succeed in that global struggle, the Iraq War had to be brought to a successful conclusion. "People have got to have confidence in the United States, that they can count on us. If the United States doesn't have the stomach to finish the job in Iraq, we put at risk what we've done in all of those other locations out there."[38]

Ultimately, then, responded his questioner, Chris Wallace, the United States would do whatever it takes to win. "I believe we will." By choosing the policy you have, Wallace said about plans for the surge, and rejecting the Iraq Study Group's proposals, "haven't you, Mr. Vice President, ignored the express will of the American people in the November election?"

VICE PRESIDENT CHENEY: Well, Chris, this president, and I don't think any president worth his salt, can afford to make decisions of this magnitude according to the polls. The polls change day by day. . . .

CHRIS WALLACE: Well, this was an election, sir.

VICE PRESIDENT CHENEY: Polls change day by day, week by week. I think the vast majority of Americans want the right outcome in Iraq. The challenge for us is to be able to provide that. But you cannot simply stick your finger up in the wind and say, "Gee, public opinion's against us; we'd better quit."

The enemy, he went on, believed that the United States did not have the stomach for the fight, and the election had added to that belief.

They believe it. They look at past evidence of it: Lebanon in '83 and Somalia in '93. Vietnam before that. They're convinced that the United States will, in fact, pack it in and go home if they just kill enough of us. They can't beat us in a stand-up fight, but they think they can break our will.

Cheney was undoubtedly right that most Americans did not want to "lose" in Iraq, despite the polls that Wallace cited showing that 67 percent of the nation wanted to change course. But the implications of the Cheney "doctrine" were frightening, even after the Democrats shriveled before the White House mantra of supporting the troops, or an attorney general candidate who refused to say what the world knew to be true: Waterboarding is torture. Suddenly aroused from five-year torpor, other normally friendly commentators, like CNN's Wolf Blitzer, took up the question of winning and losing, and who was responsible. Commenting on the president's 2007 State of the Union speech, which brought Osama bin Laden back onstage, Blitzer said the speech was all about the consequences of failure, but how much responsibility did the administration have for this scenario? The following dialogue revealed much of what the war had been about.

VICE PRESIDENT CHENEY: Saddam Hussein would still be in power. He would, at this point, be engaged in a nuclear arms race with Ahmadinejad, his blood enemy next door in Iran—

WOLF BLITZER: But he was being contained, as we all know—

VICE PRESIDENT CHENEY: He was not being contained. He was not being contained, Wolf . . . the entire sanctions regime had been undermined by Saddam Hussein. He had—

WOLF BLITZER: But he didn't have stockpiles of weapons of—

VICE PRESIDENT CHENEY: —corrupted the entire effort to try to keep him contained. He was bribing senior officials of other governments. The oil-for-food program had been totally undermined, and he had, in fact, produced and used weapons of mass destruction previously, and he retained the capability to produce that kind of stuff in the future.

WOLF BLITZER: But that was in the eighties.

VICE PRESIDENT CHENEY: You can go back and argue the whole thing all over again, Wolf, but what we did in Iraq in taking down Saddam Hussein was exactly the right thing to do; the world is much safer today because of it. There have been three national elections in Iraq, there's a democracy established there, a constitution, a new democratically elected government. Saddam has been brought to justice and executed, his sons are dead, his government is gone, and the world is better off for it.[39]

Bush had just introduced the surge as his new policy, the reinsertion of nearly thirty thousand troops in an effort to quell the insurrection and sectarian violence. Bush had put General David Petraeus in command, after praising him as the best qualified man in the military to complete the mission. There were no dissenting votes in Congress on Petraeus, but there was only party-line support for the surge. Bush resorted to the LBJ argument about withdrawal during the Vietnam War: His opponents had no other plan, by which he meant, of course, no other plan for an endgame that would keep the dream alive.

> One of the things I've found in Congress is that most people recognize that failure would be a disaster for the United States. And in that I'm the decision maker, I had to come up with a way forward that precluded disaster. In other words, I had to think about what's likely to work.
>
> And so I worked with our military and I worked with Secretary Gates to come up with a plan that is likely to succeed. And the implementor of that plan is going to be General Petraeus. And my call to the Congress is, is that I know there is skepticism and pessimism, and that they are—some are condemning a plan before it's even had a chance to work. And they have an obligation and a serious responsibility, therefore, to put up their own plan as to what would work.[40]

Cheney seconded the president's insistence, in the Blitzer interview, that critics must have a better plan to achieve the administration's goals, or keep silent. "They haven't put anything in place. All they want to do, all they've recommended is to redeploy or to withdraw our forces. The fact is, we can complete the task in Iraq. We're going to do it. We've got Petraeus—General Petraeus taking over. It is a good strategy. It will work. But we have to have the stomach to finish the task."

Bush cited Petraeus 6 times in January, but more than 150 over the next six months. The general who had written his dissertation at Princeton on "The American Military and the Lessons of Vietnam" had been given the job of saving Iraq from becoming a worse example of a misguided military effort than Vietnam. Conservative critics of the American war in Vietnam usually took as their starting point the CIA-engineered coup against Ngo Dinh Diem at the end of October 1963, blaming liberals in the Kennedy administration for the series of unstable military regimes that lasted little more than ten years before final defeat. Petraeus soon teetered close to a deep conflict with the Iraqi prime minister, Nouri al Maliki, over a whole range of policies, including control of the Iraqi military. It was rumored that Maliki told the general on one occasion, "I can't deal with you anymore. I will ask for someone else to replace you."[41]

When it became evident that the jerry-built Iraqi government could not get itself together to enact new oil legislation, Dick Cheney made a trip to Baghdad to attempt to get things moving. The oil question had been a controversial issue since before the invasion, with administration officials vehemently denying it had any connection to Iraq policy—except to say that removal of Saddam Hussein would restore Iraq's oil to world markets, and thus help the Iraqi people. As matters stood before the invasion, the UN oil-for-food program and sanctions instituted after Gulf War I had proved a failure, especially in terms of bringing pressure on Saddam; but there was also the central issue of what the dictator would do if the sanctions were withdrawn, an outcome that could have led to a scramble for concessions in which the United States—as a long-time opponent—would lose out to other countries seeking to get a foothold in what could become, said experts, a "second Saudi Arabia."[42]

Optimism about oil futures ran so high at the time of the invasion in March 2003, that administration officials insisted Iraq could itself pay for the costs of reconstruction after the war. It seems ridiculous in retrospect, but the idea bruited about by Bush officialdom was that the only thing that stood in the way of Iraq's progress and prosperity—in cooperation with the United States—was Saddam Hussein. It was not a new idea, of course, and it went back to Walt Rostow and *The Stages of Economic Growth*, and his belief that what set things in motion for third world countries was—nine times out of ten—a powerful external stimulus.

But four years after the invasion the great bonanza had not been realized. Cheney made an unannounced visit to Baghdad to press Maliki to speed up efforts at reconciliation among the three main groups in Iraq. As Cheney met with the prime minister a mortar shell rattled windows in the Green Zone, the enclave/embassy housing all the young Americans who had come to help the Iraqis create a free-market democracy. These stepchildren of the Peace Corps had become frustrated that they were now being required to wear helmets and vest armor even inside the Green Zone sanctuary. While accompanying newspaper reporters were hustled into a shelter, a Cheney spokeswoman said he was not disturbed: "His business was not disrupted. He was not moved." Especially, it became clear, he was not moved from insisting upon action on the oil legislation, which had bogged down over distribution of the revenues to the various interested groups. A senior official traveling with the vice president said his message boiled down to this: "We've all got challenges together. We've got to pull together. We've got to get the work done. It's game time."[43]

Oil legislation drafts had been making their way up the ladder for quite some time and, impatient Westerners insisted, should now be acted upon. The principal features of the proposed law were the PSAs, production sharing arrangements, that awarded a share of profits to the companies for providing infrastructure. Neither Saudi Arabia nor Iran, the current number one and two producers, had entered into these long-term arrangements. Nor had most countries in the Organization of Pe-troleum Exporting Countries (OPEC). PSAs were a wedge or lever to reenter oil-producing states on something like the old terms, before na-tionalization in 1972. The PSAs paid to foreign countries were supposed to offset exploration and development costs, including, especially in Iraq, the assumed costs associated with security risks. The proposed con-tracts, however, locked in high percentages, up to 20 percent for thirty years. At a June 14, 2006, press conference, President Bush reaffirmed the denial that oil mattered, "The oil of the Iraqi people . . . is their wealth. We did not [invade Iraq] for oil." In 1999, however, CEO Dick Cheney of Halliburton had voiced a different concern: "By 2010 we will need [a further] 50 million barrels a day. The Middle East, with two thirds of the oil and the lowest cost, is still where the prize lies."[44]

After his talks with Maliki, Cheney declared, "I did make it clear that we believe it's very important to move on the issues before us in a timely fashion, and that any undue delay would be difficult to explain." Despite pressure from Washington, the oil law stalled. At one level it was a con-test over divvying up the proceeds between regions, with the Sunni lead-ers especially fearing they would not get a fair share; on another level, it was the nature of the risk-free PSA contracts the law envisioned, by which the companies would not even have to begin investment until stability was restored—postponing any contribution oil could make to Iraq's recovery. At a third level, the oil question was a matter of self-determination in the old Wilsonian sense. "Oil is Iraq's sovereignty," said a leader of the Federation of Oil Unions. "It is the only wealth in Iraq. It unifies Iraqis. When we give it to a foreign investor, this means the sovereignty is taken away."[45]

With the oil legislation stymied, Cheney held a joint press conference with Petraeus and Ambassador Ryan Crocker, both of whom gave the usual upbeat reports, including the general's hailing of progress in building an Iraqi army. "Some 9,000 Iraqi soldiers graduated from training this month alone, just to give you an example," he said, providing evidence "of their own surge." As for the September 15, 2007, congressional deadline on reporting progress, he hedged, saying it would take "several months" after he had all the forces on the ground to provide grounds for assessing the impact, but, yes, by that date, there would have been, "we think, enough of a period to assess the joint security effort." When a reporter asked if there had really been serious progress on the political front, Cheney repeated that he had seen "a greater sense of urgency."

"But no specific time commitments?"

"It's difficult to do with our own Congress, let alone somebody else's."[46]

That was interesting wordplay, using the new Democratic Congress as a backhanded way of excusing lack of action in the Iraqi Parliament. Back in the United States, Cheney addressed the graduating class at West Point, telling them that the enemy they faced sought to impose a world "dictatorship of fear" under which "every man, woman, and child lives in total obedience to their ideology. . . . Their ultimate goal is to establish a totalitarian empire, a caliphate, with Baghdad as its capital. They view the world as a battlefield, and they yearn to hit us again. And now they have chosen to make Iraq the central front in their war against civilization. . . . America is fighting this enemy in Iraq because that is where they have gathered."[47]

But in Iraq the Parliament scattered for an August break. Maliki did not even risk presenting the oil legislation before the legislators departed. In the final days, a Sunni bloc of forty-four announced its intention not to return after the break, further weakening the government amid calls for Maliki to resign. "This is bad news," said a *Wall Street Journal* article, contradicting a positive assessment of the war in a *Times* op-ed piece, "A War We Just Might Win," by Kenneth Pollack and Michael O'Hanlon, who had just returned from a fact-finding trip to Iraq. The op-ed piece talked mostly about military progress as a result of the surge and the new morale of the troops under Petraeus's command. The White House distributed the piece to the press corps as evidence the strategy was working, that morale was high among American troops, and the Iraqi forces were performing much better. Petraeus was determined to hold areas, the two wrote, until they were truly secure, and therefore the increasing competence of the Iraqis was having a critical effect: "[N]o more whack-a-mole, with insurgents popping back up after the Americans leave." The authors did admit, "[W]e still face huge hurdles on the political front." If these continued, all the military success could go up in smoke, as the newly trained Iraqi army splintered along ethnic and religious lines. "The surge cannot go on forever. But there is enough good happening on the battlefields of Iraq today that Congress should plan on sustaining the effort at least into 2008." The coy title "A War We Might Just Win" covered over the echoes of the Vietnam War era's last-ditch call for "Five More Minutes, Five More Minutes." The *Journal* was less optimistic. The Kurds in the north wanted to make the "oil capital," Kirkuk, part of an autonomous Kurdistan, infuriating the Shiite majority that wanted the city under central control. The Congressional Research Service, it noted, had reported that even if the oil legislation finally survived, it remained to be seen whether it would promote reconciliation, or "contribute to deeper political tension." Baghdad, moreover, remained "a particularly bloody place," as bombing attacks killed another seventy people the day the op-ed piece appeared. "But even if Baghdad were quiet, the parliament—including Mr. Maliki's wobbly coalition—would still be on vacation."[48]

Bush reacted to the latest bad news by summoning Maliki to yet another of their periodic videoconferences, opportunities for face-to-face frankness, light-years ahead technologically from anything Kennedy or LBJ could convey during the Vietnam War. "The president emphasized that the Iraqi people and the American people need to see action—not just words—but need to see action on the political front," White House press secretary Tony Snow said. "The prime minister agreed."[49]

There was apparently no way Dick Cheney could help Maliki establish a unitary premiership in Iraq, however. Bush had meanwhile pursued the surge strategy as an alternative to the Iraq Study Group's proposals, and others from critics, that would set a course for a phased withdrawal. At a July press conference he confronted a series of questions about what role Congress should play in Iraq decision making. It could appropriate money, he said, but it should not be running the war. "Congress has all the right in the world to fund. That's their main involvement in this war, which is to provide funds for our troops." It was an interesting example, both of the president's language rules and usage, and his conception of the presidency behind the language. He did not say that it had all the right in the world to fund, *or not to fund*. Therefore, it could not, according to a literal translation of his phrase, determine troop strength or tell the military how to conduct operations.

Bush constantly shifted perspective from "we're making progress" to his insistence that Iraq was only the "beginning" of a supposed decades-long struggle. "As I say, this is the beginning stages of what I believe is an ideological conflict that—where you've got competing visions about what the world ought to be like. . . . And it's in our interest to spread an alternative ideology. . . . We've done this before in our nation's history. We have helped people realize the beginnings of liberty, even though they may have been our enemy."

Over and over again Bush repeated that he had a higher obligation than the polls or critics. He had a higher obligation to protect the nation. "I'm pretty confident our military do not want their commander in chief making political decisions about their future." Harry Truman, a neocon idol in the post–Cold War era, would have done a double take at this statement. So would Dwight Eisenhower, a cautious president who was careful about giving his generals too much say.

"You know," Bush said at the end of this press conference, "I guess I am like any other political figure—everybody wants to be loved, just sometimes the decisions you make and the consequences don't enable you to be loved." Like other presidents in deep trouble, Bush expected to be vindicated by history. He would be able in retirement down at Crawford to look in the mirror and say he had acted on principle.[50]

By late fall 2007 the violence in Baghdad had subsided to levels not seen since the beginning of the insurgency in 2004. The White House, while obviously delighted by the casualty figures, remained cautious about the future. On November 1, 2007, Bush spoke at the Heritage Foundation, a neocon stronghold. He called the terrorists, with Osama now taken off the forgotten-about-as-irrelevant list as the dark force threatening the entire world. "In pursuit of their imperial aims," he said, "these extremists say there can be no compromise or dialogue with those they call infidels—a category that includes America, the world's free nation [*sic*], Jews, and all Muslims who reject their extreme vision of Islam." The [*sic*] appears in the transcript of the president's remarks, almost as if to emphasize Bush's error was a subconscious acceptance that the United States was now alone in Iraq, even if his other words talked about allies. "They're at war with America because they hate what they

[*we*] stand for—and they understand we stand in their way." It was a global fight to the end. "We will not rest, or retreat, or withdraw from the fight until this threat to civilization has been removed."[51]

The president's speeches, which had seemed so appropriate immediately after 9/11, now sounded disjointed, even confused at points. At the July 2007 press conference veteran correspondent Helen Thomas had challenged him directly: "Mr. President, you started this war, a war of your choosing, and you can end it alone, today, at this point—bring in peacekeepers, UN peacekeepers. Two million Iraqis have fled their country as refugees. Two million more are displaced. Thousands and thousands are dead. Don't you understand you brought the al Qaeda into Iraq?"

The president responded with a remarkable statement: "Actually, I was hoping to solve the Iraqi issue diplomatically. That's why I went to the United Nations and worked with the United Nations Security Council, which unanimously passed a resolution that said disclose, disarm, or face serious consequences. That was the message, the clear message to Saddam Hussein. He chose the course." On other occasions Bush had acknowledged the absence of WMD in Iraq, and had taken his stand on the grounds that Saddam Hussein was an evil force in the world no matter the state of his weapons programs. Faced with Thomas's question, however, the president truly left the reality-based world behind. The administration could not get the Security Council to authorize an invasion in 2003, at least not until the inspections had been completed; but more than that, given what everyone in the room that day knew, and had known for at least four years, there was nothing to disclose. The president had chosen the course.

Journalist Ron Suskind's 2002 interview with a White House aide was the best clue to understanding the president's state of mind when confronted by the doubting Thomases of the world. The reality-based community, said the aide, believed that solutions emerged from a "judicious study of discernible reality." Suskind nodded and started to say something about enlightenment principles and empiricism, but the aide cut him off. "'That's not the way the world really works anymore,' he continued. 'We're an empire now, and when we act, we create our own reality. And while you're studying that reality—judiciously, as you will—we'll act again, creating other new realities, which you can study too, and that's how things will sort out. We're history's actors . . . and you, all of you, will be left to just study what we do.'"[52]

How the nation finally deals with the Iraq War is secondary to its response to the implications of such statements in the future—indeed, in the near future. From the first moments of shock at the attack on the World Trade Center and the Pentagon, the Bush doctrine of preemption began to take shape. It would brook no disagreement, whether in the form of Colin Powell's troubled attempts to guide the president to safer ground, or from anyone still living in the reality-based community. September 11 had changed the United States, Bush said. On that point there could be no argument.

WHAT LIES AHEAD, IN WHICH THE MEANING
OF THE WAR IS REVEALED

A point was reached during the Vietnam War when the domestic debate became so bitter as to preclude rational discussion of hard choices. Administrations of both political parties perceived the survival of South Vietnam as a significant national interest. They were opposed by a protest movement that coalesced behind the conviction that the war reflected an amorality that had to be purged by confrontational methods. This impasse doomed the U.S. effort in Vietnam: it must not be repeated over Iraq.

> —Henry A. Kissinger, "The Lessons of Vietnam," May 31, 2007

In the end, we need to recognize that our presence may have released Iraqis from the grip of a tyrant, but that it has also robbed them of their self-respect. They will soon realize that the best way to regain dignity is to call us what we are—an army of occupation—and force our withdrawal.

> —Seven noncommissioned officers, "The War as We Saw It,"
> August 19, 2007

We will not let our people be taken by the Iraqis. In an ideal sense, if there was wrongdoing, there could be a trial brought in the Iraqi court system. But that would imply that there is a valid Iraqi court system where Westerners could get a fair trial. That is not the case right now.

> —Erik Prince, founder and CEO of Blackwater Inc., October 17, 2007

Rumsfeld's successor, Robert Gates, told reporters on June 1, 2007, that he was looking at a "mutual agreement where some force of Americans" would be in Iraq "for a protracted period of time," perhaps on the model of Korea or Japan. That would be the only way to assure America's allies in the Middle East that the United States would not withdraw from Iraq as it had from Vietnam, "lock, stock, and barrel." Six weeks later, however, the House of Representatives passed a resolution banning permanent U.S. bases in Iraq. Speaker Nancy Pelosi vowed, "The Democratic Congress will go on record—every day if necessary—to register a judgment in opposition to the course of action that the president is taking in Iraq."[1]

The bitter partisan debate Kissinger warned about had apparently begun. As the 2008 presidential race began to take shape, however, the leading Democratic hopefuls were by no means so definite about withdrawing American forces from Iraq. On the hustings, Hillary Clinton vowed that she would end the war if elected. But in a half-hour interview with two *Times* reporters her position came out sounding very different. We have "vital national security interests in Iraq," she said. Protecting those interests would require keeping troops there. If Iraq was allowed to become "a petri dish for insurgents and al Qaeda," it would threaten American security, and endanger friendly regimes in the area, especially Israel. And, of course, "it is right in the heart of the oil region." Neither she, nor any of the other candidates, would estimate how many American troops they would keep in Iraq. Like Bush, she said such decisions depended upon advice from the military officers assigned to carry out the strategy.[2]

The force would be what was needed to defeat al Qaeda and deter Iranian aggression, she said. On Iran, indeed, the senator had even gotten out in front of the Bush administration in demanding that the United States take action to pressure the UN to impose sanctions to prevent Tehran from obtaining nuclear weapons. In a speech at Princeton University in 2006 she argued that a nuclear Iran would threaten the state of Israel. U.S. policy must be clear and unequivocal, she said. To prevent Iran from acquiring nuclear weapons, "we must have more support vigorously and publicly expressed by China and Russia, and we must move as quickly as feasible for sanctions in the United Nations." That was why, she added in subsequent campaign speeches, she voted for a resolution labeling Iran's Revolutionary Guards a terrorist organization. It was not a vote, she insisted, to give the president a back door to war.[3]

Freshman senator Jim Webb opposed the resolution, calling it "Dick Cheney's fondest pipe dream."

> We haven't had one hearing on this. I'm on the Foreign Relations Committee, I'm on the Armed Services Committee. We are about to vote on

something that may fundamentally change the way the United States views the Iranian military, and we haven't had one hearing. This is not the way to make foreign policy. It's not the way to declare war.

It passed by a wide margin, with several Democratic senators voting with Republicans. Clinton later joined with Webb on a resolution that prohibited funds appropriated for Iraq to be used for military actions against Iran without congressional approval. Her statement on October 1, 2007, in support of Webb's proposal tried to have it both ways.

Iran has gained expanded influence in Iraq and the region as a result of the Bush administration's policies, which have also rejected diplomacy as a tool for addressing Iranian ambitions. I continue to support and advocate for a policy of entering into talks with Iran, because robust diplomacy is a prerequisite to achieving our aims. I also support strong economic sanctions against Iran, including designating the Iranian Revolutionary Guards as a terrorist organization, to improve our leverage with the Iranian regime.

As the campaign evolved in the early months leading to showdowns in the primaries, Clinton's 2002 vote for Bush's much-desired resolution authorizing the use of military force against Iraq became a central issue as she tried to halt the momentum of Senator Barack Obama. She consistently refused to apologize for the vote, unlike other contenders such as former senator John Edwards. Finally, under intense questioning by Tim Russert, she backed into a statement that she would not have voted that way again.

CLINTON: I've said many times that, although my vote on the 2002 authorization regarding Iraq was a sincere vote, I would not have voted that way again.

I would certainly, as president, never have taken us to war in Iraq. And I regret deeply that President Bush waged a preemptive war, which I warned against and said I disagreed with. . . .

RUSSERT: But to be clear, you'd like to have your vote back?

CLINTON: Absolutely. I've said that many times.[4]

Not quite, but it was still difficult on any matter touching on the Iraq War for a candidate to be as clear as Russert or anybody wished. In this case Senator Clinton did come very close to apologizing, while still calling it a "sincere vote." That curious phrase apparently meant she was sincere in thinking she was not voting for war. Her subsequent votes portray a senator very much concerned about being in line with support for a popular president. Sincere became naive when rivals pointed out she had not bothered to read the 2002 National Intelligence Estimate before the roll call. Had she done so, it was argued, she could have laid a better claim to sincerity. But again, the fact was very few senators bothered to read the document in that atmosphere, and those who did were mostly (but not all) overwhelmed by the slightly hedged assertions that Saddam Hussein was apparently running a WMD program. Senator Jay Rockefeller, for example, who became an opponent of the war and a supporter of Clinton's most serious rival, Barack Obama, was in full-throated hue and cry even after reading the NIE.

> There has been some debate over how "imminent" a threat Iraq poses. I do believe that Iraq poses an imminent threat, but I also believe that after September 11, that question is increasingly outdated. It is in the nature of these weapons, and the way they are targeted against civilian populations, that documented capability and demonstrated intent may be the only warning we get. To insist on further evidence could put some of our fellow Americans at risk. Can we afford to take that chance? We cannot![5]

Only a close study of the document would alert readers that the hedges it contained were not so slight. No one questioned such votes, of course, so long as the war went well. Short wars, to paraphrase an old quip, tell no tales.

But in the fall of 2007 there was a new NIE to debate, one that seemed to catch President Bush unaware. The report, portions of which were made public on December 3, 2007, stated that Iran had discontinued its nuclear weapons program four years earlier. The NIE undercut strident administration warnings and blandishments that had continued even after the White House learned what the report said during the summer. Indeed, only a few weeks before its release, President Bush said Iranian possession of an atomic bomb could lead to "World War III."[6] In reaction to the NIE, White House aides said at first that it demonstrated Washington's tough stance had given Tehran pause. But that did not seem to be enough, especially for Israel, and Bush had to go farther to re-assure the Israelis, according to what *Newsweek* magazine learned. "In private conversations with Israeli prime minister Ehud Olmert last week, the president all but disowned the document, said a senior administra-tion official who accompanied Bush on his six-nation trip to the Mideast. 'He told the Israelis that he can't control what the intelligence community says, but that [the NIE's] conclusions don't reflect his own views' about Iran's nuclear-weapons program."[7]

On his Middle Eastern tour in mid-January 2008—in which he hoped to persuade Saudi Arabia and other OPEC members that the rising price of oil would eventually rebound to their disadvantage by lowering con-sumption in the industrial world—the president was asked to clear up the ambiguity the White House displayed in regard to the NIE on Ira-nian nuclear programs. Asked what he had told Olmert, the president responded:

> I assured him that our intelligence services came to an independent judg-
> ment. I reminded him of what I said at my press conference when we got
> involved with that story: they were a threat, they are a threat, and they
> will be a threat if we don't work together to stop their enrichment. So we
> spent a fair amount of time on Iran. I have spent a fair amount of time on
> Iran in every stop.

But did he mean to distance himself from the NIE?

THE PRESIDENT: No, I was making it clear it was an independent judgment, because what they basically came to the conclusion of, is that he's trying—you know, this is a way to make sure that all op-tions aren't on the table. So I defended our intelligence services, but made it clear that they're an independent agency; that they come to conclusions separate from what I may or may not want.

Q: And on the issue of Iran, did the question of a possible military strike either by the United States or Israel come up?

THE PRESIDENT: I just made it clear that all options are on the table, but I'd like to solve this diplomatically—and think we can, and talked about making sure consistent messages emanated from all parts of the world to the Iranians.[8]

In this instance, as in some others, Bush found himself wearing a sandwich board on which the message on the front contradicted the one on the back. On one side it appeared the NIE drafters were "trying to make sure that all options aren't on the table," but on the other, "I just made it clear that all options are on the table." The uncertainty over how to handle the NIE left the administration in a new WMD debate. It was also embroiled at the beginning of Bush's last year in a controversy over a proposed security pact with Iraq that some in the White House claimed would not have to be approved by Congress. After five years of occupation, an Iraqi government had emerged—it was fervently hoped—that could negotiate itself into a protectorate. There was no question violence in Baghdad had diminished, although 2007 would still witness the bloodiest year for American forces. The surge was partly responsible, but the policy of arming Sunni tribal leaders to fight al Qaeda as paid hirelings was a big factor, and probably accounted as well for Shiite prime minister Maliki's sudden eagerness to embrace Washington's proposals for an enduring security pact, out of a preemptive desire to stay in power.

General David Petraeus, now not only the surge leader, but also the would-be soldier-diplomat of the war, kept his options open. He offered praise for an inveterate opponent of the occupation, Muqtada al-Sadr, the cleric who had declared a six-months' truce in his fight—but no lasting peace until the Americans were gone. "I speak to the head of evil Bush," al-Sadr declared, even as Petraeus praised his restraint on the ground, "go out of our land, we don't need you or your armies, the armies of darkness, your aircrafts, tanks . . . your fake freedom." The general was singularly remarkable for ignoring such rhetorical assaults. "Nobody says anything about turning corners, seeing lights at the ends of tunnels," he said. "You just keep your head down and keep moving."[9]

Keeping Up Appearances

Behind all the to-ing and fro-ing of congressional resolutions on one or another aspect of the Iraq War, and efforts to co-opt elements of the insurgency, the reality of the administration's successful power grab in the name of the war on terror defied critics who argued about infringements on constitutional rights. No serious move was made to repeal the Patriot Act, and its spawn, the Protect America Act, which removed many restrictions on federal spying authority by allowing "basket warrants," which authorized the government to target whole organizations or groups of people if it could prove one party being tapped was outside the United States. While proponents of such measures had argued they were needed to keep up with the technology available to potential terrorists, they rolled back constitutional barriers to unlawful searches in the Fourth Amendment. The administration's primary legacy threatened to be a color-coded state of permanent emergency, achieved with a citizenry mesmerized into acquiescence by the blinking lights atop the Homeland Security offices.

In the aftermath of the attacks on the World Trade Center, on the other hand, President Bush had asked for no material sacrifices from the nation. Quite the opposite. To win the war on terror it was necessary to consume more—of everything. That would show our enemies, who hated Americans' freedom to go to the mall of their choice, that this country would not be driven out of the Middle East. On September 20, 2001, the president set forth his agenda. "Americans are asking: What is expected of us? I ask you to live your lives, and hug your children. . . . I ask for your patience, with the delays and inconveniences that may accompany tighter security; and for your patience in what will be a long struggle. I ask your continued participation and confidence in the American economy. Terrorists attacked a symbol of American prosperity. They did not touch its source. America is successful because of the hard work, and creativity, and enterprise of our people. These were the true strengths of our economy before September eleventh, and they are our strengths today. [Applause.]"

Bush did not ask the country for the backdoor sacrifices the war demanded, however, both in the present and for the long-term future. Once again it was a case of assuming a short war at a cost of only $50 or $60 billion, money that would be well spent, it was argued, to get rid of the monster of Baghdad and his WMD. The backdoor sacrifices in lost services began to come into clearer focus as the war went on, but there was still no good accounting of what the war had done to undermine the American economy.

Confronting the nation, Bush said, was nothing less than the paramount ideological struggle of the twenty-first century. Yet unlike previous wars, tax cuts and increased consumer spending were to be understood as acts of defiance against an enemy who wanted to destroy the blessed American "way of life." The peculiar logic espoused in these declamations demanding no sacrifice at home except "delays and inconveniences" was underscored as the occupation/war dragged on, requiring American soldiers to return for second and third tours of duty. A lot longer than World War II, Iraq threatened to overtake Vietnam as America's longest war. It had become a test to see if Americans had the stomach to prevail over its enemy. Well, only for some Americans, because to talk about a draft was taboo. The strain Iraq had imposed on the military did not presage a serious debate about renewing the draft, because even to think about going back to those methods for raising an army was not only unpopular with Congress but also an admission that the experiment in a small professional army on the plan of earlier imperial forces had failed, and thus that a force equipped with every new weapons system the Pentagon invested taxpayer money buying could not do the job. Iraq had already forcefully demonstrated that shock and awe, high-tech wars fought from lily pads, or, indeed, SOCOM wars, were not the future. Indeed, Iraq looked very much like a bad colonial war, if on terrain more like Algeria than Vietnam. Washington during the Vietnam War or the Iraq sequel simply could not admit that the United States fought colonial wars, or that what the "enduring" security arrangement looked like was anything resembling the British raj in India.

No one in Washington would own up to such descriptions, of course, but the use of interrogation techniques copied from the colonial era should have—but, alas, did not—provide a different take on what had happened to the American ethos than the continuing invocation of the metaphor of progress. In the later years of the war, as he sought to rally his political backers, Bush usually spoke of the "enemy" in the singular, as in a speech to a friendly audience at the Heritage Foundation on November 1, 2007: "It's been now more than six years since the enemy attacked us on September the eleventh. . . . With the passage of time, the memories of the 9/11 attacks have grown more distant. And for some, there's a temptation to think that the threats to our country have grown distant as well. They have not."

Here was a clue to understanding what Iraq presaged for the future.

Costly as it had become—with some estimates that it would reach as much as $1.5 trillion or more—ultimate "victory" there, bringing the troops home, would not mean the enemy had been defeated. To be fair, he had promised a long war on terrorism, with inconclusive moments along the way, but all these statements reaffirmed what had been there from the beginning for all to see: Iraq was not about Saddam Hussein, it was about the American objective of establishing a new Middle East. It was the mirror image of the administration's charge that Islamofascists, headed by Osama bin Laden, sought to establish a new caliphate in Baghdad to extend their power worldwide. White House press secretary Tony Snow was asked about Bush's use of the term "Islamofascism" to describe the reclassified enemy. In response he pointed to Osama bin Laden's purported desire to reestablish the "Islamic Nation," or caliphate, in Baghdad, a desire that he claimed went back to 1492 and the expulsion of the Moors from Spain. The president was absolutely right to want to preempt that, said Snow. The enemy's strategy was to "create failed states, so that you can go in, you can use their land for training, but also you can make use of their resources. He's [Bush] spoken a couple of times recently, for instance, of the dangers of such a state that would have access to oil and the ability to bring Western and industrialized nations economically to their knees."[10]

The more elusive the enemy was, moreover, the better chance for obtaining congressional votes on war-related issues, a task thus made easier by the sporadic broadcast visits Osama bin Laden made to the world. One could even argue that bin Laden and Bush needed one another to keep their forces disciplined. Had there been no William Lloyd Garrison attacking the South in his newspaper, *The Liberator*, a famous Civil War historian once said, the slaveholders would have had to invent him to prevent a serious debate about the "Peculiar Institution." Writing about the ideological conflicts of the twentieth century, William Pfaff put his finger on the meaning of Iraq: "Ideological war, which is to say utopian war, in the twentieth century tested human or spiritual possibility, implying a test of our understanding of existence, demanding in nearly every case that 'conventional' morality be sacrificed to the demands of a utopian vision."[11]

Going to war with a preemptive strike against an enemy who *might* have done us harm while leaving unfinished an effort to search out an enemy who *had* done us harm qualified fully as some form of a utopian vision. Had the war ended quickly, with the establishment of a friendly Iraq, complete with the ability and willingness to provide the American military with bases to replace those lost out of concern for safety in Saudi Arabia, then the economic costs, at least, of the invasion would have been minimal. The inability to find the stockpiles of WMD would not have mattered. When the war could not be concluded quickly, the administration shifted its rationale to Osama bin Laden and the new al Qaeda in Iraq as the enemy to be overcome. Now it was there for all to see that the axis of evil speech was a brochure advertising Perpetual War for Perpetual Peace. Herman Melville would have understood Bush well.

The utopian vision has always been expressed, however, as a form of Wilson's famous assertion that America's duty was to make the world safe for democracy. In Wilson's time it really meant a League of Nations dominated by Europe and the United States, with little more than a passive role for the rest of the world. The hope some had that this would change after World War II was aborted by the Cold War and its dark shadow over the conflicts of decolonization, and with Washington's emergence as the ambivalent successor to the British and French, in what would become the third colonial age after Christians and spices, raw materials and markets. Call it the "new American century," or whatever, the newest meaning of the Wilsonian creed in our time has come to be to make the world safe for *our* democracy, using a shifting coalition of the willing. As Defense Secretary Rumsfeld put it so forcefully in a 2001 speech after the invasion of Afghanistan, from this point forward the mission would determine the coalition, never the other way around. In part his speech was about the defection of allies in the Vietnam War, but it was also meant as an announcement of the rules in the new American century. "The enemy we face today is different from the enemies we have faced in the past," Rumsfeld wrote in a 2006 op-ed article in the *Los Angeles Times*, "but its goal is similar: to impose its fanatical ideology of hatred on the rest of the world."[12]

It was never made clear by Rumsfeld or any other government official how this fanatical ideology would be able to impose its will on the rest of the world. Bush insisted promoting democracy throughout the Middle East, the new domino thesis, would ultimately eliminate the terrorist threat. Pursuing stability, he said in an August 31, 2006, speech to the

American Legion, was the wrong approach. "In the space of a single morning, it became clear that the calm we saw in the Middle East was only a mirage. . . . Instead, the lack of freedom in the Middle East made the region an incubator for terrorist movements."

"Young people who have a say in their future are less likely to search for meaning in extremism," he insisted. "Dissidents with the freedom to protest around the clock are less likely to blow themselves up during rush hour." There was no serious encounter here with the real issues connected to the Arab-Israeli conflict, or the political economy of the regions where the Taliban was once again on the rise. Funny quips about rush hour satisfied carefully chosen audiences, which applauded loudly at all the proper points, but almost as soon as he spoke the words, they seemed outpaced by events. "Our enemies saw the transformation in Afghanistan, and they've responded by trying to roll back the progress. . . . The days of the Taliban are over. The future of Afghanistan belongs to the people of Afghanistan. And the future of Afghanistan belongs to freedom. [Applause.]"[13]

The Taliban's resurgence belied such optimistic assurances. The *Christian Science Monitor* reported how the Taliban had learned from the Iraqi experience. "That's part of our strategy," said a wounded fighter. "We are trying to bring [the Iraqi model] to Afghanistan," says the fighter. "Things will get worse here." It was not supposed to happen that way, of course. Iraq was to be the model of democracy. On his sixth visit to Iraq, in early December 2007, Defense Secretary Gates turned down a Marine general's request to "transition the Marine Corps mission to Afghanistan." "Transition" was a wonderful example of the Pentagon's penchant for turning nouns into verbs, and in this instance, conveying assumptions about the two wars, but Gates nixed the idea. Things were much better in Iraq, he said, but counterinsurgency in Anbar province, where the Marines were located, had not eliminated the threat. "He doesn't believe the time is now to do that," said his press secretary. "Anbar is still a volatile place."[14]

Promoting democracy was a good talking point to use with friendly American audiences, who always rallied to grand themes, but in practice it required turning the whole area upside down, with totally unpredictable results, as elections in Lebanon and Gaza also illustrated. Asked about the untoward results in those elections, Secretary of State Rice rejected the implication that Washington had misjudged what would happen with the dangerously simplistic approach that elections were a cure-all: "What we're seeing here, in a sense, is the growing—the birth pangs of a new Middle East. And whatever we do, we have to be certain that we are pushing forward to the new Middle East, not going back to the old one."[15]

So while the administration decided it could pick and choose what elections meant, and how to deal with (or ignore) the results, Bush told *Washington Post* reporters that failure would embolden the "external threat. . . . And I'm going to keep repeating this over and over again, that I believe we're in an ideological struggle that is—that our country will be dealing with for a long time."[16]

The Biggest Ever

Like Dick Cheney, Bush treated the 2006 election as nothing more than an opinion poll, one that could be interpreted to mean that the nation desired only a new victory strategy. With thirty thousand additional troops in Iraq by midsummer, violence in Baghdad began to decline, whether from exhaustion on both sides of the Shiitte/Sunni struggle, or a realization that the best way to get the Americans to leave was to stop the attacks.

But the Americans were not going to leave. They were building an embassy that would occupy a piece of real estate in central Baghdad that would be about two-thirds the size of Washington's National Mall, a twenty-one-building complex with desk space for one thousand people behind high, blast-resistant walls. It was envisioned, wrote Anne Gearan, "as a headquarters for the democratic expansion in the Middle East that President Bush identified as the organizing principle for foreign policy in his second term." Secretary Rice's chief Iraq expert, David Satterfield, told Congress, "We assume there will be a significant, enduring U.S. presence in Iraq."[17]

Eliminating Saddam Hussein had only been the first step. The ultimate goal had been to build the embassy, a project on the order of Howard Roark's skyscraper in *The Fountainhead*, as a permanent presence in the region to protect American interests diplomatically and by other means. While Congress might pass resolutions against permanent military bases in Iraq, the administration rushed ahead with its plans for a security pact with Maliki's government, believing that if it could nail down the agreement, no future government (in Baghdad or Washington) could afford to lose the proposed benefits of such an American presence. The British at Suez might be the model, with Egypt forced to allow the British to use the Suez Canal as a military strong point to project its power in the Middle East. With military bases and the largest embassy in the world, there would never again have to be a "dual" containment policy that had confounded Washington's aspirations after the Iranian Revolution.

Whether it would all work out to allow for such a happy ending in either the near future or over a longer time period depended upon events only partly under American control. Both Vietnam and Iraq had demonstrated that the ability to create political solutions did not emerge from the barrel of a gun. Iraq was supposed to demonstrate the efficacy of creative destruction, a notion that had seduced American policy makers—not just George W. Bush—since the end of World War II and the regeneration of Germany and Japan as free-market capitalist nations competing happily in the world marketplace.

Dick Cheney had promised that the Americans would be greeted as liberators, as they had been in Europe after V-E Day. Donald Rumsfeld had gone to Iraq soon after V-I Day and talked about how Iraq's oil could pay for its reconstruction. "Tourism is going to be something important to that country as soon as the security situation is resolved. . . . In the last analysis, they have to create an environment that's hospitable to investment and enterprise."

Creating an environment that was hospitable to the oil companies was still a far-off aspiration, as the Maliki government had not secured laws by the end of 2007 that would resolve disputes over how to divide the potential oil revenues equitably. The prospects for his government were uncertain on a number of fronts, especially in the failure to satisfy the largest Sunni bloc's demands for a larger role in the ministries. How long he could govern with a cabinet made up largely of Shiite Muslims and Kurds, absent some reconciliation with the Sunni Accordance Front and other political leaders, was a big question mark. Waiting in the wings was Ayad Allawi, the once and future hopeful political leader, who had hired a PR firm headed by Robert Blackwill, the former White

House point man on Iraq's future, to promote his interests. Allawi wasted no words in describing the fate of the Maliki regime: "There will be no lasting political reconciliation under Maliki's sectarian regime."[18]

Maliki's survival might be determined by any number of fateful choices surrounding the levels of violence throughout the country, his ability to reach out to the Sunni leaders, his relationship with the American authorities, finding a way to deal with the oil legislation, and his handling of the Blackwater crisis. The Blackwater crisis began with a shooting spree in Baghdad by private security guards on September 16, 2007, that left several Iraqis dead, though even the number killed remained in dispute as the investigation into the incident proceeded. Unlike his usual conciliatory stance when dealing with American authorities, Maliki did not wait for the investigation to be completed before declaring, "We will not allow Iraqis to be killed in cold blood."[19]

Blackwater officials insisted that the guards had been fired upon, and that that was what triggered the incident, but their account was challenged by eyewitnesses to the shooting. While the Iraqi government insisted that Blackwater must leave Iraq, and the FBI launched its own investigation, Secretary of State Condoleezza Rice pleaded with Maliki not to attempt to expel Blackwater, a step that would create an immediate logistical problem, as the security guards provided very necessary protection to all diplomats traveling outside the Green Zone. Other officials pointed out that there was no way other than using American troops that would enable the diplomats to travel around Baghdad and the country. The shooting had opened a window on the American occupation, exposing its fragile existence outside the boundaries of the Green Zone.

The crisis posed more than a "hearts and minds" dilemma. Maliki said Blackwater was "a serious challenge to the sovereignty of Iraq and cannot be tolerated." He then presided over a cabinet meeting that pronounced Rule 17, prohibiting the trial of foreigners in Iraqi courts, no longer had the force of law. Whether Maliki would actually use the shooting as a test case to challenge the limits of American rule, or contrariwise the extent of Iraqi sovereignty, remained unclear. It was also unclear under what law the guards could be tried in an American military or civilian court.

Nor did the ripples from the crisis end there. Blackwater USA was twelfth on the list of companies receiving contracts from the U.S. government between 2004 and 2006, with $485 million. Of course, that fig-ure was small compared to the $16 billion awarded to KBR, formerly a subsidiary of Halliburton, the company headed by Dick Cheney before he became vice president. Iraq was consuming "more than 10 percent of all the government's annually appropriated funds," said the Congres-sional Budget Office's report to a House committee. Even if American troops were reduced to a level of 30,000 by 2010, Congress will still have to appropriate an additional $500 billion beyond the current costs of the war, which had already totaled $500 billion. If 75,000 troops remained in Iraq by that time, the additional cost would run to $900 billion. Un-der either scenario the plan for fighting Islamofascism with tax cuts was in shambles. "It is being paid for on the national credit card," said Rep-resentative James P. McGovern. "It is being put on the backs of our kids and grandkids. That is indefensible."[20]

The Iraq War had a disastrous impact on the American economy in other ways as well, by stimulating an inflationary spiral and causing a soaring price rise in oil—which has to be the best example of the saying, "Results are what you expect; consequences are what you get." Writing in *Vanity Fair*, economist and Nobel laureate Joseph Stiglitz pointed to the irony: "It seems unbelievable now to recall that Bush-administration officials before the invasion suggested not only that Iraq's oil revenues would pay for the war in its entirety—hadn't we actually turned a tidy profit from the 1991 Gulf War?—but also that war was the best way to en-sure low oil prices. In retrospect, the only big winners from the war have been the oil companies, the defense contractors, and al Qaeda." The war increased oil prices not so much by curtailing Iraqi production, but by heightening a sense of insecurity all up and down the production line.[21]

The response to such bad news about where things had gone so awry was offered by Karl Rove, strategist of the prewar WHIG campaign for war, now safely back in Texas off the front lines as Bush faced the conse-quences of his war. Rove was set up by Fox News reporter Chris Wallace in an interview on March 2, 2008: Wallace asked about Democratic can-didate Barack Obama's assertions that the nation was spending $12 bil-lion a month on the war, money that could go into infrastructure at home as well as health and education needs.

WALLACE: Obama has found a clever way to link the war in Iraq to our domestic problems with the economy here at home. . . . If he's able to define Iraq in terms of where do you spend that $12 billion, on the battlefield over there or on infrastructure and social programs here, doesn't Obama win?

ROVE: Well, Obama—it's a good argument for Obama, but I'm wondering where it goes, because it really is a very neo-isolationist argument. It basically says, you know, "We should not be involved in the world because of the consequences to the budget here at home."

Well, we were not involved in the world before 9/11, and look what happened. Look at the cost to the American economy after a terrorist attack on the homeland. We lost a million jobs in 90 days after 9/11.

If we were to give up Iraq with the third largest oil reserves in the world to the control of an Al Qaida regime or to the control of Iran, don't you think $200 a barrel oil would have a cost to the American economy?

So you know, it's a cute thing in a primary. I'm not certain over an 8-month general election that you can make the argument that we ought to take a look at every foreign policy commitment in the United States and measure it on the basis of the number of dollars that we've got there.

I happened to be in Los Angeles on Monday, and somebody had heard Obama say this [. . .] and they were Democrat [. . .] and at dinner they said, "I'm worried about that, because does that mean he's going to be looking at our support, for example, for the state of Israel and looking at it in terms of what could we be doing at home with those dollars?"

And it was a nice line, but I'm not certain how durable a line it necessarily is.[22]

Rove's gas-pump monster reaching out to steal American wallets was akin to the WHIG campaign's mushroom cloud. With oil already at $100 a barrel, the thought of it going that high was, in fact, not beyond the range of possibilities—not at all. His defense of a failed imperial policy on those grounds was, however, another deception no more solid than any other argument for the war had turned out to be. In the effort to portray what withdrawal would mean for the average citizen—with Is-rael's welfare thrown in for good measure—Rove had in fact pinpointed how the profits and losses from empire were never distributed evenly.

In March 2006, Secretary of Defense Don Rumsfeld traveled to Vail, Colorado, and met with a small group of wounded soldiers. It was the third year that Iraq veterans had been entertained by the Vail citizenry, as they sought to work through their injuries with special instructors to help them. "These people," he told a TV interviewer, would never have had "a chance to come to Vail, Colorado, never in their lives, to come here and spend several days and just have a fantastic time and under-stand that they are capable of going up on that mountain and beating the mountain." Aside from this revealing commentary about the men and women doing the fighting in Iraq, Rumsfeld also commented on their wounds: "They're folks who have lost legs or arms or sight and have demonstrated a determination to be able to go out and live a life, a nor-mal life."

Asked by the interviewer how he would change public perception of the war and, implicitly, his own role in pushing for an invasion of Iraq, Rumsfeld launched into a long discussion of how wars had never been popular in the United States, from the time of Washington and the rev-olution. "George Washington was almost fired. . . . And Franklin Roo-sevelt was one of the most hated people in the country. . . . He was commander in chief." People did not study history anymore, he com-plained, and journalists ought to do a better job of providing context, "rather than just running around trying to win a Pulitzer by dramatizing something that's negative that in fact is negative [! *Positive?*]."[23]

But in the last days of the Bush administration everything that was said to be negative was, in fact, negative. The violence in Baghdad had diminished, perhaps offering a chance to withdraw American forces with honor. There was little otherwise to compensate the nation for the disaster the administration had imposed on it by going to war, as General Bradley once said about Korea, in the wrong place against the wrong en-emy, and, in the case of Iraq, on false pretenses.

Perhaps Iraq will bring about some serious reconsiderations of the role the world's superpower should play in terms of leading by example across a range of critical questions, starting with the issues of climate change and energy resources. Alan Greenspan, longtime chair of the Federal

Reserve board of governors, wrote in his memoir, "I am saddened that it is politically inconvenient to acknowledge what everyone knows: the Iraq war is largely about oil."[24]

It is unanswerable to wonder about whether the Bush administration would have gone to war absent the oil question. That may be, as Greenspan wrote, the place to start, and no doubt for many it was sufficient cause. But oil is only one aspect of an American way of thinking about the world, and what it owes us as the "great republic." In the first hours after the 9/11 attack, Bush made a stentorian announcement to a European conference on terrorism, "Over time it's going to be important for nations to know they will be held accountable for inactivity. You're either with us or against us in the fight against terror." September 11 made that seem real, and the terrorist threat was genuine, but the justification for the continuing war in Iraq now became the idea that Osama bin Laden was out to close off a part of the world to American access, and build up an evil empire in the ruins.

If we don't fight them there, Bush said, when the insurrection began they will come over here—again. "Failure in Iraq will cause generations to suffer, in my judgment," Bush said again and again. "Al Qaeda will be emboldened. They will say, 'Yes, once again, we've driven the great soft America out of a part of the region.' It will cause them to be able to recruit more; it will give them safe haven. They are a direct threat to the United States." Critics focused on the intelligence "failure," if that was what it was, that allowed the administration to obtain the fateful votes in Congress to attack Iraq in March 2003. But Greenspan's point identified a more important intelligence failure that went back to Vietnam, at least. Defense Secretary Robert McNamara famously called Vietnam a tragedy of misperceptions, but there were no missed perceptions. The rationales for war in Vietnam and Iraq were not to be found in a communist blueprint for world conquest, or in an Islamofascist plan to reestablish a caliphate.

There were a thousand variations on this theme in Bush's speeches and press conferences—all to the point that the war had to be waged to make Iraq safe for our democracy. But even if the insurgency were quelled, even if a democratic regime emerged, even if the new government granted us military bases and oil concessions, would that bring about an end to terrorism of the sort that had killed three thousand Americans in one day? Here is Greenspan again on 9/11 and the aftermath: "Why no second attack? If al Qaeda's intent was to disrupt the U.S. economy, as bin Laden had declared, the attacks had to continue. Our society was open, our borders were porous, and our ability to detect weapons was weak." He asked this question of a lot of people at the highest levels, he added, but no one seemed to have a convincing response. "The expectation of additional terrorism affected virtually everything the government did. And, inevitably, the defensive bubble we'd created to protect our institutions influenced every decision."[25]

As a conservative in an older tradition, he was worried about the infringements on individual liberties, and found out he could not get good answers to his questions about the problem of whether there really was an Islamofascist enemy capable of, or determined to, carry out a campaign to destroy the American economy. But more to the point, Greenspan had raised the issue of whether fighting the enemy in the way the Bush administration had done by attacking Iraq could preempt future terrorist attacks like 9/11, or worse? The reports of diminished violence in Iraq provided an answer to the question, but still not one likely to win favor in the White House. American officers in Baghdad spoke openly about the new surge tactic of handing out money to alleviate the "soaring unemployment that can turn young Iraqi men into insurgents-for-hire." The other side had long been supplying money to men desperate for work. "I tell a lot of my soldiers: A good way to prepare for operations in Iraq is to watch the sixth season of *The Sopranos*," said Major General Rick Lynch. "You're seeing a lot of Mafioso kind of activity."[26]

If it was awkward politically to say that the Iraq War had been about oil, was it equally so to say that it was not hatred of America and a determination to strike a blow against capitalism that motivated the insurgency? If the case for war because of Saddam's phantom WMDs had long ago collapsed, the argument for the occupation that Iraq was the center of *the* ideological struggle of the twenty-first century did not stand up to close examination.

The invasion of Iraq in March 2003 had its origins in the Vietnam defeat and the perceived need to reassert American primacy over the Soviet Union in contests in the third world, but this drive was also connected root and branch to a need to reassure the nation that what had not been lost in Vietnam was confidence in the American metaphor of progress. Had it been a quick war the promise might have been fulfilled, it was argued. *Had the surge been employed earlier. Had the Iraqi army not been dismantled*. And so on. Critics were ready with answers to why things had gone so terribly wrong. But none of them confronted the reality of the limits of power, even power overflowing with smart bombs and global positioning systems, night goggles and Stryker fighting vehicles.

It is obviously much easier to say what went wrong than to prescribe hard-and-fast solutions for the future. In this case, however, there was a procedure in place, the UN inspections that offered an alternative to war. But the problem went back to Walt Rostow's assumptions that Vietnam could be the "final throes," as Dick Cheney talked about the Iraq insurgency, of the antiliberal revolutions promoted by the Soviet Union, or Brzezinski's assumption that strong Islamic movements could block communism, or George W. Bush's assumption that America needed no further reason for going to war than to remove Saddam Hussein to open the way to democracy's spread all across the region.

But those were not the only dangerous assumptions. Perhaps the most dangerous over the long run was Cheney's conception of the presidency as separate from, but more equal than the other branches of the federal government. The future of the republic may well depend upon the willingness and ability of the next president to resist the temptation to continue holding onto all those special powers Cheney and his loyal aides maneuvered after 9/11 to obtain for a president with unlimited ambitions.

If the Iraq War began as a bad war, it threatened to end as an even worse war. The argument that the United States could not run away from the devastation it had caused, that the nation's enemies were waiting to set up an Islamofascist state in Iraq, approached that obvious truth from the wrong end. It put a negative spin on America's obligation to reconstruct a viable Iraqi state. In Washington General Douglas Lute, the administration's special coordinator of Iraqi affairs, announced at the end of November 2007 that the two countries had signed a Declaration of Principles on future relations. Lute was effusive about Iraq-America prospects. "The basic message here should be clear: Iraq is increasingly able to stand on its own. That's very good news, but it won't have to stand alone."[27]

The agreement did not spell out the number of troops to be stationed in Iraq in the future. That was to be the subject of negotiations, as were questions like who would have jurisdiction over the American military in criminal cases and such—thereby putting off a confrontation over Order 17, even as the Blackwater case remained unresolved. Lute observed that the agreement offered assurances to America's friends and allies in the region that the United States would continue to have a military presence in Iraq. Prime Minister Maliki issued a statement after the signing praising the agreement. "It was built by the brave sacrifices made by both peoples for a democratic and free Iraq."

Bush committed the United States to support Iraq in "defending its democratic system against internal and external threats," and to aiding economic development with financial resources and technical assistance. He would work to see that Baghdad obtained "preferential trading conditions" in the World Trade Organization and most-favored-nation trading status in the United States. In return, Iraq pledged to encourage "the flow of foreign investments to Iraq, especially American investments, to contribute to the reconstruction and rebuilding of Iraq."

Lute was very clear about what the declaration would lead to in the negotiations. There would be no formal treaty, he said. "We don't anticipate now that these negotiations will lead to the status of a formal treaty, which would then bring us to formal negotiations or formal inputs from the Congress." Instead, these would be handled by an executive agreement that did not require congressional assent. "The two negotiating teams, Iraq and the United States, now have a common sheet of music with which to begin the negotiations." And Bush added that he had signed the declaration because it had become clear to Iraqi leaders "that their success will require U.S. political, economic, and security engagement that extends beyond my presidency."[28]

The Declaration of Principles came just as the new embassy opened, "a self-contained city with no need for Iraqi electricity, food or water." Outside Baghdad, the aptly named Camp Anaconda occupied fifteen square miles, with a pool, a gym, a theater, a beauty salon, a school, and six apartment buildings. Maliki had hesitated before deciding not to present the declaration to the Iraqi Parliament. When it was announced, both Sunni and Shia members of Parliament charged that it would lead to "U.S. interference for years to come." Muqtada al-Sadr was furious with Maliki for going outside Parliament. It was in response to the declaration that the Shiite leader had reasoned, "I speak to the head of evil Bush, go out of our land, we don't need you or your armies, the armies of darkness, your aircrafts, tanks . . . your fake freedom."

"The Sadrists, who had been flirting with Maliki for 10 days, immediately cut off contacts," said *Asia Times*, "claiming that the agreement 'sets the ground for long-term occupation.' Muqtada was furious that Maliki never presented the agreement to Parliament before signing it off with the US President. One of his top commanders, Falah Shanshal, said that it 'contradicted' with everything the Sadrists had been working for (in terms of a rapprochement with Maliki)."[29]

Neither Petraeus nor Sadr was very happy about Maliki, who had apparently signed the declaration under pressure from Bush, who wanted to force things along in the Iraqi Parliament, especially the much-desired oil law that was no nearer accomplishment than it had been at the beginning of the year. It did appear that efforts to bring the Sadrists into the tent, as the American general hoped would happen, had been dealt a serious blow by Washington's preemptive diplomatic strike. In the United States the Declaration of Principles was sure to have a major impact on the presidential campaign. Perhaps, one could hope, it would force a clarifying debate, at last, on the policies that had set the nation on the road descending to Baghdad.

Signs did appear that the days of imperial privilege in the executive branch were coming to an end—if only because it was proving too costly. Karl Rove might fret about neo-isolationism and conjure up a $200 price tag for a barrel of oil to scare war critics, but Congress looked to be taking a stand on the Declaration of Principles. Unable to achieve enough of a majority to force a full-scale debate on war financing or a timetable for troop withdrawals, Democrats on Capitol Hill had a somewhat better chance of denying the administration achievement of its full agenda. They could do nothing about the signatures of Bush and Maliki on the declaration itself, but the legality of the subsequent document that would be negotiated to carry into effect the "principles" was under sharp attack even before negotiations began. The Pentagon hoped to avoid congressional review by making it a status-of-forces agreement like others negotiated with nearly eighty countries, rather than facing a fight over a treaty.

The negotiations were to cover many of the same topics as did Order 17, the original document L. Paul Bremer imposed on his Iraqi council, such as immunity for American soldiers from Iraqi prosecution and the continuing ability of American forces to take and hold prisoners. Beyond that, said to be some of the easier conditions to negotiate, the American side wished to secure immunity for contractors as well, especially security organizations like Blackwater. Here, aside from the obvious irritation of such a provision to the Iraqis, the American position revealed the Achilles' heel not only in the Iraq transformation project, but also the Pentagon's new high-tech lean and mean machine and the financial sustainability of remaining the world's greatest empire. If it could not secure immunity protection from Iraqi laws for more than 10,000 private security guards, let alone 160,000 contractors, their places would have to be taken by uniformed soldiers (especially the security guards), raising the specter of a new draft. To downplay the importance of the draft, one senior Bush official said, "More than 90 percent of this will be pretty standard status-of-forces agreement. It is not something that will tie the hands of the next president." Senator Jim Webb, who has emerged as one of the most thoughtful of the war critics, replied bluntly to these assurances. "There's no exit strategy, because the administration doesn't have one. By entering this agreement, they avoid a debate and they validate their unspoken strategy."[30]

As the 2008 presidential debate went on, meanwhile, an echo of the 1965 national teach-in could be heard in an exchange between Barack Obama and Senator John McCain. Obama had qualified his statements about withdrawing American forces from Iraq in a timely fashion by saying that he would reserve the right to send troops back if "al Qaeda is forming a base in Iraq." McCain pounced on the remark. "I have some news," he said in Tyler, Texas. "Al Qaeda is in Iraq. It's called 'Al Qaeda in Iraq.' My friends, if we left, they wouldn't be establishing a base. They'd be taking a country, and I'm not going to allow that to happen." Obama, campaigning in Ohio, shot back. "I have some news for John McCain. There was no such thing as Al Qaeda in Iraq until George Bush and John McCain decided to invade Iraq."[31]

John McCain reprised the role of those who argued that how the United States had gotten into Vietnam was no longer relevant—if in the more strident tones of a presidential campaign instead of the prowar professors of that earlier era. Obama's position insisted that ignoring the matter of how the nation became involved narrowed the perspective about an exit strategy into a matter of tactics, avoiding fundamental issues.

How that debate played out, and how Congress ultimately deals with Bush's plan for avoiding a debate over the Declaration of Principles, whether under a Republican or a Democratic president, will tell the nation much about what lies ahead. As he entered the final months of his presidency, Bush vowed, to a loudly applauding audience of religious broadcasters, that he would never waver in fighting the war on terror. "The reason why the enemy uses such brutal tactics is they're trying to shake our nerve," he said. "And frankly, that's not hard to do in America because we're a compassionate people."[32] Aside from the odd juxtaposition of these sentences, Bush's speech was an amplification of brief remarks a few days earlier when he vetoed a congressional bill that would have banned waterboarding, asserting then that he would not tie a future president's hands on such an issue involving national security. Like Lyndon Johnson, who feared he would be blamed for bugging out of Vietnam, and Richard Nixon, who announced the 1970 incursion into Cambodia, saying, "If, when the chips are down, the world's most powerful nation, the United States of America, acts like a pitiful, helpless giant, the forces of totalitarianism and anarchy will threaten free nations and free institutions throughout the world," Bush had personalized the war as a struggle with his enemies at home. His concern about American compassion and shaky nerves sounds very much as if he believes the nation has deserted him and he must stand alone, if necessary, like Will Kane in *High Noon,* to defend the town against killers. Politics will not divert him from his course, he promises, which, in this context, also updates what Vice President Cheney said after the 2006 elections, that Americans—even Marine veterans like John Murtha—were too soft to be trusted with serious matters of national security.

The actions he took signaled that he saw himself as endowed (and commanded) by special providence to ignore the nation's weak nerves and press ahead against all opposition. His commander in the Middle East, Admiral William Fallon, had raised serious questions about the threats to use military force against Iran as a dangerous diversion from the far more serious fight against a resurgent Taliban in Afghanistan. Talk of war with Iran was not helpful to his mission, he said. Fallon was forced to retire. When Congress voted against permanent bases in Iraq, Bush used a favorite tactic, the signing statement, to announce he would not abide such an incursion into presidential prerogatives. Secretary Rice and Defense Secretary Gates attempted to back off a bit in an op-ed piece for the *Washington Post,* insisting that nothing would be negotiated with Iraq that would tie a future president's hands. "We seek to establish a basic framework for a strong relationship with Iraq, reflecting our shared political, economic, cultural and security interests." Further-more, "nothing will authorize permanent bases in Iraq (something nei-ther we nor Iraqis want). And consistent with well-established practice regarding such agreements, nothing will involve the U.S. Senate's treaty-ratification authority[.]" They promised consultations with appropriate committees and complete transparency.[33]

Later that same day, February 13, 2008, however, White House press secretary Dana Perino stepped back, in turn, from Rice and Gates; talk-ing about the question of "permanent" bases, she pointed out that none of the nations where American forces had been stationed since World War II had asked for their removal. "And if they did, we would *probably* leave" (emphasis added). The president's emissaries then came to Capi-tol Hill to inform Congress that it would have no role in approving the "status of forces agreement" and "strategic framework agreement" ex-pected to result from negotiations with Baghdad undertaken to flesh out the Declaration of Principles Bush signed with Prime Minister Malaki in November 2007. Secretary Rice's top adviser on Iraq, Admiral David Satterfield, justified the White House position, in testimony before a House committee, as stemming from the 2002 vote to authorize military action and subsequent votes. "Congress," he said, "has repeatedly pro-vided funding for the Iraq war, both in regular appropriations cycles and in supplemental appropriations."[34]

Satterfield's nonchalant reference to "the Iraq war" reveals much about how the Bush administration felt about constitutional questions relating to the power to declare war. It could have been Under Secretary of State Nicholas Katzenbach declaring, as he did in 1967, that the Gulf of Tonkin Resolution was the functional equivalent of a declaration of war in the thermonuclear age—thus empowering the president to keep half a million troops in Southeast Asia until that resolution had been re-pudiated. But in this case, Satterfield's position even went beyond what Katzenbach had claimed for Lyndon Johnson. He was saying that the initial authorization to use military force against Saddam Hussein gave the president the power to negotiate a binding agreement about the use of the American military with a new government. This was the rationale supplied to Congress after months of unanswered questions about the Declaration of Principles as the secret negotiations got under way. Con-gressman Bill Delahunt, who chaired a series of hearings into the administration's plans for Iraq, vowed to continue "until the administration finally comes clean about its intentions here." Their position, he added, "creates the basis for a constitutional confrontation."[35]

When Katzenbach made his pronouncement about the 1964 Gulf of Tonkin Resolution, there had also been an outcry about how the constitutional responsibilities and obligations of Congress were being ignored by an obsessed occupant of the White House. Once again the nation faces a political crisis; as Robert Byrd said just before the war, "This coming battle, if it materializes, represents a turning point in U.S. foreign policy and possibly a turning point in the recent history of the world." He warned then that the nation was sleepwalking through history and faced a rude awakening. After five years of struggle in Iraq, however, Bush instead told the religious broadcasters that he was certain he had acted right and could feel their prayers of support: "I feel your prayer. I can't tell you how meaningful they have been, to help Laura and me deal with—do our job. And I can report to you this: that the prayers of the people have affected us, and that being the President has been a joyous experience. (Applause.)"[36]

It was a troubling valedictory for those seeking to come to terms with the long road to Baghdad—and the reality of where the journey had led afterward.

NOTES

Introduction

1. John Batiste and Pete Hegseth, "Getting Beyond Stalemate to Win a War," *Washington Post*, December 8, 2007.

2. "Obama Plan Has a Critic in Australia," *New York Times*, February 12, 2007.

3. Joshua Partlow, "List of 'Willing' U.S. Allies Shrinks Steadily in Iraq," *Washington Post*, December 8, 2007.

Chapter 1: Beyond Baghdad

1. Quoted in Lloyd C. Gardner, "The Atomic Temptation," in Lloyd C. Gardner, ed., *Redefining the Past: Essays in Diplomatic History in Honor of William Appleman Williams* (Corvallis: Oregon State University Press, 1986), p. 171.

2. Lou Cannon, *President Reagan: The Role of a Lifetime* (New York: Simon & Schuster, 1991), p. 321.

3. John Foster Dulles, draft, "The 'Big Three' Alliance," July 11, 1954, The Papers of John Foster Dulles, Subject File, Box 8, Mudd Library, Princeton University, Princeton, New Jersey.

4. Donald Rumsfeld, speech to the Center for Security Policy Keeper of the Flame award dinner, November 6, 2001, defenselink.mil/transcripts/2001 (emphasis added); Dave Eberhart, "Rumsfeld: 'Coalition Must Not Determine the Mission,'" NewsMax.com, November 7, 2001, archive.newsmax.com/archives/articles/2001/11/7/152709.shtml.

5. Philip Zelikow and Condoleezza Rice, *Germany Unified and Europe Transformed: A Study in Statecraft* (Cambridge: Harvard University Press, 1995), p. 197.

6. Condoleezza Rice, "Special Briefing on Travel to the Middle East and Europe," July 21, 2006, state.gov/secretary/rm/2006/69331.htm.

7. Draft memorandum to President Lyndon Baines Johnson, November 3, 1965, U.S. Department of State, *Foreign Relations of the United States, 1964–1968*, volume III (Washington, DC: G.P.O., 1966), pp. 514–25.

8. United States Senate, Committee on Foreign Relations, *Supplemental Foreign Assistance, Fiscal Year 1966—Vietnam. Hearings*, 89th Cong., 2nd sess. (Washington, DC: G.P.O., 1966), pp. 73–74.

9. Quoted in Peter Singer, *The President of Good and Evil: The Ethics of George W. Bush* (New York: Penguin, 2004), p. xi.

10. Gardner, "The Atomic Temptation," p. 184.

11. William Appleman Williams, *Empire as a Way of Life* (New York: Oxford University Press, 1980), p. 183.

12. AP, "Send the Marines, Rostow Proposes," *New York Times*, April 5, 1975.

13. Rostow to Jackson, August 20, 1953, Papers of C.D. Jackson, The Dwight D. Eisenhower Library, Abilene, Kansas, Box 6.

14. Rostow to Secretary of State, et al., April 24, 1961, John F. Kennedy Papers, John F. Kennedy Library, Cambridge, Massachusetts, President's Official File, Box 115.

15. Rostow to McNamara, November 16, 1964, Department of State, *Foreign Relations of the United States, 1964–1968: Vietnam 1964* (Washington, DC: G.P.O., 1992), I, 906–8.

16. William Conrad Gibbons, *The U.S. Government and the Vietnam War: Executive and Legislative Roles and Relationships, Part IV* (Washington, DC: G.P.O., 1994), pp. 297–98.

17. *The Pentagon Papers*, Gravel Edition, vol. IV, pp. 666–67 (Boston: Beacon Press, 1971).

18. Helms to Johnson, September 12, 1967, cited in Lloyd Gardner, Introduction, p. xxvi, Memorandum, "Implications of an Unfavorable Outcome in Vietnam," September 11, 1967, National Intelligence Council, *Estimative Products on Vietnam, 1948–1975* (Washington, DC: G.P.O., 2005).

19. Notes of the President's Meeting with Australian Broadcast Group, September 20, 1967, Papers of Lyndon B. Johnson, Lyndon B. Johnson Library, Austin, Texas, Meeting Notes File, Box 3.

20. Congressional briefing by General Westmoreland, President Johnson, and Mr. Rostow, November 16, 1967, Johnson Papers, Congressional Briefings, Box 1.

21. Note dated 3/25/68, Johnson Papers, Files of Walt Rostow, Box 6.

22. Lloyd C. Gardner, *Pay Any Price: Lyndon Johnson and the Wars for Vietnam* (Chicago: Ivan R. Dee, 1995), p. 454.

23. W.W. Rostow, "The Case for the Vietnam War," *Parameters*, Winter 1996–97, pp. 39–50.

24. On Reagan, see Beth Fischer, *The Reagan Reversal: Foreign Policy and the End of the Cold War* (Columbia: University of Missouri Press, 1997). Fischer suggests that viewing the apocalyptic-style film *The Day After* shaped his diplomacy and willingness to change his rhetoric. See p. 122 for a discussion.

25. President George Bush's press conference in Kennebunkport, Maine, September 2, 1991, presidency.ucsb.edu/ws/?pid=19931. Emphasis added.

26. See Alex Danchev, "'I'm with You': Tony Blair and the Obligations of Alliance: Anglo-American Relations in Historical Perspective," in Lloyd C. Gardner and Marilyn B. Young, eds., *Iraq and the Lessons of Vietnam: Or, How Not to Learn from the Past* (New York: The New Press, 2007), pp. 45–58, on the Blair doctrine speech, April 22, 1999, pbs.org/newshour/bb/international/jan-june99/blair_doctrine.

27. Debate transcript, October 3, 2000, debates.org/pages/trans2000a.html.

28. Condoleezza Rice, "Responsibilities of Freedom," address to the International Institute for Strategic Studies, June 26, 2003, www.iiss.org.uk/recent-key-addresses/condoleezza-rice-address/.

29. Secretary Rice's remarks at Princeton University's celebration of the seventy-fifth anniversary of the Woodrow Wilson School of Public and International Affairs, September 30, 2005, state.gov/secretary/rm/2005/54176.htm.

30. Office of the Press Secretary, "Remarks by President Bush and Prime Minister Howard of Australia, Hanoi, Vietnam," November 17, 2006, fpc.state.gov/fpc/76236.htm.

31. Ibid.

Chapter 2: Zbig at the Khyber Pass, or the Last Flight of the Persian Rug

1. James T. Wooten, "A Moralistic Speech," *New York Times*, January 21, 1977.

2. William Safire, "Pedestrian Inaugural," *New York Times*, January 24, 1977.

3. See David F. Schmitz and Vanessa Walker, "Jimmy Carter and the Foreign Policy of Human Rights: The Development of a Post–Cold War Foreign Policy," *Diplomatic History*, vol. 28: no. 1 (January 2004): 113–43.

4. Norman Podhoretz, "The Red Menace," *New York Times*, May 14, 1978.

5. David Binder, "Carter Requests Funds for Big Increase in Broadcasts to Soviet Bloc," *New York Times*, March 23, 1977; "Rebuffs at Home, Flak from Abroad," *Time*, July 11, 1977, time.com/time/printout/0,8816,919042,00.html.

6. Zbigniew Brzezinski, *Power and Principle: Memoirs of the National Security Adviser, 1977–1981* (New York: Farrar, Straus & Giroux, 1983), p. 49.

7. *New York Times*, February 16, 1965; "The Debate," *Time*, July 2, 1965,

8. James Reston, "Japan Demands Equality," *New York Times*, March 2, 1973.

9. Brzezinski, *Power and Principle*, p. 5.

10. Ibid., pp. 43–44.

11. Richard Burt, "Zbig Makes It Big," *New York Times*, July 30, 1978.

12. Brzesinski, *Power and Principle*, pp. 62–63.

13. Memorandum of conversation, January 28, 1977, The Papers of Jimmy Carter, James E. Carter Library, Atlanta, Georgia, NSA, Box 33.

14. Piero Gleijeses, "Moscow's Proxy? Cuba and Africa 1975–1988," *Journal of Cold War Studies* 8 (Spring 2006): 3–51. The following paragraphs are largely drawn from this excellent study of Soviet-Cuban policy.

15. Ibid.

16. SCC meeting on the Horn of Africa, February 22, 1978, turnerlearning.com/cnn/coldwar/goodguys/good_re6.html.

17. Ibid.

18. Hedrick Smith, "Lashing Out at Soviet: Product of Frustration," *New York Times*, May 30, 1978.

19. Interview with Dr. Brzezinski, June 13, 1997, gwu.edu/~nsarchiv/coldwar/interviews/episode-17/brzezinski2.html.

20. President Jimmy Carter's address at Wake Forest University, March 17, 1978, presidency.ucsb.edu/ws/index.php?pid=30516&st=&st1=.

21. Brzezinski, *Power and Principle*, p. 189.

22. Patrick Tyler, "The (Ab)normalization of U.S.–Chinese Relations," *Foreign Affairs* 78 (September/October 1999):93–122.

23. "President Carter's Instructions to Zbigniew Brzezinski for His Mission to China, May 17, 1978," in Brzezinski, *Power and Principle*, Annex I, pp. 551–55 (unnumbered).

24. Ibid.

25. Fox Butterfield, "Brzezinski in China: The Stress Was on Common Concerns," *New York Times*, May 24, 1978.

26. Memorandum of conversation, September 23, 1977, Carter Papers, NSA-7, Box 35; Richard Burt, "Asia's Great Game . . . ," *New York Times*, July 9, 1978.

27. Bernard Gwertzman, "Brzezinski Charges Moscow Violates 'Code of Conduct,'" *New York Times*, May 29, 1978.

28. Bernard Gwertzman, "Young Voices Dissent on Policy in Africa," *New York Times*, May 22, 1978; Terence Smith, "Debate in Washington, DC: How to Meet Soviet Challenge," *New York Times*, May 27, 1978; George McGovern, "A Cool Foreign Policy," *New York Times*, June 26, 1978.

29. Bernard Gwertzman, "Top Government Science Mission Being Sent to China Next Week," *New York Times*, June 28, 1978; Bernard Weinraub, "U.S., in Reversal, Will Sell China Equipment Withheld from Soviet," *New York Times*, June 9, 1978.

30. Anatoly Dobrynin, *In Confidence: Moscow's Ambassador to America's Six Cold War Presidents* (New York: Times Books, 1995), pp. 404–10.

31. Kathleen Teltsch, "China, at U.N., Says Moscow May Cause 'A New World War,'" *New York Times*, May 30, 1978.

32. William Borders, "Afghanistan Vows 'Active Neutrality,'" *New York Times*, May 5, 1978.

33. Karl E. Meyer, *The Dust of Empire: The Race for Mastery in the Asian Heartland* (New York: PublicAffairs, 2003), p. 125; Diego Cordovez and Selig S. Harrison, *Out of Afghanistan: The Inside Story of the Soviet Withdrawal* (New York: Oxford University Press, 1995), pp. 14–32.

34. Cordovez and Harrison, *Out of Afghanistan*, pp. 32–34.

35. Shah Reza Pahlavi to Carter, May 8, 1978; Carter to Pahlavi, June 2, 1978, Carter Papers, Plains Files, Box 23.

36. Mohammed Heikal, *Iran: The Untold Story* (New York: Pantheon Books, 1982), p. 16; Helms to Kissinger, December 31, 1975, The Papers of Gerald R. Ford, Gerald R. Ford Library, Ann Arbor, Michigan, Confidential File, Box 14.

37. Shah Reza Pahlavi to Carter, June 1, 1977, Carter Papers, Plains File, Box 23.

38. Falk to Brzezinski, May 19, 1977, Carter Papers, White House Central File, Box F-08.

39. Carter to Shah Pahlavi, July 15, and August 27, 1977, Carter Papers; James Bill, *The Eagle and the Lion: The Tragedy of American-Iranian Relations* (New Haven: Yale University Press, 1988), pp. 228–32.

40. Jimmy Carter, *Keeping Faith: Memoirs of a President* (New York: Bantam Books, 1982), pp. 436–37.

41. David Harris, *The Crisis: The President, the Prophet, and the Shah—1979 and the Coming of Militant Islam* (Boston: Little, Brown, 2004), p. 69.

42. Visit of the Shah of Iran toasts of the President and the Shah at a dinner honoring the Shah, November 15, 1977, presidency.ucsb.edu/ws/?pid=6938.

43. Barry Rubin, *Paved With Good Intentions: The American Experience and Iran* (New York: Oxford University Press, 1980), pp. 188–89.

44. Heikal, *Iran*, p. 106ff.

45. Harris, *The Crisis*, pp. 74–75.

46. Heikal, *Iran*, p. 123.

47. "The Iranian Revolution: An Oral History with Henry Precht, Then State Department Desk Officer," *Middle East Journal* 58 no. 1 (Winter 2004): 9–31.

48. Ibid.

49. Ibid.

50. Ibid.

51. Brzezinski to Carter, December 2, 1978, Carter Papers, Brzezinski Donation, Box 42.

52. Robert L. Huyser, *Mission to Iran* (New York: Harper & Row, 1986), p. 17.

53. Ibid.

54. Bernard Gwertzman, "A Former Envoy Says Brzezinski Hurt U.S. in Iran," *New York Times*, September 7, 1980.

55. Brzezinski to Carter, February 2, 1979, Carter Papers, Brzezinski Donation, Box 42.

56. "The Crescent of Crisis," *Time*, January 15, 1979, time.com/time/printout/0,8816, 919995,00.html.

57. Meeting with King Hussein, March 18, 1979, Carter Papers, NSA-7, Box 33.

58. "Interview with Zbigniew Brzezinski," *Le Nouvel Observateur*, January 15–21, 1998, trans. by William Blum, members.aol.com/bblum6/brz.html.

59. Ibid.

60. Hamilton Jordan, *Crisis: The Last Year of the Carter Presidency* (New York: Putnam, 1982), pp. 31–32; Harris, *The Crisis*, p. 201.

61. Steve Coll, *Ghost Wars: The Secret History of the CIA, Afghanistan, and Bin Laden, from the Soviet Invasion to September 10, 2001* (New York: Penguin Press, 2004), pp. 47–49.

62. State of the Union address, January 23, 1980, presidency.ucsb.edu/ws/print.php?pid=33079.

63. Ibid.

64. Interview with Dr. Brzezinski, June 13, 1997, gwu.edu/~nsarchiv/coldwar/interviews/ episode-17/brzezinski2.html; "Brezinski at the Pass: Bonhomie, Bullets," *New York Times*, February 4, 1980.

Chapter 3: The First Gulf War, in Which the Realists Make Their Last Stand

1. Quoted in Patricia Nelson Limerick, *The Legacy of Conquest: The Unbroken Past of the American West* (New York: W.W. Norton & Co., 1987), p. 324.

2. Interestingly enough, the Star Wars speech, March 23, 1983, in which Reagan announced the planned research for an antimissile program, probably would not measure up to today's neocon standards of bellicosity for presidential defense initiatives. It was, in fact, prefaced with a kind of disclaimer about American policy: "The defense policy of the United States is based on a simple premise: The United States does not start fights. We will never be an aggressor. We maintain our strength in order to deter and defend against aggression—to preserve freedom and peace." Reagan even ad-

mitted that, taken in conjunction with his offensive arms buildup, it might be judged by the Soviets as a plan for preemptive attack. He tried to make additional disclaimers about such fears later in the speech, such as: "I clearly recognize that defensive systems have limitations and raise certain problems and ambiguities. If paired with offensive systems, they can be viewed as fostering an aggressive policy, and no one wants that." Again, by certain of today's standards, Reagan's rhetoric was measured and sophisticated.

3. Edwin Meese, *With Reagan: The Inside Story* (Washingon, DC: Regnery Gateway, 1992), p. 244.

4. See Theodore Draper, *A Very Thin Line: The Iran-Contra Affairs* (New York: Hill & Wang, 1991) for a discussion of the implications of the affair, and its implications for the future.

5. March 11, 1992, Office of the Federal Register, National Archives and Records Administration, *Public Papers of the Presidents of the United States, George Bush, 1992–93,* 2 vols. (Washington, DC: G.P.O., 1993), vol. 1, pp. 428–32 (hereafter *Public Papers*).

6. Rachel Bronson, *Thicker Than Oil: America's Uneasy Partnership with Saudi Arabia* (New York: Oxford University Press, 2006), p. 147.

7. Ibid., p. 149.

8. Richard A. Clarke, *Against All Enemies: Inside America's War on Terror* (New York: Free Press, 2004), p. 52.

9. One can follow the twists and turns in this story in Gary Sick, *October Surprise* (New York: Random House, 1991).

10. Haig, undated [1981] "Talking Points," as a reprinted attachment to Robert Parry, "Missing US-Iraq History," February 27, 2003, consortiumnews.com/2003/022703a.html.

11. Stephen R. Shalom, "The United States and the Iran-Iraq War," Z, February 1990, zmag.org/zmag/articles/ShalomIranIraq.html.

12. Meese, *With Reagan*, p. 249.

13. A good short summary is Walter LaFeber's *The American Age: United States Foreign Policy at Home and Abroad Since 1750* (New York: W.W. Norton & Co., 1989), pp. 690–92.

14. Sick, *October Surprise*, p. 109.

15. Bob Woodward, *Veil: The Secret Wars of the CIA, 1981–1987* (New York: Simon & Schuster, 1987), pp. 439–40.

16. Joyce Battle, ed., "Shaking Hands with Saddam Hussein: The U.S. Tilts Toward Iraq, 1980–1984," National Security Archive Electronic Briefing Book No. 82, February 25, 2003, gwu.edu/~nsarchiv/NSAEBB/NSAEBB82/.

17. Press conference, July 16, 1989, Public Papers, 1989, II, 969–77.

18. *Public Papers*, 1990, I, pp. 130–31.

19. Stephen Kinzer, *Overthrow: America's Century of Regime Change from Hawaii to Iraq* ((New York: Henry Holt & Co., 2006), p. 252.

20. Operation Just Cause is well treated in ibid., pp. 239–59.

21. Glaspie's cable on this part of the conversation is much briefer, and almost an afterthought. "The Ambassador," it reads, "said that she had served in Kuwait 20 years before; then, as now, we took no position on these Arab affairs." Easy cross-references to the transcripts can be found in the article "April Glaspie," in Wikipedia, en.wikipedia.org/wiki/April_Glaspie.

22. Joseph Wilson, *The Politics of Truth: Inside the Lies that Led to War and Betrayed My Wife's CIA Identity* (New York: Carroll & Graf Publishers, 2004), p. 102.

23. April Glaspie transcript, July 25, 1990, whatreallyhappened.com/ARTICLE5/april.html.

24. Herbert S. Parmet, *George Bush: The Life of a Lone Star Yankee* (New York: Scribner, 1997), p. 454.

25. George H.W. Bush and Brent Scowcroft, *A World Transformed* (New York: Alfred A. Knopf, 1998), p. 315.

26. Remarks and an exchange with reporters on the Iraqi invasion of Kuwait, August 5, 1990, margaretthatcher.org/archive/displaydocument.asp?docid=110704.

27. Martin Walker, "American Caesar's Dream," *The Guardian*, January 12, 1991.

28. General H. Norman Schwarzkopf with Peter Petre, *The Autobiography: It Doesn't Take a Hero* (New York: Bantam Books, 1992), pp. 297–98.

29. Ibid., pp. 303–4.

30. "Oral History: Richard Cheney," PBS, *Frontline: The Gulf War* (program originally broadcast January 6, 1996), pbs.org/wgbh/pages/frontline/gulf/oral/cheney/1.html.

31. Colin Powell with Joseph Persico, *My American Journey* (New York: Ballantine Books, 1996), p. 451.

32. Ibid., p. 457.

33. Michael Duffy and Dan Goodgame, *Marching in Place: The Status Quo Presidency of George Bush* (New York: Simon & Schuster, 1992), p. 155.

34. Scott Ritter, *Target Iran: The Truth About the White House's Plans for Regime Change* (New York: Nation Books, 2006), p. 5.

35. Bush and Scowcroft, *A World Transformed*, p. 382.

36. "Oral History: James Baker," *Frontline: The Gulf War*, pbs.org/wgbh/pages/frontline/gulf/oral/baker/1.html.

37. Quoted in Maureen Dowd, "Mideast Tensions: Bush Intensifies a War of Words Against the Iraqis," *New York Times*, November 1, 1990.

38. Bush and Scowcroft, *A World Transformed*, p. 385.

39. Ibid., p. 418.

40. Center for Media and Democracy, "How PR Sold the War in the Persian Gulf," prwatch.org/node/25.

41. Ibid.

42. John R. MacArthur, *Second Front: Censorship and Propaganda in the Gulf War* (New York: Hill and Wang, 1992), pp. 65–68.

43. "Gulf War Stories the Media Loved—Except They Aren't True," *Extra!*, special Gulf War issue 1991, fair.org/index.php?page=1515.

44. Press conference, November 1, 1990, text available at bushlibrary.tamu.edu/research/papers/1990/90110102.html.

45. Dowd, "Mideast Tensions," *New York Times*, November 1, 1990.

46. See Steven Hurst, "The Rhetorical Strategy of George H.W. Bush during the Persian Gulf Crisis 1990–91: How to Help Lose a War You Won," 32 *Political Studies: 2004*, 376–92.

47. Lawrence Freedman and Efraim Karsh, *The Gulf Conflict, 1990–1991: Diplomacy and War in the New World Order* (Princeton: Princeton University Press, 1993), p. 220.

48. Ibid., pp. 291–95.

49. Michael R. Gordon, "U.S. Aides Press Iraqi Nuclear Threat," *New York Times*, November 26, 1990.

50. Richard Rhodes, "Iraq's Atomic Red Herring," *New York Times*, November 27, 1990.

51. Address to the Nation, January 16, 1991, *Public Papers*, 1991, I, pp. 42–45.

52. Bush and Scowcroft, *A World Transformed*, p. 440.

53. S.H. Kelly, "Bush Tells Gulf Vets Why Hussein Left in Baghdad," *Army Link News*, March 3, 1999, fas.org/news/iraq/1999/03/a19990303bush.htm.

54. pbs.org/wgbh/pages/frontline/gulf/oral/powell /5.html.

55. Robert Jay Lifton, "Last Refuge of a Hi-Tech Nation," *The Guardian*, March 12, 1991.

56. "Analysis," *The Guardian*, February 5, 2003.

57. Ibid., and Scott Peterson, "Some US Assertions from the Last War Still Appear Dubious," *Christian Science Monitor*, September 6, 2002.

58. The Strategic Assessment document is discussed in Ritt Goldstein, "Oil Wars Pentagon's Policy Since 1999," *Sydney Morning Herald*, May 20, 2003.

Chapter 4: The End(s) of History, in Which the Theory and Practice Conflict

1. Remarks at Maxwell Air Force Base, April 13, 1991, Public Papers, 1991, I, pp. 364–68.

2. Excerpts from news conference, April 1, 1992, U.S. Department of State Dispatch, April 6, 1992, pp. 261–62.

3. Thomas P.M. Barnett, *The Pentagon's New Map: War and Peace in the Twenty-first Century* (New York: G.P. Putnam's Sons, 2004), p. 94.

4. See Jonathan Randal, *Osama: The Making of a Radical* (New York: Alfred A. Knopf, 2004), pp. 99–114.

5. Ibid., 105.

6. Ibid., 109.

7. George Will, "The Case Against Bush's Foreign Policy," *Home News* (New Brunswick, NJ), January 12, 1992.

8. Interview with Brent Scowcroft, "We Won't Let Him Do That," *U.S. News & World Report*, December 24, 1990.

9. Interview, "America Can't Afford to Turn Inward," *New Perspectives Quarterly*, Summer 1992, pp. 6–10.

10. The document is excerpted at pbs.org/wgbh/pages/frontline/shows/iraq/etc/wolf/html.

11. James Mann, *Rise of the Vulcans: The History of Bush's War Cabinet* (New York: Viking Penguin, 2004), p. 113. The quoted figures on allied financial help in Gulf War I are taken from the Civil War History Center Web site, cwc.lus.edu.

12. The National Security Strategy document of September 17, 2002, with the covering letter can be found at whitehouse.gov/nsc/nssall.html. I have added the italics.

13. See Ron Suskind, "Without a Doubt," *New York Times Sunday Magazine*, October 17, 2004, downloaded from Truthout, January 31, 2005, truthout.org/docs_04/printer_101704A.shtml.

14. Fukuyama's essay "The End of History" can be found in the summer 1989 issue of *The National Interest*. The liberalism Fukuyama was talking about, of course, was the pre–New Deal, nineteenth-century liberalism of nationalism and laissez-faire. Fukuyama paid great homage in the essay to free markets, not as the Marxist engine of capitalist striving, but as carriers of the ideals of liberalism.

15. Richard Holbrooke, "The Paradox of George F. Kennan," *Washington Post*, March 21, 2005.

16. Ibid.

17. Suskind, "Without a Doubt."

18. SourceWatch, "Iraqi National Congress," sourcewatch.org/index.php?title=Iraqi_ National_ Congress.

19. This discussion is largely drawn from Peter Bergen, "Armchair Provocateur, Laurie Mylroie: The Neocons Favorite Conspiracy Theorist," *Washington Monthly*, December 2003, washingtonmonthly.com/features/2003/03/12.bergen.html.

20. Laurie Mylroie, "The World Trade Center Bomb: Who Is Ramzi Yousef? And Why It Matters," *The National Interest*, Winter 1995/96, fas.org/irp/world/iraq/956–tni.html.

21. Bergen, "Armchair Provocateur."

22. The letter can be found at newamericancentury.org/iraqclintonletter.html.

23. The letter, dated February 19, 1998, can be found at iraqwatch.org/perspectives/rumsfeld-openletter.

24. Seymour Hersh, "Did Iraq Try to Assassinate ex-President Bush in 1993? A Case Not Closed," in Christoper Cerf and Micah Sifry, *The Iraq War Reader, History, Documents, Opinions* (New York: Touchstone Books, 2003), pp. 140–62.

25. The Clinton quotations in this paragraph and the one following are from Stephen F. Hayes, "Democrats for Regime Change: The President Has Some Surprising Allies," *The Weekly Standard*, September 16, 2002. Hayes's purpose was to demonstrate that Clinton was the true author of regime change.

26. CNN, "U.S. Policy on Iraq Draws Fire in Ohio," February 18, 1998, cnn.com/WORLD/ 9802/18/town.meeting.folo/.

27. NBC, *Today*, February 19, 1998, quoted in members.aol.com/bblum6/albright.html.

28. Madeleine Albright, *Madam Secretary: A Memoir* (New York: Miramax Books, 2003), p. 283.

29. Ibid., pp. 368–69.

30. See Norm Dixon, "Richard Butler—Servant of the UN or Washington?" reprinted on the Web at globalpolicy.org/security/issues/butler2.html. Dixon provides a catalog of articles dealing with the strikes from the *Washington Post* and the *New York Times*.

31. Albright, *Madam Secretary*, pp. 274–75.

32. Albright's speech, March 26, 1997, at fas.org/news/iraq/1997/03bmd970327b.html.

33. Sandy Berger, "Change Will Come to Iraq," National Press Club address, December 23, 1998, mtholyoke.edu/acad/intrel/berger2.htm.

Chapter 5: Axis of Evil, in Which the Nation's Enemies Are Revealed

1. Conversation with David Frum, January 20, 2004, Conversations with History: Institute of International Studies, University of California, Berkeley, globetrotter.berkeley.edu/people4/Frum/frum-con4.html.

2. Gordon Corera, "Iran's Gulf of Misunderstanding with US," BBC News, September 25, 2006, news.bbc.co.uk/2/hi/middle_east/5377914.stm.

3. Remarks by the President at the American Society of Newspaper Editors annual convention, April 5, 2001.

4. "Bush, Cheney Meet with 9/11 Panel," CNN.com, April 30, 2004, cnn.com/2004/ALLPOLITICS/04/29/bush.911.commission/index.html.

5. David Ignatius, "Cheney's Enigmatic Influence," Washington Post, January 19, 2007, washingtonpost.com/wp-dyn/content/article/2007/01/18/AR2007011801511.html.

6. "Cheney in His Own Words," PBS, Frontline: The Dark Side, pbs.org/wgbh/pages/frontline/darkside/themes/ownwords.

7. "Cheney's Views on Presidential Power Forged During Iran-Contra," Daily Herald (Everett, WA), June 25, 2007.

8. Nick Turse, "The Pentagon as Global Landlord," July 11, 2007, tomdispatch.com/post/print/174818/Tomgram%253A%.

9. Patrick Tyler, "After the War: U.S. Juggling Iraq Policy," New York Times, April 13, 1991.

10. "Dick Cheney Ain't Studyin' War No More," BusinessWeek, March 2, 1998, businessweek.com/1998/09/b3567127.htm.

11. Cheney, "Defending Liberty in a Global Economy." Speech at the Cato Institute, June 23, 1998, cato.org/speeches/sp-dc062398.html.

12. Barton Gellman and Jo Becker, "Angler: The Cheney Vice-Presidency, Part One: A Different Understanding with the President," June 24, 2007, blog.washingtonpost.com/cheney/chapters/chapter_1/.

13. Ron Suskind, The One Percent Doctrine: Deep Inside America's Pursuit of Its Enemies Since 9/11 (New York: Simon & Schuster, 2006), pp. 60–63.

14. George W. Bush, "Remarks at the annual meeting of the Associated Press," April 30, 2001.

15. Larry Everest, "Cheney, Energy and Iraq Invasion/Supreme Court to Rule on Secrecy," San Francisco Chronicle, March 21, 2004.

16. Ron Suskind, The Price of Loyalty: George W. Bush, the White House, and the Education of Paul O'Neill (New York: Simon & Schuster, 2004), p. 72.

17. Ibid.

18. Ibid., p. 74.

19. Bob Woodward, Plan of Attack (New York: Simon & Schuster, 2004), p. 175.

20. Jane Perlez, "Powell Proposes Easing Sanctions on Iraqi Civilians," New York Times, February 27, 2001.

21. Frank Bruni and David E. Sanger, "Attack on Iraq," New York Times, February 17, 2001.

22. Woodward, Plan of Attack, p. 27. Emphasis added.

23. William Safire, "Team B vs. C.I.A.," New York Times, July 20, 1998.

24. Prepared testimony of U.S. secretary of defense Donald H. Rumsfeld, Senate Armed Services Committee, June 21, 2001, armed-services.senate.gov/statemnt/2001/010621rumsfeld.pdf.

25. "Plans for Iraq Attack Began on 9/11," CBS News, September 4, 2002, cbsnews.com/stories/2002/09/04.

26. Dan Balz and Bob Woodward, "America's Chaotic Road to War," *Washington Post*, January 27, 2002.

27. Richard A. Clarke, *Against All Enemies: Inside America's War on Terror* (New York: The Free Press, 2004), pp. 30–32.

28. Woodward, *Plan of Attack*, p. 25.

29. The vice president appears on *Meet the Press*, September 16, 2001, whitehouse.gov/vicepresident/news-speeches/speechesvp20011209.html.

30. Ibid.

31. Rowan Scarborough, *Rumsfeld's War: The Untold Story of America's Anti-Terrorist Commander* (Washington, DC: Regnery, 2004), pp. 1–2.

32. Karen Kwiatkowski, "The New Pentagon Papers," undated, informationclearinghouse.info/article/5829.html.

33. David L. Phillips, *Losing Iraq: Inside the Postwar Reconstruction Fiasco* (Boulder, CO: Westview Press, 2005), p. 61.

34. Ibid.

35. James Dao and Eric Schmitt, "Pentagon Readies Efforts to Sway Sentiment Abroad," *New York Times*, February 19, 2002.

36. Mike Allen, "White House Angered at Plan for Pentagon Disinformation, *Washington Post*, February 25, 2002.

37. Defense Department briefing, February 26, 2002, fas.org/sgp/news/2002/02/dod022602.html.

38. DoD news briefing—Secretary Rumsfeld and General Myers, October 24, 2002, defenselink.mil/transcripts/transcript.aspx?transcriptid=3798.

39. Bradley Graham and Dana Priest, "Pentagon Team Told to Seek Details of Iraq–Al Qaeda Ties," *Washington Post*, October 25, 2002.

40. Suskind, *One Percent Doctrine*, pp. 33–34.

41. Vice President Cheney delivers remarks to the Republican Governors Association, October 25, 2001, whitehouse.gov/vicepresident/news-speeches/speeches/vp20011025.html; President delivers State of the Union address, January 29, 2002, whitehouse.gov/news/releases/2002/01/20020129–11.html.

42. The vice president appears on *The NewsHour with Jim Lehrer*, October 12, 2001, whitehouse.gov/vicepresident/news-speeches/speeches/vp20011012.html; the vice president appears on NBC's *Meet the Press*, December 9, 2001, whitehouse.gov/vicepresident/news-speeches/speeches/vp20011209.html.

43. "Anthrax Culprit 'Probably Domestic,'" BBC News, November 10, 2001, news.bbc.co.uk/2/hi/americas/1648159.stm.

44. Transcript of interview with Vice President Dick Cheney on *Meet the Press*, September 8, 2002, mtholyoke.edu/acad/intrel/bush/meet.htm.

45. Deputy Secretary Wolfowitz interview with BBC, October 31, 2001, defenselink.mil/transcripts/transcript.aspx?transcriptid=2294.

46. "The Impact of Bush Linking 9/11 and Iraq," *Christian Science Monitor*, March 14, 2003. The fullest account of the anthrax scare and its momentous impact on the public and the case for war is Phillip Sarasin's *Anthrax: Bioterror as Fact and Fantasy*, trans. by Giselle Weiss (Cambridge: Harvard University Press, 2006). Despite its occasional lapses into postmodern jargon, Sarasin's book provides an excellent account of the politics of anthrax.

47. Secretary Rumsfeld on CBS *Face the Nation*, September 23, 2001, defenselink.mil/transcripts/transcript.aspx?transcriptid=1922; Secretary Rumsfeld interview with NBC *Meet the Press* with host Tim Russert, September 30, 2001, defenselink.mil/transcripts/transcript.aspx?transcriptid=1947.

48. Secretary Rumsfeld interview with *USA Today*, October 24, 2001, defenselink.mil/transcripts/transcript.aspx?transcriptid=2173.

49. Woodward, *Bush at War*, p. 194.

50. Bill Keller, "The Sunshine Warrior," *New York Times*, September 22, 2002.

51. Ibid.

52. A good example of Rice's post-9/11 rhetoric can be found in her speech to the Paul H. Nitze School of Advanced International Studies at Johns Hopkins University on April 29, 2002, whitehouse.gov/news/releases/2002/04.

53. President Bush delivers graduation speech at West Point, June 1, 2002, www.whitehouse.gov/news/releases/2002/06/20020601-3.html.

54. Nicholas Lemann, "The Next World Order: The Bush Administration May Have a Brand-New Doctrine of Power," *New Yorker*, April 1, 2002, posted on the Web March 25, 2002; "Dr. Condoleezza Rice discusses president's national security strategy," October 1, 2002.

55. Interview with Condoleezza Rice, September 8, 2002, CNN *Late Edition*, downloaded from mtholyoke,edu/acad/intrel/bush/wolf.html. Emphasis added.

56. Glenn Kessler, "Powell Says Weapons Inspections Needed First," *Newark Star-Ledger*, September 2, 2002.

57. "President Bush, Prime Minister Blair Discuss Keeping the Peace," September 7, 2002, whitehouse.gov/news/releases/2002/09.

58. See Mark Danner, *The Secret Way to War: The Downing Street Memo and the Iraq War's Buried History* (New York: New York Review Books, 2006), pp. 88–89.

59. President Bush, Prime Minister Blair discuss keeping the peace, September 7, 2002, whitehouse.gov/news/releases/2002/09/20020907-2.html; Arms Control Association, "Iraq: A Chronology of UN Inspections and an Assessment of their Accomplishments, 1990–2002," Washington, DC, October 2002.

60. See Roger Morris, "The Source Beyond Rove: Condoleezza Rice at the Center of the Plame Scandal," eGP@360, Green Institute, July 27, 2005, greeninstitute.net/node/186?q=node/39.

61. Vice President speaks at VFW 103rd national convention, August 26, 2002.

62. Julian Borger, "White House in Disarray over Cheney Speech," *The Guardian*, September 2, 2002.

63. President Bush's remarks at the UN General Assembly, September 12, 2002, whitehouse.gov/news/releases/2002/09/20020912-1.html.

64. Robert Draper, *Dead Certain: The Presidency of George W. Bush* (New York: Free Press, 2007), p. 182.

65. Wil S. Hylton, "The Angry One: Republican Senator Chuck Hagel Sounds Off on the Sorry State of Congress, the President's Lies, and the Vote for War That He Now Regrets," GQ, January 2007, men.style.com/gq/features/landing?id=content_5326.

66. Maureen Dowd, "Lemon Fizzes on the Banks of the Euphrates," *New York Times*, September 18, 2002.

67. See Michael Isikoff and David Corn, *Hubris: The Inside Story of Spin, Scandal, and the Selling of the Iraq War* (New York: Crown Publishers, 2006), pp. 35–44, 144–47.

Chapter 6: Shock and Awe, in Which We Learn How Some Democracies Go to War

1. Tyler Drumheller, *On the Brink: An Insider's Account of How the White House Compromised American Intelligence* (New York: Carroll & Graf, 2006), pp. 102–4.

2. Carl Bernstein and Bob Woodward, "Blue State Methodist, Red State Methodist," posted on "On Faith: A Conversation on Religion with Jon Meacham and Sally Quinn," June 26, 2007, newsweek.washingtonpost.com/onfaith/guestvoices/2007/06/bernstein.html.

3. Elisabeth Bumiller, "Traces of Terror: The Strategy; Bush Aides Set Strategy to Sell Policy on Iraq," *New York Times*, September 7, 2002.

4. Michael R. Gordon and Judith Miller, "Threats and Responses: The Iraqis; U.S. Says Hussein Intensifies Quest for A-bomb Parts," *New York Times*, September 8, 2002.

5. Michael Isikoff and David Corn, *Hubris: The Inside Story of Spin, Scandal, and the Selling of the Iraq War* (New York: Crown, 2006), pp. 34–41.

6. The story of the Niger caper can be followed in detail in ibid., pp. 85–100.

7. Joan Didion, "Cheney: The Fatal Touch," *New York Review of Books*, October 5, 2006, nybooks.com/articles/19376 Key Judgments (from October 2002 NIE), "Iraq's Continuing Programs for Weapons of Mass Destruction," declassified excerpts released by the White House on July 18, 2003.

8. Anne Penketh, "How Blair Has Stood by Niger Claim," *The Independent*, March 7, 2007. In fact, Blair stood by his report long after it was totally discredited in the United States and the Bush administration admitted error in making the assertion.

9. Matt Kelley, "Bush Seeks OK for Military Force Against Iraq," AP, September 19, 2002, salon.com/news/wire/2002/09/19/iraq_congress/print.html. Inside the Pentagon, Lieutenant Colonel Karen Kwiatkowski, who would become a thorn in Rumsfeld's side after she retired and exposed the intelligence operations of the Office of Special Plans, observed the way the Iraq War was being plotted out in regard to information about WMD. In a press interview in 2004, Kwiatowski said, "We knew from many years of both high-level surveillance and other types of shared intelligence, not to mention the information from the UN, we knew what was left [from the Gulf War] and the viability of any of that. Bush said he didn't know. The truth is, we know [Saddam] didn't have these things. Almost a billion dollars has been spent—a billion dollars!—by David Kay's group to search for these WMD, a total whitewash effort. They didn't find anything, they didn't expect to find anything."

Marc Cooper, "Soldier for the Truth," *L.A. Weekly*, February 20, 2004, truthout.org/docs_04/022304B.shtml.

10. Kelley, "Bush Seeks OK"; President Bush discusses Iraq with reporters, September 13, 2002, whitehouse.gov/news/releases/2002/09.

11. See, for example, Secretary Rumsfeld interview with Jim Lehrer, *NewsHour*, September 18, 2002, defenselink.mil/transcripts/transcript.aspx?transcriptid=3656.

12. Eric Schmitt, "Rumsfeld Says U.S. Has 'Bulletproof' Evidence of Iraq's Links to Al Qaeda," *New York Times*, September 28, 2002.

13. George Tenet with Bill Harlow, *At the Center of the Storm: My Years at the CIA* (New York: HarperCollins, 2007), pp. 360–65.

14. Bryan Burrough, Evgenia Peretz, David Rose, and David Wise, "The Path to War," *Vanity Fair*, May 2004, p. 228ff.

15. ABC News, "Powell Calls U.N. Speech a 'Blot' on His Record," AOL News, September 5, 2005, articles.news.aol.com/news/_a/powell-calls-un-speech-a-blot-on-his/20050908231709990004.

16. Bob Woodward, "Cheney Was Unwavering in Desire to Go to War," *Washington Post*, April 20, 2004.

17. Don Van Natta, "Bush Was Set on Path to War, British Memo Says," *New York Times*, March 27, 2006.

18. Transcript of Bush-Aznar consultation in Crawford, Informed Comment, February 22, 2003, juancole.com/2007/09/bush-aznar-transcript-war-crime-of.html.

19. Hans Blix, "Oral Introduction of the 12th Quarterly Report of UNMOVIC," UN Security Council briefing, March 7, 2003, un.org/Depts/unmovic/SC7asdelivered.htm.

20. Hans Blix, *Disarming Iraq* (New York: Pantheon, 2004), pp. 118–19.

21. Ibid., pp. 167–68.

22. "Blix Stung by Pentagon 'Smear,'" BBC News, June 11, 2003, news.bbc.co.uk/2/hi/middle_east/2980332.stm; Anne Penketh, "Blix Criticizes UK's Iraq Dossier," BBC News, September 18, 2003, news.bbc.co.uk/2/hi/uk_news/politics/3118462.stm; Anne Penketh, "Hans Blix: Bush and Blair Behaved as if They Were on a 'Witch Hunt' over Iraqi Weapons," *The Independent*, March 8, 2004, www.independent.co.uk/news/people/hans-blix-bush-and-blair-behaved-as-if-they-were-on-a-witch-hunt-over-iraqi-weapons-565577.html.

23. Gary Younge, "Blix Attacks 'Shaky' Intelligence on Weapons," *The Guardian*, April 23, 2003.

24. Elisabeth Bumiller, David E. Sanger, and Richard W. Stevenson, "A Nation at War: The President; How 3 Weeks of War in Iraq Looked From the Oval Office," *New York Times*, April 14, 2003.

25. Transcript, NBC News, *Meet the Press*, March 16, 2003. Emphasis added.

26. Eric Schmitt, "Pentagon Contradicts General on Iraq Occupation Force's Size," *New York Times*, February 28, 2003.

27. Scott Peterson, "US Mulls Air Strategies in Iraq," *Christian Science Monitor*, January 30, 2003.

28. Quotations taken from shockandawe.com/index1.html.

29. Secretary Rumsfeld briefs at the Foreign Press Center, January 22, 2003, dod.gov/cgi-bin/dlprint.cgi?http:www.dod.gov/transcripts. Here was a curious parallel to the signing statements

President Bush used to put his own spin on congressional bills he signed, so that law enforcement became a series of options instead of an absolute mandate—as in the case of the antitorture legislation passed in the wake of Abu Ghraib.

30. Andrew West and agencies, "800 Missiles to Hit Iraq in First 48 Hours," *Sydney Morning Herald,* January 26, 2003, smh.com.au/articles/2003/01/25/1042911596206.html.

31. Mary McGrory, "The 'Shock and Awe' News Conference," *Washington Post,* March 9, 2003.

32. "Bush: Saddam Has 48 Hours to Leave Iraq," CNN.com, March 18, 2003.

33. Bumiller, Sanger, and Stevenson, "A Nation at War."

34. Bob Woodward, *State of Denial: Bush at War* (New York: Simon & Schuster, 2006), pp. 154–55. These exchanges recorded by Woodward indicate how early a nagging sense of incompleteness had set in during Oval Office discussions, even in the midst of the military triumph.

35. Jay Nordlinger, "Rumsfeld Rules," National Review Online, December 31, 2001.

36. DoD news briefing—Secretary Rumsfeld and General Myers, April 11, 2003, defenselink.mil/transcripts/transcript.aspx?transcriptid=2367.

37. Ibid.

38. Fox News, "Iraqis—with American Help—Topple Statue of Saddam in Baghdad," April 9, 2003, foxnews.com/printer_friendly_story/0,3566,83580,00.html.

39. Oliver Poole and David Blair, "The Toppling of Saddam," *Telegraph,* April 10, 2003.

40. Bumiller, Sanger, and Stevenson, "A Nation at War."

41. Ibid.

42. David Zucchino, "U.S. Military, Not Iraqis, Behind Toppling of Statue," Honolulu Advertiser.com, July 5, 2004.

43. "Saddam Statue Toppled in Central Baghdad," CNN.com, April 9, 2003, cnn.com/2003/WORLD/meast/04/09/sprj.irq.statue.

44. Elisabeth Bumiller and Doughlas Jehl, "A Nation at War: Washington; Bush Tunes In and Sees Iraqis in Celebrations," *New York Times,* April 10, 2003.

45. Ibid.

46. Eric Rosenberg, "Rumsfeld Retreats, Disclaims Earlier Rhetoric," *Ocala Star Banner,* November 9, 2003, truthout.org/docs_03/printer_1111031.shtml.

47. Deputy Secretary Wolfowitz interview with Sam Tanenhaus, *Vanity Fair,* May 9, 2003, defenselink.mil/transcripts/transcript.aspx?transcriptid=2594.

48. "Wolfowitz Comments Revive Doubts over Iraq's WMD," *USA Today,* May 30, 2003.

49. Ibid.

50. Thomas M. Freiling, *George W. Bush on God and Country* (Washington, DC: Alliance Press, 2004), p. 10; Anne Norton, *Leo Strauss and the Politics of American Empire* (New Haven: Yale University Press, 2005), pp. 134–35.

51. Draper, *Dead Certain,* p. 194.

52. President Bush announces major combat operations in Iraq have ended, May 1, 2003, whitehouse.gov/news/releases/2003/05/20030501–15.html.

53. President discusses economy, national security in California, May 2, 2003, z22.whitehouse.gov/news/releases/2003/05/20030502–7.html.

54. "Commander in Chief lands on USS Lincoln," CNN.com/Inside Politics, May 2, 2003.

Chapter 7: The Occupation, in Which We Learn What Followed Shock and Awe

1. "Pentagon's No. 2 Flubs Iraq Casualties," AP, April 29, 2004, commondreams.org/headlines04/0429–11.html.

2. Thomas E. Ricks, *Fiasco: The American Military Adventure in Iraq* (New York: Penguin Press, 2006), pp. 330–31.

3. Ibid., pp. 331–32.

4. Woodward, *State of Denial: Bush at War* (New York: Simon & Schuster, 2006) pp. 298–99.

5. Jim Lobe, "'Phantom Fury' Poised to Become Phantom Victory," Inter Press Service, November 9, 2004.

6. Ricks, *Fiasco*, pp. 405–6.

7. Ali A. Allawi, *The Occupation of Iraq: Winning the War, Losing the Peace* (New Haven: Yale University Press, 2007), pp. 175–80.

8. Ibid., pp. 354–55.

9. "Text of Bush's Wednesday Comments," *USA Today*, July 2, 2003, usatoday.com/news/washington/2003–07–02–bush-speech-text_x.htm.

10. Eric Schmitt, "The Struggle for Iraq: The Military; Forces Strained in Iraq Mission, Congress Is Told," *New York Times*, September 10, 2003.

11. Ibid.; BBC News, "Iraq Contracts Bar War Opponents," December 12, 2003, newsvote.bbc.co.uk/mpapps/pagetools/print/news.bbc.co.uk/2/.

12. David E. Sanger and Douglas Jehl, "Bush Seeks Help of Allies Barred from Iraq Deals," *New York Times*, December 11, 2003.

13. Ibid.

14. Eric Schmitt, "Rumsfeld Says More G.I.'s Would Not Help U.S. in Iraq," *New York Times*, September 11, 2003.

15. Ibid.

16. Quoted in Lloyd C. Gardner, "Present at the Culmination," in Lloyd C. Gardner and Marilyn B. Young, eds., *The New American Empire: A 21st Century Teach-In on U.S. Foreign Policy* (New York: The New Press, 2005), p. 8.

17. Ibid., 9. The above four paragraphs are close paraphrases of paragraphs in this article.

18. Deputy Secretary Wolfowitz interview with Sam Tanenhaus, *Vanity Fair*, May 9, 2003, defenselink.mil/transcripts/transcript.aspx?transcriptid=2594.

19. "Defense Chief Makes Unannounced Visit to Iraq," CNN.com, February 11, 2005.

20. The interviews appear several places. I have taken these quotations from Amy Svitak Klamper, "Former Iraq Administrator Sees Decades-Long U.S. Military Presence," *Government Executive*, February 6, 2004, govexec.com/story_page.cfm?articleid+27.

21. Paul Wolfowitz, prepared statement before the House Armed Services Committee, June 23, 2004.

22. Kurt M. Campbell and Celeste Johnson Ward, "New Battle Stations?" *Foreign Affairs* 82 no. 5 (September/October 2003): 95–103.

23. David R. Francis, "US Bases in Iraq: Sticky Politics, Hard Math," *Christian Science Monitor*, September 30, 2004, csmonitor.com/2004/0930/p17s02–cogn,html; Tom Englehardt, "Everlasting US Pyramids in Iraqi Sands," *Asia Times*, June 9, 2007, atimes.com/atimes/Middle_East/IF09Ak05.html.

24. Larry Diamond, *Squandered Victory: The American Occupation and the Bungled Effort to Bring Democracy to Iraq* (New York: Times Books, 2005), pp. 160–61; Joshua Hammer, "Digging In," April 13, 2005, houston.indymedia.org/news/2005/04/38703.php.

25. Downloaded from the UCLA International Institute Web site, September 29, 2005.

26. Simon Ostrovsky, "US Working to Boost Forces in Oil-Rich Caspian," September 21, 2005, bakutoday.net/view.php?d=14714.

27. Ann Scott Tyson, "US forces are repositioning overseas forces, opting for smaller, transitory bases in places like Kyrgystan," *Christian Science Monitor*, August 10, 2004, csmonitor.com/2004/0810/po6s02–wosc.html.

28. Remarks by the president to the Philippine Congress, October 18, 2003, whitehouse.gov/news/releases/2003/10/print.

29. Fred Kaplan, "From Baghdad to Manila," *Slate.com*, October 21, 2003, slate.com/id=2090114.

30. Walter LaFeber, *The American Age: United States Foreign Policy at Home and Abroad Since 1750* (New York: W.W. Norton & Co., 1989), p. 198. Wood came back in 1921 as governor general of the Philippines, and once again earned a reputation for harshness that left behind a bitter taste in the islands.

31. Josh White, "Abu Ghraib Tactics Were First Used at Guantánamo," *Washington Post*, July 14, 2005; and Josh White, "Abu Ghraib Dog Tactics Came from Guantánamo," *Washington Post*, July 17, 2005.

32. Woodward, *State of Denial*, pp. 236–37.

33. Bob Drogin, *Curveball: Spies, Lies, and the Con Man Who Caused a War* (New York: Random House, 2007), pp. 276–77.

34. Deputy Secretary Wolfowitz interview on *Fox Sunday*, July 27, 2003, defenselink.mil/transcript.aspx?transcriptid=2906.

35. Joseph Wilson, *The Politics of Truth: Inside the Lies that Led to War and Betrayed My Wife's CIA Identity* (New York: Carroll & Graf, 2004), pp. 330–35.

36 David E. Sanger and David Barstow, "Iraq Findings Leaked by Cheney's Aide Were Disputed," *New York Times*, April 9, 2006.

37. Jason Leopold, "Wolfowitz Emerges as Key Figure in Intel Manipulation," "Truthout Report," February 12, 2007, truthout.org/docs_2006/ printer_021207A.shtml.

38. Press gaggle with Ari Fleischer, July 9, 2003, fas.org/irp/news/2003/07/wh070903.html. Emphasis added.

39. Ibid.

40. Barton Gellman, "A Leak, Then a Deluge," *Washington Post*, October 30, 2005.

41. Michael Isikoff and David Corn, *Hubris: The Inside Story of Spin, Scandals, and the Selling of the Iraq War* (New York: Crown Publishers, 2006), pp. 262–78.

42. Ibid., pp. 282–92.

43. Gellman, "A Leak, Then a Deluge."

44. Carol D. Leonnig and Amy Goldstein, "Ex-Aide Says Cheney Led Rebuttal Effort," *Washington Post*, January 26, 2007.

45. Deputy Secretary Wolfowitz with the *Jerusalem Post*, September 22, 2003, defenselink.mil/Transcripts/Transcript.aspx?TranscriptID=3173.

46. Deputy Secretary Wolfowitz interview on CBS *Face the Nation*, July 27, 2003, defenselink.mil/transcripts/transcript.aspx?transcript=2912.

47. *Meet the Press*, transcript for September 14, 2003.

48. Dana Priest and Glenn Kessler, "Iraq, 9/11 Still Linked by Cheney," *Washington Post*, September 29, 2003.

49. Michael Kranish and Bryan Bender, "Bush Backs Cheney on Assertion Linking Hussein, Al Qaeda," *Boston Globe*, June 16, 2004.

50. "Cheney Blasts Media on al Qaeda–Iraq Link," CNN.com, June 18, 2004, cnn.com/2004/ALLPOLITICS/06/18/cheney.iraq.al.qaeda.

51. "President Bush Speaks Exclusively to ABC News," Yurica Report, December 16, 2003, yuricareport.com/PoliticalAnalysis/BushInterviewByDianeSawyer12_16_03.html.

52. David Corn, "MIA WMDs—For Bush, It's a Joke," Capital Games, March 5, 2004, thenation.com/blogs/capitalgames?pid=1336.

53. Jeffrey Gettleman, "The Struggle for Iraq: The Occupation," *New York Times*, April 1, 2004.

54. Edward Helmore, "US Relied on 'Drunken Liar' to Justify War," *The Observer*, April 3, 2005; Jane Mayer, "The Manipulator," *New Yorker*, June 7, 2004, newyorker.com/archive/2004/06/040607fa_factl?print.

55. Steven R. Weisman, Ian Fisher, and Warren Hoge, "Transition in Iraq: New Government," *New York Times*, June 29, 2004.

56. Steven R. Weisman and Warren Hoge, "The Struggle for Iraq," *New York Times*, May 15, 2004.

57. Romesh Ratnesar, "From Friend to Foe," Time Online, May 22, 2004, time.com/time/printout/0,8816,641077,00.html.

58. Thom Shanker, "The Reach of War: Strategy," *New York Times*, June 23, 2004; Mayer, "The Manipulator," *New Yorker*, June 7, 2004.

59. Dexter Filkins, "Where Plan A Left Ahmed Chalabi," *New York Times Magazine*, November 5, 2006, nytmes.com/2006/11/05/magazine/05CHALABI.html; Helen Thomas, "Iraqi Exile Attains His Goal," *Seattle Post-Intelligencer*, March 2, 2004, seattlepi.nwsource.com/opinion/162728_thomas02.html.

60. Michael Rubin, "The Growing Gap," National Review Online, May 21, 2004, nationalreview.com/script/printpage.p?ref=/rubin/rubin2.

61. Ratnesar, "From Friend to Foe."

62. President Bush discusses the Iraqi interim government, June 1, 2004, whitehouse.gov/news/releases/2004/06/print/20040601–2.

63. L. Paul Bremer, *My Year in Iraq: The Struggle to Build a Future of Hope* (New York: Simon & Schuster, 2006), p. 369.

64. Mayer, "The Manipulator."

65. David E. Sanger, "Transition in Iraq: News Analysis," *New York Times*, June 29, 2004.

66. John Tierney, "The World: The Hawks Loudly Express Their Second Thoughts," *New York Times*, May 16, 2004.

67. Joel Brinkley, "Ex-C.I.A. Aides Say Iraq Leader Helped Agency in 90's Attacks," *New York Times*, June 9, 2004.

68. Melinda Liu, "Betting on an Old Horse," Newsweek online updated October 17, 2007, newsweek.com/id/53973; "Gwertzman Asks the Experts: Ex-Iraq Adviser Blackwill: Impact of Iraq's 'Extraordinary' Elections Likely to Spread to Iran," Council on Foreign Relations, February 14, 2005, cfr.org/publication/7787/exiraq_adviser_blackwill.html.

69. Jake Tapper and Avery Miller, "Pushing for a New Leader in Iraq," ABC News, August 24, 2007, abcnews.go.com/print?id=3521820.

Chapter 8: The Dream Dies Hard, in Which the Administration Loses the Mandate of the People

1. Jim VandeHei and Michael A. Fletcher, "Bush Says Election Ratified Iraq Policy," *Washington Post*, January 16, 2006.

2. Robert F. Worth, "Blast Destroys Shrine in Iraq, Setting Off Sectarian Fury," *New York Times*, February 22, 2006.

3. Hannah Allam and Warren P. Strobel, "Amidst Doubts, CIA Hangs on to Control of Iraqi Intelligence Service," Knight Ridder Service, May 8, 2005, globalpolicy.org/security/issues/iraq/occupation/2005/0.

4. David E. Sanger and David Rohde, "U.S. Is Likely to Continue Aid to Pakistan," *New York Times*, November 5, 2007.

5. Benazir Bhutto, "Musharraf's Martial Plan," *New York Times*, November 7, 2007.

6. Gareth Porter, "Despite Charges, No Evidence Iran Sending IED's to Iraq," AntiWar.Com, January 17, 2007, antiwar.printthis.clickability.com/pt/cpt?action=cpt&title=Desp.

7. Secretary Rumsfeld town hall meeting in Kuwait, December 8, 2004, defenselink.mil/transcripts/transcript.aspx?transcript=1980.

8. *Washington Post*, December 9, 2004.

9. Rumsfeld remarks, SOCOM Change of command, September 2, 2003, defenselink.mil/speeches/2003/sp20030902–secdef0422.html.

10. Ibid.

11. Radio interview with Secretary Rumsfeld and Eileen Byrne, WLS 890 AM Chicago, Ill., at the Pentagon, September 11, 2006, defenselink.mil/transcripts/transcript.aspx?transcriptid=3721.

12. Gregory L. Vistica, "'Kick Down the Doors' Everywhere?" *Washington Post National Weekly Edition*, January 12–18, 2004, p. 6; Barton Gellman, "Secret Unit Expands Rumsfeld's Domain," *Washington Post*, January 22, 2005.

13. Gellman, "Secret Unit Expands Rumsfeld's Domain."

14. Ann Scott Tyson and Dana Priest, "Pentagon Seeking Leeway Overseas," *Washington Post*, February 24, 2005.

15. Ann Scott Tyson and Dana Priest, "Bin Laden's Trail Has Gone Cold," *Washington Post*, September 11, 2006.

16. Ann Scott Tyson, "Rumsfeld OK's Wider Anti-Terror Role for Military," *Washington Post*, April 23, 2006.

17. James Brooke, "On Farthest U.S. Shores, Iraq Is a Way to a Dream," *New York Times*, July 31, 2005.

18. Peter Spiegel, "Army Warns Rumsfeld It's Billions Short," *Los Angeles Times*, September 25, 2006.

19. Katherine McIntire Peters, "Funding Shortfalls Jeopardize Army Operations, Chief Says," Government Executive.Com., July 17, 2006.

20. Ian Traynor, "The Privatisation of War," *The Guardian*, December 10, 2003, guardian .co.uk/print/0,3858,4815701–10355.

21. Jonathan Franklin, "US Hires Mercenaries for Iraq Role," March 6, 2004, theage.com.au/ cgi-bin/common; Danna Harman, "Firms Tap Latin Americans for Iraq," *Christian Science Monitor*, March 3, 2005, csmonitor.com/2005/0303/p06s02–woam.html.

22. "Anne Garrels Reporting from Baghdad," *All Things Considered*, NPR, October 3, 2005.

23. David Phinney, "Asia's Poor Build U.S. Bases in Iraq," Information Clearing House, October 3, 2005, informationclearinghouse.info/article10514.html; Matthew D. LaPlante, "Third World Warriors Fight U.S. Wars—for Dollars a Day," *Salt Lake Tribune*, December 2, 2007, origin .sltrib.com/fdep?1196778449215.

24. Dina Razor and Robert Bauman, *Betraying Our Troops: The Destructive Results of Privatizing War* (New York: Palgrave Macmillan, 2007), p. 234.

25. Ibid., p. 231.

26. Walter Pincus, "Defense Agency Proposes Outsourcing More Spying," *Washington Post*, August 19, 2007.

27. "Joint Chiefs Chairman Slams Murtha Comments," MSNBC.com, January 5, 2006.

28. Fred Barbash, "Rumsfeld, Murtha Continue War of Words Over Iraq," *Washington Post*, November 20, 2005.

29. Jones quoted in "The Education of Rep. Walter Jones," Carpetbagger Report, May 26, 2005, thecarpetbaggerreport.co/wp-print.php?p-4297.

30. Adam Nagourney and David D. Kirkpatrick, "Bad Iraq War News Worries Some in G.O.P. on '06 Vote," *New York Times*, August 18, 2005; Caspar Weinberger and Peter Schweizer, *Chain of Command: A Thriller* (New York: Atria Books, 2005).

31. Francis Fukuyama, "Invasion of the Isolationists," *New York Times*, August 31, 2005.

32. Sam Coates, "Weak Responses Led to 9/11 Cheney Asserts," *Washington Post*, October 4, 2005.

33. Jonathan S. Landay, "Bush Plays al Qaeda Card to Bolster Support for Iraq Policy," McClatchy Newspapers, June 29, 2007.

34. Interview of the vice president by Wolf Blitzer, June 23, 2005, whitehouse.gov/news/ releases/2005/06/20050623–8.html.

35. Ibid., and Leonard Doyle, "Cheney, Master of Stealth, Readies Himself for the Final Act of 'Imperial' Vice-Presidency," *The Independent*, June 29, 2007.

36. "Cheney Roars Back: The *Nightline* Interview During His Trip to Iraq," December 18, 2005, abcnews.go.com/print?id=1419206.

37. Neil A. Lewis, "The Reach of War: Questions, Pledges, and Confrontations; Furor Over Cheney Remarks on Tactics for Terror Suspects," *New York Times*, October 28, 2006; Vice President's remarks to the traveling press, December 20, 2005.

38. "Transcript: Vice President Cheney on 'Fox News Sunday,'" January 14, 2007, http:www .foxnews.com/story/0,2933,243632,00.html.

39. Interview of the vice president by Wolf Blitzer, CNN *Situation Room*, January 24, 2007.

40. President Bush congratulates General Petraeus on Senate confirmation, discusses way forward in Iraq, January 26, 2007, whitehouse.gov/news/releases/2007/01/20070126.html.

41. Steven R. Hurst and Qassim Abdul-Zahra, "Heat Rises Between Iraq PM and Petraeus," *Washington Post*, July 28, 2007.

42. Sandy Tolan and Jason Felch, "Beyond Regime Change," *Los Angeles Times*, December 2, 2006.

43. "Cheney Visits Iraq," *Bay Post*, May 10, 2007, batesmansbay.yourguide.com.au/ printerFriendlyPage.asp?story.

44. "Blood and Oil: How the West Will Profit from Iraq's Most Precious Commodity," *The Independent*, January 7, 2007.

45. Tina Susman, "Iraqis Resist U.S. Pressure to Enact Oil Law," *Los Angeles Times*, May 13, 2007.

46. Press availability with Vice President Dick Cheney, Ambassador Ryan Crocker, and General David Petraeus, May 9, 2007, whitehouse.gov/news/releases/2007/05/20070509–5.html.

47. Vice President's remarks at the United States Military Academy commencement, May 26, 2007, whitehouse.gov/news/releases/2007/05/20070526–1.html.

48. Matt Phillips, "Iraqi Reversal," *Wall Street Journal*, August 1, 2007; Michael E. O'Hanlon and Kenneth M. Pollack, "A War We Just Might Win," *New York Times*, July 30, 2007.

49. Hamid Ahmed, "Sunnis Asked to Reconsider Quitting Government," AP, August 2, 2007, truthout.org/docs_2006/printer_080207P.shtml.

50. Press conference by the president, July 12, 2007, whitehouse.gov/news/releases/2007/07/ print/20070712–5.

51. President Bush discusses global war on terror, November 1, 2007, whitehouse.gov/news/ releases/2007/11/print/20071101–4.

52. Ron Suskind, "Without a Doubt," *New York Times Magazine*, October 17, 2004.

Chapter 9: What Lies Ahead, in Which the Meaning of the War Is Revealed

1. Ann Scott Tyson, "Gates, U.S. General Back Long Iraq Stay," *Washington Post*, June 1, 2007; "House Votes to Ban Permanent Bases in Iraq," *The Gavel*, July 25, 2007.

2. Michael R. Gordon and Patrick Healy, "Clinton Sees Some Troops Staying in Iraq if She Is Elected," *New York Times*, March 14, 2007.

3. Dan Balz, "Sen. Clinton Urges U.N. Sanctions Against Iran," *Washington Post*, January 20, 2006.

4. Transcript of the Democratic presidential debate, February 26, 2008.

5. Senator John D. Rockefeller IV, "Floor Statement: On the Iraq Resolution," October 10, 2002, rockefeller.senate.gov/press/record_floor.cfm?id=292570&&.

6. William J. Broad and David E. Sanger, "Meeting on Arms Data Reignites Iran Nuclear Debate," *New York Times*, March 3, 2008.

7. Michael Hirsh, "Bothersome Intel on Iran," *Newsweek*, January 21, 2008.

8. Roundtable interview of the President by print, wire, and television reporters, January 15, 2008, whitehouse.gov/news/releases/2008/01/print/20080115–1.

9. Ann Scott Tyson, "Petraeus Says Cleric Helped Curb Violence," *New York Times*, December 7, 2007.

10. Press briefing by Tony Snow, September 13, 2006, whitehouse.gov/news/releases/2006/09/print/20060913–3.

11. William Pfaff, *The Bullet's Song: Romantic Violence and Utopia* (New York: Simon & Schuster, 2004), p. 127.

12. Donald Rumsfeld, "New Enemies Demand New Thinking," *Los Angeles Times*, September 1, 2006.

13. President Bush addresses American Legion National Convention, August 31, 2006, whitehouse.gov/news/releases/2006/08/print20060831–I.

14. Scott Peterson, "Taliban Adopting Iraq-Style Jihad," September 13, 2006; *New York Times*, Thom Shanker, "Gates Decides Against Marines' Offer to Leave Iraq for Afghanistan," *New York Times*, December 6, 2007.

15. "Secretary Rice Holds a News Conference," transcript, *Washington Post*, July 21, 2006.

16. "President Bush on Iraq, Elections and Immigration," *Washington Post*, December 20, 2006.

17. Anne Gearan, "US Embassy in Iraq to Be Biggest Ever," AP, May 19, 2007.

18. Ayad Allawi, "A Plan for Iraq," *Washington Post*, August 13, 2007.

19. Megan Greenwell, "Maliki Denounces Blackwater 'Crime,'" *Washington Post*, September 30, 2007.

20. Bryan Bender, "Analysis Says War Could Cost $1 Trillion," *Boston Globe*, August 1, 2007.

21. Joseph Stiglitz, "The Economic Consequences of Mr. Bush," *Vanity Fair*, December 2007, vanityfair.com/politics/features/2007/12/bush2007127?print.

22. "Transcript: Karl Rove on 'Fox News Sunday,'" March 2, 2008, foxnews.com/story/0,2933,334408,00.html.

23. Secretary Rumsfeld interview with Plum Television, March 3, 2006, defenselink.mil/transcripts/transcript.aspx?transcriptid=1166.

24. Alan Greenspan, *The Age of Turbulence* (New York: Penguin Press, 2007), p. 463.

25. Ibid., 237.

26. Amit R. Paley, "Iraqis Joining Insurgency Less for Cause Than Green," *Washington Post Foreign Service*, November 20, 2007.

27. Thom Shanker and Cara Buckley, "U.S. and Iraq to Negotiate Pact on Long-Term Relations," *New York Times*, November 27, 2007.

28. Marjorie Cohn, "Bush Negotiates Permanent Presence in Iraq," Information Clearing House, December 3, 2007, informationclearinghouse.info/article18820.html.

29. Sami Moubayed, "US 'Declaration' a Setback for Maliki," Asia Times Online, December 1, 2007.

30. Thom Shanker and Steven Lee Myers, "U.S. Asking Iraq for Wide Rights in Fighting War," New York Times, January 25, 2008.

31. John M. Broder and Elisabeth Bumiller, "McCain and Obama Trade Jabs on Iraq," New York Times, February 28, 2008.

32. President Bush attends National Religious Broadcasters 2008 convention, March 11, 2008, whitehouse.gov/news/releases/2008/03/20080311–3.html.

33. Thomas E. Ricks, "Top U.S. Officer in Mideast Resigns," Washington Post, March 12, 2008; Condoleezza Rice and Robert Gates, "What We Need Next in Iraq," Washington Post, February 13, 2008.

34. "US: No Permanent Bases Anywhere in the World," Agence France-Presse, February 13, 2008; Karen DeYoung, "No Need for Lawmakers' Approval of Iraq Pact, U.S. Reasserts," Washington Post, March 6, 2008.

35. "Delahunt Says Constitution Being Ignored in Iraq Agreement," press release from Congressman Bill Delahunt, March 4, 2008; and DeYoung, "No Need for Lawmakers' Approval."

36. President Bush attends National Religious Broadcasters 2008 convention.

INDEX

Abdullah, Prince, 79

Abizaid, John, 178

Abu Ghraib prison, 7, 193, 210, 234

Acheson, Dean, 15

Addington, David, 131

Afghan Refugee Service, 107

Afghanistan: American aid to anti-Russian
   Taliban, 60, 65; Brzezinski and covert aid to
   Islamic insurgents, 47–48, 56–57; first air
   attacks against (2001), 138; Soviet invasion
   (1980), 58–61; and Soviet Union, 47,
   55–57, 58–61; Soviet-Afghan war, 60–61;
   Taliban resurgence, 233, 257, 270; Taraki's
   1978 coup, 46–47; U.S.-led war in, 1–2, 138

Agee, Philip, 198

agent theory of international relations, 10, 13,
   105

Ajami, Fouad, 144

Albright, Madeleine, 92, 110–12, 113–14, 211

Allawi, Ali A., 208–12, 216, 259–60; and the
   interim government, 208–12, 216; and the
   Iraq insurgency, 179, 211; and Maliki, 216,
   260

American embassy in Baghdad, 177, 258–59,
   267

American Enterprise Institute, 16, 108

Amin, Hafizullah, 58–59

Amnesty International, 84

Andropov, Yuri, 59, 61

Angola, 39

Annan, Kofi, 165

anthrax letters, 114, 118–19, 130, 134–37

Arafat, Yasir, 179

Armitage, Richard, 198, 225

Army, U.S. See military, U.S.

Askew, Ruben, 36

Atta, Mohammed, 134–35, 136, 137, 153, 202–3

Australia, 6

Azerbaijan, 190

Aziz, Tariq, 86, 141

Aznar, José Maria, 157–61

Ba'athist Party, 179, 208

Baer, Robert, 206

Baker, James A., 82, 85, 86, 121, 182

Bandar, Prince, 79

Barbour Griffith & Rogers, 212

Barnett, Thomas P. M., 94, 96

Barre, Siad, 39–40

Bauman, Robert, 228

Bay of Pigs (1961), 18, 73

Bazargan, Mehdi, 57–58

Bechtel, 182

Beirut bombings (1983), 233

Berger, Sandy, 110–11, 114–15, 155

Berlin Wall, fall of (1989), 70, 71

Bhutto, Benazir, 217–18

Biden, Joe, 146

bin Laden, Osama: and anthrax letters, 134–35;
   changed attitudes about search for, 1–2,
   137–38, 214; Cheney interview on whereabouts, 234; quest to sever U.S.-Saudi relationship, 95; supporters in Saudi Arabia, 94,
   106; and Taliban, 65, 94, 138; U.S. attacks on
   hideouts in Pakistan/Sudan (1998), 112;
   videotaped messages, 211–12, 255

Black, Clint, 232

Black, J. Cofer, 225

Blackwater USA: ambush on, 178, 204–5; Blackwater crisis (2007), 260–61; contracts and
   recruiting, 227, 228, 260–61

Blackwill, Robert, 210, 212, 259–60

Blair, Tony, 116; alliance with Bush, 26–28, 29,
   141–43, 145, 154, 157, 160, 167, 202; and
   British goals in Middle East, 26–27; calling
   for UN role, 142, 153; Camp David meeting
   with Bush, 141–43; and historic principle of
   noninterference, 27, 29; and intelligence

Blair, Tony, (cont.)
    dossier on Saddam's WMD, 143, 154, 202;
    and the missing WMD, 173; and neoliberal-
    ism, 139; and Niger yellowcake story, 143,
    154
Blitzer, Wolf, 141, 185, 234, 235, 237–39
Blix, Hans, 159, 161–62, 194
Boehner, John, 111
Boland amendment, 63, 68
Bosnia, 97–98
Botha, R.F., 38
Boucher, Richard, 171
Brahimi, Lakhdar, 208–10
Bremer, L. Paul, 178, 183, 206–7, 210, 215, 268
Brezhnev, Leonid, 35
British International Institute for Strategic
    Studies, 28
Brown, Harold, 40–41
Brzezinski, Zbigniew, 2–3, 32, 35–61, 236; and
    Afghanistan, 46–48, 56–57; Angola crisis,
    39; background/career, 36; and Carter
    administration foreign policy, 35–61; and
    Carter's human rights campaign, 35–36;
    China mission, 42–46; and China/Soviet
    relations, 42–46; and covert aid to Islamic
    insurgents, 47–48, 56–57; and Iran, 37,
    53–55; and NSC redesign/national security
    advisor's role, 2–3, 38; Somalia/Ethiopia
    conflict, 37–42; and Soviet influence in
    Middle East/central Asia, 37–42, 55–57; and
    Soviet threat in Africa, 37–42; and Soviet-
    Afghanistan war, 60–61; and U.S.-Pakistan
    relations, 60–61; and Vance, 36–37, 38, 41,
    42, 53; and Vietnam, 36, 37–38
Bumiller, Elisabeth, 151
Bundy, McGeorge, 15–16, 20
Burt, Richard, 44
Bush, George H.W.: alleged assassination attempt
    on, 109–10; and American exceptionalism,
    92; and the CIA, 72; decision not to go into
    Baghdad, 62, 64, 86, 89–91, 93, 105, 170;
    and free trade, 93; and George W. Bush,
    204; and Gorbachev/Russia, 70–71, 93–94;
    on Gulf War I, 9, 25–26, 88, 89, 92–93; and
    incubator raid story, 84–85; and invasion of
    Panama, 72–73; and Iraq's nuclear weapons/
    nuclear program, 86–87, 88, 90–91; loss to
    Clinton (1992), 96; and new world order, 9,
    25–26, 71, 78, 92–94, 105; Persian Gulf
    policies, 64, 82; post–Cold War policies and

challenges, 62, 70–73, 93–94; Saddam-
    Hitler comparison, 85, 86; securing congres-
    sional approval for war, 78, 81–84, 86, 96;
    securing UN resolutions, 78–79, 96; and the
    "siren's call" to not cut defense, 26; and
    Vietnam syndrome, 88, 91
Bush, George W.: and administration's attack on
    Murtha, 230; on anthrax letters, 119; "axis of
    evil" speech, 1, 116–19, 147; and Blair,
    26–28, 29, 141–43; Camp David meeting
    with Blair, 141–43; and Cheney, 119–20; and
    the Declaration of Principles, 267; on
    Fallujah siege, 178; and George H.W. Bush,
    204; on Gulf War II, 9, 13–14, 60, 61,
    157–61, 243–46; later speeches/press confer-
    ences, 243–46, 256–58; and Lincoln, 173–74;
    linking Saddam/Iraq and 9/11, 118–19,
    128–29, 146–47, 203; and National Defense
    Strategy covering letter, 100–102; neoliberal-
    ism and foreign policy, 139–40; and the 9/11
    attacks, 28, 138–39; on the occupation, 177,
    180, 209, 214–15; and permanent U.S. bases
    in Philippines, 191–93; prayers, 151, 272;
    reelection and presumed mandate for war
    (2004), 213–14; and Saddam statue scene,
    170, 174; self-perceptions of his presidency/
    the war, 269–70, 272; shifting perspectives
    on the war's meaning/progress, 243–46; and
    2007 NIE, 250–52; 2000 presidential cam-
    paign/election, 27–28, 119; 2002 State of the
    Union, 1, 116–19, 147; 2003 State of the
    Union, 156, 195–96, 197–98; 2004 State of
    the Union, 208; 2007 State of the Union,
    237–38; UN speech, 145, 152, 153; and
    uranium yellowcake disinformation, 156,
    195–96, 197–98; USS *Abraham Lincoln*
    speech, 173–76; on Vietnam (the country),
    31; on war on terror, 116, 192; on the White
    House leak of Wilson's wife's identity, 198–99
Bush administration and post-invasion Iraq.
    See post-invasion Iraq and the Bush
    administration
Bush administration and selling the war on Iraq,
    118–48, 149–62; "axis of evil" speech, 1,
    116–19, 147; and British intelligence
    dossier, 143, 153, 202; Bush-Blair alliance,
    26–28, 29, 141–43, 145, 154, 157, 160, 167,
    202; Bush's UN speech, 145, 152, 153;
    Card's marketing analogy, 151; Cheney,
    119–23, 129–30, 131, 134–37, 143–45,

152–53, 201; and CIA, 124–25, 132, 135, 143, 155–56; congressional authorization for war, 145–46, 154–55, 249–50; disinformation about alleged Niger uranium/yellowcake purchase, 143, 152–54, 156, 195–99, 201–2; early military strike on Iraq's radar installations, 125–26; final round of warm-up speeches before war, 143–48; first meeting of Bush's NSC (2001), 124–25; linking 9/11 and Saddam/Iraq, 118–19, 128–30, 133–37, 141, 146–47, 150, 155, 203, 233, 234–35, 269; mushroom cloud image, 141, 147, 152, 233; neoconservatives and National Defense Strategy (2002), 100–102; Office of Special Plans (OSP), 131–32, 133–34, 189, 207; Office of Strategic Influence and disinformation, 132–33; and oil policy, 123–24, 223, 241, 264; and Powell, 124–25, 129, 141, 144, 149–50, 155, 156–57; and preemptive action, 100–101, 140–41, 144–45; and Rice, 124, 141, 152, 159, 161–62; Rumsfeld, 118, 126–34, 137–38, 154–55, 223; Saddam and the anthrax letters, 118–19, 130, 134–37; and Saddam's WMD, 124–25, 141, 142–44, 152–56, 181, 194–99, 201, 204; State of the Union speeches, 1, 116–19, 147, 156, 195–96, 197–98; surveillance photos of alleged WMD facility, 124–25; and UN resolutions, 143, 145, 152, 153, 155, 156–62, 165, 245; and UN weapons inspections, 115, 141, 144, 154–55, 159–63, 165; and WHIG, 149–57, 162; and Wolfowitz, 129, 131, 134, 137, 139, 157. See also Gulf War II

Bush Doctrine: and American exceptionalism, 140; and preemptive action, 140–41, 144–45, 246

BusinessWeek, 122

Butler, Richard, 112–13

Butterfield, Fox, 43–44

Byrd, Robert, vii, 83, 232, 272

Camp Lejeune, 231, 232–34

Canada, 182

Cannistraro, Vincent M., 134

Cannon, Lou, 10

Card, Andrew, 144, 151

Carter, Jimmy: and Carter Doctrine, 59–60, 63–64; covert aid to Islamic extremists in Afghanistan, 56–57; foreign policy and Brzezinski, 35–61; human rights campaign,

34, 35–36, 49; and Iranian hostage crisis, 58, 66, 221; and Iran-Iraq War, 66–67; and Israel-Egypt peace agreement, 44–45; Notre Dame speech, 34–35; plans for anti-imperial presidency, 33–35; and Reagan, 62; and Shah of Iran, 48–53, 57; and Soviet invasion of Afghanistan, 59–61; and Vietnam War, 34

Carter Doctrine, 59–60, 63–64

"The Case for the Vietnam War" (Rostow), 24–25

Casey, George W., 215

Casey, William, 68, 222

Castro, Fidel, 18, 39–40, 73

Cato Institute, 122

Center for International Studies, 16

Center for Security Policy, 11

Center for Strategic and International Studies, 164

Central Intelligence Agency (CIA): and anthrax letters, 135; Bush administration and selling war on Iraq, 124–25, 132, 135, 143, 155–56; and Cheney, 121, 156; Cold War, 15; countercoup in Iran (1953), 32, 50–51, 54, 65; covert aid to Islamic insurgents in Afghanistan, 47, 65–66; creation of (1947), 15; and Iran-Iraq War, 67, 68; and the occupation, 216; Rostow's feud over domino thesis, 21; and Rumsfeld, 126–27, 133–34; and Saddam's WMD, 143, 153; Scowcroft's draft memorandum on intelligence reform, 134; and Shahwani's INIS, 216; Tenet and first meeting of Bush's NSC, 124–25; and White House leak about Wilson's wife, 196–99, 201–2

Chain of Command (Weinberger and Schweizer), 231–32

Chalabi, Ahmed, 109; and Curveball, 195, 205–6; and missing WMD, 207–8; and neocons, 106, 109, 207–8, 211; and post-invasion Iraq, 109, 205–10; and Saddam statue scene, 171

Cheney, Dick, 119–23; and administration's attack on Murtha, 230; attacks on intelligence, 121, 144, 156, 234; background/career, 120–21; on bin Laden's whereabouts, 234; Blitzer interviews, 234, 235, 237–39; and Bush's USS Abraham Lincoln speech, 176; Camp Lejeune speech (2005), 232–34; Cheney "doctrine," 237; and the CIA, 121, 156; and Defense Department, 121; defining war on terror, 129–30, 131; expectations of being welcomed as liberators, 144, 163, 259; and first meeting of Bush's NSC (2001), 124–25;

Cheney, Dick (*cont.*)
  and Guantánamo Bay, 193, 235; and Gulf
  War I, 25, 79–80, 87, 90, 91, 121–22; and
  Gulf War II, 9, 21, 144, 163, 259; and
  Halliburton, 120, 122, 182, 261; and the
  insurgency, 234, 266; and interrogation
  techniques/torture, 235–36; and Iran
  sanctions, 122; linking Saddam and anthrax
  letters, 130, 134–37; linking Saddam/Iraq
  and 9/11, 124–25, 129–30, 153, 233; and
  the missing WMD, 200–204, 234; and
  national energy policy, 123; and oil legislation in Iraq's new government, 240–42; and
  oil/energy reserves, 122, 123, 190; "one
  percent doctrine," 123; and Powell, 80, 118,
  125, 150, 156–57; Russert interviews,
  129–30, 135–37, 152, 200–202; and secret
  wiretapping program, 235–36; selling war on
  Iraq/Saddam, 119–23, 129–30, 131, 134–37,
  143–45, 152–53, 201; and the UN resolution, 156; on UN weapons inspections, 115,
  141, 144; the uranium yellowcake story,
  152–53, 201–2; VFW speech, 143–44; view
  of presidential powers, 120–21, 266; on
  winning/losing in Iraq, 237–38, 239
Chicago Tribune, 189
chief-of-mission authority, 224–25
Chile, 160, 227
China, 20–21, 42–46, 235
Chirac, Jacques, 144–45, 159
Christian Science Monitor, 164, 257
Church, Frank, 13
civilian contractors and security guards in Iraq,
  182, 226–29, 260–61, 268–69; and Blackwater crisis, 260–61; division of labor and pay
  scales, 228; future of war service industry,
  228–29; and immunity protection, 268–69;
  impact on regular military, 228–29; lifestyle
  of, 227; monetary value of contracts, 228,
  229, 261; recruiting from Eastern Europe/
  Latin America, 227; Rice on, 228, 260;
  TCNs (third-country nationals), 228
Clarke, Richard, 65–66, 128–29
Clinton, Bill/Clinton administration, 3, 4, 95; and
  military strikes against Iraq, 109–13; and
  neoconservatives, 96, 108–15; PNAC letter
  to, 108–9; and regime change in Iraq, 109,
  112; and Saddam's weapons, 108–15; and
  UN weapons inspections in Iraq, 108, 110,
  112–13, 115, 155; victory in 1992, 96

Clinton, Hillary, 147, 248–50
Coalition Provisional Authority (CPA), 178, 180,
  186, 206, 210
coalitions: Gulf War I, 83, 87, 97, 99; Gulf War II,
  6–7, 73, 100, 156, 188, 256; Vietnam War,
  7, 100
Cockburn, Alexander, 84
Cohen, William, 110–11, 112
Cold War foreign policy: and American metaphor
  of progress, 14–15; containment policies/
  worldview, 3; and détente, 103; and imperialism, 7–8; military diplomacy, 15; mutually
  assured destruction (MAD), 15; and notion
  of "creative destruction," 12; realist worldview, 4, 13, 26, 30, 98, 103–4, 105, 139–40;
  Rice on post-9/11 transformation away from,
  28–30; Rostow/Eisenhower and U.S.-Soviet
  relations, 17; Truman Doctrine, 15, 146, 154,
  192. *See also* post–Cold War thinking
Congress, U.S.: banning permanent bases in Iraq,
  248, 270; Bush on the surge and role of,
  243–44; and Declaration of Principles with
  Iraq, 268, 269; and Gulf War I approval, 78,
  81–84, 86, 96; Iraq War resolution, 145–46,
  154–55, 249–50; resolutions regarding Iran/
  expansion of Bush's war, 248–49
Congressional Human Rights Foundation, 83–84
containment policies, 3, 103, 108–9, 126, 238
Cooper, Matt, 199
Corn, David, 198, 204
Council on Foreign Relations, 1, 123
"creative destruction," notion of, 12, 16, 18, 259
Crocker, Ryan, 241–42
Cuba: and Angola, 39; and axis of evil, 117; Bay
  of Pigs, 18, 73; Cuban Revolution, 18;
  Guantánamo Bay military base, 193; and
  Somalia/Ethiopia conflict, 39–40, 45; and
  Spanish-American War, 192–93
Curveball, 195, 205–6

Daily Telegraph (London), 207
Daoud, Mohammed, 46
Daschle, Tom, 134
Dayton, Keith, 173
de Gaulle, Charles, 14, 100
Dearlove, Richard, 142
Declaration of Principles (2007), 266–72; and
  Bush, 267; and Maliki, 267–68; and new
  embassy in Baghdad, 267; and Order 17/
  immunity protection issues, 268–69; and

Sadr, 267–68; and status-of-forces agreement, 268–69, 271; and 2008 U.S. presidential campaign, 268; and U.S. Congress, 268, 269

Defense Department: Cheney and power of, 121; and civilian contractors/security guards in Iraq, 229; Cold War, 15; global network of bases, 121; selling war on Iraq/Saddam, 131. See also Rumsfeld, Donald

Defense Intelligence Agency (DIA), 131, 133, 229

defense planning guidance (draft DPG) (1992), 98–100, 108

Defense Policy Board (DPB), 131–32

Delahunt, Bill, 271–72

Deng Xiaoping, 43

Desert Fox, 112–13

détente, 103

Diamond, Larry, 189–90

Diego Garcia, U.S. navy base at, 44, 59–60, 188

Diem, Ngo Dinh, 19, 54, 239

domino thesis, 21–22

Dowd, Maureen, 146

Dulles, John Foster, 10–11, 13, 15, 17

Edwards, John, 249

Eisenhower, Dwight D., 17, 21, 50–51, 146, 244

El Salvador, 227

Ethiopia, 38–42, 45

exceptionalism, American, 88, 92, 111, 140, 149

Face the Nation (CBS), 137–38, 200

Fahd, King, 79–80, 90, 94–95

Fallon, William, 270

Fallujah battle (2004), 178–79, 204–5, 207

Fascell, Dante B., 82

Federation of Oil Unions, 241

Feith, Douglas, 131–32, 134, 187, 192, 206, 207

Fitzgerald, Patrick, 199

Fleischer, Ari, 197

Ford, Gerald, 16, 34, 120

Foreign Affairs, 102, 187

former Soviet republics, 122, 190–91

Fox News, 169, 195, 213, 236, 261

France: and Bush's war on terrorism, 144–45, 159; and Cold War security, 14; colonial wars, 7; and Iraq's debts, 182; and Vietnam War coalition, 100

Franks, Tommy, 166, 168

"freedom fries," 231

Freeman, Charles, 81

Frieling, Thomas, 173

Front for the Liberation of Iran, 67, 69

Frost, David, 141

Frum, David, 117

Fukuyama, Francis, 102–4, 108, 232

Garner, Jay, 186–87, 188, 189, 190, 205

Garrels, Anne, 227

Gates, Robert M., 65, 218, 247, 257, 270

Gearan, Anne, 258

Germany: and Iraq's debts, 182; U.S. military bases in, 187, 189

Gerson, Michael, 116, 147

Gingrich, Newt, 126, 131

Glaspie, April, 73–77

GlobalSecurity.org, 189

Gorbachev, Mikhail, 25, 63, 70, 78, 93

Graham, Bob, 1–2, 153

Great Britain: Blair and British goals in Middle East, 26–27; Blair-Bush alliance, 26–28, 29, 141–43, 145, 154, 157, 160, 167, 202; Gulf War I and critics of Glaspie Affair, 76–77; and intelligence dossier/white papers on Saddam's WMD, 143, 154, 202

Green Zone, 178, 180, 184, 240

Greenspan, Alan, 263–65

Gromyko, Andrey, 44, 45–46

Guantánamo Bay military base, 193, 234–35

Guardian, 117, 163

Gulf of Tonkin incident/resolution (1964), 19–20, 82, 126, 146, 271–72

Gulf War I, 25–26, 73–91; air war/beginning of bombing, 87–88, 89–90; assault on retreating Iraqi soldiers, 89–90; awaiting provocation, 82–83; baby-milk factory bombing, 167; Bush on, 9, 25–26, 88, 89, 92–93; and Cheney, 25, 79–80, 87, 90, 91; the coalition, 83, 87, 97, 99; congressional approval, 78, 81–84, 86, 96; and containment worldview, 3; decision not to go into Baghdad, 62, 64, 86, 89–91, 93, 105, 121–22, 163, 170; demonization of Saddam, 83, 85, 86, 88, 89; Glaspie Affair, 73–77; ground campaign, 88–89, 91; incubator raid story, 84–85; Iraq's invasion of Kuwait, 64, 73–79; and neoconservatives, 3–4, 26, 88, 104; persuading Saudis to accept American military force, 79–81, 90, 94–95; postwar self-congratulations/triumphalism, 92, 96; public relations/propaganda campaign, 83–88, 91, 132; retrospect, 89–91; and Saddam's WMD/nuclear ambitions, 86–87,

Gulf War I (*cont.*)
88, 91, 105, 108–15; satellite images showing Iraqi tank buildup on Saudi border, 79, 90; and UN Security Council resolutions, 78–79, 85–86, 87, 96; and Vietnam memories, 25–26, 88, 90, 91

Gulf War II, 4–5, 91, 157–71; Bush on America's world mission in, 13–14; Bush's impatience, 157–61; Bush's prewar ultimatum to Saddam, 166–67; Bush's USS *Abraham Lincoln* speech, 173–76; and Cheney, 9, 21, 144, 163, 259; coalition of the willing, 6–7, 73, 100, 156, 188, 256; as colonial war, 254; expectation to be welcomed as liberators, 144, 163, 168, 259; expectations/predictions for, 157–61, 163–64; expected costs, 164; and historic principle of noninterference, 27, 29; Iraqi looting and lawlessness, 168–69, 194; issue of removing Saddam, 160, 163, 166–67, 172; the looting of antiquities, 168–69, 184; and oil policy, 123–24, 223, 241, 264; propaganda and PSYOPs, 167–71; Rumsfeld's plan for victory, 164–66; Rumsfeld's press conferences, 168–69; Saddam statue scene, 169–71, 174; shock and awe, 159, 164–66, 175; and Vietnam memories, 30, 265–66. *See also* Bush administration and selling the war on Iraq; post-invasion Iraq and the Bush administration

Gwertzman, Bernard, 45

Hagel, Chuck, 146
Haig, Alexander, 67
Halliburton, 120, 122, 182, 227–28, 261
Hannah, John, 156
Hannity, Sean, 213
Harnish, Reno, 190
Heikal, Mohamed, 51, 52
Heller, Jean, 90
Helms, Richard, 21, 23
Heritage Foundation, 244, 254
Hill & Knowlton, 83–85
Holbrooke, Richard, 104
House, Edward M., 2
House Armed Services Committee, 154, 187, 231
House Foreign Affairs Committee, 82, 120
Howard, John, 6
Huang Hua, 46
Hughes, Karen, 105, 133
Human Rights caucus, 83–84

Humphrey, Hubert, 36
Huntington, Samuel P., 41
Hussein, King, 55–56
Hussein, Saddam: and anthrax letters, 118–19, 130, 134–37; and anthrax stocks, 114; and chemical/biological weapons, 68–69, 108–9; and Clinton military strikes, 109–13; Clinton-era neocons and case for removal/regime change, 107–15; early statements about attacking Israel, 81; and George H.W. Bush's Hitler comparison, 85, 86; Glaspie Affair, 73–77; Gulf War I and demonization of, 83, 85, 86, 88, 89; and Gulf War I sanctions, 110, 113–14, 240; Gulf War II and Bush's prewar ultimatum to, 166–67; Gulf War II and issue of removing, 163, 166–67, 172; Gulf War II and prewar attack on bunker, 167; and Iran-Iraq War, 66–67, 69, 74; linking to 9/11, 118–19, 128–30, 133–37, 141, 146–47, 150, 155; linking to Yousef/first WTC bombing, 107–8; oil prices and Iraq's war debt, 69–70, 74–75; supposed assassination attempt on George H.W. Bush, 109–10; and UN weapons inspections (Gulf War I), 108, 110–13, 115, 155; and UN weapons inspections (Gulf War II), 115, 141, 144, 154–55, 159–63, 165; and U.S. presidential campaign (2000), 27–28; and WMD (Gulf War II), 124–25, 141, 142–44, 152–56, 181, 194–99, 201, 204; and WMD/nuclear ambitions (Gulf War I), 86–87, 88, 91, 105, 108–15. *See also* Gulf War I

Huyser, Robert, 52–55

Ibn Saud, King, 95
improvised explosive devices (IEDs), 179–80, 218–19
In Retrospect (McNamara), 24–25
Intelligence Identities Protection Act, 198
interim governing council (IGC), 206–7
interim government in Iraq, 171, 180, 208–12, 215–17
International Criminal Court (ICC), 100
interrogation techniques, 193, 224, 234–35
Iran: and Brzezinski, 37, 53–55; Bush administration accusations of "foreign agents" operating in Iraq, 218–19; Bush administration attempts to expand war on terror, 248–52; and Bush's axis of evil speech, 117; CIA countercoup (1953), 32, 50–51, 54, 65; early

show of support for America after 9/11, 117; and Gulf War I, 78; and Hillary Clinton, 248–49; hostage crisis, 58, 66, 221; Iranian Revolution (1979), 3, 32–33, 51–55, 65; and Maliki government in Iraq, 216; nuclear program, 50–51, 248–49, 250–52; Revolutionary Guard, 248–49; Savak, 47, 52; Shah Reza Pahlavi, 32–33, 48–53, 57–58; and 2007 NIE, 250–52; U.S. arms sales to, 47–49; U.S.-imposed sanctions on, 122

Iran-Contra scandal, 63, 67–68, 120, 222

Iran-Iraq War, 56, 66–67, 68, 69, 74

Iraq, post–World War I creation of, 64

Iraq insurgency, 177, 178–85, 195, 215, 234; and Allawi, 211; Blackwater ambush, 178, 204–5; Cheney on, 234, 266; and the CPA, 180; Fallujah battle, 178–79, 204–5, 207; and Iraqi army, 183; and Maliki, 215; Rumsfeld on, 179, 181, 183, 210–11; Sunni/Shiite violence, 215; tactics (IEDs), 179–80; troops needed for, 181–82, 183, 215; and Vietnam, 210–11

Iraq Liberation Act (1998), 112

Iraq National Accord, 211

Iraq Study Group, 237, 243

Iraq Survey Group, 173

Iraq War resolution, 145–46, 154–55, 249–50

Iraq wars. See Gulf War I; Gulf War II

Iraqi army, 183, 241–42

Iraqi National Congress (INC), 69, 106, 109, 132, 171, 195, 205, 207, 208

Iraqi National Intelligence Service (INIS), 215–16

Islamic Army of Iraq, 179

Islamic extremism, 5–6; covert aid to movements in Afghanistan, 47–48, 56–57; Iranian Revolution, 51–55

Israel, 44–45, 67, 81

Ivanov, Sergei, 154

Jackson, C.D., 16–17

Jerusalem Post, 199

Johnson, Lyndon, 270; and Gulf of Tonkin, 19, 82, 126; peace speeches, 23; and Rostow's call for invasion of Laos/North Vietnam, 23–24; and Rostow/Vietnam War policy, 19–25

Jones, Walter, 231

Jordan, 55–56

Justice Department, 107

Kaplan, Fred, 192

Karmal, Babrak, 59

Katzenbach, Nicholas, 271–72

Kay, David, 194–95, 200, 201, 203

Kazakhstan, 190

Keller, Bill, 139

Kellogg Brown & Root, 182, 227–28, 261

Kendall, J.P., 88

Kennan, George, 102–5

Kennedy, John F., 18, 54, 73, 239

Kerry, John, 198, 211

Kessler, Glenn, 203

Khalilzad, Zalmay, 98–100

Khomeini, Ayatollah: and Iran-Iraq War, 66, 69; and Iran's nuclear ambitions, 50; revolution and the Shah, 52–53; rise to power/Islamic revolution, 51–55

Khrushchev, Nikita, 73

Kim Jong-il, 128

Kissinger, Henry: and Angola, 39; and détente, 103; on lessons of Vietnam, 247; and Shah of Iran, 33, 52, 57

Korean War, 17, 187, 263

Kosygin, Alexi, 36

Kurdistan, 243

Kuwait: Iraq's invasion of, 64, 73–79; and Iraq's/Saddam's debts, 70, 74–75; and OPEC/oil prices, 70, 74–75, 77; pre-invasion geopolitical situation, 77

Kwiatkowski, Karen, 131, 189

Kyoto treaty, 28

Kyrgyzstan, 190–91

Late Edition (CNN), 141. See also Blitzer, Wolf

League of Nations, 145, 156

Leahy, Patrick, 134

Ledeen, Michael, 92

LeFeber, Walter, 193

Lehrer, Jim, 135

Lesar, David, 122

Leviathan (Hobbes), 101

Lewis, Bernard, 131

Libby, I. Lewis "Scooter," 131, 156, 196, 198–99

Lifton, Robert, 89

Lincoln, Abraham, 173–74

Lodge, Henry Cabot, 156

Los Angeles Times, 84, 256

Lugar, Richard, 146

Lute, Douglas, 266–67

Luti, William, 131

Lynch, Rick, 265

MacArthur, John, 84

Magofna, Olympio, 226

al-Maliki, Nouri: and Allawi, 216, 260; and
    Blackwater crisis, 260; and the Bush admin-
    istration, 215–17, 239, 243, 252; and the
    Declaration of Principles, 267–68; and the
    insurgency, 215; and the interim govern-
    ment, 212, 215–17; and oil legislation, 240,
    241, 242, 243, 259; and Petraeus, 239; and
    post-invasion Iraq, 212, 215–17, 239–43,
    252, 259–60, 267–68; and proposed security
    pact, 252, 259; and Rule 17, 260

Manley, John, 182

Mann, James, 99

Martin, Cathie, 199

Matalin, Mary, 202–3

McCain, John, 269

McClellan, Scott, 230

McGovern, George, 45, 83

McGovern, James P., 261

McGrory, Mary, 166

McKinley, William, 150–51, 193

McNamara, Robert, 12–13, 20, 24–25, 264

McPherson, Harry, 23–24

Meese, Edwin, 63

Meet the Press (NBC), 45, 129–30, 135–37, 138,
    197

military, U.S.: the "all-volunteer" army, 220;
    armor/equipment, 219–20; draft, 254;
    equipment repair issues, 226; funding/budget
    problems, 226; Gulf War II troop level
    expectations, 163–64; National Guard troops
    in Iraq, 182, 220, 222; the occupation and
    soldiers killed, 177; Pacific region recruiting,
    225–26; and private contractors/war service
    industry, 228–29; recruiting problems, 220,
    225–26, 230; Rumsfeld's 2004 town hall
    meeting, 219–21; Rumsfeld's plan to restruc-
    ture, 187–88, 220–25; and SOCOM,
    221–25; stop-loss program/extended tours,
    181–82, 183, 220; troop levels/troop reduc-
    tion issue, 181–82, 183, 214–15, 261

Miller, Geoffrey D., 193

Miller, Judith, 198, 199

Milošević, Slobodan, 27

Mondale, Walter, 33

Moore, Michael, 230

Moran, Terry, 235

Mubarak, Hosni, 75, 160

Murtha, John P., 229–30, 270

Musharraf, Pervez, 217–18

Myers, Richard B., 181, 206, 207

Mylroie, Laurie, 107–8, 129

National Defense Strategy (2002), 100–102

National Guard troops in Iraq, 182, 220, 222

national intelligence estimates (NIEs): (2002),
    153–54, 201, 250; (2007), 250–52; and
    Iran's nuclear weapons program, 250–52;
    and Niger uranium yellowcake story,
    153–54

National Public Radio, 227

National Review, 168

National Security Council (NSC): Brzezinski and
    redesign, 2–3, 38; Bush administration and
    Iraq focus, 124–25, 128; Cold War–era,
    15–16; first post-9/11 meeting, 128

NATO expansion in Eastern Europe, 104

Negroponte, John, 163

neoconservatives: anti-Carter offensive, 34–35;
    building case for Saddam's removal/regime
    change, 107–15; and Chalabi, 106, 109,
    207–8, 211; and Clinton administration, 96,
    108–15; and defense planning guidance
    (draft DPG) (1992), 98–100, 108; end of
    history argument, 102–5; and Gulf War I,
    3–4, 26, 88; late critics of Bush's war, 232;
    and Lincoln, 173–74; and National Defense
    Strategy (2002), 100–102; and neoliberal-
    ism, 139–40; PNAC letters to Clinton,
    108–9, 232; and Reagan, 4; and Strauss, 99

neoliberalism, 139–40

Neto, Agostinho, 39

New York Times: and Brzezinski, 36, 41; Bush
    administration's strategies in selling of the
    war, 146, 151–52; Cheney and secret wire-
    tapping program, 235–36; and Gulf War I
    propaganda, 84; and the insurgency, 215;
    leaked story about OSI, 132–33; and the
    occupation, 183; and Pakistan crisis, 218;
    the uranium yellowcake story, 152–53, 195,
    198; Wilson's op-ed, 195, 198; Wolfowitz's
    rendition of Bush administration logic, 139

Newsom, David, 47

Newsweek, 251

Niger. *See* uranium yellowcake disinformation story

Nightline (ABC News), 235

9/11 attacks, 7; and George W. Bush, 28, 138–39;
    linking Saddam/Iraq to, 118–19, 128–30,
    133–37, 141, 146–47, 150, 155, 203

9/11 Commission, 120, 203

Nixon, Richard: and China, 42; and détente, 103; and George H.W. Bush's Soviet policies, 71; and Shah of Iran, 32–33; and Vietnam, 16, 270; and War Powers Act, 120

noninterference, principle of, 27, 29

Noriega, Manuel, 72

North American Free Trade Agreement (NAFTA), 93

North Korea, 1

Novak, Robert, 198

Nunn, Sam, 82

Obama, Barack, 6, 249, 250, 261–62, 269

occupation of Iraq, 177–93, 204–12, 214–15, 265. *See also* post-invasion Iraq

O'Connell, Thomas, 224

Office of Reconstruction and Humanitarian Aid (ORHA), 205

Office of Special Plans/Projects (OSP), 131–32, 133–34, 189, 207

Office of Strategic Influence (OSI), 132–33

O'Hanlon, Michael, 242

Ohio State University forum and Clinton cabinet, 110–12

oil legislation and Iraq's new government, 240–42, 243, 259, 268; and Cheney, 240–42; and Maliki, 240, 241, 242, 243, 259; PSAs (production sharing arrangements), 241; regional disputes, 243

oil policy and Gulf War II, 123–24, 223, 241, 264

oil revenue and Iraq reconstruction, 183, 259

oil/natural gas and permanent bases in former Soviet republics, 190–91

Oklahoma City bombing (1995), 107

Olmert, Ehud, 250–52

O'Neill, Paul, 124

Operation Eagle Claw, 221

Order 17 and immunity protection issues, 206–7, 217, 260, 266–67, 268–69

Organization of American States (OAS): and George H.W. Bush's invasion of Panama, 72–73; OAS Charter, 73

Organization of Petroleum Exporting Countries (OPEC), 33, 70, 75, 77, 241

Pace, Peter, 229–30

Pahlavi, Shah Reza, 32–33, 48–53, 57–58; and Afghanistan, 47–48; arms sales to, 47–49; and Carter, 48–53, 57; and Khomeini's

revolution, 52–53; and nuclear program, 50–51; shelter in U.S., 57–58

Pakistan: and Afghanistan's 1978 coup, 47; Brzezinski and U.S.-Pakistan relations, 60–61; Bush administration and Musharraf/Bhutto crisis, 217–18; U.S. attacks on bin Laden hideouts (1998), 112

Panama invasion (1989), 72–73

Pearl Harbor, 214, 219, 230, 232–33

Peck, Edward, 177

Pelosi, Nancy, 248

Perino, Dana, 271

Perle, Richard, 107, 131, 211, 231

permanent bases in Iraq, 185–93, 205, 248, 270–71; and American embassy in Baghdad, 258–59; and bases in former Soviet republics, 190–91; congressional resolution banning, 248, 270; costs of, 189; and Rumsfeld, 186, 187–88; and status-of-forces agreements, 189

Petraeus, David, 5, 215, 238–39, 242–43, 252

Pfaff, William, 255

Philippines: permanent U.S. bases in, 186, 188, 191–93; Spanish-American War, 150–51, 186, 188, 192–93

Pike, John, 189

Pincus, Walter, 198

Plame, Valerie, 198, 199

Podhoretz, Norman, 35

Poland, 6

Pollack, Kenneth, 242

Pollman, Robert, 189

Popular Movement for the Liberation of Angola (MPLA), 39

post–Cold War thinking, 97–105; future coalitions and unilateral expectations, 99–100; Kennan's "X" article, 102–5; neocons and 1992 draft DPG, 98–100, 108; neocons and end of history argument, 102–5; neocons and National Defense Strategy (2002), 100–102; and preemption, 100–101; Scowcroft's interviews on end of Cold War/new world order, 97–98; and "shifting coalitions," 98; and "weak states," 101

post-invasion Iraq and the Bush administration, 177–212, 213–46, 247–72; accusations of "foreign agents" operating in Iraq, 218–19; and Allawi, 208–12, 216, 259–60; American embassy in Baghdad, 177, 258–59, 267; Blackwater ambush (2004), 178, 204–5; Blackwater crisis (2007), 260–61; and Bremer,

post-invasion Iraq and the Bush administration
(cont.)
178, 183, 206–7, 210, 215, 268; and Bush's
later speeches/press conferences, 243–46,
256–58; central front for war on terror, 60,
195, 203, 211–17, 223, 233–38, 242, 244–46,
255, 264–65; and Chalabi, 109, 205–10; and
Cheney, 200–204, 232–38, 240–42, 266; and
the CIA, 216; civilian contractors and
security guards, 182, 226–29, 260–61,
268–69; costs of the occupation, 182, 189,
255, 261–62; the CPA, 178, 180, 186, 206,
210; the Declaration of Principles (2007) and
future relations, 266–72; and electricity/
electric power grids, 180; and the enduring
U.S. presence, 185–93, 205, 247–48, 258–59,
270–71; Fallujah battle (2004), 178–79,
204–5, 207; the Green Zone, 178, 180, 184,
240; the insurgency, 177, 178–85, 195, 215,
234; and interim governing council (IGC),
206–7; and interim government, 171, 180,
208–12, 215–17; and Iraqi army, 183,
241–42; January 2005 Iraqi elections, 179,
180, 186, 215; making the world safe for our
democracy, 214, 256, 257–58, 264–65; and
Maliki, 212, 215–17, 239–43, 252, 259–60,
267–68; and metaphor of progress, 254,
265–66; and the missing WMD, 155,
171–73, 193–204, 207–8; necessity of victory,
223, 236–37, 239, 258; the occupation,
177–93, 204–12, 214–15, 265; oil legislation,
240–42, 243, 259, 268; Order 17/immunity
protection issues, 206–7, 217, 260, 266–67,
268–69; and Pakistan crisis, 217–18; Pearl
Harbor analogies, 214, 219, 230, 232–33; and
permanent bases in Iraq, 185–93, 205, 248,
270–71; and Petraeus, 238, 242–43, 252;
post-invasion weapons inspections, 162–63;
and Powell, 184–85; proposed security pact
with Maliki government, 252, 259; and al
Qaeda in Iraq, 233, 234–35, 269; and quest
to transform Middle East, 7–8, 26–29,
175–76, 217–18, 223–24, 255–58; and
reconstruction, 183, 184, 259; the regular
Army/troops, 177, 181–83, 214–15, 219–21,
225–30, 261; and Rice, 228; and Rumsfeld,
155, 171–73, 179, 181, 183, 186, 187–88,
210–11, 219–25, 259; and Sadr, 267–68;
Shahwani and the INIS, 215–16; SOCOM,
221–25; and status-of-forces agreements, 189,

268–69, 271; Sunni/Shiite/Kurdish disputes,
215, 259–60, 267; the surge, 5, 22, 215, 237,
238–39, 242–44, 252, 265–66; and transi-
tional national government, 180; and 2008
presidential race, 248–50, 268; and U.S.
Congress, 268, 269; utopian visions, 255–56;
and Vietnam, 210–11, 239; and Wolfowitz,
177, 182, 185–86, 211
Powell, Colin: and air attacks against Afghan
targets, 138; and American exceptionalism,
149; and Bush administration efforts to sell
the war, 124–25, 129, 141, 144–45, 155; and
Cheney, 80, 118, 125, 150, 156–57; and
containment of Iraq, 126; and Guantánamo
Bay detentions, 235; and Gulf War I, 78,
79–81, 89, 94–95; and Iraq focus at first
NSC meeting (2001), 124–25; and Iraq
sanctions, 125, 126; Iraq/Vietnam analogies,
185; on the occupation, 184–85; Pottery
Barn rule, 205; on reconstruction of Iraq,
184; and Rumsfeld, 118, 138; UN Security
Council testimony, 114, 149–50, 156–57,
195; and UN weapon inspections, 141, 144
Prague connection and Mohammed Atta, 135,
153, 202–3
Precht, Henry, 53
preemptive action, 100–101, 140–41, 144–45
presidential campaign of 2000, 27–28, 119
presidential campaign of 2004, 203, 211–12
presidential campaign of 2008, 248–50, 268
Presidential Emergency Operations Center, 128
Priest, Dana, 203
Prince, Erik, 247
private contractors. See civilian contractors and
security guards in Iraq
progress, metaphor of, 9–14; the agent theory of
international relations, 10, 13; Bush administration's quest to transform Middle East,
26–29; and "coalitions of the willing," 13;
Cold War foreign policy, 14–15; Dulles on
differences of American/European ap-
proaches to world affairs, 10–11, 13; and
erasing Vietnam memories, 25–26, 30, 88;
and faith in American ingenuity (science/
technological fixes), 9–10, 30; and Gulf
War I, 25–26, 88; and Iraq as central front
for war on terror, 254, 265–66; notion of
"creative destruction," 12, 16, 18; and Reagan, 62–63; and realist interpretation of
world affairs, 13, 26, 30

Project for a New American Century (PNAC), 96, 106, 108–9, 232

A Promise to Keep (Bush), 173

Protect America Act, 253

PSYOP (army psychological warfare team), 170–71

Putin, Vladimir, 158, 160

al Qaeda, 107, 129; linking Iraq and, 128–29, 133, 147, 155, 203, 233, 234–35, 269; in post-invasion Iraq, 233, 234–35, 269

Quayle, Dan, 122–23

Radio and Television Correspondents' Association Dinner (2004), 204

Radio Free Europe, 35

Rahman, Sheikh Omar Abdel, 107

Razor, Dina, 228

Reagan, Ronald/Reagan administration: and arms to Iran, 66; and Carter, 62; faith in American ingenuity, 10; foreign policy and precursors to Gulf Wars, 62, 63–64; and Gorbachev, 25, 63, 70; and Iran-Contra scandal, 63, 67–68, 222; and Iranian hostage crisis negotiations, 66; and Iran-Iraq War, 67; and Iraq/Saddam's chemical weapons, 68–69; and neoconservatives, 4; and progress metaphor, 62–63; and Soviet "evil empire," 4, 63, 103–4; "Star Wars," 4, 63; and Vietnam syndrome, 25

realist worldview: and Cold War foreign policy, 4, 13, 26, 30, 98, 103–4, 105, 139–40; and neoliberalism, 139–40; and post-invasion Iraq, 245–46; Rice on, 30, 139–40

Rendon, John, 106, 132

Rendon Group, 106, 132

Rhodes, Richard, 87

Ricciardone, Francis J., 177

Rice, Condoleezza: accusations of Iranian "foreign agents" operating in Iraq, 219; and Blackwater crisis, 260; and Blix's reports of UN weapons inspections, 159, 161–62; on Bush Doctrine and American exceptionalism, 140; on Bush Doctrine and preemptive action, 140–41; and Bush's prayers, 151; and civilian contractors and security guards, 228, 260; on elections in Lebanon and Gaza, 257–58; and first meeting of Bush's NSC, 124; on "multipolarity," 29; and neoliberalism, 139–40; and notion of "creative destruction," 12; and Pakistan crisis, 217; on post-9/11 transformation away from Cold War alliances, 28–30,

32; and question of permanent bases, 270–71; on realist worldview, 30, 139–40; selling the war on Iraq, 124, 141, 152, 159, 161–62; smoking gun/mushroom cloud remark, 141, 152; and SOCOM's challenge to chief-of-mission authority, 225; on untrustworthiness of Iraqis, 167, 171; on war on terrorism, 213

Ricks, Thomas, 179, 221

Rise of the Vulcans (Mann), 99

Ritter, Scott, 81, 141

Rockefeller, David, 36, 57

Rockefeller, Jay, 250

Roosevelt, Franklin, 70, 71, 95, 116

Rosenberg, Julius and Ethel, 10

Rostow, Walt Whitman, 16–25; background and early career, 16–18; "The Case for the Vietnam War," 24–25; on the "crossover point," 22; and domino thesis, 21–22; and Eisenhower/Cold War U.S.-Soviet relations, 17; and Gulf of Tonkin resolution, 19–20; and invasion of Laos/North Vietnam, 23–24; and Johnson administration, 19–25; and Johnson's peace speeches, 23; and Kennedy, 18; and McNamara, 20, 24–25; and notion of creative destruction, 16, 18; on old concept of wars of national liberation, 20–21; on risks of failure/defeat in Vietnam, 19, 21, 24–25; slogan "the New Frontier," 18, 26; *The Stages of Economic Growth*, 17–18, 20, 240; and Tet offensive, 23; Vietnam War policy, 2, 18–25, 266

Rove, Karl, 105, 150–52, 198, 261–63

Rubin, Barry, 51

Rudd, Kevin, 6

Rumsfeld, Donald, 1; accusations of Iranian "foreign agents" operating in Iraq, 218–19; and administration's attack on Murtha, 230–31; and air attacks against Afghan targets, 138; and antiballistic missile system, 126–28; calls for resignation, 211; and CIA/intelligence community, 126–27, 133–34; on coalitions, 11–12, 256; Defense Policy Board (DPB), 131; on the enemies faced today, 256; expectations for Iraq's reconstruction, 183, 259; expectations of being welcomed as liberators, 168; "going massive," 112, 128; and Gulf War II troop levels, 163–64; and the hidden WMD, 155; immediate response to 9/11, 128; on the insurgency, 179, 181, 183, 210–11; linking Iraq/Saddam and 9/11, 2, 128–29,

Rumsfeld, Donald (*cont.*)
    133, 155; and looting of antiquities, 168–69,
    184; meeting with Saddam (1983), 68; and
    the missing WMD, 155, 171–73; and OSI,
    133; and permanent bases in Iraq, 186,
    187–88; plan for Gulf War II victory,
    164–66; plan to restructure U.S. military,
    187–88, 220–25; and PNAC letter to
    Clinton, 108; and Powell, 118, 138; press
    conferences, 168–69; on public perceptions
    of the war, 263; on Saddam statue scene,
    169–70; and search for bin Laden, 137–38;
    selling war on Iraq/Saddam, 118, 126–34,
    137–38, 154–55, 223; shock and awe,
    164–66; and SOCOM, 221–25; "stuff
    happens" quip, 168–69; and Tenet, 134;
    terrorism network theory, 118; town hall
    meeting with soldiers, 219–21; on troop
    levels for the occupation, 181, 183; and UN
    weapons inspections, 115, 154–55, 165;
    Vietnam analogies, 210–11, 231; on the war
    on terrorism, 130–31, 213, 223; worldview,
    127; and wounded veterans, 263
Rusk, Dean, 13, 15–16
Russert, Tim: Cheney interviews, 129–30,
    135–37, 152, 200–202; Hillary Clinton
    interview, 249–50; Rumsfeld interview, 138;
    and Valerie Plame leak, 199
Russia: and Eastern Europe, 93–94; and George
    H.W. Bush, 93–94; and Gulf War II coali-
    tion, 158, 160; and Iraq's debts, 182

al-Sadr, Muqtada, 252, 267–68
Safire, William, 33, 126–27
SALT treaty (strategic arms limitation talks), 35,
    40, 41
Satterfield, David, 258, 271
Saudi Arabia: and American aid to anti-Soviets,
    65–66; bin Laden supporters, 94, 106; bin
    Laden's quest to sever U.S.-Saudi relation-
    ship, 95; and Gulf War I, 77, 79–81, 90,
    94–95; and Iraq's invasion of Kuwait, 77;
    and oil, 64–65; persuasion of Fahd to accept
    American military force, 79–81, 90, 94–95;
    proposed scale-down of U.S. bases, 185–86,
    189
Sawyer, Diane, 203–4
Scarborough, Rowan, 130–31
Schieffer, Bob, 200
Schlesinger, Arthur M., Jr., 5–6

Schlesinger, James, 149
Schoomaker, Peter, 226
Schwarzkopf, Norman, 78, 79, 90, 94
Schweizer, Peter, 231
Scowcroft, Brent, 3, 77, 81–82, 87, 97–98, 102, 134
SEATO (Southeast Asia Treaty Organization), 100
Selassie, Haile, 39
Senate Armed Services Committee, 181
Shah of Iran. *See* Pahlavi, Shah Reza
Shahwani, Mohammed Abdullah, 215–16
Shanshal, Falah, 268
Shinseki, Eric, 163, 226
shock and awe, 159, 164–66, 175
Shulman, Marshall, 42, 45
Shultz, George, 140, 182
Sick, Gary, 68
Snow, Tony, 189, 243, 255
Somalia, 37–42, 45
The Sopranos (HBO), 212, 265
South Africa, 38
South Korea, 1, 187, 189
Soviet Union: and Afghanistan, 47, 55–57, 58–61;
    Brzezinski and China/Soviet relations,
    42–46; Brzezinski and influence in Middle
    East/central Asia, 37–42, 55–57; Brzezinski
    and military threat in Africa and Middle
    East, 37–42; and Carter's initiatives, 35;
    Cold War foreign policy and U.S.-Soviet
    relations, 17; George H.W. Bush and
    post–Cold War challenges, 70–71; Kennan's
    portrayal, 103; and Reagan's "evil empire," 4,
    63. *See also* Russia
Spain: Aznar-Bush meeting on eve of war,
    157–61; and Gulf War II coalition, 6
Spanish-American War (1898), 150–51, 186, 188,
    192–93
Special Operations Command (SOCOM),
    221–25; budget, 225; and chief-of-mission
    authority, 224–25; interrogation techniques,
    224; and Rumsfeld, 221–25; Strategic
    Support Branch, 224
"spheres of influence," 71
St. Petersburg Times, 90
The Stages of Economic Growth (Rostow), 17–18,
    20, 240
Stahl, Lesley, 113
State Department: Cold War, 15; and Glaspie
    meeting with Saddam, 73–74; and post-
    invasion Iraq, 182, 205; SOCOM and chief-
    of-mission authority, 225

status-of-forces agreements: and the Declaration of Principles, 268–69, 271; and issue of permanent bases in Iraq, 189

Stiglitz, Joseph, 261

stop-loss program, 220

Strategic Defense Initiative ("Star Wars"), 4, 63

Strauss, Leo, 99

Study of Revenge (Mylroie), 108, 129

Sudan, 112

Sullivan, William, 52, 53, 54–55

Sumida, Mike, 191

Suskind, Ron, 101–2, 105, 245

Syria, 117

Taliban: American aid to, 60, 65–66; and bin Laden, 65, 94, 138; Cheney on, 143; resurgence in Afghanistan, 233, 257, 270

Tanenhaus, Sam, 185, 194

Taraki, Noor Mohammad, 46–47, 58

Taylor, Maxwell, 19

Telegraph (London), 169

Tenet, George: and Cheney, 156; and first meeting of Bush's NSC, 124–25; and Rumsfeld, 134; and the "slam dunk" case for war, 155–56, 197; tip leading to prewar attack on Saddam's bunker, 167; and uranium yellowcake story, 196–97

terrorism, war on, 1–2; Bush administration attempt to expand to Iran, 248–52; Bush and the backdoor sacrifices, 253–54; Bush on, 116, 192; Cheney's definition, 129–30, 131; and domestic economic messages, 253–54, 262; domestic measures, 234–35, 253–54; and elusive enemies, 254, 255–56; interrogation techniques, 234–35; Iraq as central front for, 1–2, 60, 195, 203, 211–17, 223, 233–38, 242, 244–46, 255, 264–65; necessity of victory, 223, 236–37, 239, 258; Rumsfeld's idea for, 130–31; strain on the military, 254; wiretaps, 234, 235–36. *See also* Bush administration and selling the war on Iraq

Tet offensive, 23, 210–11

Thatcher, Margaret, 76–77, 82–83, 114, 211

Thomas, Helen, 245

Thurman, Max, 72

tourism and Iraq reconstruction, 183, 259

Treaty of Westphalia (1648), 29

Trilateral Commission, 36, 57

Truman, Harry, 244; and American metaphor of progress/distaste for diplomacy, 14; and

atomic bomb, 10, 14–15; Truman Doctrine, 15, 146, 154, 192

Truman Doctrine, 15, 146, 154, 192

Turki, Prince, 65

Tyson, Ann Scott, 191, 225

Ullman, Harlan, 149, 164–65, 166

UN General Assembly, 72–73

UN Security Council resolutions: Gulf War I, 78–79, 85–86, 87, 96; Gulf War II, 143, 145, 152, 153, 155, 156–62, 165, 245

UN weapons inspections: Albright's Georgetown speech on, 113–14; Cheney on, 141, 144; Clinton era, 108, 110, 112–14, 115; Gulf War I, 108, 110–13, 115, 155; Gulf War II, 115, 141, 144, 154–55, 159–63, 165; PNAC letter to Clinton, 108; post-Iraq invasion, 162–63; Powell on, 141, 144

UNESCO, 145

United Arab Emirates, 74

University of Chicago, 99

uranium yellowcake disinformation story, 143, 152–54, 156, 195–99, 201–2; Bush's 2003 State of the Union speech, 156, 195–96, 197–98; and Cheney, 152–53, 196, 197, 199, 201–2; and CIA, 143, 153, 196–97, 201–2; and the NIE (2002), 153–54, 196; White House anti-Wilson campaign, 196–99, 201–2; Wilson's op-ed, 195–99; and Wolfowitz, 195–96

U.S. News and World Report, 97

USA Patriot Act, 130, 134, 234, 253

USA Today, 138

USS *Cole* bombing (2000), 233

Vance, Cyrus: and arms sales to Shah/Iran, 48; and arms talks with Russia, 45–46; and Brzezinski, 36–37, 38, 41, 42, 53; and Carter, 42; and Somalia/Ethiopia conflict, 40, 41; and U.S. shelter for Shah, 57

Vanity Fair, 261

Vietnam War: and agent theory of revolution, 13; and Brzezinski, 36, 37–38; and Carter, 34; and domino thesis, 21–22; "five o'clock follies," 184–85; Gulf of Tonkin incident/resolution, 19–20, 82, 126, 146, 271–72; and Gulf War I, 25–26, 88, 90, 91; and Gulf War II, 30, 265–66; and Johnson administration, 19–25; and Kennedy, 54; and McNamara, 20, 24–25; and post-invasion Iraq, 210–11, 239;

Vietnam War (*cont.*)
and Rostow, 2, 18–25; Rostow on risks of failure/defeat, 19, 21, 24–25; Rostow on the "crossover point," 22; Tet offensive, 23, 210–11

Vietnam/Iraq parallels: the coalitions, 7, 100; "five o'clock follies," 184–85; home front defections, 231; Johnson's argument about withdrawal/Bush on failure, 239; "many flags campaign"/coalition of the willing, 7; not admitting defeat, 30; rationales for war, 264; refighting Vietnam in Iraq, 30; Rostow on "crossover point"/Bush on success of the surge, 22; Rostow's remarks/Rice's reprise, 20; Rostow's/Cheney's battles with CIA, 21; SEATO experience and disappearing allies, 100; Tet offensive/Iraq insurgency, 210–11; worldwide communist conspiracy/Islamic extremism, 5–6

Viguerie, Richard A., 231

Walker, Martin, 78
Wall Street Journal, 123, 196, 242, 243
Wallace, Chris, 236–37, 261–62
Wallis, Jim, 101–2
Walters, Barbara, 157
War Powers Act (1973), 120, 121, 222
Washington Post, 47, 132–33, 134, 162, 198, 202–3, 214, 221, 224
waterboarding, 237, 270
weapons of mass destruction (WMD): and Chalabi, 207–8; and Cheney, 200–204, 234; Curveball and faulty intelligence, 195, 205–6; Gulf War I, 86–87, 88, 91, 105, 108–15; and Kay, 194–95, 200, 201, 203; missing, 155, 171–73, 193–204, 207–8; and Rumsfeld, 155, 171–73; and selling of Gulf War II, 124–25, 141, 142–44, 152–56, 181, 194–99, 201, 204; surveillance photos of alleged Iraq WMD facility, 124–25; uranium yellowcake disinformation, 143, 152–54, 156, 195–99, 201–2; and Wolfowitz, 172, 193–94, 195, 199–200. *See also* UN weapons inspections

Webb, Jim, 248–49, 269
Webster, William, 86
Weinberger, Caspar, 108, 231–32
Westmoreland, William, 22–23
White House Iraq Group (WHIG), 149–57, 162
Will, George F., 96
Wilson, Harold, 26
Wilson, Joseph: and Cheney, 199, 201–2; and Glaspie Affair, 76; op-ed exposing uranium yellowcake story, 195–99, 201–2; *The Politics of Truth*, 76; White House campaign against, 196–99, 201–2
Wilson, Woodrow, 2, 156, 256
wiretapping, secret, 234, 235–36
Wolfowitz, Paul: and anthrax letters, 134, 137; and Chalabi, 206, 207–8; and defense planning guidance (1992), 98; Gulf War II expectations, 163–64; linking Saddam/Iraq and 9/11, 129; and the missing WMD, 172, 193–94, 195, 199–200; and Mylroie, 107, 108; and the occupation, 177, 182, 185–86, 211; rendition of Bush administration logic, 139; selling war on Iraq/Saddam, 129, 131, 134, 137, 139, 157
Wood, Leonard, 193
Woodward, Bob, 125, 126, 151
Worden, Simon, 132
World Trade Center bombing (1993), 107

Yalta Conference (1945), 71–72
Yazdi, Ebrahim, 57–58
Yeltsin, Boris, 93
Yom Kippur War (1973), 33
Young, Andrew, 45
Yousef, Ramzi, 107–8
Yugoslavia, former (Balkan wars), 97–98, 104

Zahedi, Ardeshir, 53
Zarif, Jared, 117
al-Zarqawi, Abu Musab, 179
Zelikow, Philip, 212
Zimmerman, Peter, 90
Zinni, Anthony, 229